THE
COSTELLO
MEMOIRS

THE
COSTELLO
MEMOIRS

THE AGE OF PROSPERITY

PETER COSTELLO
WITH PETER COLEMAN

MELBOURNE
UNIVERSITY
PRESS

MELBOURNE UNIVERSITY PRESS
An imprint of Melbourne University Publishing Limited
187 Grattan Street, Carlton, Victoria 3053, Australia
mup-info@unimelb.edu.au
www.mup.com.au

First published 2008
Text © Peter Costello, 2008
Design and typography © Melbourne University Publishing Ltd 2008

Text and cover design by Phil Campbell
Typeset by Megan Ellis
Printed by Griffin Press, SA

National Library of Australia Cataloguing-in-Publication entry
Costello, Peter, 1957–

The Costello memoirs / Peter Costello with Peter Coleman.

9780522855821(hbk.)

Includes index.

Costello, Peter, 1957–
Politicians—Australia—Biography.
Australia—Politics and government—1996–
Coleman, Peter, 1928–

994.066092

PREFACE

Peter Costello has never been a predictable politician. Whatever they may say, most of them do not go into Parliament to bring about particular reforms; they go in because they find the life is irresistible. They want to be in it all their lives. They enjoy its exhilarating highs and take its miserable (and tedious) lows in their stride. They face long years in the wilderness with equanimity. They take for granted the slander of fools. They also believe that the voters will get it right in the end. Their day will come. They are politicians in the way others are poets. They can't help themselves.

Peter Costello is not like that. To him all that stuff is the excuse of the seat-warmer, the hack, the careerist, or at best the adventurer. He belongs to a different parliamentary tradition. He went into Parliament to make changes to the Australian settlement. He wanted to liberalise the economy, especially the system of taxation. (A dental technician with gallows humour drilled the letters GST on a crown for one of his teeth damaged beyond repair by constant grinding during the GST debates.) He wanted to strike a blow for individual rights against union bullies. (He first came to public notice as the champion of the small company Dollar Sweets against the thugs of the Federated Confectioners Association.) He wanted to bring indigenous Australians into the mainstream. (He was gratified to see Noel Pearson reading FA Hayek's *The Road to Serfdom*.) He was determined to advance liberal multiculturalism within the Australian tradition of tolerance and freedom. (Why come to the country at all if you despise everything about it?) From the containment of communism to the war on terrorism, from voluntary student unionism to the republican referendum, he has been an agent of liberal change.

Throughout his eleven to twelve years in Government he was an indefatigable, totally committed Treasurer. He is also a splendid parliamentary performer. In my years in state and federal Parliaments I never saw his equal. Yet when he is no longer able to achieve the changes he believes in, he wonders whether it is worth sticking around. These memoirs may be either an *apologia* or a platform.

Several political currents meet in Peter Costello: conservative, liberal, radical. One key to his life and work is that he is a Christian reformer. His religious faith has always been important to him. It has become even more important as he has grown older. He believes that divine intervention helped Tanya, his wife (and my daughter), recover from a grave illness in 1987. His hope for redemption and God's forgiveness is central to his life.

Christian reformism is a continuing, if minority, tradition in Parliament. Ordinary members—worldly, sceptical, practical—often dub the men and women of faith 'the God Squad'. At one time in the House of Commons, cynical conservatives labelled them the YMCA. Yet these reformers have leavened the lump. They have been at the heart of most successful movements for social reform.

Throughout his years as Treasurer (and before that, in Opposition) Costello has been a leader in all the principal decisions of the Coalition. His Budgets and tax reforms restored the economy, stimulated investment and employment, and underpinned major policies ranging from the family to the arts. He brought the Australian economy back from being the 'sick man of Asia' to becoming one of the very few able to withstand the Asian meltdown of the late 1990s—and to revive Indonesia, Thailand and South Korea. He contributed significantly to the strategic decisions on East Timor, Iraq and Afghanistan.

His policies do not command universal assent, even among reformers. I, for one, do not always agree with him. As an in-the-bone federalist I cannot accept his centralist hostility to the states and states' rights. I am not as convinced as he is that a republic would be a beneficent influence on Australian freedoms or self-respect. But these differences could not disrupt our collaboration. We discussed, edited and improved on each draft as we worked through the themes we agreed were central to the book. I did not press my disagreements.

These are his memoirs, not mine. In any case I found some of his reformist positions persuasive enough for me to reconsider my own. He supported the apology to Aborigines for their dispossession and associated grievances—provided any apology be accompanied by the policies now known as the Northern Territory Intervention. He wanted the Government to ratify the Kyoto Protocol since Australia (unlike some countries that had already signed it) was meeting the Kyoto targets. Both may be symbolic, but I agree with him that symbols have a potency of their own.

Costello's story is one of high achievement. He helped create—and managed—the Age of Prosperity in Australia. He should have been Prime Minister. It was his misfortune to come up against a man whose determination to hang on to power, while not Mugabe-esque, was unyielding. John Howard is not an unusual case. The pain and frustration in dislodging Prime Minister Hawke or Premiers Askin and Bjelke-Petersen are fresh in memory. Tony Blair was as unwilling to vacate 10 Downing Street as Howard was to vacate Kirribilli House (although Blair finally made way for his successor). The United States set the world an example in constitutionally limiting the number of years a president may remain in office (and even there Bill Clinton strove mightily to return to the White House on the coat-tails of his wife).

These memoirs record the long saga of the Howard–Costello contest. Costello writes of Howard in a restrained and generous way. He declares plainly that he regards him as Australia's greatest Prime Minister after Sir Robert Menzies. But he also tells the story of the agreement, understanding, deal or whatever, summarised in the McLachlan Memorandum, about the proposed transition of Liberal Party leadership from Howard to Costello—and the differing inter-pretations of that memorandum. It is a dispiriting record of loyalty and frustration, of egoism and betrayal. Should Costello have resigned in protest? He believes that would have badly damaged the Government. The dismal details, through to the final catastrophe, are all here. The reader will judge.

Peter Coleman
Saturday, 2 August 2008

CONTENTS

Preface		v
Author's Note		xi
1	What Went Wrong?	1
2	The Making of a Politician	10
3	From Confectionery to Canberra	33
4	Defeat from the Jaws of Victory	48
5	Out of the Wilderness and into Government	69
6	Balancing the Books: Setting Monetary Policy	90
7	Unchain My Heart: A New Tax System	119
8	Second Term Blues: 1998–2001	147
9	Meltdown: The Asian Financial Crisis	168
10	War and Terrorism: The Third Term	188
11	From Mabo to Mal: Indigenous Australia	205
12	Leadership: From Memo to Madness	223
13	Bringing Home the Bacon: The Fourth Term	258
14	Going Cactus: The 2007 Election	290
15	Unfinished Business	310
Appendices		338
Index		377

Author's Note

The number of Australian Members of Parliament and Ministers that have recorded accounts of their time in office is small. Very few of those are on the Liberal side of politics. Some claim that this shows Liberals lack an interest in history. This book will, I hope, prove to the contrary.

In Australia the writers of contemporary politics come overwhelmingly from a left or 'progressive' perspective. In their accounts Labor usually emerges as the hero and the Liberal Party as the villain. Because some will try to make this the story of the nearly twelve years of the Howard-led Coalition Government I wanted to record what actually happened—to describe the achievements as well as to acknowledge the failures.

Three people served in Cabinet for the entirety of those four terms of Government—John Howard as Leader of the Liberal Party and Prime Minister, Alexander Downer as Foreign Minister and me as Deputy Leader of the Liberal Party and Treasurer. As the Deputy Leader of the Liberal Party from 23 May 1994 to 29 November 2007, I held that office longer than anyone else in the history of the party. I have served the longest term as Treasurer and brought down more Budgets than anyone else in that Commonwealth office. This, I think, gives me a perspective to write an inside account of the Government and indeed this part of Australia's history, particularly its economic performance over the 1990s and most of the first decade of the twenty-first century.

As a former Minister I have access to minutes that were prepared for me as Treasurer—in all, some 32 000. In order to keep the account readable I have not cited many of them!

In preparing an account of political events, particularly the leadership discussions, I was able to rely on contemporaneous notes

I made of important meetings. As a young solicitor I was taught to make a note of every phone conversation or conference with a client. These notes could be referred to later if there was a dispute about an agreement or negotiation. We were trained to write down the actual words that were spoken—not an interpretation of the words, which would be of no evidentiary value.

After significant political meetings I would prepare a note for the file on what had been said. In this book I have used the actual words said, although on some occasions they were ungrammatical, even nonsensical. This is how people actually speak, rather than in rounded sentences.

I kept a record of the matters raised in the party room during our period of Government. Both the Leader and the Deputy Leader sit at the head table. The Leader chairs the meeting. I recorded the matters raised by Members and Senators so they could be followed up and attended to. I have not referred to particular matters raised by particular Members or Senators in this book but I have used the notes to inform myself of the tenor of the party meetings and the political climate at certain times and over particular events.

In the Cabinet room I also recorded views expressed on major decisions. There is an official note-taker present throughout Cabinet meetings and the note-taker's records will—after the statutory period— be released. I have been careful here not to disclose any material that is sensitive from a national security or defence perspective, writing only about perspectives and facts that are already known to the public.

I have been fortunate in public life to have been served by exceptional personal assistants. Pat Herman, who first joined me when I was a barrister in the private sector, came over to my electorate office when I first became a Member of Parliament and stayed with me there for a decade. When I became Deputy Leader of the Opposition in 1994, Lizzie McCabe became my executive assistant and served in that role for more than a decade, until the end of 2005. Gabe Doye, who had been in my office many years, took over from Lizzie until the election in November 2007. Since the 2007 election Philippa Campbell, who has been with me for a total of nine years in various roles, has taken over Gabe's role.

A mark of their organisation and competence was that even though we were required to vacate our ministerial office and shred more than one hundred bins of material in less than one week, all my personal records were kept intact and my notes of meetings preserved and filed in a way that enabled me to find and access them. I would especially like to thank Philippa Campbell for all the extra hours she put in on weekends and at night while I was preparing the manuscript for this book, and also for the first-class support she gave me while I was writing it.

In Australia, no one can serve as a Minister without first being elected as a Member of Parliament. Be you ever so high, you cannot represent our country on the international stage without first winning and then holding the trust and support of your local community and electors. I thank the people of Higgins for the honour they have given me to represent them in the Australian Parliament. I especially wish to thank the chairmen of my Electorate Committee—friends and valued confidants all—for all they have done to help me in my election campaigns and my representational duties in my electorate—Anthony Starkins, Christopher Leach, John Allen, Helen Maxwell-Wright, Andrea Coote, Ross Liebmann and Alan Cullen.

I would like to thank Mrs Maureen Santora of New York for permission to use her letter to me about her son, Christopher.

Most of the photos and illustrations for this book came from my personal collection. I'd like to thank cartoonists Bill Leak, Peter Nicholson, Mark Knight, Alan Moir, Todd Davidson and Patrick Cook for their work. Thanks are also due to the many photographers whose work is reproduced here. I'd like to acknowledge the other cartoonists and photographers who have, over the course of the past seventeen years, captured my every other grimace and chronicled the key disasters of my career.

The indefatigable Louise Adler at MUP first approached me about a book when she spotted me on an aeroplane flying from Canberra before the fatal 2007 election. The conversation began in transit and concluded only at the luggage carousel. In that time Louise succeeded in extracting my agreement to a further discussion about writing my memoirs after the election. Louise is highly entertaining, and after the election I discovered how determined she can be. Before I wrote this book I had no idea what a publisher does. Now I know how important they are to the finished product. I thank Louise and MUP's Executive Publisher, Foong Ling Kong, for their intelligent and robust engagement. I am particularly grateful to Foong Ling for her management of the editorial process and meticulous attention to details. Any errors, of course, are my own.

This book would not have been possible without the encouragement of my co-author and father-in-law, Peter Coleman. This collaboration has been an immensely rewarding experience, and through the process I have developed great respect for the craft and commitment that is required to produce a book. Peter is a brilliant writer and, for Australia, a rare and valuable person—both an intellectual and a conservative.

My greatest debt is to my wife, Tanya, and my children Seb, Maddy and Phoebe. There were many times when my public duties and profile caused them difficulties—for example, when protestors against the Iraq War set up on the nature strip outside our home. Demonstrations outside my offices were as regular as the news cycle, but the purpose of that particular demonstration was to intimidate my family—I was not even home at the time.

There were other political crises during which news outlets took to staging cameras and journalists outside our home in a quiet suburban street, hoping for an early-morning news grab. Since I did a daily press conference there was no need for it. But on those days, bad days, my children (particularly Phoebe) had to walk through the cameras on the way to school. They endured the fact that at every public place we went as a family, someone would come up and talk to their father with good-natured advice, which tore him away from family time.

My family was my refuge of sanity through all the ups and downs of political life. I thank them for their understanding. They, too, came on the roller-coaster ride that is public life and they never once wavered in their support.

Peter Costello
Saturday, 2 August 2008

WHAT WENT WRONG?

The night before the 2007 election we met in a popular restaurant in Melbourne's Chinatown. It was Friday 23 November. We knew in our bones we were defeated. We joked and tried to look on the bright side. You never give up hope.

Twenty or so of us—mostly aged under thirty but some older—sat around a large table. We had different ethnic backgrounds and different religions. Some had grown up on farms, some in the cities. Some were married, some were in established relationships, some had children. When you work together in a political office seven days a week and travel together and eat together, you all live the same highs and lows. You become family.

This was my last chance to thank my team for all they had done in our doomed campaign and for their personal sacrifices over our eleven and a half years in Government. Our press team began at 5 a.m. each day. We were running on adrenalin. My wife Tanya came to thank them. Our son, Seb, joined us, down from the country after he had finished his regional radio program.

Our talk turned to a host of 'what if?' issues. What if the party had made the leadership transition? How would we have done things differently? What if John Howard had stood down after APEC in September? Would there have been enough time to turn around Labor's lead at that late stage?

We talked about the speech I had prepared over the APEC weekend in the event that Howard decided to go. It was designed to set a new direction for a fresh Government. We talked about some of the policy ideas we had included in that speech: ratifying the Kyoto Protocol, family and housing initiatives, new ways to deal with the water crisis. Would these have captured public attention and turned things around?

Then we talked about the disaster of the past forty-eight hours, when Liberal campaign workers in the New South Wales seat of Lindsay, including the husband of member Jackie Kelly, had been caught with a bogus leaflet trying to use anti-Muslim sentiment against Labor. How could anyone be so stupid?

My mind went back to the 1996 election when 'the forged letters affair' had blown up in Labor's face in the last forty-eight hours before it was thrown out of office. That incident had added several seats to our majority. I had no doubt that the Lindsay affair would add several seats to Labor's majority. It looked so crook, so desperate. It had dominated the media from the minute of Jackie Kelly's fateful interview on ABC Radio's *AM* program the day before. It had obliterated John Howard's last appearance at the Press Club that day, my message on the ABC's *PM* program that night and Howard's message on *AM* the next morning.

Kelly was a Howard favourite, the kind of member Howard loved. Swept into Parliament in 1996, she had no background in the Liberal Party. Her loyalty was to Howard. He had promoted her and made her a Minister—even giving her the plum appointment of Minister for Sport during the Sydney Olympics.

I could not remember a worse interview than Kelly's that morning two days before the election. Listening to it in the car, I reached out to switch off the radio. But it was so awful that my hand froze in mid-air. Kelly giggled and described it all as 'a bit of a Chaser-style prank'. After several more excruciating minutes she asked the interviewer: 'Where is this conversation going?' 'Right down the gurgler,' I muttered to no one. 'Why do these people do interviews?'

After dinner that Friday night I delivered my last speech of the campaign. I spoke about the Coalition's achievements in office. Over eleven and a half years we had delivered the most successful period of economic management in Australian history. We had lowered interest rates, brought unemployment to historic lows, eliminated Commonwealth net debt and managed the longest period of uninterrupted growth our country had ever known. We had turned Australia from the 'sick man of Asia' into a respected regional leader. We had built an Age of Prosperity. That would be the verdict of history. It was a record of which we could all be proud.

It was the best team I had ever had. The senior members were veterans of the GST campaign a decade earlier. Many of the staff in other Ministers' offices had drifted off as the parliamentary term wore on and the polls showed a looming disaster. But this team had fought out the campaign and done well. The polls showed that the Coalition parties were judged the best able to manage the economy—by a margin of 53 to 29. I told the team:

> It was a textbook campaign. Not a hitch. Not a loose word. No mistakes, by us at least. We stayed focussed and on-message throughout. Voting will begin in ten hours. It will be glory or death. But if we lose, it won't be on the issue of economic management. Everyone here can hold his or her head high. You will look back on these years in Government as the greatest days of your lives.

Phil Gaetjens also spoke. He was my chief of staff. He had been hit by a car in Canberra five months earlier and lay in intensive care in a coma for several weeks. My press secretary David Gazard, my adviser David Alexander and I had sat by Phil's bed while he was unconscious, willing him to recover and looking for signs. 'We'll know he's back when he can tell us the marginal tax rates and the tax thresholds,' Gazard said. Phil's brush with death had shaken all of us. He had not yet fully recovered and although he was still frail he came back to work on the campaign for restricted hours.

Phil spoke about what it meant to him to have these colleagues, these friends, stand by him throughout his gruelling experience. He spoke of the campaign. It had helped him. He was getting stronger. 'Tell us the rates and thresholds, Phil!' Gazard called out when Phil had finished speaking.

My personal assistant, Gabrielle Brennan, spoke of the friendships we had made for life.

I was up at six the next morning. As always I toured the polling booths in my electorate of Higgins, one every quarter-hour. Arrive, shake hands with the poll workers, speak to the voters, then on to the next booth. Ten minutes to drive between booths, five minutes to talk, thirty-seven booths in ten hours. David Alexander was the driver. My son Seb was with me all day. So was a federal policeman!

When Tanya and I voted at the Church of Christ, Camberwell, the television cameras were ready to record my last message. I asked voters to think about economic management, jobs and interest rates. Don't risk it all, our Age of Prosperity. 'You can't wake up on Monday morning and say: Oh I didn't mean that,' I said.

A posse of five journalists and two photographers trailed us in cars throughout the day. They recorded every conversation and photographed each handshake at the booths. They were looking for an incident, for colour, for movement, maybe a confrontation. Once or twice we gave them the slip but they always found us. It was a cat-and-mouse game. They trailed off in the afternoon.

The reception around the electorate was enthusiastic and positive, one of the best receptions I have had. My son was stunned by the warmth of it all. I was returned with a substantial majority. In my electorate there was a two-party preferred swing of 1.7 per cent against the Liberals. The national swing was 5.5 per cent. If we could have held the national swing to 1.7 per cent the Coalition would have been returned.

The western end of my electorate in Prahran usually delivers a majority for Labor. As I was walking down to a polling booth at a kindergarten, I heard a woman scream out from a balcony above the street: 'Peter, Peter, I love you, I love you!' A woman came racing out of her house and gave me a huge kiss. Then she demanded that her boyfriend come out and give me a hug. She called out to two of her girlfriends to come and give me a kiss. Never before had I experienced a reception like this on a polling day!

When it was all over we went to my office to wait for the results— Tanya, our children Sebastian and Phoebe, and the staff. (Our daughter

Madeleine was in Kilkenny, Ireland, working at a school for a year.) The Australian Electoral Commission website was posting results as they came in. We could see early on that the news was going to be bad. The two Tasmanian seats we had won from Labor in 2004 were going back to Labor. We held up well in Victoria, where we lost only two seats—Corangamite and Deakin. But in New South Wales we were in trouble in Eden-Monaro, Robertson, Dobell, Macquarie, Parramatta, Lindsay and Bennelong—John Howard's own seat. In South Australia it was expected that we would lose two seats we had picked up in the 2004 election—Wakefield and Kingston. The good news was we were holding in Boothby and Sturt. Queensland was an hour behind New South Wales and Victoria. We would need a miracle to hang on there. Labor needed a total of thirteen seats to form a majority. When the Queensland results came in, there were double-digit swings against the Coalition. We lost seats that were not even marginal. In total we lost nine seats in Queensland and seven in New South Wales. By nine o'clock it was all over.

I wanted to go to the St Andrew's Uniting Church Hall, where my friends and supporters had gathered, to thank them and console them. I rang John Howard at Kirribilli House. I asked him whether he had spoken to Kevin Rudd and when he proposed to make his concession speech. He had not yet rung Rudd. He said he would do that, then drive across the Harbour Bridge to the Wentworth Hotel and concede the loss of the election and the defeat of the Government. We had a brief discussion about his electorate of Bennelong. I could see he had lost it. He was not conceding. He asked: 'What will you do?' I said: 'I'm inclined to move on. I won't make an announcement until I've thought about it overnight.'

I hopped into the car with Tanya, Sebastian and Phoebe to join friends and several hundred supporters, led by my campaign manager, Andrea Coote, at St Andrew's Church Hall. Everyone was in a state of shock but they gave us a tremendous reception. We had run a great local campaign. I thanked them all for the time and energy they had volunteered on that day and over the years. My concluding words were:

I want to say two things about our country. Our ambitions for our country should be as large as the country itself. As I flew from Brisbane to Perth after our national campaign launch and I saw our broad and vast and expansive country, I thought to myself I want a country with ambitions as big as the continent itself. The second thing I want to say is that I believe in the future of Australia. The best years of our country are in front of us. We are young and we have boundless opportunity.

We were home by about midnight. Friends, colleagues and party officials were still ringing. I rang Madeleine in Kilkenny. It was morning there. She had been following the election on the internet. She was sad and disappointed. We all were. We went to bed about 2 a.m. and got up again at 6 a.m. Tanya and I talked about the announcement I had to make that day. We had already thought and talked a lot about what I would do if the Liberals lost. It had been my view for the past year that, if we lost, the best thing for me would be to make a break from politics. I had been the Deputy Leader of the party for more than thirteen years. I was conscious of the frustration people would suffer if opportunities for career advancement were not available. There would be other people in the party who had not yet had their opportunity to assume a major leadership role. They deserved a go. Tanya told me: 'You make whatever decision you think is right.'

So we went into my office. The staff were there already, cleaning out the offices, sorting documents, feeding the shredder bins. The phones were running hot. The press wanted to know whether I would take the party leadership. Colleagues were ringing to urge me to nominate. Some were making public endorsements. It was gathering momentum. I could not let this run. It had to be dealt with cleanly and immediately so that others could make their decisions and step forward if they wanted to lead the party. I spoke to each one of my staff individually and told them I did not intend to seek the leadership of the Liberal Party. I told them I would help them find other jobs. It was a shock. Most of them had hoped that I would stay on and do something after this terrible defeat we had all suffered. Philippa Campbell, my office manager, burst into tears.

Then I called in the press and made a statement. I congratulated Kevin Rudd and the Labor Party, thanked the millions who had voted for the Coalition, and paid a tribute to John Howard: 'I had the privilege of serving alongside him. I said in a recent interview that, with the possible exception of Sir Robert Menzies, John Howard is Australia's greatest Prime Minister.' But the principal purpose of the news conference was to make an announcement about my future:

> I have served the Liberal Party for seventeen years as a Member of Parliament, the first six years in Opposition, and whilst we were in Opposition I was elected the Deputy Leader, a position that I have held now for thirteen and a half years. Of course, for the last eleven and a half years I have served as Treasurer. I have given every waking hour to Government and to the people of Australia over those years.
>
> It has been a great privilege to serve with some wonderful people and I want to thank my wonderful colleagues with whom I have served, many of whom have asked me in the last twelve hours to become the Leader of the Liberal Party.
>
> I have discussed this with my family and my wife Tanya, and we have decided that the time has come for me to open a new chapter in my life. I will be looking to build a career post-politics in the commercial world.
>
> As a consequence of that, I will not seek nor will I accept the leadership or deputy leadership of the Liberal Party. I want to spend more time with my family and do something for them. They have paid a heavy price for [my] eleven and a half years as Treasurer.
>
> I believe in generational change in the Liberal Party. I came in as part of an Opposition, we took the Opposition up to the Hawke–Keating Government, we were elected and we formed Government. Now it is time for a new generation in Opposition to take the fight up to the Rudd Labor Government and to form the next Liberal Government.
>
> It is time for the young people of talent and ability, of whom there are many, to be given their go in the Liberal Party.

Just as I was given my go in the early 1990s, I think it is time for them to have their go and I am going to reprise my trust in the talented young members of the Liberal Party.

The achievements of recent years have been absolutely outstanding. I have personally been the longest serving Treasurer in Australia's history. I have brought down twelve federal Budgets. The incoming Treasurer will not inherit a situation that I did with a $10 billion deficit and $96 billion worth of debt. The incoming Treasurer will have a balanced Budget. There will be no Commonwealth debt, we are saving $9 billion a year in interest payments alone. We have reformed the tax system and introduced a broad base consumption tax, 2.2 million more Australians are in work and young people have a better opportunity for work than they have in a generation. We have established a Future Fund which now has $61 billion to provision for Australia's future ...

I want to pay tribute to other Members of Parliament, particularly those that have lost their seats in this most recent election. It may well be that John Howard has lost his seat, and Phil Barresi, a very dear colleague of mine. I think it is particularly tough on Mal Brough, who would have been part of any future leadership in the Liberal Party, and to lose him has been a heavy blow.

I concluded by thanking my magnificent staff:

All of you have been wonderful and I want to thank each and every one of you. I also want to pay tribute again to my wife, who has been absolutely wonderful. She has put up with a lot over the last eleven and a half years, raising our children single-handedly. While I have been doing my work, she has been doing much more important work.

When I had finished, one of the journalists asked Tanya: 'Mrs Costello, can I ask you what you think of your husband's decision?' I had no idea what was coming and I was not ready for her answer.

She replied:

CJ Dennis, the well-known and well-loved Australian poet, wrote in a series of poems entitled the *Songs of the Sentimental Bloke* the following lines, and I think that's where I am and where Peter is:

> Yeh live, yeh love, yeh learn; an' when yeh come
> To square the ledger in some thortful hour,
> The everlastin' answer to the sum
> Must allus be, 'Where's sense in gittin' sour?'
> ...
> Livin' an' lovin'—so life mooches on.

Then I did what I enjoy most: I invited everyone around to our home for a barbecue. It was a fine, sunny day. I cooked steaks and sausages. Tanya made salads. Phoebe made sure everyone had hats, sunscreen and drinks. We sat around talking. We talked about the campaign and the years in Government. Above all we asked each other: How did it come to this? How did a Government that had created such an Age of Prosperity, such a proud and prosperous country, now find itself in the wilderness?

2

THE MAKING OF A POLITICIAN

Some people in political life like to emphasise their hard upbringing and tough background. It shows, they say, how they understand the poor or less fortunate. They like to tell a Log Cabin to White House kind of story. But there are not as many Abraham Lincolns in our system as these people would have us believe. The hardship and deprivation usually revolve around an anecdote or two about sleeping in a car for a few nights or eating the occasional meal of bread and dripping. Memory can also play tricks, particularly when there is a hungry press to feed. It can be misleading to extrapolate from one incident a general picture of a person's background or upbringing.

There were some times of hardship during my childhood but overall I was very fortunate. By today's standards we were not affluent. We had no television or automatic washing machine or separate bedrooms for the children. It was not because we were particularly poor. Most people in Australia at that time were without these things. Living standards generally were lower than today. Consumer durables were not widely owned. Paid entertainment was a luxury out of the reach of most people and we made our own. Our imagination was more vivid and creative than if others had animated our dreams. My parents were never in a position to give their children money or property. But they had a stable home and they gave strong moral and religious guidance, which I believe is more important.

I am a baby-boomer—a late boomer but part of the generation born after World War II, raised in relative peace and rising prosperity in which families were commonly larger than today. After the war, with families feeling secure under stable economic growth and before the advent of widespread access to hormonal contraceptives, there was a huge increase in the proportion of young people in our society. Returning soldiers, or those who had put off having children during the war, began parenting. I studied demographic trends as Treasurer. The total fertility rate during the war was 2.5 children per woman, peaking in 1961 at about 3.5 per woman. From then on it fell almost continuously for forty years to a low of 1.73 children in 2001. I was born in 1957, pretty close to the peak, and our family of three children was standard for the time.

But we also lived in the shadow of our parents' formative experiences. My father's generation was formed by the Depression and the war. These events were burnt into his memory and were never far from our consciousness.

My father, Russell, was born in 1919. He was a good student and won a place at University High, a selective high school in Melbourne. But at the age of fourteen, after completing Year 10, he had to leave school and get a job to help with the family finances. This was not unusual. His parents had left school at an even earlier age. He followed a normal pattern for that place and time. He entered the workforce in 1933 in the wake of the Great Depression. Unemployment was around 18 per cent. It was a great achievement that he was able to get and hold a job. He was a machinist on shift work in a textile factory.

In 1940 he joined the Australian Military Forces and later the Australian Imperial Force. He saw action in New Guinea in 1943 and 1944. At the end of 1944 the Australian Army began to demobilise and servicemen were entitled to free tertiary education and accelerated completion of tertiary qualifications under the Commonwealth Reconstruction Training Scheme. As a mature-age student my father eventually finished school and enrolled at the University of Melbourne.

My mother, Anne, was the third of four children to Raymond and Jesse Northrop. Naturally outgoing and vibrant, she did well at school, ending up Dux and winning a place at Melbourne University. At the time the university was filling up with returned servicemen under repatriation schemes. One of them was my father.

Their plans for marriage were disrupted by illness. My mother was hospitalised for five months with rheumatic fever and their first attempt at a wedding was cancelled. When she recovered, they seized the chance to go through with the wedding, even though she had not finished her degree. In those days many, perhaps most, people thought it was not important for women to build a career outside the home. But she was one who did think it important and, after three children (including me), she returned to university, qualified and began a career. At first she was a high school teacher and later a psychologist. It must have taken a huge effort.

My parents bought a block of land and built a home in Blackburn, at that time an outer suburb of Melbourne. The purchase was financed by a war service loan, another entitlement to returned servicemen, with a fixed low-interest rate. They lived in this house for fifty-five years. They improved and renovated it on a number of occasions. At first it was not sewered and there was an 'outhouse'. It also had an external laundry. My parents added an extra bedroom to accommodate the growing family and later a further extension to allow my infirm grandmother to live with us.

My father did not pay off his mortgage until December 1996 (by which time I was the federal Treasurer). He told me he could have paid it off earlier but the 3¾ per cent fixed rate war service loan was a bargain. Indeed it was. At some periods during those times home mortgage interest rates had been as high as 17 per cent.

In the May 1998 Budget, as Treasurer I announced that servicemen who had seen active service in World War II would be eligible for a gold card, which would cover all of their medical expenses. It has proven enormously useful to them in their declining years. I was very proud to have been able to make the announcement and to benefit my father, among all the other members of his generation, who had served their country in this time of great danger.

Throughout the late 1940s and the 1950s returning servicemen and post-war immigrants were turning the semi-rural land on the outskirts of our major cities into suburban sprawls. The block of land where our house stood had been carved out of an orchard. The front was cleared but neat rows of fruit trees still stood in the backyard. For a young boy it was a chore to be ordered out in the hot summer sun to pick pears, apples and plums. It was hard to get to this fruit before the birds did, but we generally managed to gather a greater yield from these trees than our family could ever eat. The fruit would be preserved and put away to eat during the winter months or turned into jam and distributed among friends and family.

As the suburbs rapidly expanded, infrastructure lagged badly and by today's expectations was substandard. We lived on the main street in our suburb, which was, in fact, called Main Street. It was paved but most of the other streets were unmade. Around the houses of our street were empty paddocks where horses grazed on blocks yet to be developed. These unmade roads were not a great problem because many of the families, including ours, did not own a car.

The absence of motor transport meant we were essentially confined to the neighbourhood, which included parks, creeks, swamps and neighbours' homes. Since one of the neighbours had a television set, local children could usually be found around there after school, looking at this new-found luxury. Strangely, the lack of car transport also gave us an incredible amount of freedom. The boundaries of our world were set by the walking distance from home. Inside that world the local children were known to most of the neighbours, who would look out for them and send them home when it was time to eat, or give them food before sending them home to sleep. Neighbours got to know each other much better than they do today. Because shops had limited trading hours, a family that ran out of sugar or milk would borrow from the neighbour and return it at some later stage. Our neighbours were our friends and we all got on well because we had to. It was not easy to break out of the confines of the neighbourhood.

When I was old enough to go to school, I was sent to Blackburn South Primary, a government (free) school. I would walk to and from school each day. Enrolments were overflowing and during my period there were thirty to forty pupils in each class. School consisted of a preparatory class, then grades One to Six—seven years. After my first year I was put directly into Grade Two. Most of the class went to Grade One. At the time this was a matter of great pride to me. I would frequently boast that I had done so well that I had skipped a grade without doing a single day's work. It may be that overcrowding in the school led to an attempt to balance the numbers in different years by moving some pupils between the grades. This accelerated beginning meant I was younger than most of my colleagues throughout primary and secondary school.

When I started school we were given slates and taught to write, using sticks of chalk, by copying the teacher, who wrote letters and words on the blackboard. Later we graduated to inkwells with dip pens. Each child had an inkwell set into a desk and a class member chosen to be the ink monitor would fill it daily. It was a prized appointment to be ink monitor and to control the supply of ink to all of the children in the class. I was rarely entrusted with the job, either because of general clumsiness or behavioural infractions. It was as a newly minted Second Grader that I experienced my first bout of corporal punishment. I was caught playing in the wrong part of the playground and was taken before the Infant headmistress who pulled out a leather belt and strapped me five times on the left hand. Strapping was administered to the left hand because the right hand was 'the writing hand' and could not be injured. Although my left hand was bruised and suffering spasms of pain, I was packed back into class to continue my lessons.

Corporal punishment was not an everyday occurrence. It was administered to me three or four times during my primary school career. Other than in Infant school, anyone who committed an offence would be ordered to attend the headmaster's office. I was sent to see the headmaster, Mr Rafferty, quite a few times. His discipline was summary and efficient; we called it Rafferty's Rules. He had a leather strap and he would deliver ten strikes, known as 'the cuts'. This could be taken on either the legs or the hand. I preferred to take 'the cuts' on the hand because strapping on the legs would invariably leave marks that might be seen and would require a lot of explanation when I got home. I do not think corporal punishment did me any great damage, but it would be considered highly inappropriate today. The boys kept a record of the number of 'cuts' they received throughout their schooling. I was not a record-holder but I was a decent performer on the league tables, coming within the top half-dozen or so.

Most of the children in our neighbourhood went to the local government school but some enrolled at the Catholic parish school nearby. With children in our street going in different directions, I became aware for the first time of religious differences in our community. The government school children wore grey uniforms and the parish school children wore brown. Walking home from school, the two tribes would often cross and meet. Occasionally an insult would be hurled from one camp to the other, although I do not recall any serious conflict.

At the back of our school there was a church-run residential complex for orphans or children who needed to be placed in care. They came to our school but would generally stay for only short periods, while they were waiting for foster homes. These were children who had been taken from their parents for their own protection. Probably some mistakes were made but it was well intentioned. I remember my mother asking my Grade Five teacher whether these children presented problems of discipline. 'No, Mrs Costello, all my problem children come from private homes,' she said rather ominously.

Because my mother had a job, there was no one at home when I came home from school each day. From Grade Three onwards I was a 'latch key kid'. This did not trouble me in the slightest. My parents did not work too late and before they got home I could do what I liked. When we got television I spent the afternoons watching cartoons and other series that are now considered classics. Some of them I can recite by heart.

The government school had compulsory religious education. If a parent objected, the child could be removed from class for that period. Catholic children would always be excused from religious education in the government school. There were children in our class who were Exclusive Brethren and they too would be removed. We complained that they were lucky because they were allowed to play sport while the rest of us had religious education. But in my heart I knew this exclusion from normal classes branded them as separate and different.

I felt sympathy for those few children out in the playground while the rest of us were still in class. I think they would have found it difficult.

I was vaguely aware of religious differences within our extended family. As a teenager my father went to a Presbyterian church that fielded good cricket and football teams and required church attendance as a condition of playing. This was known as Church Parade. His father had been a Protestant, his mother a Catholic. He had not been exposed to any religion as a child. In those days the Catholic–Protestant differences were strictly enforced and it may have been too difficult to agree on how to raise him. As a result he was not baptised. It was against Catholic doctrine for a Roman Catholic to attend a Protestant church, even at a family wedding. When my parents married in a Presbyterian church some of my father's relatives waited outside. I would later find out that it was not just religion that created tension between different tribes in Australia.

Since the Catholic population was overwhelmingly Irish and was led in Melbourne by the charismatic Archbishop Dr Mannix, 'the Irish question' was always present. Dr Daniel Mannix, archbishop of Melbourne from 1917 to 1963, was an Irishman trained in Maynooth, Ireland, and a strong supporter of Irish nationalism. Although he deplored the Easter Uprising in Dublin in 1916, he blamed the English for it. During World War I there were two referenda in Australia on the question of conscription. Mannix was a strong opponent. This prompted some mutterings about his loyalty and the loyalty of the Irish to the British Empire. The referenda split the Labor Party, which officially opposed conscription. Mannix's Catholic church and the Labor Party were allies on the question. Leaders with ties to Irish republicanism saw the Labor Party as their political representative against the pro-conscription conservative parties, which they regarded as the establishment and pro-Empire.

About one in three Australians claims to have Irish ancestry, but fortunately 'the troubles' of Ireland never really infected Australia. There was a tendency, appropriate in my opinion, to leave the troubles of Ireland in Ireland and get on with a new start and a new life in Australia. Those seeking to further an ethnic or religious dispute with its origins in Europe are ordinarily considered fanatics in Australia and have little support outside their own enclaves. In this sense Australia has been successful in assimilation.

In my own case three of my grandparents were born in Australia. This is now unusual. Today 40 per cent of Australians were born overseas or had a parent born overseas. The one grandparent not born in Australia was my maternal grandfather, Raymond Northrop. He was born in Portsmouth, Hampshire, England, in 1893. His parents died when he was young. As an orphan at the age of twelve, he was sent from England to Sydney to be looked after by relatives. He enlisted in the Australian Imperial Force in New South Wales in August 1915. He was wounded seven weeks after being sent to the Western Front in France in 1916, then evacuated to England for treatment, and in 1917 he returned to the front. Three months later he was wounded in action a second time and again evacuated to England. When he recovered he was repatriated to Australia because of his war injuries. Being wounded twice was enough. The gunshot wounds disfigured his legs. As a child I was shocked to see them when he wore shorts in summer.

After the war Raymond worked as a book-keeper on stations in northern Victoria and southern New South Wales, where he met my grandmother, a bush nurse. He also spent a brief period in the administration of the Australian Mandated Territory in New Guinea, before he returned to Melbourne to set up an accountancy business. The business failed in the Great Depression and he was out of work for some years before he eventually joined the Commonwealth Public Service in its tax office. Like many of his generation who were scarred by the Great Depression, he took a great interest in monetary theory. Maynard Keynes published his general theory in 1936. There was considerable interest in the supply of money and the use of credit and demand to prevent unemployment. My grandfather wrote a manuscript on the subject of money, which he showed me when I was a teenager. I tried to read it but could not really understand it. It was never published as a book. Years later, when I became responsible for running the Australian monetary system, I wished I had been mature enough to talk with my grandfather about his ideas. He was once a candidate for the Nationalist Party—the non-Labor party that had been formed with Labor defectors who supported conscription during World War I. He was not elected but he and my grandmother were long-time members of the Liberal Party after its formation towards the end of World War II. His wife Jesse, my maternal grandmother, gave me a certificate issued to her father to certify that he had voted in the referendum to federate the colonies into the Commonwealth of Australia in 1899. It records that in the colony of Victoria, out of 163 783 votes, there were 152 653 votes in favour. That was a decent majority.

Costello is an Irish name. My paternal grandfather was Christopher. His grandfather was one Patrick Costello, who came from Leitrim and arrived in Melbourne on the ship *William Metcalfe* in 1841. This was some seven years after Melbourne was founded. Patrick was a successful publican and owned a string of hotels. He was elected to the city council and later Parliament as a representative of the 'Publicans Party'. In his efforts to win one election he apparently paid patrons to vote under assumed names. They were soon discovered and the game was up. He was convicted of ballot fraud and sentenced to prison, although public petitions led to his early release.

Our family was blissfully unaware of these events until a distant relative wrote a genealogical history of her family that included Patrick. A Labor backbencher launched an attack on my character in the House of Representatives on the grounds of Patrick's misdemeanours. But it is hard to blacken the character of someone for the deeds of a forebear four generations earlier. The discovery of this interesting family history allowed me to make a boastful claim whenever I addressed Irish functions. Most of the early Irish in Australia came as convicts. My great-great-grandfather came on an assisted passage, which meant he was a free and sponsored immigrant. I would boast to those of Irish background that, unlike most of their forebears, my great-great-grandfather came to Australia as a free man. In fact, as I would tell many a St Patrick's Day function, our family was so upright and law abiding that they became convicts only once they got to Australia!

Among these forebears I had two grandfathers who were of the Church of England, a grandmother who was Catholic and a grandmother who was Presbyterian. My father joined the Presbyterian church and later became a Methodist lay preacher, while my mother was raised a Presbyterian. Although my parents married in a Presbyterian church, when they built a home the nearest church was of the Baptist denomination. They attended it and sent their children to its Sunday School. I also attended a Baptist secondary school.

With this assortment of religious affiliations we did not take denominational allegiances too seriously. Our attitude was that belief was important and depended not on the theology of the church but on the faith of the believer. The best church to be part of was the one that encouraged your own faith. Although we attended a Baptist church, a Catholic priest would regularly attend our home to give the mass to my maternal grandmother, Honora, when she was infirm and living with us in her declining years.

I was badly accident prone as a child. It may have been the struggle to keep up with a brother two and a half years older. On one occasion we were playing together with a heater. When my brother, Tim, turned it on, it gave me an electric shock and I was hospitalised with severe burns to my hand. The surgeon saved my hand with skin grafts. Later I could joke that it was just the first of many attempts on my life.

Our family was close. Our parents imparted strong values—the importance of honesty, thrift, work, duty, faith, compassion. Outside the church and the local neighbourhood, my parents were not involved in civic institutions or politics but they took a keen interest in public affairs, and my father would pore over the newspapers.

Tim became a Baptist minister, having done his theological training overseas. After returning to Australia he was in charge of a couple of pastorates and became well known as a spokesman against the poker machines introduced by the State Government in Victoria in the early 1990s. At one point Cheryl Kernot, then Leader of the Australian Democrats, asked him to stand for Parliament. He considered it but decided not to run. That was a wise decision. Kernot defected from her own party shortly afterwards and it went into decline and eventually dissolved.

Tim later became chief executive of the major international aid agency World Vision. He organised a huge response to the tsunami that swept the Indian Ocean on Boxing Day 2004. The Australian Government committed $1 billion in aid to Indonesia. Tim and I flew to Aceh together to support projects of reconstruction. The devastation was awful. The Australian Government promised to rebuild a school that once had 540 students, 410 of whom had died in the tsunami. The shocked and traumatised survivors thanked us for our assistance. But how could they ever be the same again? It is hard to imagine the suffering of those who survived, let alone those who died in that shocking tragedy.

My younger sister, Janet, while not so much in the public eye, established her vocation as a careers and guidance adviser in a secondary school in my electorate. She has raised a family and obviously won a great deal of respect from her students. As the local MP I would visit the school where she taught and talk to its classes. The students were, and are, tough and intelligent questioners. I respect the teachers able to cope with such intelligence.

At the Baptist Sunday School I was taught the lessons of the Bible and the Christian faith. This faith has been very important to me throughout my life. As I grew older the gospel became more meaningful and personal to me. It has given me a framework by which to steer my direction in life. I would not claim to be exemplary in behaviour but my faith has given me the certain hope of God's forgiveness and redemption. Attending church has been important in nurturing my faith. I owe a lot to my Sunday School teachers and pastors and my parents for sharing these great truths with me.

Mark Latham, then a Labor frontbencher, attacked me in Parliament for 'changing' my religion. This is nonsense. My religion is Christian. I have attended different churches at different times, mostly Baptist or Anglican, depending on which was active in the area and the inspiration of the leader or vicar.

In one aspect my parents were different from their own parents: each had completed tertiary education. I could see the difference this had made in my father's life, where tertiary education had 'upskilled' him from repetitive factory work. The same impulse could be found in my mother's family. The Depression and the failure of her father's business led to an emphasis on the education and self-improvement of my mother and her siblings, all of whom enjoyed worthwhile careers.

My father became a secondary school teacher and spent the whole of his 30-year career at the one independent school, Carey Baptist Grammar School, in Kew, Melbourne (where I had my secondary education). He taught generations of schoolboys, earning himself a 'Mr Chips'-like reputation. Lawyers, judges, doctors and army commanders would regularly approach me to reminisce fondly about the influence of 'Russ' as their teacher. Even the odd bankrupt or career criminal would warmly remember his guiding influence! Some of his former students would later claim that they thought he was on the left of politics. But he had a conservative outlook on moral issues and I remember him being highly critical of the scandals of the Whitlam Labor Government.

Both my parents had taught high school and stressed the importance of study. As school teachers they did not earn high incomes, but the work gave them more time to spend with their children and family. My mother told me that the best any parent could do for their children was to give them a good education. There is no doubt that we learned from an early age that the path to self-improvement was to study and work hard. These were invaluable lessons.

As I was finishing my secondary education, I was drifting towards the idea of studying medicine. It was the hardest course to enter at university and our teachers encouraged us to aim for the highest. The only compulsory subject for entry into medicine was chemistry. We had an inspirational chemistry master by the name of Alan Smith. I really enjoyed chemistry and did well at it. About twenty years after I had left, I was asked to address a function for my old school. To my delight Alan moved the vote of thanks. He said he had been particularly impressed with my Year 11 Chemistry exam paper—so impressed he had kept it. He then produced it. He had given it a mark that was clearly written on the front of the paper: 22 out of 20! According to him, I had answered all the questions correctly and thought of two answers that he hadn't. I can't think what they were.

A large number of my classmates entered medical school, inspired by Alan Smith. But when the time came for me to enter university

I enrolled in Law. During my last year of school we were set to study Robert Bolt's play *A Man for All Seasons*, a story of Sir Thomas More and his struggle with Henry VIII. I was fascinated by the interplay of law, morality, conscience and politics and it gave me the idea that I should study law. Since my mother's brother had been a barrister and then a judge of the Federal Court of Australia, I had some familiarity with the life of a lawyer. My decision was clinched when I examined the schedule of law lectures and compared it with that of medical students. Law students had a lot more time out of classes to do things other than study, and I was determined to pursue interests outside of the lecture theatre.

So I enrolled to study Arts and Law at the university nearest to where we lived. I could save money on transport fares, either by hitchhiking or by getting a lift with my brother. I did not know that Monash University was then the most radical left-wing university in Australia. This decision would expose me to left-wing politics, and turn me against them, for life.

In my first year, in 1975, there were two momentous political events. The first was the fall of Saigon at the end of the Vietnam War. In the mid-1970s the Cold War was still in progress, the Berlin Wall was in place and various proxy wars were raging in Africa. People living under communism were subject to coercion and denial of liberty. I had no doubt communism was a bad system. The evidence was the number of people who escaped it, often at risk of their lives. When Saigon fell, the television footage of Vietnamese crowds trying to find refuge in the United States Embassy or fighting to get on helicopters said volumes about their fear of persecution. Soon the first wave of refugees would come to Australia by boat, fleeing the communist regime. The fall of Saigon did not strike me as a moment of great elation, but to student leaders on campus it was a great triumph.

Conscription and Vietnam dominated Australian politics in the late 1960s and early 1970s. Conscription had been a controversial issue in Australia, ever since the time of World War I when the referenda seeking to impose conscription were opposed by the Labor Party and defeated. With its history of opposition to conscription, the Labor Party would support the compulsory call-up during World War II only 'for the defence of Australia', which was expanded to include New Guinea. Australian conscripts could not be sent to fight outside that area—even to fight alongside the US forces conscripted overseas to the Pacific theatre.

The Menzies Government instituted compulsory national service for eligible young men in the 1950s but later scrapped it. It reintroduced it as part of the build-up of forces required for the Vietnam War effort. It was not universal. It depended on a person's birthday. Various dates were balloted and if you were of eligible age and born on that day, you were required to register. It was a bad system because selection was completely arbitrary.

The Labor Party originally supported Australia's engagement in the Vietnam War but later changed its position. Conscription was unpopular with young people and, as the war in Vietnam became less popular, conscription also became less popular with the wider public. Since a tertiary student could defer the call-up, some young men enrolled in tertiary campuses, and sought to continue their enrolment as long as possible, as a means of avoiding conscription. A generation of student activists did extended courses to delay the call-up. Labor promised to abolish conscription if it won the 1972 election. The Liberal Government actually ended conscription before the election but, since it had introduced it in the first place and supported the Vietnam War effort, a great part of this generation was extremely hostile to the Liberal Party.

At Monash the student activists had taken the argument to a new level when a small group collected funds to send to the National Liberation Front (NLF) of Vietnam. The NLF was the political wing of the Viet Cong, both controlled ultimately by the North Vietnamese. This meant collecting money to fund forces fighting and killing Australian soldiers. It generated huge community outrage but became a publicity bonanza for the student activists. For them the fall of Saigon in 1975 was a wonderful victory for communism and a momentous defeat for 'American imperialism'.

The other great political event of 1975 was the dismissal of the Whitlam Labor Government. This Government had been elected in 1972 and re-elected in 1974. Its second term ordinarily would have run to 1977, but because of ministerial incompetence and economic mismanagement, the Government was immensely unpopular. The Coalition parties threatened to withhold Supply from the Government in the Senate. In these circumstances the Governor-General dismissed the Government. The Coalition parties, led by Malcolm Fraser, overwhelmingly won the consequent elections.

The dismissal of the first Labor Government in twenty-three years understandably led to uproar on the left-wing campus. The return of the Liberal Government, which had supported both conscription and the Vietnam War, kept their rage smouldering for years. And Malcolm Fraser, as Minister for the Army and later Minister for Defence during Australia's engagement in Vietnam, had been one of the principal spokesmen defending the war.

I voted for the first time in that 1975 federal election—for the Liberal Party. Inflation was high, unemployment was rising, strikes were damaging the economy, and the Whitlam Government was staggering under ministerial scandals. I voted for the Liberal Movement in the Senate. This was a breakaway small-'l' liberal group that opposed the blocking of Supply but gave preferences to the Liberal Party. It was my way of saying that I did not like the blocking of Supply. I disapproved of the means but I approved the outcome!

At the Commonwealth level, the Government must go to the electorate every three years—a fairly short term. An elected Government is, or should be, entitled to expect that its money bills will pass. Under the Australian Constitution the Senate can defeat a money bill but the circumstances have to be extreme. By the time I had become Australia's longest serving Treasurer, I was less sympathetic than ever to the argument from a hostile Senate that it knew better how to allocate Budget spending.

If Malcolm Fraser had not deferred Supply but let the Parliament run, he still would have been elected, probably in an even greater landslide. What is more, he would not have had to face the argument—which he always had to face—that somehow he had got into office through illegitimate tactics. I believe Fraser felt de-legitimised by this tactic and this is one of the reasons he was cautious in office and later began to court progressive opinion.

Nobody on the left of politics supported Fraser when he was elected in 1975 or at any time through his period in office. When he attended Monash University to open a new childhood education centre on 23 August 1976, there was a riot. He was locked inside a building for several hours while hundreds of student demonstrators overwhelmed security and blockaded the exit.

Victoria Police had to call for reinforcements. They were bussed in and formed a flying wedge to get through the demonstrators to Fraser and his party and then to evacuate them. I was caught between the demonstrators and police. Although Fraser was the supreme target of the venom of that day, students of more moderate outlook were not much more popular. One of Fraser's staff, Vincent Woolcock, told the police to grab me and another student, my friend Michael Kroger, and get us out to safety with the Fraser party. Thirty years later Vincent Woolcock was still getting me out of tricky situations, but now as a member of my staff!

That day I was there just to watch what was going on and I was shocked by the violence. The student left genuinely believed that the Prime Minister had no right to attend the university or to speak in it and they saw the violence and disruption as a great success. Their view was that his attendance at a Commonwealth-funded university was 'provocation'. At Monash I had been elected to the Student Association's 15-member Public Affairs Committee as a Christian representative. The committee debated the riot. My view was that the protesters had a right to protest but Fraser had a right to free speech as much as anyone else; violence was not acceptable.

The majority of the committee was leftist and refused to recognise Fraser's right to free speech at the university. He got enough space, they said, in the 'capitalist press', and the university should be reserved for alternative (left-wing) viewpoints. I was a middle-of-the-road student, not particularly Labor or Liberal, but I was shocked by the authoritarianism of the left-wing students, who would not tolerate alternative viewpoints, not even those of the Prime Minister.

The other issue that occupied a great deal of attention in the student association at that time was the Middle East. In 1974 the Australian Union of Students (AUS) passed extremist resolutions that

'AUS informs the national union of Israeli students that AUS does not recognise the existence of the State of Israel' and that 'AUS supports the liberation forces of Palestine'. In 1975 the council of the AUS further resolved that 'AUS Travel cease all advertising and organisation, and promotion of travel to occupied Palestine until the Zionist entity is overcome and the land known as Israel is completely restored to its rightful inhabitants'.

This was in the aftermath of the Yom Kippur War, the massacre of Israeli athletes in Munich, and a hijacking and terror campaign by the Palestine Liberation Organization (PLO). Most Australian students were appalled at these sentiments. It did not reflect student opinion. What it showed was how extreme and unrepresentative the student leadership had become. All student associations had to decide whether to ratify these positions. Jewish students in particular began organising against the resolutions. They were ably led by the president of the Australian Union of Jewish Students, Joe Gersh, whom I got to know at this time and who became a great friend.

There was overwhelming opposition to these resolutions on campuses around Australia, and they were defeated. Attention turned to how the leadership of AUS had become so unrepresentative. The explanation was that a handful of leftist activists had hijacked it. Few mainstream students ran for office and only a minority bothered to vote. At the end of 1976 I stood for the position of chairman of the Monash Association of Students on a platform of moderating the extremism of the previous student leaders. I had the backing of Jewish students, Christian students, many Liberal students and quite a number of right-wing Labor Party supporters. Collectively this was known as the 'right' or 'centre'. The incumbent group we were trying to dislodge was known as the 'left' and consisted of Marxists of one kind or another, some pro-Peking, some pro-Soviet, Trotskyites, anarchists and other denominations. I won. It had been a long time since the left had been defeated at Monash University.

I enjoyed standing for election and running campaigns, although on one occasion I was ambushed and punched up by a student radical. He was convicted of assault and dined out on the notoriety for years. I enjoyed working with a broad cross-section of students against the left-wing extremists. Our campaign to change the policy of the AUS on the Middle East to one more balanced and pro-Israel was successful and it evolved into campaigns to reform the AUS generally. Eventually, disaffection with the extreme policy of the organisation led a number of constituent campuses to secede from the AUS and it collapsed. I worked with other like-minded students to aid that collapse. A number of them later entered Parliament and were colleagues—such as Tony Abbott in Sydney and Eric Abetz from Tasmania. One of the student representatives I also met at this time was Tanya Coleman from Sydney University.

In these campaigns we tried to build as broad a coalition of mainstream opinion as possible. The Liberal students were good allies. The Young Liberal movement was focussed on internal issues in the Liberal Party rather than the ideas and debate at university. There were many right-wing members of the Labor Party who were anti-communist and opposed to the leftist leadership of the AUS. The left wing of the Labor Party usually supported the socialist officials in the AUS.

During this period some of the right-wing Labor students who worked to reform the AUS asked me to join the Labor Party. They saw the left-wing student leaders in the AUS as the same kinds of extremists who ran the left-wing trade unions. These right-wing Labor types were consistently at war with their left-wing comrades and particularly with left-wing union leaders, some of whom were communists. They were keen to recruit allies. At the same time some of the Liberal students asked me to join the Liberal Party. But the Liberal Party, with a few exceptions, did not engage its members in student debates with the same enthusiasm as the left or the Labor Party. It did not take university or ideological debates seriously enough. I declined invitations from both sides.

One week in 1978 I attended the Australian Liberal Students Federation (ALSF) conference in Canberra and a Labor-run conference on social democracy in Sydney. The ALSF had as its speaker the larrikin founder of the right-wing Workers' Party, advertising man John Singleton, while the Social Democrats had the left-leaning *enfant terrible* Paddy McGuinness as theirs. Both of them in their own way were in revolt against the welfare state. Singleton later ended up working for the Labor Party on election campaigns and McGuinness later became its trenchant critic as editor of *Quadrant*.

There was considerable industrial disruption in Australia in the 1970s and 1980s. I could see that trade unions operated in much the same way as the student union operated at Monash. They were authoritarian and did not care for individual rights or for the voice of conscience if they conflicted with their position or bargaining power. When they finished as students the left-wing activists drifted into jobs with the left-wing unions, which were enormously powerful in the Australian Labor Party (ALP). All the real power in the ALP organisation was held and exercised by the union bosses.

The Liberal Party is a voluntary organisation of individual members. It has no equivalent to the bosses that run in the ALP. Some people make the mistake of thinking that the membership of the Liberal Party is run by big business. In fact, most members have backgrounds in small business and some can be quite hostile to large corporations. They do not like being pushed around by powerful unions either.

An article of faith for the Liberal Party is individual rights and individual liberty—including the right to start a business and receive just reward for hard work and effort. The Liberal Party believes in the importance of private property and in protecting it from punishing taxation. It also believes that all people should be equally subject to the law—including powerful corporations and powerful unions. Labor was born of the unions and is still subject to enormous influence from the union leadership—although, with declining union membership, perhaps less so today than was the case decades ago.

After finishing university I spent two months backpacking across Europe. My friends in Australia also organised a tour for me in Israel. Later, while travelling in Germany, I crossed the Berlin Wall through Checkpoint Charlie to look at East Berlin in the socialist East Germany. The wide streets had few cars and the cars they did have— Trabants—looked like they were relics of the 1950s. I was amazed to see long queues outside state-owned shops that had hardly any produce in them. There was no advertising on any of the shops, only omnipresent pictures of Marx and Lenin. What struck me was the economic backwardness compared with the West. It dawned on me that communism was not just a repressive political system; it was an economic failure.

In 1979 the Soviet Union invaded Afghanistan. This confirmed for me what a dangerous power the Soviet Union was and the importance of defending the other flashpoints in the Cold War. While some members of the Labor Party were strongly anti-communist, there were also a lot of fellow-travellers. The Liberal Party had never had any misapprehension about the nature of communism and its repressive system.

In 1980 I decided to join the Liberal Party. At that time a person under thirty could join the youth wing—the Young Liberal (YL) movement—or the senior party organisation. Members of the YL movement had full membership and voting rights in all the councils of the Liberal Party. I joined the YL movement at the suggestion of my friend Michael Kroger.

Michael was one of the few members of the Monash University Liberal Club who was interested in student politics. He had been engaged in re-invigorating the ALSF when he was elected as its president in 1978. The Liberal students saw the YL movement as too focussed on social activities and not enough on politics.

Michael became intent on getting elected as YL president so as to make the movement more 'political'. He ran for election as vice president in 1980 and was given strong support by Prime Minister Malcolm Fraser. At the time, former Foreign Minister and then Minister for Industrial Relations Andrew Peacock, an ex-president, was the favourite of the YL movement. Peacock was seen as more progressive than Fraser. Michael was unsuccessful but he would not be put off. He started to work on becoming president in 1981 and asked me to help. I agreed to help his campaign as long as he did not expect me to spend too much time on it. After graduating I had spent a year doing my practical training to qualify to practise law, and from March 1981 I was working long hours practising as a solicitor. I did not want to spend my time on politics. Michael asked me to stand for election to the YL state executive, which he would chair if he were elected president. In the event, he was not successful but I was. I became a member of the state executive of the Young Liberals at the end of 1981. I found that most of the YL members were still focussed on social activities and I left the executive after a year. I remained in the organisation as a branch president and member of state and federal electorate committees.

Michael Kroger later nominated for pre-selection in two different state seats (both in the federal electorate of Higgins) but he was not successful. He was too young and inexperienced. After the 1987 federal election defeat he was elected president of the Victorian Division of the Liberal Party. He was a reforming president who brought youth and vigour to the organisation and he served a record term. He has been significantly engaged in the organisational wing of the party most of his life and a great friend and supporter of mine. Missing out on state politics may have been a blessing; instead, he has had a successful business career.

The early 1980s were a bad period for the Liberal Party. It lost government in Victoria in 1982 and the Fraser Government was defeated in 1983. In 1983 Alan Jarman, the sitting member for the seat of Deakin, where I lived, was swept away in a landslide victory to the Labor Party led by Bob Hawke. As a result the local Liberal Party had to choose a new candidate for the 1984 election. It pre-selected Julian Beale, who was a breath of fresh air for the party. A self-made millionaire, he was something of a free marketeer and determined to be part of a Government more reformist than Fraser's. I supported his pre-selection and worked on his campaigns in the 1984 and 1987 elections. When I entered Parliament myself, in 1990, we became colleagues. Unfortunately Julian lost his seat before the Liberals won government in 1996. He would have made a good Minister. His career illustrates that in politics timing is everything. He was in the wrong cycle—at his peak in Opposition, and out of Parliament when we were in Government.

At the beginning of the 1980s I had my work cut out building a legal career. I was also busy with family matters. Tanya Coleman graduated from Sydney University at the end of 1980 having completed an Arts degree, majoring in French, and a Law degree.

A brilliant student, she was elected to the Students' Representative Council and the University Senate. Her father, Peter, had been an academic, journalist, editor, lawyer, member of the New South Wales state Parliament and federal Member for Wentworth in the House of Representatives. Her mother, Verna, was an accomplished biographer. I met Tanya at the annual conference of the AUS when she was still a student. After graduating she worked for Stephen Jacques and Stephens, the Sydney solicitors. I worked for Mallesons, solicitors in Melbourne. The two firms merged in the 1980s.

Tanya is vivacious, articulate, well read and highly educated. She has a wide circle of friends and has not only pursued a legal career but has also given time to many charitable and educational causes. We were married in Sydney in January 1982 and settled down to live in Melbourne. Our first child, Sebastian, was born in February 1987. After that Tanya resumed her career. By July, she was pregnant again. I had started at the Bar in 1984, which meant I was self-employed and working long hours to support the growing family and meet our mortgage repayments. One morning I left for work, before Tanya was up, to appear in the national wage case due to open in Melbourne on 21 October 1987. The world financial markets were in turmoil. On Monday 19 October 1987 the New York Stock Exchange suffered its biggest one-day fall in history—even greater than the one that started the Great Depression. The national wage case was adjourned to see how financial markets played out and the effect this would have on the world economy. I went back to my chambers much earlier than I had expected. It was lucky that I did. My secretary told me that Tanya was seriously unwell.

For a few days she had been experiencing acute headaches. She had been to see doctors who had prescribed painkillers. But on the Wednesday morning, after I was already at work, she had rung a friend to get some help. The friend, who became alarmed when Tanya was unable to speak, contacted my office and I raced home. Tanya was still conscious but she had lost movement and speech and was deteriorating fast. I rushed her to hospital, where she was diagnosed with severe cerebral debilitation, possibly tumours. She underwent immediate surgery to drain fluid from the brain and to reduce intra-cranial pressure. When no tumour was found it was clear that she had a serious inflammatory disorder of the brain itself. She hovered between life and death.

The doctors prepared me for the worst. There was not only Tanya's life at stake but also that of our unborn child. Tanya was taking massive doses of medicine to treat the inflammation and it was not known whether this medication would affect her pregnancy. It was possible that saving one life could damage the other. Tanya was in hospital for forty-five days. With a serious brain disorder there is not just the fear for a person's life but the fear that, even if they do survive, they might suffer irreparable brain damage. Tanya survived, and she recovered her speech. Our daughter Madeleine was delivered successfully. With the care of a brilliant neurosurgeon and neurologist Tanya made a slow recovery over several months. This medical assistance and, in my view, divine intervention saw her recover from an illness that threatened her life. Our family and hers were an enormous support.

The shadow of death had hung over us in late 1987 but Tanya fought back with great courage. Later she resumed her career. We had a third child—our daughter Phoebe. An event like this gives you a sense of proportion, a feeling for what is really important and what is not. I have no doubt that life, health and family are much more important than money and career. I have been blessed with a healthy and happy family. The rest is secondary.

3

FROM CONFECTIONERY TO CANBERRA

In the mid-1980s Fred Stauder, the owner of the confectionery company Dollar Sweets, became part of industrial folklore. He was the little man who stood up to trade union bullies and thugs. All his life he had been manufacturing 'hundreds and thousands' to decorate the cakes and fairy bread of children's birthday parties and other celebrations. In a small factory in Glen Iris, up the road from where I would later locate my electorate office, Fred and his workers would toss sugar and colours into machines that looked like cement mixers, whirl them around, and produce a mixture that came out as sprinkles and toppings.

Fred was an easy-going, practical man. He got on well with his twenty-seven employees, who were all members of a union, the Federated Confectioners' Association. The secretary of the union was Carlo Frizziero. Carlo was an ideologue, one of the 'tomato left', so named because they once threw rotten tomatoes at some right-wingers entering an ALP conference. The union's leaders admired and visited Colonel Gaddafi's Libya.

To understand the Dollar Sweets story and the contest between Fred and Carlo's union, we have to go back in history to another age, to 1983, when Prime Minister Hawke's 'Accord' re-introduced centralised wage fixation. The idea was that wages would be fixed in accordance with the movements of prices. If prices went up by 4 per cent, wages would be increased by 4 per cent. If prices moved by a higher amount, wages would move by the same amount—a process of automatic indexation administered by the Arbitration Commission. The commission set wage levels by amending the industrial award that stipulated an employer's legal obligations. All a union had to do was give a commitment that it would abide by the principles of the Arbitration Commission.

Fred accepted the principles of centralised wage fixation. He even paid over the award. His employees worked a 38-hour week even though the award prescribed a 40-hour week. But Carlo and his union decided to demand a 36-hour week. The union started rolling strikes in support of its claim in July 1985. Fred explained that his company could not afford a 36-hour week and the Arbitration Commission told the union it could not claim a 36-hour week. Fred said if employees wanted a 36-hour week, they would have to find it elsewhere. Twelve of the twenty-seven employees were happy to keep working on existing terms. The other fifteen, on the recommendation of the union, refused. Fred advertised for new employees to take their place. He was flooded with applications. He replaced the fifteen, who then began to picket the premises. Since he was complying with the wage-fixing principles, Fred believed that the Arbitration Commission would and should protect him, his factory and his loyal employees.

At first the picketers tried to stop employees entering and leaving the premises. Later, the focus turned to drivers. After a few weeks, events at the factory became more serious. Fred Stauder received death threats, and bomb threats were made against the factory. The locks on the factory doors were destroyed and part of the premises was set alight in an attempted arson. In mid-August 1985, a driver making a delivery was assaulted and his truck was vandalised. Some of the picketers were later convicted of common assault in relation to this incident.

Fred turned to the authorities, to the guardians of industrial law and order, for help. He appealed to Prime Minister Hawke and to Ralph Willis, the Minister for Employment and Industrial Relations. Both said they would ask the Department of Industrial Relations to 'look into' the matter. The department referred the matter to the Australian Council of Trade Unions (ACTU), which 'looked into' the matter and supported the union. Fred appealed to the Victorian premier, John Cain, who said he would get his department 'to look into' the matter. Fred asked the commissioner for police to station a police guard at the factory. The commissioner did not think this would be necessary. When the telephone and telex wires to the factory were deliberately severed, Telecom employees refused to repair them; they would not cross a picket line.

Fred's lawyers took the matter to the Arbitration Commission, which recommended the picket line be disbanded. The union ignored the recommendation. Fred was told there was nothing he could do. He began appealing to business leaders for help. Hugh Morgan, chief executive of Western Mining Corporation, recommended that Fred see me because he thought Fred needed a new lawyer. I had been a part-time tutor in industrial law at Monash University and was now a young and lean barrister. I said I would do what I could to help. I told Fred he would need a solicitor, and recommended my friend Michael Kroger.

The first step I took as Fred's new lawyer was to go back to the Arbitration commissioners and ask them to fix the situation. They gave their usual recommendation that the union lift its picket. The union ignored this. Nothing changed. I told Fred that the only thing I could think of now was to go to the Victorian Supreme Court to get an injunction—a court order—to lift the picket. It was a long shot; it was highly unusual and it would take some resources. Fred was a member of the Melbourne Chamber of Commerce (MCC), whose chairman at the time was Andrew Hay. The MCC said it would raise some funds to pay Fred's costs.

In November I drew the pleadings, and the court proceedings were initiated. For the hearing of the interlocutory injunction we brought in a QC, Alan Goldberg. Our case was that the picket line was intimidation, nuisance and a conspiracy to injure the company and interfere with its contractual relations. We wanted the union to observe the laws—laws that say you must not cut telephone lines, burn a factory, punch up drivers or stop deliveries.

Our case was that the State Supreme Court should exercise common law jurisdiction to grant injunctive relief against a union involved in acts that were civil wrongs, or torts. The union argued that the Arbitration Commission had jurisdiction in industrial disputes and that civil jurisdiction should not be invoked when the whole thing related to wage-fixing principles and industrial disputes. The Victorian Supreme Court rejected this argument. It upheld our claim.

The judge was Mr Justice Peter Murphy, who had been a World War II bomber pilot. He was not impressed by lawlessness in the suburb of Glen Iris. On 12 December 1985, he gave a judgment and said: 'If the defendants continue with their picketing, in the form in which they have chosen to conduct it, they may well succeed in forcing the plaintiff family company out of business. This indeed would seem to be their object, although I find it extremely difficult to rationalise such apparently stupid and nihilistic acts.'

The judge gave orders to restrain the picket, which ended the next day. It had lasted 143 days. Fred battled on to claim damages for the business losses his company had suffered. In April 1988 the union settled the case and paid Dollar Sweets $175000 in compensation. The Dollar Sweets company survived. It moved to bigger and newer premises and eventually was bought out by a larger concern.

The case was a significant legal milestone. It showed that the common law had jurisdiction in industrial disputes and that civil courts could be effective where the Arbitration Commission failed. Henry Bournes Higgins, 'the father of arbitration' (and the judge after whom my electorate was named), claimed he had abolished the common law in the workplace and replaced the market with arbitration. He called this, in the title of one of his publications, 'A New Province for Law and Order'. But it was the Dollar Sweets case that ushered in, at long last, a truly new province for law and order.

Throughout the dispute the media, with the exception of Melbourne's *Age*, supported the little company. They reported 143 days of picketing, violence and intimidation. They congratulated the Dollar Sweets company for relying on the law and blazing a new trail to industrial justice. While the court decision made headlines around Australia, Melbourne's *Herald* published an editorial headed 'A Sweet Result'. When I began my career as a barrister I had decided to focus on commercial and tax law—the areas I knew best. Now I found myself in the midst of a case that generated a lot more notoriety than dusty tax cases. On the afternoon and evening of the judgment, the case featured prominently on the television news. As the barrister who had advised Fred to take the action, I found it all pretty heady stuff and I was elated by his victory.

In 2005, Stauder, Morgan, Kroger, Hay, Goldberg and I celebrated the twentieth anniversary of the Dollar Sweets case at a black-tie dinner in Melbourne. Fred was the hero of the case. In a toast to him I quoted a famous speech by Teddy Roosevelt:

> It is not the critic who counts, not the man who points out how the strong man stumbles or where the doer of deeds could have done better. The credit belongs to the man who is actually in the arena, whose face is marred by dust and sweat and blood, who strives valiantly, who comes up short again and again, because there is no effort without error and shortcoming, but who knows the great enthusiasm, the great devotions, who spends himself for a worthy cause, who, at best, knows in the end the triumph of high achievement, and who, at the worst, if he fails, at least fails while daring greatly.

To Fred Stauder I said: 'You were the one marred with dust and sweat and blood. You were the one in the arena. We were just the advisers. You had your whole life's savings on the line. You had plenty of critics. But you won a place in Australian industrial history. This child of Austrian immigrants became a true Australian hero.' In an emotional response Fred said, 'Tonight is the greatest night of my life.' He died a few months later. I was privileged to deliver a eulogy at his funeral.

When the Dollar Sweets company went outside the Arbitration Commission, it undermined what political commentator Gerard Henderson had called, in an influential article in *Quadrant* in September 1983, 'The Industrial Relations Club'. This was the cosy and complacent ring of unionists, employer representatives and arbitration commissioners who settled industrial disputes between themselves according to arcane principles quite untroubled by economic realities such as capacity to pay. The process kept them all in business. The Dollar Sweets case re-wrote the manual on the acceptable limits of industrial action by unions. It encouraged hundreds of businesses to rely on their common law rights. It also contributed to the decision of the Hawke Government to withdraw its Industrial Relations Bill which had proposed to give legal immunity to trade unions.

There were other milestone cases against militant and lawless trade unionism at this time—the Mudginberri Abattoir case, the Wide Comb issue and the Robe River dispute. In the early 1970s the Mudginberri Station in the Northern Territory had developed a small abattoir to process feral buffalo for export. Pickets by the Meat Workers' Union were set up against the station to impose a unit tally system on the abattoir rather than a local award. The consequence was that export inspectors would not cross the picket line and production stopped. The station took action under the Trade Practices Act, section 45D, to lift the picket and pursue damages. The dispute was essentially over whether the Northern Territory would be forced to follow the uncompetitive terms that the Meat Workers' Union had established in some southern abattoirs.

The Wide Comb dispute arose when New Zealand shearers came to Australia and used a wider comb for shearing the fleece of the sheep. By using a wider comb the shearer could cut the fleece faster and process more sheep in a day. Since shearers are paid by the number of sheep, this enabled them to earn higher wages. The Australian Workers' Union argued that Australian shearers had always used the narrow comb and did not want technological advances, so it opposed the use of wide combs. Despite this vigorous resistance by the AWU, the wide comb took off in Australia and is now almost universally used by Australian shearers.

The Robe River dispute etched the phrase 'restrictive work practices' into the national lexicon. Robe River was an iron ore producer in the Pilbara, Western Australia, and, like other operations in the Pilbara, it had become subject to petty rules and work practices imposed by powerful unions that had established non-working full-time conveners paid by the company. These convenors had offices on-site, and any complaints by the workforce would be taken directly to the union convener, who would resolve them according to union rules. These rules determined which union's members had to perform each specific task. Peko Wallsend, the new majority owner of Robe River in 1986, attempted to remove many of these restrictive work practices and lift productivity, including directing the union conveners to work at jobs. Disputes between management and the unions culminated when the whole workforce was sacked in July 1986. When the workforce returned, production lifted substantially. Robe River eventually ended up as part of Rio Tinto and became a pace-setter for the improvement of output and productivity in other iron ore mines in the Pilbara.

The notoriety of the Dollar Sweets case brought other victims of trade union bullies my way. In October 1986 I represented a boiler-maker who had been sacked because he refused to join a trade union. Franz Hein had been born in Germany and had lived under both Nazism and Russian occupation. As a qualified boiler-maker he was employed by an engineering firm in Clayton, Victoria. The union shop steward demanded that he join the Amalgamated Metal Workers' Union. When he refused, he was reported to management, which immediately sacked him. This kind of thing was quite common at that time. Employers did not particularly like sacking people who refused to join a trade union but they did it to preserve industrial peace.

I took his case to the Equal Opportunity Board, which found in Hein's favour and awarded compensation. The basis of the case was that he refused to join the union because he disagreed with its politics. He said: 'I will not sing hallelujah to the communist Satan.' His dismissal for exercising that choice amounted to political discrimination. It was a big blow to the closed shop and in the aftermath of that case many other people who had suffered discrimination in the workplace at the hands of the unions came to see me.

One was a devout Christian by the name of Frank Marrett. He was a member of a trade union but he refused, on the basis of his religious beliefs, to pay a levy struck by the Amalgamated Metal Workers' Union to support a strike in south-east Queensland. He was declared 'black'. The employer, a petroleum refiner, removed him from the workplace. He was made to sit in a small Atco hut without a phone and given no work for twelve weeks, then the company dismissed him. Again he was successful in his case.

At this time a number of students objected to paying compulsory student fees, which universities imposed as a condition of enrolment. The head of the Victorian Liberal Students' Association, Tony Smith, took up their case. He came to my legal chambers to ask me whether I would test a case to see if this infringed human rights and equal opportunity principles. I did, but the case was unsuccessful. Tony Smith impressed me as a capable student. He worked part-time for the Institute of Public Affairs. It turned out he was the son of my old chemistry teacher. When I became a candidate for the 1990 election, he offered to work for me. He proved an exceptional recruit and stayed on my staff until he entered Parliament as the Member for Casey in 2001. Tony has been a parliamentary secretary and is now a shadow Minister. He will go a long way in politics. As a Member of Parliament it gave him great satisfaction to see legislation pass through Parliament to establish voluntary student union membership—a cause he had begun to campaign for nearly twenty years earlier.

By the 1980s there was little public sympathy for unions that ruthlessly enforced the closed shop or organised violent pickets. But the union leadership was not going to take these legal reverses lying down. Its members began to organise a counter-attack. They claimed there was a vast conspiracy—dubbed 'the New Right'—behind these events. At its centre they imagined a secret cabal—the HR Nicholls Society. This group was a loose association of people who discussed industrial relations. It had no staff, offices or resources. The society didn't even have a common view, although it was critical of Prime Minister Hawke's Accord. It was formed largely on the initiative of Ray Evans, once a Labor Party activist but now involved in more liberal and conservative causes. A former deputy dean of Engineering at Deakin University, he was an assistant to Hugh Morgan at Western Mining Corporation. He had a knack for unearthing arcane political episodes and making them famous. One of these was the story of the editor of the *Hobart Mercury*, Henry Richard Nicholls.

In April 1911 Henry Nicholls published an editorial in which he described Mr Justice Higgins as 'a political judge who does not mean to allow any reflections on those to whom he may be said to be indebted for his judgeship'. (In 1904 the short-lived Watson Labor Government had made Higgins attorney-general and in 1906 the Deakin protectionist Government had appointed him to the High Court and then to the Commonwealth Court of Conciliation and Arbitration.) The Commonwealth attorney-general brought an action in the High Court to commit the editor to prison for contempt of court. The case was dismissed. Nicholls became a Tasmanian hero and a champion of free speech.

Ray Evans' idea was to form a discussion group that would take its name from that famous editor. He called it the HR Nicholls Society. John Stone was one of the foundation members. In 1984, while secretary to the Commonwealth Treasury, Stone gave the Shann Memorial Lecture in which he called the arbitration commissioners 'latter-day arbitral Higginses'. This was a reference to the judge who was Nicholls' foe. Another foundation member was Barry Purvis, the debonair and worldly survivor of the Industrial Relations Club who ran the Australian Wool Selling Brokers. Evans invited me to join and I accepted.

The inaugural meeting was held in CWA House, the Country Women's Association's gracious old residence in Lansell Road, Toorak—in the electorate of Higgins. A number of excellent papers were given, principally about current industrial cases and the legal and political issues they raised. The speakers included Ian McLachlan, then president of the National Farmers' Federation; John Hyde, a former MP and leader of the 'dries' in the Parliament; Sir John Kerr; Gerard Henderson; and Hugh Morgan.

We all agreed on one general principle: that centralised wage fixation had failed and that Australia needed to liberalise and free up its industrial laws. A modern economy must be flexible if it is to adjust with minimum distress to inevitable shocks—whether caused by oil prices, drought, the terms of trade, an American recession or whatever. For example, during the Asian economic meltdown of the late 1990s, our floating exchange rate meant that our dollar went as low as US$0.47. This helped our exporters keep the Australian economy on an even keel. Similarly, a flexible wage-fixing system is absolutely essential to deal with a terms-of-trade shock. If commodity prices lead to increased profitability in one sector, employers can afford to pay high wages. But if these wages are applied across the board, as in a centralised system they must be, an unsustainable wages burden is placed on many other industries.

The HR Nicholls Society promptly published the papers of its first meeting and made them freely available. But journalists are less interested in anything public than in something secret. A whole industry flourished by attacking or 'exposing' this 'secretive' New Right which included conspirators such as the Institute of Public Affairs, the Centre for Independent Studies, *Quadrant* and sundry 'sinister' individuals.

The Labor Party even invoked the threat of the New Right to sell its raffle tickets. In 1986 Stephen Loosley, general secretary of the New South Wales Branch of the Labor Party, wrote to his members:

Dear Colleague,

The New Right looms very large on the Australian political landscape and has made clear its dedication to the destruction of Labor Government. The ALP is currently under political pressure. Important political contests, including the State By-Election for Heathcote assume real significance. The ALP looks to our traditional supporters to help defeat the philosophy of the New Right early and decisively. In these terms, the party is seeking your support for our Melbourne Cup Competition. We would be pleased if you could sell the enclosed book of tickets.

The raffle tickets sold like hot cakes in a determined stand to defeat the New Right. (Later Senator Stephen Loosley asked me to help him with one of the essays he was writing for a law degree. It was about Dollar Sweets.)

I received two approaches to stand for Parliament in the 1987 election. One was from Eda Ritchie, the president of the Liberal Party in Victoria. She thought I might contest the seat of Chisholm held by the Labor Party. In fact a young doctor, Michael Wooldridge, nominated for that seat. I declined Eda's offer because I was still new at the Bar and I wanted to establish myself as a lawyer. My legal career was beginning to take off.

The other approach was from John Stone, who invited me to his house in East Melbourne to meet with people like Australian Medical Association (AMA) President Bruce Shepherd and Melbourne Chamber of Commerce President Andrew Hay, who were being courted to join the Joh-for-PM campaign. There was a plan to split the federal Coalition and run candidates throughout Australia who would be led by the Queensland Premier Sir Joh Bjelke-Petersen. After a smashing election victory Joh would become Prime Minister of Australia. As far as they were concerned, they had the leader—Joh. All they needed were some candidates. I thought the idea was bizarre and politically wacky. The Joh-for-PM campaigners claimed that the Liberal Party was finished, that John Howard was finished, that Joh was going to sweep the polls, and that I had better get with the strength. I declined their approach to be a candidate. As a loyal member of the Liberal Party I supported it and its Leader, John Howard. On 11 February 1987, I told the *Australian*: 'I am not proposing to be, nor would I ever be, a candidate for a Joh Party. I believe John Howard is the best hope of winning Government at the next election. People should get behind him to make sure he will do it.'

As it turned out, the Joh-for-PM movement was a fizzer. It could not attract any high-profile candidates and Joh himself did not stand. In the end John Stone was the only one who got on board. He stood for the Senate for the Queensland National Party and was elected. He was a senator for three years. Then, in 1990, he stood for the seat of Fairfax held by the National Party in the House of Representatives. The swing against the Nationals on first preferences was 13.4 per cent. He lost the seat to Alex Somlyay, the Liberal candidate. The main consequence of the Joh-for-PM episode was to damage John Howard's campaign in 1987 and help the re-election of the Hawke Government.

Although I was not prepared to be a Liberal candidate, I contributed to the party's industrial relations policy. I drafted a bill called 'The Industrial Relations Bill 1987' to enact the party's industrial relations policy to repeal the *Conciliation and Arbitration Act 1904* and allow voluntary agreements between employees and employers.

After the 1987 election both John Howard and Andrew Peacock had led the party to a defeat. Some thought it might be time for a totally different person to lead the Liberal Party. The federal president of the party at the time was John Elliott. He was at the height of his business career and was president of the Liberal Party and the Carlton Football Club. He had played nearly three hundred games for the Carey Old Boys' Football Team. My father, who taught him at school, said he had a booming voice: 'Elliott belted out hymns in school chapel louder than anyone else.' He had joined McKinsey & Co., the management consultants, taken over a small Tasmanian jam factory which had become Henry Jones (IXL), taken over Carlton United Breweries, and was about to 'Foster-ise' the world through the Foster's Brewing Company. By 1987 he wanted to become a Member of Parliament, the Liberal Leader and then Prime Minister. To do so he needed to find a seat in Parliament. The one fixed in his sights was Higgins, then held by Roger Shipton. The next election was not due until 1990. Elliott could not wait that long. He wanted Shipton to resign so that he could enter Parliament in a by-election. In that way he could be Leader by the time of the 1990 general election and Prime Minister after that. Elliott began agitating for Roger Shipton to leave. But without Roger's agreement there was no chance of a by-election.

Roger's predecessor as Member for Higgins was John Grey Gorton. When Prime Minister Holt disappeared in the surf off Portsea on 17 December 1967, this had created a vacancy not only in the Prime Ministership but also in the seat of Higgins. When a Liberal Leader dies or resigns, the successor must be a member of the lower house. The vacancy in Higgins opened up the chance for the Senate Leader, John Gorton, to seek the Liberal leadership on the understanding that if elected he could enter the lower house through Harold Holt's old seat of Higgins. It would mean the locals would have to accept him as their candidate. They could hardly refuse a Prime Minister—and they did not. But the local party members in Higgins were always a bit resentful. They had not chosen their candidate or member. The parliamentary party had chosen him for them.

Gorton remained Prime Minister until 1971. By 1975 the rank-and-file party members in Higgins had made it clear that they would not be re-endorsing him. He stormed out of a meeting of the branches called to discuss the situation. He became an Independent and ran for the Senate in the ACT in the 1975 election. After this experience with a high-profile member parachuted in to Higgins, the branch members did not want another outsider; they wanted a local. There was a huge pre-selection, with several distinguished outsiders standing, such as Eve Mahlab and Graeme Samuel. But the members voted for Roger Shipton, a local and a solicitor.

Roger was a good-humoured, good-natured, hardworking member. But he did not become a Minister in the Fraser Government. He was briefly a shadow Minister under Andrew Peacock, from 1983 to 1985, but when Howard became Leader he was dropped. By comparison with his predecessors Roger was starting to look lightweight. John Elliott's manoeuvring for the seat was undermining him. There was talk of offering Roger a well-paid job outside politics but he was not interested. If Elliott wanted the seat he would have to work through a pre-selection for the 1990 election. Shipton was always confident that he could beat Elliott in a pre-selection. So was I. Elliott would not be popular with the branch members. He was an extremely successful businessman and apparently at that stage hugely wealthy. He would fly to football matches in a helicopter rather than waste time in road traffic. I could not see him having the patience to deal with branch members and branch meetings. As he saw it, running a political party would be like running Foster's. You give orders and expect them to be obeyed. That is not the way the Liberal Party works.

In the lead-up to the pre-selections the chairman of the Goldstein electorate asked me to contest the seat, held by Ian Macphee. But Goldstein was nowhere near the Higgins electorate, where Tanya and I lived. I knew a lot of the Higgins branch members and several asked me to run. I thought Elliott might run. Strangely enough the very day of the 1987 stock market crash, which was a day of horror for us because of Tanya's illness, may well have been the beginning of the end of Elliott's political ambitions. He was reported to have bought a lot of shares in the aftermath of the crash. But he was beginning to over-extend himself. In the end he did not run for pre-selection. Later he lost control of Foster's. His business career came to an end and eventually he was declared bankrupt.

The pre-selection was on Friday 5 May 1989. It was a cold night but a crowd gathered in Greville Street outside the Prahran Town Hall to wait for the result. The Victorian Liberal Party pre-selectors—in this case more than 120 of them—were a mix of locals and state-wide representatives. They divided into two groups, which in turn interviewed the two candidates and their wives. (One pre-selector asked Tanya if she believed that, as a young mother, she could cope with parliamentary life. She already knew the life well and answered brilliantly.) Then the candidates addressed the whole panel and answered additional questions. It was all over by 10 p.m. I won the ballot 97 to 26. When the chairman, Anthony Starkins, announced the result the people in the street cheered wildly. 'We'll be back in Government soon!' one called. The press said Shipton was stunned. But he behaved as always—with civility and dignity.

That same weekend Julian Beale defeated Ken Aldred in a pre-selection in Bruce, and David Kemp defeated Ian Macphee in Goldstein. The three of us were more or less lumped together, sometimes as the 'new blood', sometimes as the 'New Right'. The following Tuesday, Andrew Peacock and his supporters dumped John Howard as parliamentary leader in the notorious coup of May 1989. Shipton, Macphee and Aldred were all still in the Parliament. Howard refused to intervene in their pre-selections. He would have had little influence if he had tried to do so. But by staying neutral he would not have won any favour from them.

Not being in Parliament, I did not have a vote in the leadership ballot. But if anyone had asked me in 1989 whom I preferred as Leader I would have said Howard. He stood for a much more pro-market economic policy. Peacock and I came from the same state but we were not close. I was considered a conservative, Peacock a progressive.

The federal election was held in March 1990. John Hewson, the shadow Treasurer, launched my local campaign. For me the great issue of the day was interest rates. They had peaked at more than 17 per cent. As a self-employed barrister, with a wife and two children to support,

I knew that high interest rates were 'murdering' people, especially in Victoria, which was at the epicentre of the national recession. In the strip shopping centre in High Street, Armadale, where I had my campaign rooms, there were 160 shops, fifty of them vacant. In my view we should have run squarely and solidly on interest rates. But the Coalition message was confused and contradictory.

When the Reserve Bank began cutting interest rates in January 1990, Hewson attacked it, suggesting the move was political. It is possible it was. But what did this mean? Did the Coalition think they should not be cut? During the campaign John Stone suggested that interest rates could not be cut until foreign debt was reined in. Tying interest rates to foreign debt was a major mistake. But if the Coalition genuinely believed interest rates should stay high until foreign debt came down, then there was not much relief in sight by voting for the Coalition. As we look back now, the problem in early 1990 was not that the Reserve Bank was cutting rates too early but that it was acting too late. This was to lead to a deep recession. The Coalition would have been right, on economic grounds, to claim that rates needed to be cut earlier and faster. It would have been a much better political message. We achieved a rare double—wrong on the politics and wrong on the economics as well.

We lost the election. I took my seat in Parliament as a member of the Opposition. I was to stay there for six years.

4

DEFEAT FROM THE JAWS OF VICTORY

The 1990 election was the Coalition's fourth successive defeat. It was also Andrew Peacock's second defeat as Leader. He was ready to stand down. After two defeats no one expected him to win the third time around. While he was waiting for the final results to come in, I went to see him in his office in the Old Customs House in Melbourne. I was the most junior MP, elected only days before, but I presumed to suggest that he stay on for a while to give the party time to think about his successor. Howard, who had lost the leadership less than a year before, was lobbying for the job. The shadow Minister for Education, Peter Reith, was ringing around. I thought someone else might emerge.

There was no great drive in the Liberal Party to swing the revolving door from Peacock back to Howard. But Peacock decided he would have to move quickly if he was going to head off Howard. He had no intention of taking my advice. He was already anointing his successor. As I was leaving I saw John Hewson come in.

Peacock had had a charmed entry into politics, succeeding Sir Robert Menzies in the seat of Kooyong at the age of twenty-seven. Educated at Scotch College, he had moved seamlessly from president of the Young Liberals to vice president of the Liberal Party, then president in Victoria before becoming the Member for Kooyong, the seat regarded as the jewel in the Liberal Party crown. He had been Minister for the Army, for the Territories and for Foreign Affairs.

Twice married and divorced by this stage, Peacock had a fine eye both on and off the track. He had been part-owner of a Caulfield Cup winner, Lelani. During the 1990 campaign I sat next to him when he addressed a business lunch. The speech was workmanlike but he showed more interest in holding the attention of a very attractive lady across the room than that of the predominantly male business crowd. The press noticed it and got excited about the 'mystery woman' in his life. In between marriages, Peacock had been photographed with Shirley MacLaine, who was quoted as saying he was the only man she knew with a Gucci toothbrush. He cultivated a progressive position, in contrast with the more conservative, Western District outlook of Malcolm Fraser. At that time Fraser represented the right of the Victorian Liberal Party. Peacock was effective on television, if prone to tripping up on policy detail. He was always ready with a joke or with a tip on the next race. He was at home in the football change rooms. He had glamour and bonhomie.

John Howard, an old boy of Sydney's Canterbury High, had been a president of the Young Liberals and a vice president of the Liberal Party in New South Wales. Elected to Bennelong at thirty-four, he had a meteoric rise to become Treasurer in 1977 when Philip Lynch was stood aside. In contrast with Peacock, he presented himself as a conviction politician and had none of Peacock's relaxed style. He found small talk difficult. He sprang to life in Parliament, where he revelled in debate. A social conservative, he also embraced labour market deregulation, which gave him a radical reform agenda in the late 1980s. He had lost the election in 1987 and the leadership in 1989. After that he said that if he were to become Leader again, he would have to be 'Lazarus with a triple bypass'.

John Hewson worked for Philip Lynch when Lynch was Treasurer and he continued with Howard when he succeeded Lynch. Hewson was an economist, trained both in Australia and overseas. He had worked at the International Monetary Fund (IMF) at the time of the liberalisation of financial markets in the wake of the breakdown of the fixed exchange rate system. Unlike Howard and Peacock, he had not grown up in the Liberal Party. He had not been a branch member or an official of the organisation. He had little feel for the Liberal Party rank-and-file or its culture. What he had was economic zeal. He scorned the political reality which he thought contaminated 'pure policy'. Before entering Parliament, he wrote a column in *Business Review Weekly* which was regularly contemptuous of the Liberal Party, its members and its ideas. Members in safe seats included 'those who have contributed little or nothing', he complained. 'A plan needs to be developed and implemented to trim this "dead wood" (and there are at least five in New South Wales alone) by forcing resignations and, importantly, introducing new qualified members.' He criticised Peacock as Leader of the Opposition: 'The current leadership,' he wrote in *BRW* on 9 April 1985, 'is weak, and generally disinterested [*sic*] in, and lacks credibility in, economic matters.' He joined the Liberal Party not long before he ran for pre-selection in the seat of Wentworth, to which he was elected in 1987. When Peacock became Leader for the second time, in 1989, he appointed Hewson his shadow Treasurer. Although inexperienced in the Parliament, he performed well during the 1990 campaign, showing a strong grasp of economic policy—a foil to Peacock's strong political instincts.

In 1990 Howard didn't have the numbers to be re-elected to the leadership, but it was Peter Reith, a former Howard loyalist, who killed off his hopes for resurrection. Reith decided to run for the leadership himself. He declared on television that it was time for a new generation. This struck a chord. The party was sick of the Peacock–Howard rivalry and wanted to put the leadership ambitions of both men behind it. But it was not about to elect Reith.

In the ballot for the leadership Hewson easily defeated Reith and a third candidate, Alistair Webster. Reith was elected Deputy Leader. I voted for Hewson. My efforts to persuade Peacock to stay on for the time being were not successful and they earned me the displeasure of Hewson, who thought I was manoeuvring to bring in someone else. I was not. I had no other candidate and was simply worried that Hewson did not have enough experience in the party or the Parliament. I thought he could well become the Leader in due course but I thought he needed more experience and more time to get to know the Liberal Party. Despite distrusting me, Hewson made me shadow Minister for Corporate Law and Consumer Affairs, ranked last in the shadow ministry. The New South Wales MP Michael Yabsley acidly observed: 'Shadow Minister for Corporate Law and Consumer Affairs hardly rolls off the tongue.' At least I was on the front bench.

Hewson brought in two other newly elected members—Ian McLachlan and David Kemp. He wanted to demonstrate that there was a generational change and that the old Peacock–Howard rivalry was behind us. He carefully positioned both Peacock and Howard as shadow Ministers with equivalent seniority.

I found corporate law interesting. Later, as Treasurer in the Howard Government, I brought it into the Treasury portfolio and pushed through a number of reforms in the area. Our Government oversaw the demutualisation of the Australian Stock Exchange—a world first—and its public listing. We adopted international accounting standards, introduced a business judgment rule for directors and established a Takeovers Panel that could give swift adjudication on takeovers. Corporations law had been run by state Corporate Affairs offices. In the late 1980s they began cooperating through a coordinating body, the National Companies and Securities Commission (NCSC). It was under-resourced and enforcement was slack. There were several corporate collapses—Bond, Skase, Adsteam, Rothwells. Eventually the states realised we needed a national regulator. But the states used corporate regulation fees as a source of revenue and did not want to give it up. It was not easy to convince our party, particularly where there was a strong states rights feeling (as in Western Australia), to agree to a national regulator. I wanted to beef up corporate enforcement because open and transparent markets are important for investors and critical to our economic performance. But I had to wait until we came to Government in 1996 before I could introduce the necessary reforms and the necessary funding for proper enforcement.

My shadow ministry also included consumer affairs. This too was largely a state matter. There were important issues such as product liability and class actions. I was suspicious of class actions, believing that, if mishandled, they would lead to an explosion of litigation in the American style. But these were not top-of-the-agenda issues in the early 1990s. It was hard to generate front-page coverage over such issues.

As a junior shadow Minister I had no staff other than the electorate staff. Pat Herman, who had been my very effective personal assistant when I was a barrister, joined my electorate office, Kathy Thompson handled constituency matters, and Tony Smith became my researcher, press secretary, letter-writer, trouble-shooter and personal adviser.

At the time I did not think so but, as I look back, starting in Opposition was a plus. We had no resources. I wrote my own speeches and read all the bills I handled in the House. I had to learn skills from drafting a Question without Notice to writing a newspaper article. There were no public servants or press officers to do that for me. Those who start in Opposition get tougher a lot earlier because of the experience.

In April 1992, Hewson reshuffled his front bench. Peacock was the shadow attorney-general in charge of legal matters. He handled all the matters I did not. We often joked that as his junior I was only the shadow attorney-colonel. Peacock, who never liked attending to the details involved in complex legal matters, moved to Trade. But I was not promoted to shadow attorney-general, a sign that I was not in favour with Hewson. That post went to Peter Durack, a former attorney-general in the Fraser Government. A month later he was moved down the Liberal Senate ticket in Western Australia. It meant the end of his Senate career and he resigned from the shadow ministry. This time Hewson had to appoint me shadow attorney-general. When he rang to offer me the job I was at the Chardonnay Lodge in the Coonawarra, South Australia, addressing the Electorate Committee of Ian McLachlan, Member for Barker. I was thrilled. But Hewson was obviously still wary of me. Both Peacock and Durack had been in shadow Cabinet when they were shadow attorneys-general. I was not.

Every MP qualified as a lawyer imagines him- or herself as an attorney-general—the first law officer of the Crown. I would have loved the post. But I had not entered Parliament to become attorney-general. I wanted to work on economic issues. My other major policy interest was foreign affairs. However, as a barrister who had conducted litigation in the Federal Court and taken some cases to the High Court, the idea of taking responsibility for the Constitution and the courts was exciting.

To get there I would have to start with more mundane matters. I began scrutinising the accounts of the Attorney-General's Department. We noticed that the department had spent $160 000 building a barbecue for staff in the courtyard of the Canberra departmental building. Tony Smith and I managed to make this a national issue. I denounced this barbecue as a characteristic Labor waste of public moneys. As most Australians stood around their $500 gas barbecues in the summer of 1992–93, we entertained them with our revelations of the gazebo, bar and ornate facilities that some public servants enjoyed at their Canberra workplace.

My family and I were holidaying on the Mornington Peninsula at the time. I would dictate a press release to Tony Smith over the phone, with whatever new angles I could think of. Tony would put out a press release from Melbourne. The television stations would fly down camera crews in their helicopters and land at the Sorrento helipad to interview me and take the footage that they would use on the national news after flying back to Melbourne. Seeing these helicopters emerge over the bay was like the scene in the movie *Apocalypse Now*. Each morning I would ring Tony and tell him to summon the helicopters: 'I love the smell of barbecue in the morning.' Attorney-General Duffy was infuriated: I had ruined his summer. As it happens, I got on well with Duffy. He and Peacock and I were all devoted followers of the Essendon Football Club. During dull periods in the debates in the House of Representatives, Duffy would pass me notes with his views on which players should be dumped and which promoted. Australian Football conquers all. It allowed friendly relations to survive the barbecue scandals.

Most of the effort in Parliament during this period was devoted to the policy released in November 1991 called Fightback! Central to it was a 15 per cent goods and services tax (GST). This tax would fund the abolition of payroll tax and petrol excise.

Most people even today would think that Fightback! was only about a GST. In fact, it had a 20-point plan that included policies for privatisation, health, superannuation and tariffs. It pledged zero tariffs by the year 2000. It proposed restricting access to superannuation lump sums and increasing the tax on earnings in a superannuation fund. In health it proposed to abolish bulk billing except for cardholders and to reduce the Medicare rebate.

Despite these shortcomings Prime Minister Hawke was unable to respond effectively, largely because he was being undermined by his former Treasurer, Paul Keating. When Keating became Labor Leader a month later, he delivered a much tougher if more demagogic counter-punch. He would say: 'This is a life-changing tax. You pay this tax from the moment you get out of bed and brush your teeth with your toothpaste to the moment you go to bed and have your cup of milk. John Hewson's hand will always be in your pocket.' The joke was that Keating himself had championed a broad-based indirect tax known as 'Option C'. It would have taxed the same people from the moment they got out of bed to the moment they went to sleep with their cup of milk. But Hewson did not have the political skills to sustain his case against Keating's invective.

It was a difficult period. I worked devotedly for Fightback! but Hewson continued to be suspicious of me. He knew I was sympathetic to Howard, who had not relinquished his quest for the leadership. I had good relations with Howard. I had invited him to my home, where on one occasion we ordered a pizza while we talked through the political issues of the moment. Hewson also knew I was friendly with Tony Abbott, whom he thought was undermining him. Abbott was on Hewson's staff and Hewson regarded him a Howard spy. During his period in Hewson's office I gave Tony moral support as an old friend. We all had similar tales to tell about Hewson.

I first met Tony Abbott at a conference of the Australian Union of Students (AUS) in the late 1970s when, after some provocative act of political incorrectness, he was expelled. He had been a fierce critic of the AUS. But he also had a strong commitment to college life and to rugby. When I was addressing an anti-AUS rally at Sydney University at this time, Tony settled on a plan to get his college mates to vote with me. He would assemble them at a nearby hotel for beer and then lead them en masse to the rally. But as the afternoon wore on, the beer proved far more compelling than the rally. They never made it. The vote was lost. I suggested that in future he should recruit some teetotallers, but I doubt that he had met any members of that species!

After a Rhodes scholarship in Oxford, Tony decided to train for the Catholic priesthood. I asked him why he began training as a diocesan priest rather than as a Jesuit. He said that popes were ultimately drawn from the ranks of diocesan priests. He had ambition! But parish work did not really suit him. He subsequently became a journalist and press secretary to John Hewson. Later he became a Member of Parliament and a colleague of mine in the Cabinet.

Tony always saw himself as something of a romantic figure, a Don Quixote ready to take on lost causes and fight for great principles. Never one to be held back by the financial consequences of decisions, he had grandiose plans for public expenditure. At one point when we were in Government, he asked for funding to pay for telephone and electricity wires to be put underground throughout the whole of his northern Sydney electorate to improve the amenity of the neighbourhoods. He also wanted the Commonwealth to take over the building of local roads and bridges in his electorate. He wanted the Commonwealth to take over hospitals. He used to tell me proudly that he had learned all of his economics at the feet of Bob Santamaria. I was horrified. He once claimed he was 'the political love-child' of John Howard and Bronwyn Bishop.

When we got back to Canberra after John Hewson appointed me shadow attorney-general, Hewson called me down to his office. He explained that he had previously appointed Peacock to the job because he needed to give him a portfolio as senior as that held by John Howard. He told me: 'It was a clever strategy. No one caught on that in fact I had gutted the portfolio and given the substantive responsibilities to you.' I told him I was very glad to be appointed as the shadow attorney-general and looked forward to dealing with the issues.

That night he called me to his office again. When I got there he was in a totally different state of mind.

'You have been bagging me in the gallery. I have checked and I have heard from six sources. You've been telling people you will be the next Leader. You are nothing. If you don't shape up, you won't be a Minister during the next Government! There is a hot-shot lawyer coming from WA.'

I was stunned. 'Who have I supposedly been bagging you to?'

'You have been leaking to Laurie Oakes.'

'I have spoken to Oakes only once in my life and I have never bagged you to him.' (I made a mental note that if I was being accused of leaking to Oakes I had better meet him and find out what I had missed.)

'After the last election, when I was making a run for Leader, you and Kroger were trying to get Andrew to stay on so you could move in McLachlan.'

'I had no plan to move in McLachlan. I just suggested that Andrew should hang around for a bit while the party stabilised itself and had time to assess its options. I voted for you as Leader. I have been absolutely loyal and all I get is this tirade. Why didn't you raise this with me this morning?'

It was late at night and he had been out for dinner. It was not an auspicious start for me as the new shadow attorney-general.

On another occasion, closer to the 1993 election, Hewson called me in to a meeting with the campaign director Andrew Robb.

'We need some cut-through issues. We can make law and order an issue if we promise to bring back the death penalty.'

I swallowed. For a while I was speechless. After coming to, I said: 'There is no doubt that if you promise to bring back the death penalty you will capture the electorate's attention. But you won't get a message out on anything else.'

His idea was to introduce a death penalty for rapists and child molesters. 'There'd be huge support, wouldn't there?'

I had to agree with that. But I pointed out: 'Australia is a party to international conventions against the death penalty. How will we get out of them? Besides, most of the crimes you have in mind are state laws. How could the Commonwealth execute people for state crimes?'

I was sent away to investigate. My investigation took a long time. During that time the idea was dropped.

I once asked Ian McLachlan: 'Do you think we have an obligation to tell the Australian people our Leader is a maniac?' He said: 'No, the Australian people will figure it out for themselves.'

In 1993 we lost 'the unlosable election'. I had promoted Fightback! all around the country. I really believed in the GST and the way it would pay for the abolition of other taxes. The policy I had the most trouble with was the abolition of all tariffs by 2000. Unemployment was around 10 per cent. Telling workers in the car industry that a massive cut in the tariff was good for them was a hard sell.

The Industrial Relations policy that the Coalition took to the 1993 election was called 'Jobsback'. Howard was the responsible shadow Minister. It abolished compulsory arbitration. Awards would apply only where both an employer and one or more employees agreed, and either party could veto an award. Outside awards, there would be workplace agreements that would have to meet or exceed four conditions: a minimum hourly rate, four weeks' annual leave, two weeks' non-cumulative sick leave and twelve months' unpaid maternity leave. The policy provided that employers and employees were free to negotiate penalty rates or the length of the working week, the hours worked and the times at which they were worked. The policy had fewer minimum requirements than WorkChoices, the policy of the Coalition at the 1998 election. There was no fairness test.

But this was not the part that generated controversy. What did was a proposal for a youth training wage for fifteen to seventeen year olds at $3 an hour and for eighteen to twenty year olds at $3.50 an hour. Hewson announced these rates at a Coalition National Convention at Darling Harbour in Sydney. When he stated the rate, there was an audible gasp in the audience. I had no idea it was coming. It had not been discussed in any meeting I had attended. I have no idea how that rate was fixed. Undoubtedly it was a time of high youth unemployment but the announcement did not go down well. The Labor Party was able to characterise our policy as a policy to make people work for $3 an hour.

Even then we still should have won the election. The country had been through 17 per cent interest rates and a huge recession, for which people rightly held Keating responsible. Kerry Packer had famously said: 'An Alan Bond only comes along once in your life,' and Keating adapted it: 'Hewson was my Alan Bond.' There was enormous anger when we lost. People turned on us. People walked up to me in the street and said things like: 'I wanted to get rid of Keating but you made it impossible.' Keating had shown considerable political skill. But we had Hewson and Fightback!

After the 1993 election, Howard ran for the leadership against Hewson. I supported Howard and I nominated for Deputy Leader. There were seven candidates, including Peter Reith, Alexander Downer and Michael Wooldridge. Hewson, with Peacock's support, easily beat Howard 47 to 30. The same group supported Wooldridge, who won 45 votes to my 33 after all of the other candidates had been eliminated. It was not surprising that I lost: I had not voted for Hewson—why would the party make me his deputy?

But the defeat of Reith, who had been a loyal deputy to Hewson, caused trouble for Hewson. Reith realised that he had taken the fall for the election defeat. Hewson had not campaigned to save him. Straight after the ballot Reith came to my room and said: 'This will not last. I'll make sure of that.' He went to the backbench.

I thought that we had lost because of Hewson's miscalculation. He did not have the experience to know which policy issues the public would stomach and which ones he should leave alone. In the end we were engaged in fights with practically everyone. The welfare lobby was at our throat over GST and the churches were campaigning against it. Those in superannuation schemes hated our proposal to limit lump sums. The unions were fighting us on the youth wage. The health changes included the abolition of universal bulk billing. In the end Hewson stumbled in trying to explain the GST.

The worst thing a conviction politician can do is to give up his convictions. After the 1993 election defeat Hewson announced he was no longer in favour of a GST. This damaged his one great strength: his economic credibility. He gave away his chief equity. He had always said that the Fightback! program was necessary for the economy and he would not compromise on it. His appeal had been: 'I'm the tough economic leader for these tough economic times. I have the tough—but right—economic program.' He now said that Fightback! was not necessary after all and he dumped it. He abandoned his whole raison d'être. He could not re-make himself as a populist.

After defeating Howard in the leadership ballot and winning re-election as Leader, Hewson appointed me shadow Minister for Finance and Alexander Downer shadow Treasurer. He probably thought I would languish in Finance. Instead, it turned out to be a good move for me: I thrived in it. It gave me the opportunity to look at all Commonwealth expenditure and understand how the Government really works. I was also responsible for the auditor-general and his reports. It was in the course of this work in November 1993 that I came across the auditor-general's report on the Community Cultural Recreational and Sporting Facilities Program. This was a program to give grants to local communities to help with facilities. The auditor-general found the department's administration was weak, its procedures for processing applications were poor and the supporting documentation was inadequate.

Besides all that, it was clear that grants had been skewed to Labor electorates and that processing them had been accelerated in the period before the 1993 election. The responsible Minister, Ros Kelly, was unable to explain how decisions were made. When asked to produce documentation, she said that allocations had been made on 'a great big whiteboard'. The idea that $30 million of taxpayers' money had been allocated to more than 700 groups out of 2800 applications on the basis of an assessment on a whiteboard, the contents of which had now been erased, was unbelievable. If it was true, it was incompetent. But hardly anyone believed it. 'I cleaned the whiteboard' became a statement as believable as 'The dog ate my homework'. Comedy writers began using it in their routines. I asked question after question in Parliament and moved several censures of the Minister. A politician can survive many things but not ridicule. In the end Kelly had to go. It was a ministerial scalp. Later she resigned her seat in Canberra and the Opposition won the by-election. Tony Smith thought of a name for it: 'Sports Rorts'. It was a bright spot at the beginning of 1994.

As Hewson floundered, members began soundings about the next Leader. There was some speculation that it might be me. I was not seeking the leadership; I had been in Parliament only four years.

But when the bush is dry, a match can create a bushfire. Premier Jeff Kennett lit the match. In May 1994 he launched a huge personal attack on me on Radio 3AW, alleging that I had undermined Hewson and raising doubts about my integrity. Hewson had been trying to paper over the weakness of his support. He denied there was any problem at all. Kennett finished off that strategy. His attack put the leadership firmly in play. It became a front-page story and forced Hewson to call a ballot. If he had not called that ballot, he would not have been rolled, at least not then and certainly not by me. In the outcome I was elected Deputy Leader. Kennett's attack took me from number twenty in the shadow Cabinet to number two.

To explain why he did it, I have to go back a few years. The Cain Labor Government had been re-elected in Victoria for a third term in October 1988. At the time, Kennett was the Leader of the state parliamentary Liberal Party. He lost the leadership in 1989 but regained it in April 1991. By now John Cain had stepped down as premier in favour of Joan Kirner. The country was in the depths of a recession and Victoria was at the epicentre. The Kirner Government was a mile behind in the polls but an election was not due for eighteen months—in October 1992.

Kennett wanted an early election. In May 1991 he announced he had a 5-point plan to force it. He announced his plan one step at a time. If the Labor Government accepted it, they would go to the polls. If not, he would escalate the situation by moving to the next step. The first step was to ask the Government to resign. The second was to ask it to vote against its own Supply. The third was to introduce legislation to change the Constitution to allow an early election. The fourth was to confiscate the superannuation of Labor MPs. We never found out what the fifth step was.

On superannuation, Kennett's idea was that after the election of a Coalition Government, he would introduce special legislation to retrospectively take back the public component of superannuation for the entire parliamentary service of all ALP parliamentary members. This would apply to all MPs apart from those who voted then and there for an early election. Needless to say, they did not vote for an early election. In the midst of this furore the federal Labor

Government claimed that the move was in breach of the International Covenant on Civil and Political Rights. The federal attorney-general maintained that the Commonwealth would intervene to override any such state legislation.

Like everybody else in the Liberal Party, I wanted to see the end of the Kirner Government, but the idea of confiscating the superannuation of ALP members was a ridiculous tactic, an awful precedent. It was sure to run into a legal minefield and hardly likely to preserve confidence in superannuation and economic stability generally. No federal Liberal MP supported the confiscation. When asked about it, I said it was not right to confiscate an MP's superannuation if he did not vote in a particular way. Howard described Kennett's superannuation tactic as 'unorthodox' and told the Opposition to present itself as 'stable and reliable'.

That week, Kennett's disapproval went up 16 per cent and the Coalition dropped twelve points in the polls. By the end of the week Kennett had withdrawn the policy and decided to wait for the October 1992 election. It was a wise decision. He won it easily.

Until this point I had never had a disagreement with Kennett. I had not been involved in any of his leadership fights, although he harboured a grudge against the state president, Michael Kroger, in that regard. I was seen as a Howard supporter inside the Victorian Division. Kennett had bad relations with Howard and therefore had his suspicions about me. As I was to learn, Kennett was the kind of person to bear a grudge and to bear it for a long time.

The night before Kennett attacked me on 3AW, he told Petro Georgiou, the Victorian state director of the Liberal Party, that he was planning to do it. Georgiou tried to dissuade him. 'You will start World War III,' he said, but to no avail. The next morning Kennett told 3AW:

> This debacle at the moment, and that's what it is, is being generated from Melbourne by the Costello camp. I make no bones about that whatsoever. And I make those comments not because Peter and I had a disagreement over his opposition to my move on superannuation. That is immaterial. It has been

quoted many times, it was a factor, he didn't see fit to support us. That's fine. He became very supportive of us the moment we won the leadership and particularly when we won Government. But this has been a very deliberate destabilising effort where in fact ambition is clearly overriding ability and performance. And I am very concerned that, in fact, if my federal parliamentary colleagues allow the promoters of destabilisation the ultimate prize of leadership, without having earned the right, then they put the party, put Opposition, and then what I require, good Government, at risk.

Kennett's unsolicited denial that all this had nothing to do with his 'move on superannuation' was a dead giveaway; it had everything to do with that. No one raised the superannuation issue except Kennett. He went further: 'I have very real reason to be concerned about the integrity of that [Costello] camp.' What this meant was anyone's guess. Who was in this 'camp' was also anyone's guess. I issued a statement immediately repudiating the attack, especially his aspersions on my integrity. I never heard any more about this from Kennett.

Hewson was in Queensland at the time. When he heard about it, he realised that the Liberal state premier had gone to war with his federal party colleagues. Kennett had also given his advice on who was capable or not capable of taking the leadership: Peacock and Howard could not be 'recycled'; Bronwyn Bishop was a contender. Of Alexander Downer, he said: 'I think his game is improving.'

The firestorm lit by Kennett engulfed Hewson's leadership. The next day at 3.55 p.m. a journalist tipped me off that Hewson was about to hold a press conference. He announced that he had decided to declare his position as leader vacant and re-contest it in a ballot to take place the following Monday.

Since there was no challenger, Hewson thought he would be elected unopposed or that he would catch any would-be challenger unprepared. This would give him the opportunity to silence his critics. Within half an hour of hearing this news I rang Downer to ask him to run for the leadership. I had been in Parliament for only four years. I was then thirty-six. I did not have the experience to lead the Liberal

Party. Despite Kennett's claims, I was not pursuing leadership in any way. The only way to get a clean resolution of the issue would be to have two candidates. People could then vote either for Hewson or for an alternative. I told Downer I would support him and would run as deputy if he ran as Leader. I told him that the party would be a joke if no one nominated against Hewson. 'We will be a laughing stock if no one runs and we will be a laughing stock if Hewson wins. The party will go into self-destruct mode. We have to put someone over the top. I am going to make you the offer of your life. I am going to put you one election away from the Prime Ministership.' Downer said he wanted to think about it and talk to his wife and a few others.

I then decided to check with two other people who I thought might be interested in running for Leader, although I believed that neither of them would in fact nominate. One was Ian McLachlan, who said he was not interested. The other was Howard, who called me almost immediately. I told him that I wanted to make sure someone ran and defeated Hewson. I asked him: 'What are you going to do?' He said his inclination was not to run. He wanted to have a dinner in Melbourne at which we could all have a discussion about who should nominate. I told him there was no time for that. It was Friday night. The ballot was on Monday.

I called Downer back and asked whether he had made his decision. He wanted an assessment of the numbers and I ran him through the party room. I told him he could win. He still wanted time to think. I told him he had to make an announcement. I asked Tony Smith to begin drafting a press release making a joint announcement. He did a draft and I handwrote the last paragraph: 'The party must however put behind it past failure and reinvigorate itself for the challenge that lies ahead, to win Government at the next election and provide sound direction and leadership for Australia into the next century.' We faxed the press release to Downer's office.

I rang him a third time. He told me he had read the draft press release to Malcolm Fraser, who said it was good and needed no changes. Fraser, Downer said, had tears in his eyes—he was so happy. I thought this was a very strange thing to say since Fraser had been on the end of a telephone and Downer could not see his eyes. But he agreed with the release. We issued it before 7 p.m. Now there would be a real ballot on the Monday morning.

I called Howard to tell him that Downer was nominating and I was supporting him on a joint ticket. He sounded very disappointed. He could see the leadership slipping away again. Peacock then rang me. I told him that Downer was running for Leader and I was running for deputy.

'Oh mate, wrong order. Should be other way around.'

'Too late. It's all done.'

'I have got the numbers for *you*; I can't get them for Alexander.'

'Well, you've got to.'

Hewson had called the leadership ballot without consulting Peacock, who had been his chief supporter and numbers man. This was a major strategic mistake. Peacock thought it was an error to call a spill. Since Hewson was no longer consulting him, Peacock no longer felt responsible for organising Hewson's support. He came out for the Downer–Costello ticket. It took Howard a bit longer to do so. He was still ringing around colleagues on Saturday but on Sunday he too made a statement of support. On Saturday I flew to Adelaide to work on support for Downer. Nick Minchin also did a lot of work. On Sunday I flew to Adelaide again, where Downer and I did a joint interview with Laurie Oakes on the *Sunday* program. The ballot was held on the afternoon of Monday in Canberra. Alexander Downer was elected by 43 to 36. Michael Wooldridge did not contest the ballot for Deputy Leader. I was elected unopposed. The press dubbed this the 'Dream Team', a silly label but a sign of the general relief that Hewson was no longer the Leader.

Downer got off to a good start. 'I am born,' he said with assurance, 'of the Liberal Party.' This was to distinguish himself from Hewson, who had no real background in the party. A third-generation politician, Downer understood the culture of the Liberal Party and was a veteran of the factional wars in the South Australian Division. Early in his career he had worked as a staffer for Malcolm Fraser, who had a great influence on him at that time.

As Leader he called for a return to commonsense after the failures of the Hewson years. He made early commitments to small business, the states, local government, the arts, the environment, Aborigines and Asian immigrants. I did everything I could to support him. I really wanted to get into Government.

Yet Downer soon began to flounder. Although he had been in Parliament for ten years, he had never been a Minister and did not have enough policy depth at that time. He was tripped up on Aboriginal land rights in the Northern Territory. He confused the Fraser Government's land rights legislation with claims based on the High Court's judgment in the Mabo case. (He was uncertain, he said, because he had been emotionally moved by a corroboree he had attended earlier.)

Criticism came to a head in September 1994 with the launch of a joint Coalition policy document called 'The Things that Matter', our first major policy statement since Hewson's Fightback! It was one of the best policy documents that I have ever been associated with. It was well argued, well costed, well designed and easy to read. It outlined a program embracing the economy, families, communities and national pride. Unfortunately, in the course of speaking at a Liberal Party dinner at the Regent Hotel in Sydney, Downer attempted to crack some jokes, very bad jokes, based on phrases that rhymed with 'The Things that Matter'. The catastrophic low-point was when he said that we would also be announcing a policy on domestic violence to be called 'The Things that Batter'. From that moment his days as Leader were numbered.

Andrew Peacock resigned from Parliament on 17 September 1994. For John Howard the retirement of his nemesis brought new life. There was no risk now that his return would take us back to the old Howard–Peacock era; Peacock had retired from the field. Howard saw this as a decisive shift and began actively doing numbers for a return. His chief lieutenant was Western Australian backbencher Allan Rocher. The party organisation was also moving against Downer, with Party President Tony Staley urging that Downer had to go. As Deputy Leader of the party, I believed it was my duty to support Downer, but if he was going to go voluntarily I had every right to nominate for the leadership. Howard was pushing for a spill before Christmas. The last party meeting of the year was to be held on Tuesday 6 December

1994. The only other person who could credibly run for Leader at that stage, apart from Howard, was me. If I nominated, Howard would at best be elected with a substantial percentage of the party room opposing him, or at worst lose the ballot. Either way it would not be the coronation he needed if he was going to match it with Keating in the forthcoming election.

The night before that party meeting I had a visit from Howard and McLachlan, the details of which I discuss in Chapter 12. Howard wanted me to stand aside from the contest for the leadership. But if he was to regain the leadership unopposed, he also needed Downer to stand aside. The next day, the day of the last party meeting scheduled for 1994, the *Sydney Morning Herald* splashed across its front page a story by Mick Millet and Geoff Kitney: 'Lib Rebels Try to Draft Howard'. The story had been approved by Howard before publication. Behind the scenes he was actively trying to organise a spontaneous draft of himself. Even on the weekend after Parliament had risen, there was wild talk from Howard's lieutenants about petitioning a special meeting to move a spill. I told Rocher they had better calm down. I was getting sick of it. If they kept pressuring Downer, he might dig in, and they would get me offside as well.

In this situation the shadow Cabinet went to Adelaide for its meeting on 13 December 1994. After a business fundraiser at the Adelaide Hilton, Downer, Howard and I met at the Adelaide Club where I was staying. We discussed the situation frankly and openly. We were worried that Keating might call an early election. The three of us agreed that Downer should be given one last chance to see if he could pick himself up in the polls but that, if his position had not improved by Australia Day, he should stand down. If he did that I would not run against Howard but would continue as Deputy Leader so that Howard could be anointed unopposed. Howard and I would both pay tribute to Downer for his decision taken in the interests of the party and he would be appointed shadow Minister for Foreign Affairs. He would become Minister for Foreign Affairs in a Coalition Government.

Howard contacted me a few times over that summer to keep the pressure on. He did not want Downer to back out and he did not want me to nominate for the leadership myself. In my view Downer was not going to recover by Australia Day, but he had to be given a chance. It was part of treating him with respect. He had been Leader for only seven months.

I saw it as my duty as Deputy Leader to facilitate this transition. I was sick of leadership contests and the bad blood they created. At one stage Downer was Leader of a shadow Cabinet that included three of his predecessors: Hewson, Peacock and Howard. Hewson was still agitated. Downer had to sack him as a shadow Minister in August for speaking on issues outside his shadow portfolio. In January 1995 Hewson put out a press release offering himself for appointment as shadow Treasurer. I was the Deputy Leader and shadow Treasurer. It was a bizarre statement. He could not possibly have imagined that Downer would sack his Deputy Leader as shadow Treasurer. I described him as a 'suicide bomber'. The only way to win the next election was to ensure that there was an orderly transition in the leadership and that senior people in the party behaved sensibly in order to achieve it.

In January 1995 I went to London to explain our policies to the international fund managers. Then I went to France for talks with the Organisation for Economic Co-operation and Development (OECD). The London-based Australian journalists chased me to Paris. They took up positions outside the Hotel Mercure and tried to doorstop me. I refused to comment.

When I flew back to Australia, there was a swarm of media waiting as I came out of Customs at Melbourne Airport. I tried to get away but took a wrong turn. Cornered in a dead-end corridor I asked: 'Where is the way out?' Journalists had a lot of fun using that line to describe our leadership problems. But I knew the way things would work out. It was clear that Downer was not going to resuscitate himself. On Australia Day he announced that he was going to call a party meeting on the following Monday. 'I will not continue as the Leader of the Liberal Party after that time.' At the party meeting, he said, John Howard would be elected as Leader. He added, 'I hope that Peter Costello will continue uncontested as the Deputy Leader of the party.'

The party met. Howard was the only candidate. He was elected unopposed and unanimously. There was no division and no rancour.

I continued as Deputy Leader and shadow Treasurer. Downer was given the shadow Foreign Affairs portfolio. We had demonstrated that the party had got its act together. Downer was treated with respect and Howard achieved his ambition. I had brokered an arrangement to put the party on its best footing. I believed that, in turn, I would get my opportunity. This was indeed an orderly transition. We looked like we could manage our own affairs. Now we would have to convince the electorate that we could manage Australia.

5

OUT OF THE WILDERNESS
AND INTO GOVERNMENT

I have a theory that every Government wins one more term than it should. There are exceptions, but the underlying idea is that a long-running Government will overreach in a desperate bid to win re-election. It may work one last time but the electorate will punish it next time.

This theory explains Labor's defeat in 1996. In the election of 1993 (the Coalition's 'unlosable' election), Labor made promises it could not keep. Hewson's policy was to introduce a 15 per cent GST but, in compensation, he would cut income tax. In response Keating released a statement called 'One Nation', which proposed much the same income tax cuts without a GST. He even legislated those tax cuts to come into force in two instalments. During the election he boasted that his tax cuts were already 'L-A-W law'. He won the election but he could not deliver. In the 1993 Budget, after the election, the Labor Government postponed the second instalment of the 'One Nation' tax cuts to a date to be proclaimed. It was never proclaimed. It also increased wholesale sales tax by 2 per cent and raised petrol excise by 5 cents per litre.

The Coalition used this to devastating effect in the 1996 campaign. Television advertisements in regional markets showed a photograph of a Labor member, for example Jim Snow in Eden-Monaro, and asked: 'When you voted for Jim Snow, did you vote for increased taxes?' The reply was: 'Yes, you did.' Most of the Labor voters in 1993 thought they were voting against the GST. In fact, they voted for Members of Parliament who increased sales tax and petrol taxes instead.

Polling after the 1993 Budget showed that 74 per cent of Australians thought they would be worse off, while 4 per cent thought they would be better off. The Budget had a net approval rating of −42. No other Budget has come close since such polls have been conducted. It was the end of John Dawkins' career as Treasurer. He left the Parliament in December of that year.

As the shadow Minister for Finance I was in the lockup studying the Budget papers before the Budget was delivered. When I came out, Daryl Williams asked me about it. 'We'll bury this Budget,' I said, 'and we'll bury Keating.' The Labor premier of Queensland, Wayne Goss, was later famously to remark that Queenslanders were sitting on their verandas with baseball bats just waiting for Keating. 'They don't care how long they have to wait. They'll get him whenever he comes.' The public thought they had been swindled. They *had* been swindled. They were waiting to square up the ledger. The only thing that got in the way was the weakness of the Opposition.

Keating had the ability to believe something with great fervour and argue for it in hyperbolic language. He could then switch positions and argue an opposite opinion with equal fervour and self-belief. When he began as Treasurer, he was committed to stimulating fiscal policy. Then, in 1986, he declared that Australia was at risk of becoming a banana republic and tried to tighten fiscal policy. Before becoming Treasurer he railed against the entry of foreign banks into Australia. When they were given licences, he claimed it was one of his great achievements. He boasted in March 1990: 'There won't be a recession' and in December 1990 declared: 'This is a recession that Australia had to have.' He fell in and out of love with pet economic theories such as the 'J Curve' and the 'Twin Deficits theory'. When the first negative quarter of what would prove to be a prolonged recession was released, Keating proclaimed: 'This is a beautiful set of numbers for us.'

He backed up all of these contradictory and strongly held positions with fierce rhetoric. This made him effective in the Parliament, if unpopular with the public. When he was Treasurer, his brutal attack was useful to Hawke because it allowed Hawke to float above the fray as a consensual, non-partisan figure.

In 1995 the Liberal Western Australian Government set up a royal commission into the circumstances surrounding the death of Penny Easton, a Perth solicitor who had committed suicide shortly after a petition relating to her bitter divorce had been tabled in the Western Australian Parliament. The petition claimed that she had perjured herself in the Family Court. It was tabled by a Labor MP. The Labor premier, Carmen Lawrence, claimed she knew nothing about it in advance.

Lawrence moved to federal politics and became a Minister in Keating's Government. A former Labor Minister in her old Western Australian Cabinet alleged that Lawrence had lied to the Western Australian Parliament when she denied knowledge of the petition. The royal commissioner who examined the matter eventually found that Lawrence had lied about her involvement. Obviously the inquiry and the testimony of her former colleagues raised questions about her fitness for office. During Question Time on 28 August 1995, Howard asked Keating if he accepted that Lawrence had told the truth about the Easton affair when she addressed the National Press Club on 13 April 1995. In his answer Keating called Howard 'the same old shop-soiled, shop-worn political hack he has always been,' adding: 'You are a joke; you are an immoral fraud.' He also said: 'I have not read the complete text of her Press Club address. Why should I?'

I then sought leave to table Lawrence's Press Club speech. When leave was refused, Keating invited me to table it. I tossed a copy across the table. Unfortunately it was held together by a large bulldog clip. The clip went up in the air and landed on Keating. I was very surprised. I was not aiming at him. Keating immediately jumped up as if to take a swing at me. The Speaker called for order and, invoking Standing Order 304A, threw me out of Parliament for an hour. Keating had behaved badly and so had I. When I was returning home from Canberra at the end of that week, a taxi driver at the airport walked across to me and said in broken English: 'Mr Costello, you throw papers in Mr Keating's face. Next time you throw brick.' Ron Walker, then Treasurer of the Liberal Party, asked for a copy of the papers. He thought they would go for a fortune at a fundraiser. I gave them to Tony Smith for safe keeping. He still has them.

MPs and Senators are required to make a disclosure of all their financial interests, including shares. These disclosures are placed on the parliamentary record and are available to the media. After our election in 1996, the Labor Party went through these registers, as they were entitled to do, to find any items with which they could embarrass a serving Minister. I owned no company shares and made it a deliberate policy not to do so. It was safer not to have to deal with arguments about conflicts of interest, even though it cost me financially. But I declared the fact that my wife Tanya owned some shares in the Commonwealth Bank. The Labor Party attacked me in the press over it. They said it was a conflict of interest for the Treasurer's wife to own bank shares.

Since Labor was afraid to ask me a question about it in Parliament, I arranged a question myself. I pointed out that my wife had bought some two hundred shares in a public float and that I had declared it two years before. I reminded Labor that it was the Labor Party that had privatised the Commonwealth Bank in the float. The shadow Treasurer, Gareth Evans, was attacking my wife for doing what his children had done. 'If you think my wife does not have the right to buy and make investments out of her own earnings, you are entirely wrong.' I think Labor regretted bringing my wife into its attack. The Labor Party's Senator Nick Sherry raised the issue of shareholdings held by my assistant Treasurer, Senator Jim Short, which included shares in the ANZ Bank. In his ministerial capacity he signed off on a routine banking licence for an ANZ subsidiary as recommended by the Treasury. Any other Minister would have done the same. It would have been unthinkable to deny the licence. But since Jim had signed a document affecting a company in which he had shares, he felt he had to resign on the grounds of a conflict of interest. It was a sad end to his ministerial career. Jim had been a talented member of the Opposition front bench. After serving more than a decade in Opposition, he lasted only some seven months as a Minister.

Senator Sherry and the Labor Party were buoyed by this and they now focussed their attack on my parliamentary secretary, Senator Brian Gibson, who had shares in a company in the energy business. Brian had signed off on a routine declaration allowing the trading of energy futures as recommended by the department. He would hardly have known what the application related to, let alone been influenced by his own share portfolio. It is unthinkable that any Minister would not have signed off on this application. But he too was forced to stand down.

In August 1996 Mal Colston, a Labor Senator for Queensland, resigned from the Labor Party to become an Independent. As a result he was elected to the post of deputy president of the Senate. The Labor Party was infuriated by his defection and began releasing information about irregularities in his claims for allowances and entitlements. Although Labor figures had known of these irregularities for years, they had kept silent while Colston was a Labor Senator. By leaving the Labor Party he lost its protection. He was forced to refund a substantial sum that had been incorrectly claimed. Labor hoped to drive him from the Senate.

The events set in motion by this episode spread out in every direction. In the wake of the Colston issue the relevant presiding officers of the Senate and the House tabled all Members' and Senators' claims for allowances going back several years. Labor began investigating Ministers for allowances they had claimed while they were in Opposition. With Colston's claims under attack, the press began to take interest in the conduct of other MPs.

In September 1997 Transport Minister John Sharp resigned after revising his claims and repaying money to which he was not entitled. John Howard then sacked David Jull, the Minister who had accepted the repayment from John Sharp. When Jull's staff pointed out that members of Howard's office had known that Jull was taking this action, Howard sacked two of them, including his chief of staff, Grahame Morris. The Minister for Science, Peter McGauran, also revised his claims and resigned as a Minister. In the short space of a week the Government lost three Ministers and two senior staffers. There was a state of paralysis. At the time I was in Hong Kong at a meeting of the IMF. When I got back I could not believe the damage done to the Government. There were dead political bodies everywhere and no end in sight.

When a Minister is wounded, the press always goes into a frenzy. It becomes a race among journalists over who can discover or report the knock-out blow. The journalist who delivers this blow can claim the ministerial scalp, which may win him or her a media award, a promotion or the admiration of his or her peers. If one journalist or one paper seems to have wounded a Minister, another journalist or paper will look out for a similar set of circumstances to go after another. It is like a shark attack. Once there is blood in the water, the shark goes into a frenzy. Once there is blood in politics, the press goes into a frenzy. The victims of that attack might include the person who was originally bitten or others nearby.

There is no doubt that there were breaches of the travelling allowance rules. But once the frenzy begins, there is no such thing as an innocent mistake. Every mistake is culpable. Simple mistakes that would hardly raise an eyebrow in more normal times suddenly become grounds for dismissal. Every mistake is pounced upon.

Labor was on a roll. Its party members alleged that corruption and dishonesty were endemic in the Howard Government. They could point to three Ministers stood down over 'travel rorts' and two who had resigned in the previous year over 'conflict of interest'. In reality these travel rorts were not confined to the Coalition and the amounts involved were not on the scale practised by some on the Labor side, including Senator Nick Sherry.

I have never been interested in reading the parliamentary Register of Members' Interests, nor could I be bothered investigating the travel returns of other members. These are not the big issues in politics. But when I returned from Hong Kong, Chris Miles, a Tasmanian MP, pointed out to me the much more egregious travel allowance claims of Nick Sherry, a Labor Senator from his state. Senator Sherry nominated Burnie in north-west Tasmania as his home but claimed he had to travel to southern Tasmania for business on an awfully regular basis. He claimed allowances for this travel, including expenses for accommodation, even though he stayed with his mother. He claimed that he was entitled to expenses at a higher rate because his mother's residence was in Hobart. In fact, she lived at a place called Opossum Bay. If there had been a ferry down the Derwent River it might have been considered Hobart, but to reach it required a journey around a bay of 49 kilometres by road. All this combined to deliver an exceptionally large expense bill for the benefit of Senator Sherry, far larger than anything claimed by the Ministers who had lost their jobs.

Senator Sherry had shown great interest in the personal expenses of senators Jim Short and Gibson, who had lost their ministries. He should not have been surprised that our members would show great interest in him. During the height of Labor's hue and cry against the Government, I directed the attention of the House of Representatives to Senator Sherry:

> Senator Sherry spends some 140 nights in a place he calls Hobart—49 kilometres away at Opossum Bay. So we have weekends at Burnie and then we have weekdays with Mum in Opossum Bay. Senator Sherry claims $300 to stay with Mum at Opossum Bay while he is on parliamentary business. Can you imagine the kind of welcome he gets? He gets paid $300 to go home to Mum's. Can you imagine the welcome? 'Oh Possum,' she says, 'Oh Possum, you're home!' On Sunday the Leader of the Opposition said: 'If Labor people are rorting, Labor people go.' It is time for Senator Sherry.

The House of Representatives erupted in laughter. The story played on all the national television news bulletins. The joke lay partly in the impossible name of the place where Senator Sherry was staying—Opossum Bay, a place Dame Edna Everage could only dream about—and partly in the idea that a grown member of the Australian Parliament was claiming money from the taxpayer to stay at his mother's house. Senator Sherry was a second-generation politician who had assisted to end the careers of two Coalition Senators. He should have been careful about his own conduct.

The next evening Senator Sherry dined with members of the Labor leadership group at the Tang Dynasty Chinese restaurant in Kingston. By all accounts nothing was amiss. No one was prepared for what happened next. He returned to his parliamentary office, wrote a note which was delivered to the press bureau, went home and attempted suicide. The journalist who discovered the note the next morning alerted staff in the office of the Leader of the Opposition, who rushed Sherry to hospital.

When I heard the news that morning, I was shocked. I rang the Labor Leader, Kim Beazley, and expressed my sympathy. Beazley was gracious. He told me that he had been at a dinner with Sherry the night of the event and had not noticed anything untoward. He said that no one could have foreseen it and that I bore no responsibility.

There had been nothing untrue in what I said in Parliament. I did not anticipate that result. If I had, I would not have said it. Nothing is worth the loss of a life and I would hate to contribute in any way to that outcome. Fortunately Senator Sherry made a complete recovery. After that incident I toned down my parliamentary performances. There were times when I could have been tougher, but I deliberately held back. You are never quite sure what is going on in another person's life. You never know how a person will respond to pressure in Parliament.

During my time in Parliament there was a suicide by a federal member, the Member for Isaacs, Greg Wilton. There have also been some attempted suicides at state level. I doubt this is because the world of politics has become rougher. It is more related to the increased reach of the media. Failure in politics, even an indiscretion, is now quickly broadcast so far and so wide that there is no relief and there is no hiding.

In my later years as Treasurer, YouTube was also emerging as a powerful medium. Bloggers pick up parliamentary broadcasts carried on television and post them on YouTube. Some of my attempts at humour can be viewed there. I had great fun one day reciting the words to a Midnight Oil song, which had been sung by Labor member Peter Garrett in his previous life. As I began, the Opposition demanded that I sing it. I couldn't quite come to that, so I mimed Garrett's actions. He enjoyed it; so did I. YouTube had not been developed in the early part of my parliamentary career and many of my performances at that time, mercifully, have been lost.

John Howard was elected Leader of the Liberal Party unopposed on 30 January 1995. When we returned to Canberra for the first sitting of the year, Parliament House was blockaded by logging trucks protesting about the Government's forestry policy. Commonwealth cars were unable to get to the doors and MPs had to walk through the blockade. Keating was no exception and the cameras captured footage of him walking into his office. It was a surprise that he was coming into the office mid-morning. It was a late start. Apparently he would sit at the Lodge in his pyjamas listening to the morning media before going in to the office. He had also instituted a system by which Ministers attended Question Time only every second day when the House of Representatives sat. This allowed the Opposition to claim that Labor was treating Parliament with contempt.

Ros Kelly, who stood down as a Minister in the wake of the Sports Rorts affair, resigned from the seat of Canberra at the beginning of the year. In March 1995 the Liberal Party won Kelly's seat with a swing of more than 16 per cent. It was clear that Labor was in trouble. But in voting terms Canberra is the most unrepresentative town in Australia. No one could be too sure how a swing of this dimension would translate outside that peculiar atmosphere.

Keating was bogged down defending Carmen Lawrence through much of July and August. When she finally appeared before the royal commission in Western Australia, her standard answer to questions was: 'I cannot recall' or 'I am unable to recall'. This may have helped in the royal commission but it did not add much to her credibility as a Minister. I dubbed her 'Lawrence of Amnesia'.

Throughout this period the Coalition was identifying savings in Government programs that we could use to fund our election promises, especially the Family Tax Initiative. Alistair Davey in my office did much of the leg work for this policy. The idea was to increase the tax-free threshold for parents by $1000 for each child. A family with three children would get an increase of $3000 in their tax-free threshold. We had designed this as a tax cut, consistent with our philosophy. It would also illustrate that the Coalition was prepared to deliver tax reductions—in contrast to Labor, which had abolished the second round of its 'One Nation' tax cuts after the 1993 election.

There would be some families that did not pay tax. Our policy was to give them the equivalent of the increase in the tax-free threshold by way of a payment of $200. Throughout his career Howard had championed the cause of mothers who stayed at home to look after their children. He felt that they were not properly recognised and they did not receive assistance with childcare. By definition the increase in the tax-free threshold would benefit all families, whether the mother was working or not. Howard wanted an additional benefit to assist families where the mother stayed out of the workforce.

I added a Part B to the Family Tax Initiative, which was an increase in the tax-free threshold of $2500 for a single-income family. Again this could be taken as a benefit of $500 by those families that did not pay tax. This policy was the origin of the family payments structure known as Family Tax Benefit Part A and Part B. Part A was for me and Part B was for Howard. Over the years these payments have been increased. We reformed the tax system in 2000 and amalgamated other family assistance allowances into them.

The day after New Year in January 1996 I left home for Sydney to attend what would be the most crucial meeting in our preparation for the 1996 election. The plane was almost empty. I was the only person flying into Sydney to work that day. John Howard interrupted his holidays for the meeting. We assembled in Phillip Street in Sydney's CBD: the leadership group, our campaign director, Howard's economic team and mine—Stephen Joske, Alistair Davey and Tony Smith. The meeting was to go as long as it took to settle all our policies for the 1996 election. We thought it would last two days, but it took four. For me the fact that we worked all day and all night was something of a relief. I was staying at a hotel in Kings Cross. One night, in the room next to mine, paramedics came in and took a body out—apparently a drug overdose. It was not a luxurious hotel and I had no desire to spend any more time in it than was necessary.

I arrived armed with my list of proposals to cut expenditure to produce savings. I took the group through them one by one. There was a lot of resistance. We had lost the 1993 election with our Fightback! program, which involved significant expenditure cuts. Andrew Robb, the campaign director, preferred to have no expenditure cuts at all. But I was insistent. We could not fund our election promises without offsetting savings. I had been working on a Family Tax Initiative for most of the year. We had to fund it. My plan was to have expenditure savings in excess of our campaign promises so that we would still improve the bottom line of the Budget. It would also give us useful insulation if Labor claimed our promises were more expensive than we had allowed. Our other most important promise was in health, where we planned to give a rebate for private health insurance of $450 for families—the first incentive for private health insurance since Medicare.

We also had to do something about privatisation—an issue left over from Fightback!, in which, we had promised to privatise the Australian and Overseas Telecommunications Corporation, now Telstra. This was never a popular policy. It remained unpopular until it was finally achieved more than a decade later. Labor had no compunction about privatising the Commonwealth Bank or Qantas but it opportunistically decided, as a matter of principle, that Telstra should never be privatised and fought us every step of the way.

We considered whether we should go ahead with the privatisation, although to not do so would look like a backward step on economic reform. John Howard came up with the idea that we could soften our policy by restricting privatisation to one-third and using some of the proceeds to establish a Natural Heritage Trust. This would give a purpose to the privatisation and it would be useful to appeal to the conservation movement, which was offside with Labor over logging policy. It was a novel idea and a good one. I had been extremely critical of the way Labor had mistreated privatisation by using the proceeds of asset sales to pay for recurrent expenditure. I had promised that we would use the proceeds of a capital sale for either debt retirement or building a capital asset. At this meeting we agreed that the bulk of the proceeds from the one-third privatisation of Telstra would be used to retire debt, but we would set aside $1 billion for capital projects in the Natural Heritage Trust.

In order to use the $1 billion for capital projects it was necessary to distinguish between environmental spending properly viewed as 'recurrent' and spending that was truly 'capital'. Whereas the National Party wanted projects of interest to rural Australia, our shadow Environment Minister, Rod Kemp, wanted projects that would be seen as more purely environmental. The argument about capital/revenue and rural/environment went on and on and round and round. John Anderson, the shadow Primary Industry Minister and Deputy Leader of the National Party, and Rod Kemp were asked to come to an arrangement. A day later they declared they had been unable to do so.

The frustration of the participants in the Phillip Street room was growing. We had already gone longer than we expected. At one point I took Anderson and Kemp outside the room. I pointed out that if the privatisation of Telstra did not go ahead, both of them would lose out, that neither of them could get all of their projects funded and that they would have to lose some to win some. I told them that if they did not reach agreement I would decide the projects. Both of these men are friends of mine and it was extremely difficult to arbitrate between them. Such is the gruelling business of politics. Compromises have to be found in the allocation of limited resources. Eventually we got one.

In the four days in Sydney we settled our campaign announcements and all of our policy for the election. I had a score sheet of savings and a tax policy. It was one of the most fruitful meetings I have ever had in politics. I was determined that Labor would never knock a hole through our costings and undermine our economic credibility as they had during Howard's 1987 campaign. I had these costings double-checked by Access Economics and we drew them together in a document called 'Meeting Our Commitments'.

From the day the campaign began I was conscious that all of our promises would stand or fall on our ability to defend their cost and explain how they would be funded. In those days an Opposition had no right to have its policies costed independently by Treasury or Finance, departments that worked exclusively for the Government. The Government could ask them to cost the policies of the Opposition. The Opposition was not even told about it or the results. The Government could choose to release these costings if they were politically helpful. I spent much of the 1996 campaign defending our policies against attacks launched by the Government on the basis of work they had had done in the departments. It was a complete mismatch of resources. After the election I ended all that by legislating the Charter of Budget Honesty, which allowed an Opposition to have independent costing by Treasury and Finance, with the costings to be released to both Government and Opposition—not merely to the Government—simultaneously.

When the day came to release our costings we set up a press conference at the Golden Sands Reception venue in Blackburn Road, Burwood East, Victoria. I knew the venue well—I had driven past it every day on my way to university—but I had never been inside. We should have done an advance reconnaissance. The room was tiny, the day was fearfully hot and a barrage of cameras was there to greet us. They had been primed by the Government. The traffic was unbelievable and the documents that were being printed in my Melbourne office took a long time to be delivered. They were not there when we arrived. The press was angry and ill-tempered in the heat. We waited. And waited. Packed in to a tiny room with the press, perspiring in the heat and facing a wall of cameras, Howard and I began our press conference. Our backs were to the wall—literally! If the campaign was going to fall apart it was going to fall apart that day.

The next morning on *AM*, the Finance Minister, Kim Beazley, opened the attack by saying: 'The figures don't stand up to scrutiny. They are shonky.' I rang in to *AM* to rebut his propositions. Beazley came back, complaining to the interviewer, Fran Kelly: 'You asked him the wrong questions. These figures are shonky. And the job is to ask questions about the shonkiness.' I got another chance to reply. The debate was technical and for the listeners quite incomprehensible. But there were no errors. Labor was unable to land a blow.

Beazley also got into awful trouble later over the state of the Budget before the 1996 election. He was not dishonest; he was just too inexperienced to have a real feel for the state of the books. He repeated lines on the economy rather than giving them serious thought. The great love of his life was defence policy, which he had administered in the Hawke Government.

When Keating called the election, he had emphasised the experience of his team, which he compared with the inexperience of the Coalition. He said he wanted debates between Ministers and their shadows. Immediately I asked my staffer Tony Smith to arrange a debate with Ralph Willis as soon as possible. Tony contacted the Seven Network and told them that I would debate Willis, the Treasurer, on their *Today Tonight* program. *Today Tonight* issued an invitation to both of us. Willis accepted.

On the Tuesday after the election was called, Willis and I went head to head. I challenged him to rule out increasing taxes if Labor was re-elected. He replied: 'No. But there will be no increase in the overall burden of taxes.' We all knew that, before the 1993 election, Labor had said nothing about new taxes and had brought them in anyway. The fact that they were keeping their options open before this election showed they might have a plan for a repeat performance. Most people thought it was a bad political error by Willis. I think his answer was a considered one. He might have known how bad the Budget position was (which I did not). He wanted to keep his options open. But the public did not trust Labor on tax after the 1993 Budget. Equivocal answers were bad answers in an atmosphere of distrust. I rang our federal director from the studio at the end of the debate and told him what Willis had said. I urged him to get the footage and use it for new television advertisements. He did. It was useful to remind people that Labor had broken its word on tax before and could do so again.

Willis kept a low profile for the rest of the campaign. I joked that he had gone into witness protection because he had told the truth about Labor's tax plans. He emerged again in spectacular fashion three days before polling day.

A federal election campaign usually runs for five weeks. A party leader will generally visit twenty or thirty marginal seats in that campaign. There are set-piece events—the opening statement on what the campaign is about; the leaders' debates; the campaign launch; the final address to the Press Club. In between it is hand-to-hand combat to try to win favourable media coverage in the daily news cycle. Each day a party will usually have a positive announcement and a negative attack on the other side. In the best campaigns the positive and negative themes will be covered in the free media and then be backed up with paid advertising. It is important for political leaders to keep focussed and avoid distractions. The message for the day should complement the advertising schedule and the overall theme. Leaders are constantly urged to stay 'on message'.

Keating was floundering and flailing about at the start of the 1996 campaign; he was badly off message. His first big announcement was to be a Youth Policy. Since the election had been called the Government had officially gone into caretaker mode, in which public servants can still work for the Government but are not supposed to initiate new policies. It was a point I made loudly when the campaign began. But Keating somehow got it into his head that I had threatened the secretary of the Department of Employment, Education and Training over Labor's Youth Policy. I had not. I had not spoken to him although one of my colleagues had. Keating even claimed that I had threatened a criminal prosecution of the secretary. This false and ridiculous allegation completely overshadowed Labor's positive message of the day—the Youth Policy.

The next day Keating was asked whether he would apologise to me for making this false claim. He replied: 'Will he apologise for ringing Bernie Fraser and threatening him as Governor of the Reserve Bank? Will he? And he did, he rang him and threatened him. Will he apologise to him?' No sooner had the earlier allegation about the secretary run into the sand than he came up with a new one! This was even more astounding. I have no idea what he was on about. I could not take it seriously. It showed that Keating was badly agitated. If he stayed like this we were going to have a good campaign. The Labor organisation dubbed him 'Captain Wacky'.

Our campaign had a few stumbles of its own. Howard announced the Family Tax Initiative at the campaign launch in Ryde. It went extremely well. The next day John Laws interviewed Howard on radio. The policy was income-tested but the income test varied according to the number of children in the family. Laws asked about the test and Howard said the benefit cut out at $70 000. Laws pointed out that the income test increased by $3000 for each child in a family. Howard denied it. Laws noted that it had been widely reported that this was the case. Howard said it was wrong. Laws went on and on, hammering the point until a member of Howard's staff brought a note into the studio to correct Howard while he was still on air. It looked bad. Later that day Howard addressed a Women's Party Launch. As he was walking off the stage he tripped on the stairs. The footage was manna from heaven for the television networks. John Howard's physical stumble was all the footage they needed to report the policy stumble.

By 1996 our party had lost the past five elections. The principal cause was leadership instability arising out of the debilitating Howard–Peacock rivalry. We were determined now to run a tough and disciplined campaign. We could not afford break-outs from ill-disciplined candidates who would capture headlines and de-rail our national campaign. In Far North Queensland, in the seat of Leichhardt, the Nationals' candidate was reported as describing citizenship ceremonies as 'de-wogging'. We immediately reprimanded him. Such a remark is offensive in itself but it also opened the way for Labor to attack the Coalition over racial insensitivity. Back in 1988 Howard had once suggested that the Asian immigration to Australia was too high. He was widely condemned for it. For years he was accused of dragging racism into Australian politics. In 1995, he went on the *Sunday* program with Laurie Oakes to repudiate his 1988 comments. We could not afford to let the issue out again.

Shortly after this the Liberal candidate for Oxley in Queensland declared that Aborigines were getting too much welfare and too many handouts. This was a second candidate who was inserting race into the campaign. Howard and I were in Melbourne together when the issue erupted. We agreed that the candidate should be cut adrift as soon as possible. Andrew Robb, our campaign director, spoke to us by telephone. He was in touch with the Queensland Division of the Liberal Party, which was preparing to dump the candidate that night. We agreed. I did not worry too much about it. The seat in question was the safest Labor seat in Queensland. Since there was no way she would win the seat, there would be no electoral harm in sacking her as a Liberal candidate. But the sacking was so late in the day that nominations were closed and her name was already on the ballot paper. The sacking helped her enormously by making her a martyr. She went on to win the seat with a swing of 19.3 per cent—the largest swing in the election. Her name was Pauline Hanson.

On the Wednesday before polling day, John Howard addressed the National Press Club at lunchtime in his last formal speech of the campaign. I was in Canberra to do another press conference that afternoon on our policy costings. Ten minutes before I was due to start, Treasurer Ralph Willis hastily convened a press conference of his own at which he released two letters. The first was, he said, from Premier Jeff Kennett to John Howard saying that he had been informed 'by a reliable source' that there was a Coalition proposal to cut state grants by 15 per cent to finance Coalition election promises. The second was a letter from my chief of staff, Dr Barbara Hayes, to Arthur Sinodinos, John Howard's economic adviser, commenting on the first letter and saying that the cut was only 12 per cent, throwing in some gratuitous insults about Kennett and telling Arthur to falsely reassure Kennett that no substantial changes were anticipated. It was marked 'SECRET'.

Willis said these letters showed we had a secret agenda to cut payments to the states, which would cut services. He said we were lying to Jeff Kennett about it and 'lying to the whole of Australia'. He told the journalists that they could go and ask me about it right away.

I delayed my press conference and got a copy of the letters that Willis had released. When I saw them I knew immediately that the letter from Barbara Hayes was a forgery. There was no such plan. Barbara was in my Melbourne office working on the campaign. She was not dealing with the policy costings. I contacted her immediately and warned that her signature had been forged. I predicted that journalists would soon be all over the campaign office looking for the creator of this alleged smoking gun. I suggested she stay out of the spotlight.

Getting to the bottom of the other letter was more difficult because it was allegedly signed by Jeff Kennett. Howard had never received such a letter. He and I rang Kennett from Parliament House. Kennett said he could not remember signing such a letter. The signature looked quite genuine but it could have been taken from a signature block or photocopied from another letter. He said he would check his files. This sent shivers down our spines. After about an hour

Kennett rang back to confirm that his office could find no copy of such a letter. He told us the telephone number on the letterhead was not used by him, that he would have used a different salutation and that he was now using a new logo on his correspondence.

Howard came with me to the press conference I had already scheduled. The reporters thought it was a bombshell. All through the campaign Labor had been saying it would explode our financial credibility. Now—three days before polling day—Labor had found what it claimed was the evidence of deceit and cover-up. Howard denounced the letters as forgeries. In fact, he was so angry that he stormed out of the conference and left me to answer further questions. The forgeries were clever. They were designed to exacerbate tensions known to exist between Kennett and us, tensions that had arisen earlier in the campaign when Kennett had stumbled over questions about the federal Budget.

The signatures were so accurate that it is likely they had been photocopied from actual correspondence. But the forger made two mistakes—using a letterhead of Kennett's that was slightly out of date and bringing Barbara Hayes into the issue when she had not been working on costings. In my opinion the letters were forged by someone who knew something about Commonwealth–state financial arrangements. This is an arcane subject. Few people, except those who have worked in the area, know much about it. Before I became Treasurer I knew very little about it. From what I now know, it is clear to me that the author had worked on the issue.

The journalists would have liked such a sensational story, but they knew we were innocent. No one in their right mind would have written a letter in the terms attributed to Barbara. The whole thing was too fantastic to believe. All of the parties allegedly involved vehemently denied it.

Willis had demonstrated a huge lapse in judgement in relying on these anonymous documents. They had also been sent to the Australian Democrats, who concluded they were fake and did not use them. The ALP organisation approved the Willis attack, which was a sign of great desperation. Later that afternoon a humiliated Ralph Willis withdrew all the allegations. He said he accepted the letters were forgeries although, he said, at the time when he released them he thought they were genuine. He had the decency to apologise. The forged letters dominated the last two days of the campaign, denting Keating's morale and killing his last appearance at the National Press Club the next day.

That should have been the end of the forged letters affair. But the next morning on Melbourne radio, Kennett claimed that the forgeries had been made in the office of Ralph Willis. He said he had given the name of the person he believed was the forger to the Australian Federal Police, who by this stage were investigating the whole affair. On the other side the ALP machine also had not yet finished with the issue. They now came up with the theory that the letters had been forged in my office with the very tricky and evil intention of hoodwinking Labor into damaging itself by releasing them.

The next day, the day before the election, the ALP National Secretariat put out a press release headed 'Fraudulent Letters':

> A Statutory Declaration was today passed to the AFP identifying the likely author of the forged letters as a person with direct access to the Offices of Messrs Jeff Kennett and Peter Costello, and spelling out a substantial body of circumstantial evidence in support of that identification.
>
> The maker of the Declaration has been interviewed by the AFP today, and it is hoped that this information will assist the speedy conclusion of the police investigation.
>
> It is also to be hoped that the police investigation, assisted by this material, will put to rest once and for all the outrageous allegation made by Mr Kennett yesterday (supported by him passing a name to the AFP) that the author of the letters was in fact someone on the staff of the Treasurer.
> 1 March 1996

It turned out that the statutory declaration had been sworn by a member of the ALP, then an articled law clerk, who subsequently became a barrister doing mostly defence work in criminal trials. On Thursday night she rang a student who did volunteer work in my office, Scott Ryan, whom she knew. He had also done part-time work for the Kennett Government. She engaged him in conversation about the issue that was now occupying national attention and asked him how such things could be done. They discussed how computers could be used in that manner. At no stage did he say he had been involved. Nor did the informant say he had said so. Scott had no knowledge of Commonwealth–state financial relations. He had no capacity to write such a letter. After Labor tried to finger him I questioned him about it. There was no way he was involved. The subsequent Australian Federal Police investigation cleared him. But Labor was still able to circulate the suspicion that somehow, rather than being the perpetrator of the forgery, it was the victim. Gareth Evans, the Minister for Foreign Affairs, assiduously pushed this line. We debated the issue in an angry exchange on radio the morning before the election.

Later that afternoon television journalists were stationed outside my office trying to interview the accused staff member about the so-called Coalition involvement in the forgery. The ABC's *7.30 Report* was going to run Gareth Evans pushing this particular theory and it wanted me to go on camera. I thought this would only make the story bigger when there was no evidence at all to support it. Howard called me at about 5 p.m. He wanted me to go on the program. I told him I had already answered the whole story on radio that morning. I did not want another angry confrontation. Howard asked me to give him an assurance that no one in my office was involved. It was an assurance I had no difficulty in giving. He got quite agitated and demanded I go on the *7.30 Report*. He said: 'We could lose this election and this might be the reason.'

I did not want to carry on my shoulders the suggestion that I could have saved the election but declined to do so. I finally agreed to go on. I was so incensed about this completely baseless allegation that I insisted on being interviewed separately from Evans. I thought if we sat together I might want to hit him.

It was a dramatic end to a tough campaign. For the agitated players exhausted by travel and lack of sleep these matters assumed monumental proportions. The next day the ALP got the headline it wanted in Melbourne's *Age*: 'ALP Links Letters to Libs'.

People will claim that the election was a foregone conclusion. It might seem that way in retrospect. But at 5 p.m. on the night before polling day, Howard thought we could lose. So did I. That was the reason I was down in an ABC studio angrily arguing about forged letters which had been designed to set me up and which were now being said to be a clever plot instigated by me or my staff.

Twenty-four hours later it seemed of no consequence. We were elected with a majority of thirty seats. A few days later I moved into the office vacated by Ralph Willis—the very same office where he had received the forged letters, read them and decided to use them in one last attempt to undermine our financial credibility.

The office was empty except for an old CD player, left there by Keating several years before. It was said that he used to play music composed by Gustav Mahler as he composed his Budgets. Since there were no CDs from his collection left in the office, I brought in a few of my own. I used to play Marvin Gaye's 'I Heard It on the Grapevine' for mood music at Budget time.

My musical taste raised a few eyebrows within the Labor Party. Once, when my regular driver Kim Simpson was on holidays, another Commonwealth driver took over his duties. The relief driver was known as a classical music aficionado with a serious collection in his own CD stack. Driving in my car, he picked up Labor MP Barry Jones, who got into the car not knowing it was mine. He asked the driver: 'What shall we listen to today? An opera, or perhaps Mozart?'

'No, Mr Jones. This is the Treasurer's car. We only have his CDs in the player.'

'So we shall listen to some of his music. What does he have? A concerto?'

'No, Mr Jones.'

'Mahler?'

'No, Mr Jones.'

'What does the Treasurer listen to?'

'He listens to a Mr Meatloaf, sir.'

From the symphonies of Mahler to the rock opera of Meatloaf, things had changed in Canberra.

6

BALANCING THE BOOKS:
SETTING MONETARY POLICY

It was not until Monday 4 March 1996 that I was at last briefed on the true state of the Australian Budget. The whole election campaign had been conducted on the basis that the Budget was in surplus. I learned the truth at a meeting in Sydney with the Treasury Secretary, Ted Evans, and some of his senior officials.

Ted Evans is an avuncular man with a sense of humour and a penchant for Delphic comments that project an aura of deep contemplation. He had begun his career in the public service as a linesman for the Postmaster-General's Department and was said to have an encyclopaedic knowledge of the telephone line layout throughout Queensland. He had educated himself as a mature-age student and risen through the Treasury ranks with stints at the International Monetary Fund in Washington before the Keating Government appointed him Treasury Secretary when Tony Cole was transferred to the Department of Health.

Before our meeting, Ted would have been concerned about his future, since no assurances had been sought or given that he would be kept on as permanent head. In fact, few of the previous departmental heads were kept on. Departures included Dr Michael Keating (secretary to the Department of Prime Minister and Cabinet), Michael Costello (Foreign Affairs and Trade), Dr Stephen Duckett (Health), Derek Volker (Employment, Education and Training), Chris Conybeare (Immigration and Ethnic Affairs), Stuart Hamilton (Environment, Sport and Territories) and Peter Core (Transport).

Ted asked to see me privately before the other officials came in. He offered his resignation; it was the right thing to do. I brushed it aside. I told him that I wanted him to stay as departmental secretary. He stayed for the remainder of his term. I appointed him to a second term, which ended with his retirement at sixty in 2001, when I appointed Dr Ken Henry as his successor.

I asked Ted to bring in the officials. When they entered I asked about the state of the Budget. Ted took a breath and softly stated that the Budget deficit that year, in underlying terms, was $9 billion. The starting point for the next year was a deficit of $7.6 billion—about 1.5 per cent of GDP. The words hit me like a sledge hammer. I had worried about the possibility that there would be a slight deficit. I had contemplated nothing like this.

We had been elected on a program of balancing the Budget. We had proposed a tax relief program but it had been carefully offset with savings measures. The savings exceeded the spending and would add $8.6 billion to the bottom line over the three years. I had published a table carefully showing that. I thought this would give us padding to pay for our policy and balance the Budget if it turned out to be in slight deficit.

Now we were being told that the starting point had just been ripped away. We were miles behind the starting line: our savings would not cover this Budget deficit. Our whole program had been drawn on a false premise. Far from implementing our policies, we would spend the whole term fixing Labor's Budget hole. I wasn't sure it could be done. My head began swimming.

The previous May the Labor Government had announced that the Budget for the year ending 30 June 1996 would be in surplus. This included proceeds from the sale of the Government's equity in the Commonwealth Bank. These proceeds were counted as a 'negative outlay'—that is, a reduction of expenses in the Budget. It was an accounting trick and one I had railed against in Opposition. When I became Treasurer I stopped it.

More importantly the 1995–96 Budget had reported an expected surplus of $3.4 billion for the 1996–97 year. Treasurer Ralph Willis had stated in his Budget speech: 'Importantly the Budget for 1996–97 will be in surplus excluding asset sales and special debt and capital repayments.' This foreshadowed a real surplus in the first year of the new Government.

In December 1995 Willis had announced an update of the Budget position—a mid-year review. He stated that the surplus expected for 1995–96 had diminished but that the Budget was still in surplus. As was the practice at the time, he did not report on any of the forward years, including the 1996–97 year.

On 10 February 1996, as shadow Treasurer, I had written to Ted Evans:

> You will be aware that there is considerable speculation as to whether the Budget projection of revenue, outlays and outcome for the 1996–97 financial year is still accurate.
>
> I am writing to ask whether the Treasury and Finance Departments have prepared more up-to-date projections (on the basis of no policy change) and, if so, whether you will inform me of the result.
>
> If the Departments stand by the projections for 1996–97, I request official written confirmation of that position.
>
> I have written to the Treasurer, Mr Willis, and asked him to authorise the release of this information if that is required.

Ted had replied that this was a matter for the Treasurer. Willis replied on 12 February:

> The mid-year review is confined to updating Budget estimates for the current year. This is because it is only for the current year that significant new data, on both the economy and Government outlays and receipts, has become available since Budget time ... The Government decided not to publish revised forward estimates outside the Budget context because of the false impression of precision in these estimates that such an exercise would imply.

Apparently it would have been a false precision to have updated the forward estimates between May and December. That false precision might have shown that a 0.6 per cent surplus was now looking like a 1.5 per cent deficit. It was a pretence. On 12 February I was told there was no update. On 4 March—twenty days later—the Treasury gave it to me. Somewhere along the line we had lost more than $8 billion.

It was in this meeting that the fateful decision was taken to move the Australian Budget from deficit to balance. Treasury advised me that the magnitude of the task meant it could not be done in one year without risking a severe contraction. It recommended a two-year program requiring tightening by 1.5 per cent. Even then, Treasury warned: 'The macroeconomic effect of a tightening of fiscal policy of this magnitude would most likely lead to lower activity.' We briefly discussed balancing the Budget over three years, but that would take us into an election year. It would be hard to maintain discipline. I preferred to make the tough decisions early and hope to get some return by the time of the next election. We would halve the Budget deficit projected for 1996–97 to around $4 billion and close the deficit in 1997–98.

The Prime Minister's Department was floating the option of a hard-hitting May Statement. But the magnitude of the task was so great that we had no idea where we would find the savings. I decided to wait for an August Budget. This would give me the time required to go through Commonwealth spending line by line. It would be no fun but it had to be done. If done properly it would set the Government up for the immediate term and beyond. We did not know then how important this decision would turn out to be when the Asian financial collapse began the next year, in 1997.

But first I had to be sworn in by the new Governor-General, Sir William Deane, who had himself been sworn in during the election campaign. He was formerly a High Court judge. In 1992 he had delivered the influential judgment in the Mabo case, in which he had referred to Australia's record of 'unutterable shame'. For this reason, and because he had been appointed Governor-General in the dying days of the Keating Government, some Coalition members regarded him with a certain suspicion. For my part I found him and his wife thoughtful and gracious hosts at state events at Yarralumla, their official residence. I did not have a lot to do with Sir William since I attended the Executive Council only three or four times in our eleven and a half years in Government. (Junior Ministers usually make up the quorum at the Executive Council, senior Ministers attending only when the agenda includes a matter in their portfolio.)

There was some tension between Howard and Sir William over the proper role of the Governor-General. Holders of the vice-regal office should not comment on partisan or political matters but they do have a role in advancing altruistic causes, in times of national grief or when national healing is needed. Sir William ably represented the nation at the memorial service at the scene of the Interlaken tragedy in Switzerland in 1999, when fourteen young Australians lost their lives in a canyoning accident. While Sir William saw it as part of his role to speak publicly on non-partisan national issues, Howard thought a Governor-General should be more circumspect. When Sir William ended his term and Howard was considering a successor I suggested Tim Fischer, a former politician in the tradition of Sir William McKell, Baron Casey, Sir Paul Hasluck or Bill Hayden. Howard said he would not have an ex-politician; they would have too much to say.

Although Howard is a constitutional monarchist, he does not believe the monarch's representative should have a major role in Australian public life. He himself liked to perform the role of comforting victims at times of national mourning, such as the families who lost loved ones in the Bali terrorist attacks. In my time in Government the various occupants of the vice-regal office played a representational role less and less at moments of national suffering or emergency, while the Prime Minister played it more and more. One of the arguments in support of constitutional monarchy is that the monarch or the vice-regal representative is an alternative source of authority which can operate as a check-and-balance on the executive, especially the Prime Minister. Despite the theory, John Howard did not like it being too much of a brake on the elected Government.

My father came to the swearing-in at Yarralumla. It was a thrill for him and a great honour for me. We had lunch in the parliamentary dining room afterwards. Tim Fischer joined us. He had just been sworn in as Deputy Prime Minister. Tim, the Leader of the National Party, had a shrewd, even cunning, understanding of his rural constituency.

He tended to mangle his syntax, which led many people to think he was not sharp, but it added to his political appeal. He was a bit like Joh Bjelke-Petersen: his sentences might not have been always clear and precise, but he communicated his intentions. He said later, of this day at Yarralumla, that being sworn in as Deputy Prime Minister gave him a terrible attack of insecurity, almost a blackout. This was not my feeling at all. For me it was the culmination of six years of hard effort in Opposition, the chance at last to do something, including to build a stronger economy, tempered only by the thought that there was a huge Budget repair job to be done. And I had been left with the responsibility of doing it.

I held my first press conference the next day in the Blue Room across the corridor from the Prime Minister's office. Only the Prime Minister and senior Ministers use it. I did so for all important press conferences—for example, on the national accounts. Altogether I did more than forty of these. Howard tended to do his press conferences in the Prime Minister's Courtyard. I did not have that option. In the Blue Room the journalists can sit and ask questions, whereas in the courtyard they have to stand, which means the conferences tend to be shorter, particularly in the fearfully cold Canberra winter.

At this conference I released the Treasury's estimates for the current year, 1995–96, and the future year, 1996–97—the figures Labor had refused to release during the election campaign. I homed in on Beazley because he had maintained during the campaign that 'We're operating in surplus and our projections are for surpluses in the future'. Beazley had been an inexperienced Finance Minister; it is unlikely he had had a genuine understanding of the true position. Willis had been more discreet because he had a better understanding of the real position.

I announced our strategy of balancing the Budget over two years. The Expenditure Review Committee (ERC) of Howard, myself, John Anderson (Primary Industry), Michael Wooldridge (Health), John Fahey (Finance) and Jim Short (Assistant Treasurer) began work immediately. I also announced the Charter of Budget Honesty. This would, by law, require a pre-election statement to be produced by the secretary of Treasury and Finance which would disclose the true state of a Budget before the election. It would, by law, require a mid-year review updating the Budget for the current and forward estimate years—something Labor had refused to do in response to my request in February 1996. The review, which under Labor was two pages, had grown to 260 pages by my last mid-year review. In effect, it became a second Budget statement.

Finally I announced a National Commission of Audit, to be chaired by Professor Bob Officer. It was to report on the state of Commonwealth finances, identify contingent liabilities, produce a balance sheet and examine the efficiency of Commonwealth/state delivery of services. The commission was also charged with reporting on matters to be included in the Charter of Budget Honesty. Some idea of the effectiveness of that charter can be found in the events surrounding the change of Government in 2007. There were no skeletons, no undisclosed liabilities, no Budget black holes. If anything, there was an embarrassingly (for the Labor Government) large surplus, which was revised upwards after the election.

The press conference set the tone for the first term, making it clear that an enormous financial challenge and many tough decisions lay ahead of us. It gave the Government a financial framework and set out the work program leading up to the August Budget. Months would be needed to deal with the deficit. I would spend almost the whole of the next six months in the bleak surroundings of an icy Canberra winter working on my first Budget.

The ERC was nominally chaired by the Prime Minister. As the years wore on, John Howard attended less and less. At the end he would attend only when we were finalising decisions. He would come in with a list of the decisions with which he disagreed, which had been prepared by his staff. Ministers who had their expenditure proposals cut would commonly complain to him and ask him to intervene and overrule the committee. It was known as 'the back door', which opened wider and wider as the Government went on. At the beginning the Prime Minister was more involved in the committee's decision-making. If he was there for the decision, had heard the argument and agreed with it, the Minister was unlikely to get him to overrule it at a second hearing. But if he had not been there and had not heard the argument, he might think the decision was unwise or too tough. He also wanted to project to Ministers and the public an air of compassion and reason—a kindly face that stepped in to protect the public from the more heartless economic Ministers.

The ERC sat with officials in the Cabinet room. Each department prepared a Budget submission. This became a Cabinet paper. (The ERC is a committee of the Cabinet.) Some submissions would run to hundreds, even thousands, of pages. The Family and Community Service Department might have a Budget proposal to increase the level of the benefit. This would form a paper of, say, twenty or thirty pages explaining what the payment was, what the increase was, whom it would affect. Then there would be financial tables at the back to show the costs and the effect of the proposal on the forward estimates. The department might have hundreds of such proposals running to thousands of pages. If you multiplied this across all of the departments, the submissions would be metres deep. In my time as Treasurer, we very rarely accepted a submission on face value. We would go point by point through each proposal. If we accepted a new proposal, we would usually ask for an offsetting saving. In that first Budget we had no new proposals for spending, just new proposals for saving.

The Finance Department would prepare a table summarising the financial implications of all submissions. The Finance comments and tables gave arguments against those of the spending departments. Revenue was not a matter for the ERC; there was a separate Revenue Committee of Cabinet for that purpose, and proposals on revenue could come to that committee only on the submission of the Treasurer.

The room in which the ERC met had no windows, no fresh air, no telephones. During that first winter we generally would be there for twelve hours a day. Not all members attended all day every day, but the Treasurer and the Finance Minister did. There was no point in meeting without them. A brotherhood tends to develop among the Ministers on the ERC—and it was particularly strong during our first year in Government as we sat freezing night after freezing night in Canberra away from our families and with all our other colleagues back in the electorates or travelling to much more interesting places.

I got to know John Fahey, former premier of New South Wales and the Government's first Finance Minister, well. He became a valued friend during this process. He was a great raconteur. Like all the Irish, he could talk. Sometimes as a punishment for long-winded Ministers I would ask John to reply to their arguments. He could go a lot longer in reply than they did in making their submissions. Letting John loose was a tactic designed to wear down even the most loquacious of the other Ministers.

At the end of the process, after months away from home, John said to me one night, 'I haven't seen much of Colleen [his wife] lately. And I guess you haven't seen much of Tanya. In fact, we now spend more time with each other than we spend with our wives ...' I cut him off: 'I'm getting a little uncomfortable about where this conversation is heading, John!'

In the ERC we would go though the papers, proposal by proposal. We got to know every department and the way every Minister worked. In some cases the Minister would present the submission. In other cases the departmental head would do it. Sometimes it became clear that the Minister did not understand his own submission. In my experience, as time went by in Government, the departmental heads began to dominate the Ministers. The first Cabinet comprised Ministers who had formed plans from Opposition and wanted to tell the departments what to do. Later, Ministers were appointed from the backbench and came to their portfolios assuming that policy had already been set by the Government or their predecessor.

After twelve Budgets I understood the thinking of these departments. I had been through more Budget rounds than any of the departmental heads. There were occasions where a departmental head would present a proposal for new spending. After listening I would say: 'We rejected this back in 1998. Can you remind me of the reasons why?' The departmental head would have no idea that it had been rolled up before or why it had been rejected. Most were in the job only a few years. Long-held ambitions in the departments bubbled their way up and up, again and again, and would work their way onto the agenda of a new departmental head, just as they had bubbled their way up to the agenda of an old departmental head.

Some Ministers were intimately involved in their departments. Others let the department run itself. Peter Reith was a very good Minister. Another Minister who was always on top of the issues was David Kemp (Schools, Vocational Education and Training; later Employment, Education and Training). In my time the department that managed to dominate the Ministers more than any other was Defence. This was not because the Defence planners had a good grip on their Budget submission: quite the contrary. They could not explain it well to their Minister and as a result their Minister could not explain it well to the ERC. When I first became Treasurer, Defence would not even itemise its Budget submissions or state where the funds were being spent. It used to insist on a global budget which, if the Government agreed to it, would enable the department to allocate funds between projects as it saw fit. I fought Defence over this practice. After several rounds over several years I managed to get the Defence Budget itemised and then reviewed by the ERC.

I also succeeded in putting in place capital acquisition programs which actually allocated money to specific projects. We discovered, for example, that in listing projects for capital acquisition Defence never allowed for depreciation or in some cases repairs. Having obtained money for the acquisition of a major plane, there was no money for repairs or parts. As a consequence, at any given time several planes in a fleet would be unable to fly. If for some reason they needed money to increase the number of serviceable aircraft, it might, under the global budgeting system, be taken out of another capital project of another branch of the services.

During our period in Government we had a number of Ministers for Defence who served for a short time, generally as their last ministerial appointment. They did not have time to really get on top of all the ins and outs of the various programs and capital acquisitions. Defence Command, which consists of dedicated and loyal servicemen, are trained for combat. They are good at that. They are not generally chosen for their expertise as financial analysts. There is a high turnover of people in the various Defence hierarchies. All the services protect their own areas. Every step in achieving more efficiency involved a tussle over whether or not the central Government was entitled to a line-by-line disclosure of how Defence spent its budget.

Defence is now making disclosures on a scale it has never done previously. After eleven and a half years I had a handle on all this simply because I had been involved in these decisions for longer than any of the Defence chiefs. I could actually remember the reasons why we had decided on certain acquisitions. They had to rely on the oral traditions passed down the chain of command. I was able to remind the Defence chiefs of previous undertakings they had given about containing costs. It will take the new Government, with no collective memory of problems and solutions, some time to learn these lessons.

The period in the ERC leading up to the August 1996 Budget gave me the opportunity to go line by line through Commonwealth expenditures. I was able to get a grip on every department and program, and indeed on every permanent head and every Minister. We were looking to balance the Budget in two steps. Apart from Defence, which was quarantined from overall cuts, there was no area of Commonwealth spending off limits. At the same time our political opponents were preparing to attack the Government for its heartlessness. The Labor Party did not support balancing the Budget and was determined to defeat expenditure reductions on the grounds that, along with balancing the Budget, they would have a contractionary effect in the economy and bring on a recession.

Labor's first shadow Treasurer, Gareth Evans, was a strong opponent and had been an accomplished Minister for Foreign Affairs but he was more interested in the international stage. I developed a grading system for the five shadow Treasurers I faced (Evans, Simon Crean, Bob McMullan, Mark Latham and Wayne Swan). For a low rating I used the label 'WTG'—Worse than Gareth. Most of them came in at that level. Crean was the best.

The secretary of the Australian Council of Trade Unions (ACTU), Bill Kelty, had promised before the 1996 election that he would give the Government 'the full symphony'. The union movement organised a huge protest outside Parliament House on the day before the Budget. Kim Beazley, the Labor Leader, and Cheryl Kernot, the Democrats

Leader, addressed the rally, as did various trade union leaders. They whipped the crowd into a frenzy over the unemployment the Budget would cause and the recession it would bring on. Some of the trade union militants stormed Parliament House. The security guards and a small contingent of police were unable to block them. Some Coalition staffers, including my microeconomic adviser, Alistair Davey, at that time the ACT shot-put champion, went down to try to hold the glass doors against the insurgents. They were unsuccessful. The mob smashed down the doors and began running through the building. Cut by the glass on the doors they had smashed, they left trails of blood on the floor. The bodyguards assigned to the Prime Minister took me out of the Cabinet room and locked me in my office. After several hours, when the rioters finally left, we were given an all-clear to unlock the office compound and come out. In the end, the riot backfired on the Labor Party and the ACTU.

I delivered the Budget the next day. It was a tough one—it had to be, to achieve $8 billion of cuts over two years. But it was one of the best received Budgets in Australian history. People knew there was a problem and they also knew the Government was trying to do something about it. As I said: 'Although we did not create it, we will take the responsibility to fix it.'

Tanya came with me to Canberra for the Budget and we asked my mother to look after our children. The Budget was carried live on television at 7.30 p.m. My mother turned on the television and called our 9-year-old son Sebastian to watch.

'No, it's boring,' he said.

'How do you know it's boring if you haven't heard it?'

'I saw the speech on Dad's desk in his study yesterday and I read it. It is boring.'

Some time later I recounted the story to Laurie Oakes, the veteran journalist of the Nine Network.

The following year, on the Sunday before the Budget, he rang me at home. 'Can I speak to Sebastian?' he asked.

'Why?'

'I want to ask him if he has read any speeches on your desk in the study.'

After that first Budget I came home utterly exhausted. On the Saturday afternoon I decided to have a sleep. Tanya was out. I said to Sebastian: 'I am going to sleep. If the phone rings, I don't care who it is, tell them Dad is not to be woken.'

When I woke up a couple of hours later, I asked him: 'Did the phone ring?'

'Yes.'

'Who was it?'

'John Howard.'

'What did you tell him?'

'Dad doesn't care who it is, he is not to be woken.'

Bernie Fraser was the Governor of the Reserve Bank when I became Treasurer. He had been appointed from the Treasury, where he had been secretary. He had been a career public servant with no previous experience in the Bank. This was unusual since, at least from the days of 'Nugget' Coombs, the Governor had been a career officer in the Bank. The Reserve Bank is located in Sydney, which was thought to put it outside the reach of the Commonwealth Public Service and the Government located in Canberra. Some saw the appointment of Fraser, a former department head in Canberra, as an attempt by the Government to further control the Bank. This was made worse when Treasurer Keating boasted that he had 'the Reserve Bank in his pocket'. He was widely taken to mean that he had the Governor (his previous secretary) in his pocket. The comment was extremely damaging to Fraser and, in my view, did him a great disservice. Although he was close to Keating it was clear that he was his own man and made his own decisions, and I am sure Keating was unhappy with a few of them. Keating's vain boasting also damaged the Bank.

Fraser is a softly spoken man—so much so that he sometimes sounds as if he can only whisper. Central bank governors are Delphic enough, but when they whisper they are doubly hard to penetrate. Yet the fact that he was barely audible did not mean that Fraser lacked a punch. He was not afraid of controversy and this got him into some ugly exchanges with the Hewson-led Coalition after the 1990 election.

In the lead-up to that election the cash rate target, the benchmark for interest rates, was 17 to 17.5 per cent. Homeowners were paying standard mortgage interest rates of 17 per cent if they could get finance from a bank and much more if they borrowed it from other institutions. The economy was moving into recession. The election was in March. Growth in the subsequent June and September quarters was negative. The recession was confirmed at the end of the year. As a young homebuyer myself I knew just how punishing these interest rates were, and it was particularly obvious in Victoria just how sick the economy had become. I thought that the level of interest rates was the strongest reason for a change of Government—patently, Labor had mismanaged the economy and was in the process of strangling it.

In those days, and right up until the time I became Treasurer, the Treasurer and the Reserve Bank Governor would simultaneously make an announcement about a change in monetary policy. The first cut which signalled an easing of policy was announced on 23 January 1990—two months before the election. Treasurer Paul Keating issued a release:

> Following consultations which I have had with the Reserve Bank it has been decided to ease monetary policy. The Government and the Reserve Bank Board are agreed that demand has slowed to the point where some response on the interest rate front is now warranted. To this end the Reserve Bank has been operating in the money market today with a view to effecting a modest reduction in interest rates.

Because an election was looming when the Treasurer made the announcement, the decision was viewed as being political. Since the inflation rate at the time was around 8 per cent, it could not be said that an interest rate cut was warranted on those grounds. These days we would regard that level of inflation with horror. But an 8 per cent inflation rate was not abnormally high for the Hawke Government, which averaged inflation at 5.2 per cent over its term—and the Government would not have brought it even that low but for the recession, which pulled the average down considerably.

On 15 February 1990 rates were cut again and on the following day Bob Hawke went to Yarralumla to seek an election. The Opposition naturally felt that interest rates had been manipulated for political ends. Hewson, then shadow Treasurer in Peacock's Opposition, said the move was a blatant political act: 'If interest rates can be put down with no justification prior to the election they will just as easily be put up again after it.'

As a candidate in the election my view was that the problem was not that interest rates were being cut too early but that they were being cut too late: they should have been decreased long before, and they were squeezing the life out of the economy. Peacock's political instincts were akin to mine. In December he had said there would be massive reductions in interest rates under a Coalition Government. His shadow Finance Minister, John Stone, immediately corrected him, and Howard (who had been the Coalition's last Treasurer) insisted that interest rates couldn't be cut until foreign debt was reined in, something that would take some considerable time. This, of course, was political pay dirt for the Labor Party struggling to be re-elected with oppressive interest rates. It pointed out that the Liberal Party was offering no short-term relief. As it turned out, Peacock was also right and Hewson was wrong. The economy did need substantial reductions in interest rates to avoid the depths of the 1990–91 recession. From January 1990 there were eleven rate cuts over three years totalling nearly 13 per cent. But they came too late.

After the 1990 election the Hewson-led Coalition proposed an inflation target of 0 to 2 per cent. Under the Hawke Government inflation had been nowhere near these levels except when the recession hit. The suggestion of a target was a great step forward in the debate over monetary policy. But whether the target was the right one was a critical issue. Hewson and Reith made it clear that if this was done they would expect the Reserve Bank to meet the target. It was something that should have been debated between the Government and Opposition. But the Governor, Bernie Fraser, joined the fray, famously telling the *Sydney Morning Herald*: 'I won't go just to appease some dickhead Minister who wants to put Attila the Hun in charge of monetary policy.' He was telling the Opposition that he would not implement their policy and he would not make way for someone who would. He was also saying that the shadow Minister proposing such a policy was a 'dickhead'. It was inflammatory stuff and quite wrong. Fraser was also widely quoted as opposing the Coalition's policy on GST, again a matter of political controversy which a Reserve Bank Governor should have avoided.

Although Fraser always opposed giving the Reserve Bank an inflation target, he started to talk, after the 1993 election, about getting inflation down to around 2 to 3 per cent over the course of the economic cycle. By this stage Hewson had lost the leadership and the Coalition had not renewed the 0 to 2 per cent target.

As shadow Treasurer, I had spoken with fund managers and foreign investors in London about Australia's economic and monetary policy. Australia was considered to be a high inflation risk (and in fact was). Much concern was expressed about the independence of the central bank. The controversy surrounding Keating's claims and Fraser's appointment had been followed closely. Australia was unfavourably compared to New Zealand. The international investors' perception was that New Zealand truly had an independent central bank, with an independent central bank governor. New Zealand had moved to an inflation-targeting regime regarded as the tightest in the world. I was shocked to be lectured about how far we were trailing the Kiwis.

The Reserve Bank of New Zealand had a formal contract to deliver inflation between 0 and 2 per cent. This was the Fightback! target. I was not sure about the target but I was convinced that it was important for the Government, for the Reserve Bank of Australia, for the public and for investors to know the objectives of monetary policy and for these to be published. I decided that we would implement such a system in Australia if we were elected. The appointment of a new Reserve Bank Governor would give me the opportunity to set it up.

Immediately after the election I was approached by various people who wanted to become Governor of the Reserve Bank. One was John Stone, a former Treasury secretary and National Party Senator. Given our experience with Bernie Fraser, a former Treasury secretary, and given Stone's views as shadow Minister for Finance on the rate cut in the lead-up to the 1990 recession, this offer was not compelling.

It is the practice for the Governor of the Reserve Bank to meet with the Commonwealth Treasurer after each monthly board meeting to brief the Treasurer on the matters discussed. If the board has decided to move the cash rate, this will have already been reported to the Treasurer, but the debrief gives a regular opportunity to discuss the state of the economy and also differences of opinion between the Bank and the Treasury. In 1996 Bernie Fraser led these meetings for the RBA, but also present was the Deputy Governor, Ian Macfarlane, a member of the board at the time.

Not having been personally involved in the stoush I bore no personal animus towards Fraser and I assured him that I would not continue the war that had erupted with Hewson and Reith. In my view this had not been good for him or for them. A lot of water had passed under the bridge. Our relations were cordial. It struck me there was a difference in outlook between the career officers of the Bank, who tended to be more technical, and Fraser, who had had much broader experience of Government and political issues. Macfarlane impressed me as somebody who was exceptionally strong on economic policy, quite neutral on political issues, and personally very affable. He seemed to me to be a sensible appointment to replace Fraser, but I was intent on reaching an agreement with the Reserve Bank on an inflation target. It was essential that the new Governor, whoever that be, agree on such a proposal. I discreetly raised the matter with Macfarlane, who was very supportive.

Choosing a central bank governor is a critical economic decision. The most important thing is to assess how the person will react to various challenges in the economy. I did not think it was right to audition candidates for the job or ask them their policies—the parameters would be set by my Statement on the Conduct of Monetary Policy—but it was crucial to get a feel for the way they would think.

I recall the advice I was given by an American investment banker. He told me that the most important thing was to get a central banker who was physically short. 'Look at Paul Volker. He was 6 feet 10 inches and because he was so tall interest rates always looked low to him. If you get a short man as your central banker, interest rates will always look high to him and he will be much more inclined to cut them.'

Macfarlane was a little over average height. I assessed him to be moderately hawkish! I offered Macfarlane the appointment and put to him a statement that would represent our common understanding of how monetary policy would be conducted. My chief of staff, Peter Boxall, flew to Sydney to show him the statement, which he accepted with some minor wording changes.

The essence of the statement was firstly that there would be an explicit target. This would make clear that monetary policy would be directed towards inflation. The target would be 2 to 3 per cent over the course of the economic cycle—more flexible than the New Zealand target and less harsh than the Fightback! target. Ian could hardly disagree since it was the target towards which the Bank itself had been moving.

The second feature was that the Treasurer would no longer make a parallel announcement of movements in monetary policy. The decision would be seen as the decision of the Bank and it would be clear to both domestic and foreign investors that the Bank was independent in this respect. My predecessors had all undertaken an announcement themselves. The last movement in monetary policy under the Keating Government was on 14 December 1994 when Ralph Willis announced: 'The Reserve Bank, after consulting with the Government, today announced an increase of 1 percentage point in the official overnight cash rate.' The purpose of these statements was to make it clear that the RBA was consulting, and would not move without consulting, the Government. These consultations gave the Government the right to influence or veto the decision. My agreement would remove this right. The Government still has the right to veto a monetary decision under the Act. But the Act prescribes a very difficult process for doing so. The Treasurer may submit a recommendation to the Governor-General to issue an order to determine the policy to be adopted by the Bank. The board is required to give effect to that order but the Treasurer has to table in each house of Parliament a statement of the board's position, a statement by the Government on the difference of opinion, and the order. This then becomes a matter for debate. This statutory process has never been invoked.

The decision to withdraw the parallel announcement and to guarantee the independence of the board made it clear that the Government would not exercise the right of influence or veto behind the scenes and would restrict its powers, should they ever be exercised, to the open and transparent procedures prescribed by the Act.

The statement, to which Macfarlane agreed, had as its third element an intent to increase the accountability of the Bank by prescribing a semi-annual Statement on the Conduct of Monetary Policy and a report from the Governor twice a year to the House of Representatives Standing Committee on Economics, Finance and Public Administration. Later the statement on monetary policy was upgraded to a quarterly release.

I announced these arrangements on 14 August 1996 when also announcing the appointment of Macfarlane as the new Reserve Bank Governor. The agreement plainly stated: 'The Government recognises the independence of the Bank and its responsibility for monetary policy matters and intends to respect the Bank's independence as provided by statute.' It was a major step forward and was well received by financial markets. It has formed a basis for the conduct of monetary policy ever since and it contributed enormously to the successful economic expansion through the late 1990s and beyond.

The agreement also stated that 'consistent with its responsibility for economic policy as a whole the Government reserves the right to comment on monetary policy from time to time'. Sometimes it would be asserted that the Government had no right even to comment on monetary policy. This is absurd. The Treasurer or Prime Minister is required to answer questions in the media on a daily basis and must account to the Parliament in Question Time on economic policy. To suggest that they could not comment on interest rates would be to prevent them from being able to answer questions about key areas of the economy. But I made it a practice never to comment on future movements or anticipate future decisions. I made this a rule so that it would be clear that I was not directing the conduct of future decisions. Almost on a daily basis I would be asked whether a particular piece of economic news would lead to a rate rise or a rate cut. I had a stock standard answer: 'I do not comment on future movements in monetary policy.'

Naturally I would be asked about inflation and inflationary expectations. I could not avoid discussing these issues and some people thought this was a way to talk about monetary policy. It was my duty to comment upon these matters and I would always remind my questioners that they, like everybody else, could work out how monetary policy would be applied in various inflationary scenarios: 'I do not comment on future movements in monetary policy.' The agreement made it quite clear that monetary policy would be applied to medium-term price stability with the objective of keeping underlying inflation between 2 and 3 per cent, on average, over the cycle.

I had an early lesson in how careful you have to be in this area. In a visit to Washington I did an interview with Australian journalists. I had just had a meeting with Alan Greenspan, chairman of the US Federal Reserve. Asked about the meeting, I said: 'He indicated to me he saw no threats to inflation down the track.' In Australia the *Australian Financial Review* ran the story under the headline 'Greenspan to Costello: Inflation Not a Problem'.

Bond traders back in the United States picked up the story and took it as a sign that US interest rates would not rise. It was said to have moved the US bond market. In Australia the Opposition called for my head. The papers described it as a terrible gaffe. My comment had been loose—accurate but loose. I gave the paper the opportunity to write the story and it took it. I learned a big lesson: caution is best. After that I developed my own defensive replies to questions that sought to elicit information that could have an effect on markets. If you wonder why Treasurers or central bankers sound boring on these issues, this is why. They are trying to avoid saying anything that will influence traders and affect markets.

It did not affect my relationship with Alan Greenspan, who is an extraordinary intellect and a charming and lively conversationalist. We met many times. I always enjoyed these occasions. He apparently enjoyed them too, judging from the reference he made to our meetings in his memoirs.

Bernie Fraser was not involved in negotiations regarding the Statement on the Conduct of Monetary Policy. Nor did I consult him on the appointment. As a matter of courtesy I informed him that I proposed to appoint Macfarlane before the announcement was made. I knew Fraser would not support the adoption of a formal agreement and inflation target. In his farewell address to the National Press Club after the statement was made he explained his reasons: 'I think at the margin it does tend to move the inflation target more into centre stage than I personally would have liked to see it.' This was a fair expression of his views and a respectable argument. However, I did not agree with it. Keating ferociously attacked the agreement. The Labor Opposition followed him.

On 13 August 1996, spurred on by Keating, Beazley released a statement:

> Federal Opposition Leader Kim Beazley says preliminary legal advice available to him suggests Mr Costello's plan may well be illegal ... Requiring the Reserve Bank Governor to pursue a hard line inflation first strategy seems inconsistent with the clear obligation and guarantee to protect jobs contained in the Reserve Bank's legislative Charter.
>
> The fact is the Charter is designed to protect Australian jobs and is the law of the land. Any attempt to get around this legislation by an exchange of letters or any non-legislative instruction from the Treasurer must be called into question.
>
> The Federal Opposition will be treating this issue seriously and will not allow the Government to subvert the Reserve Bank's legislative charter ...
>
> This is why we will be seeking further legal opinion on the legality of the Costello proposal and the option of the federal Opposition going to the High Court to force the Government to abide by all of the provisions of the RBA Act.

The Reserve Bank Act required the board to exercise its power in such a manner as would best contribute to the stability of the currency of Australia, the maintenance of full employment in Australia and the economic prosperity and welfare of the people of Australia. My view was that by setting an inflation target at 2 to 3 per cent we were effectively defining what was required to ensure the 'stability of the currency' and if it did its job properly this would, over the long term, contribute to employment and the ultimate objective of 'economic prosperity and welfare'. The Keating/Beazley argument was that we were focussing the Reserve Bank on the inflation objective at the expense of the objectives of employment, prosperity and welfare. They asserted that the agreement was therefore contrary to the Act. If so, then it would be an illegal agreement. This was not such a bad legal argument. But if it ever came to legal proceedings it would require the court to decide whether or not an inflation focus was contrary to an employment objective. This is a pure economic question and I doubt that any court would want to decide it.

Our Government's argument was borne out by history. Although it took time, we maintained our inflation objective and eventually began to bring down unemployment. We delivered on our inflation target and reduced unemployment to the lowest level in more than thirty years. The Statement on the Conduct of Monetary Policy was absolutely crucial to that.

It is true that the Reserve Bank had a statutory objective of maintaining 'full employment', but since Australia had been a long way from full employment for a long time, it could hardly have been argued that the Bank felt obliged in the conduct of monetary policy to achieve that objective, particularly when, at the height of the recession, unemployment had been in double figures. Nobody had suggested suing the RBA for a breach of this statutory objective. It was ridiculous to suggest that the Government be sued for putting these arrangements in place. But it indicated how opposed the Labor Party was to this agreement and how hard we had to fight partisan opposition for reform that is now considered a cornerstone in the economic fabric of Australia.

The Labor Party never began legal proceedings over this agreement. When elected in 2007 it committed itself to the same agreement that I initiated. I am pleased to say that no one on the Coalition side threatened to sue its members for doing so.

The Statement on the Conduct of Monetary Policy of 1996, and the conduct of the Government in recognising and abiding by it, established the Reserve Bank of Australia as one of the most respected independent central banks in the world. The Blair Government followed our lead in establishing new arrangements with the Bank of England when it was elected in 1997. The IMF held up our arrangements as a model for other countries.

These arrangements now seem obvious because they have worked so well, but they were controversial at the outset and it took time for all parties to accept them. Early on in our term, when we were having trouble with unemployment, Howard suggested that we cut interest rates. I told him this was beyond the Government's control since we had ceded this power to the Reserve Bank. 'When I was Treasurer we used to set the rates,' he told me. And they did. But we had improved things a bit since then.

The fact that the RBA is independent should not mean that it is free from scrutiny or criticism. Quite the reverse. Ceding such a significant power to an independent body means the body has to be subject to critical scrutiny. Governors are intelligent human beings who, like all human beings, are fallible. Sometimes they will get their decisions right. Sometimes they will get them wrong—as during the late 1980s. There is no doctrine of Bank infallibility.

We rightly submit Governments to scrutiny and criticism on a continuous basis. Public service departments are also subject to a lot of critical scrutiny. In my time as Treasurer a whole industry sprang up around second-guessing economic forecasts, the Budget position and the economic effects of various policy options. This is right and it keeps the Treasury on its toes. But there has been a tendency, particularly among financial journalists, to assume that, because a decision has been made by the central bank, it must be right. They no doubt see this as defending the independence of the bank—an important principle. It is also important to defend the independence of the judiciary. But this does not mean that every decision made by a court is right or that court decisions should not be critically evaluated.

The Reserve Bank did have a practice of talking to journalists off the record. This meant that financial journalists felt there were real gains to be made in cultivating good relations and maybe muting their criticism. If there was a movement in monetary policy coming, journalists would often predict or preview it. In my time Alan Wood and Alan Mitchell were generally the best informed.

There is a good purpose in the RBA keeping the market informed and talking to journalists: it is attempting to set a market rate. If its announcement produces that rate, then it has achieved its objective. If its announcement does not produce that rate, then it will have to intervene in the market to try to produce it. In a situation where the Bank tries to move to a rate that is out of line with the market, it will not have the resources to do so. The Bank does not have financial reserves deep enough to take on and prevail against the weight of money in the private sector. If the Bank is intending to move to a rate, quite often it will start to condition expectations.

Sometimes the process works the other way. If the market is beginning to price a certain outcome, the RBA may feel under pressure to make an announcement. At the end of the day it is trying to influence a market outcome. It cannot defy the prices that are being set by transactions in that market.

When the Bank sets out to target a cash rate it does so by buying or selling securities. Taxpayers' money is being used for this purpose, which is another reason why there should be strong accountability. If the board is given a role—to produce a particular inflation outcome—then it should be expected to do so. There is no point in giving this role to the board and then holding some other institution responsible for the failure to deliver it. The Government and other instrumentalities must ensure that they are working towards the same goal but they should be clear where responsibilities lie.

If a Government makes an error, then it can be voted out, but if a central bank governor makes an error he cannot be voted out. The only way to make an independent central bank accountable in a modern democracy is through press scrutiny. The responsible Minister (the Treasurer) should also, in my view, use their private meetings to challenge officials and make them critically evaluate their forecasts. The board members should do the same by challenging the officials on their forecasts and assessments.

When I put the arrangements in place for the RBA to be fully independent of Government, I had the support of Treasury. But Ted Evans, the secretary, sounded a note of warning: 'The cult of the independent central bank will pass. It is too much power without enough accountability.' In my view the independence should remain but accountability and scrutiny should be intense.

During my period as Treasurer the announcement of a cash target was nearly always sufficient to produce the outcome. I doubt that the RBA ever had to intervene to produce its desired outcome. When my son was studying for his Year 12 economics exam, he asked me to help him with one of the questions in his textbook—whether the Reserve Bank would have to buy or sell securities if it wanted to raise the cash rate. 'Buy,' I said. 'The book says sell,' he said. I told him I was meeting the Governor the next day and would check. At the end of our meeting with the RBA Governor and senior staff, I said, 'Governor, if you wanted to raise the cash rate would you buy or sell securities?' 'Buy,' he said. 'No, sell,' said his head of trading. The two began arguing about it. Eventually the Governor said: 'In practice we do neither. We just announce it.' 'That may be OK for you,' I said, 'but my son has his school economics exam tomorrow. He needs to know the answer.'

The announcement of a cash rate provided a convenient mechanism for interest rates to be transmitted in the real economy. Banks would move their rates in line with official rates. They could use the Reserve Bank as cover for their decisions. In reality they were not obliged to move their interest rates in accordance with movements in the cash target rate but it became a convenient mechanism for all concerned. Since the 2007 election the banks have begun moving interest rates by more than official movements. They argue that they are moving in accordance with market rates. This may be the case. But in my view, having broken the nexus, they have moved into a whole new environment. If banks raise rates outside official movements, then when conditions change they should be expected to cut them outside official movements. If they add margins on to official rate rises, then they can be expected to narrow margins on official rate cuts. What is more, they now have to explain their pricing. They cannot say it is all the decision of the Reserve Bank. They should be subject to transparency and critical analysis in justifying their prices. If such a system develops they might look back with fondness to the days when they could explain all their decisions by reference to the official cash rate.

One of my early decisions as Treasurer was to commission an inquiry into the financial system. It was chaired by Stan Wallis, formerly managing director of Amcor. It was a comprehensive inquiry and laid down a blueprint for many regulatory changes. One of the changes it recommended was that a single Commonwealth agency should be established to carry out prudential regulation in the financial system. Previously, this supervision for banks was undertaken by the Reserve Bank. Prudential regulation for credit unions and building societies was undertaken by different bodies. I moved to establish a single regulator, which we named APRA—the Australian Prudential Regulatory Authority. This involved taking away prudential supervision of the banking system from the Reserve Bank. The RBA opposed this decision. I proceeded with it. I think it was the right decision.

This meant that the Reserve Bank was left with only its role in monetary policy and the payments system, which gave it a very specific focus. I think this improved its operations in relation to monetary policy. With an exclusive focus and enormous resources, the Bank is better placed to make monetary policy decisions and should be held accountable for them.

Ian Macfarlane proved to be an exceptionally good appointment as Governor of the Reserve Bank. He served a full 7-year term and I offered him a reappointment. He asked that it be limited so that in total he served only ten years. He thought a maximum of ten years would be good for the Bank and would also give the opportunity for younger people in the Bank to be considered for the role of Governor.

When Macfarlane stepped down I considered both internal and external appointments. There were some outside candidates with banking experience whom I carefully considered, some internal candidates, and a very strong candidate from the Treasury. In the end I appointed Glenn Stevens, who had been Deputy Governor. Having gone to such lengths to put the Bank on an independent footing I thought the appointment of a Treasury officer would re-open the whole argument that occurred when Bernie Fraser was appointed back in 1989. Macfarlane's retirement—four years earlier than if he had served a full second term—had been timed to make way for younger people in the Bank. There was some opposition inside the Government to Stevens' appointment but I pushed it and the Prime Minister agreed with it.

Stevens was to demonstrate his independence by raising interest rates some three weeks before election day. Nobody would ever again doubt the independence of the central bank. There was no movement in December and there was no urgent reason that required a rate rise in November. I thought in the latter part of 2007 the Bank was underestimating the likely flow-on from the sub-prime crisis in the United States and had to be very careful about adding to credit costs. But the press was turning this into a test for the new Governor: he was under pressure from the economic commentators. A more experienced Governor would not have felt the same need to prove himself. I had seen this happen before, with Macfarlane. In December 1996 the Reserve Bank board decided to reduce the cash rate by 50 basis points and prepared a media release for the next day, 4 December. On the evening of the board meeting, before this release was issued, Bernie Fraser did an interview on the *7.30 Report* in which he said the Bank should have cut rates more aggressively the month before. With Fraser calling for more aggressive rate reductions and a decision taken which was going to be announced the next morning, Macfarlane felt that it would be assumed that he was responding to pressure from his predecessor. He took the unusual step of withholding the announcement of the decision until eight days after the board meeting, by which time fallout from the Fraser comments had worked its way through the press. This was his decision and I supported him in it. It illustrates how a new Governor naturally enough wants to make his own mark.

For reasons I deal with in Chapter 14 I do not think the rate rise during the election campaign worked entirely to the disadvantage of the Coalition. Some of my colleagues criticised the Governor to me, but there was no public criticism, which was very disciplined given the heat of the election campaign. I believe that the system we implemented was the right one. It was my decision to appoint Stevens; I take full responsibility for it.

Balancing the Budget, targeting inflation and establishing the independence of the Reserve Bank of Australia were fundamental pillars of our program of economic reconstruction. They maintained confidence in Australia during the Asian financial crisis, insulating us from that crisis when there was a serious flight of foreign capital from countries in our region that had once been considered much more attractive as investment destinations. As the region moved into recession and worse, Australia continued growing.

In May 1999 the Asia-Pacific Economic Cooperation (APEC) Finance Ministers' meeting was in Langkawi, Malaysia. Far from still being the new Minister on the block, as I naturally had been at my first APEC meeting, in Kyoto in 1996, I was now one of the longest serving Ministers. The crisis swept many Finance Ministers in the region out of office. Some had been sacked, some placed under house arrest, some imprisoned.

My experience at Kyoto in 1996 was that Australia was tolerated as a regional partner but not respected. We were viewed as a country that had seen its best days and was now in decline. But in Langkawi in 1999 we were seen as one of the strong economies of Asia. We had survived the crisis. We had given financial assistance to other countries in trouble.

At the Langkawi meeting, the United States was focussed on the Asian weakness. It saw a recovery in Japan as critical to lifting the regional economy and balancing world growth—then reliant almost exclusively on the United States. 'The world economy cannot fly on one engine,' said Larry Summers, the US Deputy Treasury secretary, to the Japanese representative, the highly respected, urbane Eisike Sakakibara, known in financial markets as 'Mr Yen'. (When he spoke, the Yen moved.) Sakakibara looked up in his wily way at Larry

Summers. 'The world economy does not fly on one engine,' he said. 'It has a second engine. There is the Australian economy too.' He was only half joking!

7

UNCHAIN MY HEART:
A NEW TAX SYSTEM

Three days before the 1998 election I walked through the Myer department store in Melbourne with Ray Martin, host of the Channel 9 program *A Current Affair*. Ray had a camera crew. As his scrum of sweating cameramen with boom microphones and bright lights passed through the store followed by a herd of reporters, the alarmed shoppers moved aside to watch. I was being tested on the GST. Any mistake I made would be widely reported.

Some shoppers were happy to join in. 'Go Labor!' called one. 'Stick it up 'em, Pete!' yelled another. We walked from floor to floor, product to product. Ray pointed to individual items and asked whether the price would move up or down if we were re-elected and our tax changes came into effect. Would people buy more of them or fewer? How much would a cooked chicken increase in price? What would be its GST? What about liquorice? Would linen sheets go up in price or down? What about perfume? Gift wrapping? A can of Coke? It lasted two hours. Like most men, I hate shopping. But in the late 1990s I was the nation's expert on the price of everything and how it would be affected by the largest tax reform in Australian history.

It's a sickness. I have always been fascinated by tax policy. I studied taxation law as part of my degree at Law School. It was the one course for which I won a prize! As part of that course I had a look over the Taxation Review conducted by Mr Justice Kenneth William Asprey. The Liberal McMahon Government had commissioned Justice Asprey in 1972 and he reported in 1975. He emphasised the importance of efficiency, simplicity and neutrality in a tax system. He recommended a broad-based tax on goods and services. That seemed a sensible idea to me—efficient, neutral and in concept quite simple. If I had read Asprey more carefully I would have noted his conclusion:

> The introduction of any major new tax such as VAT is a major task for Government, and the Committee is under no illusions that its proposals in this chapter are administratively easy …
>
> Once an official decision has been made, staff has to be recruited and trained and a widespread education program will be necessary to prepare the public and the business community. It is to be hoped that in the preparatory period much ill-informed criticism would be quelled and the ancillary benefits of VAT become increasingly appreciated.

I was to find each of these warnings accurate!

The Fraser Government was elected in 1975. It did not do much to reform the indirect tax base. Labor was elected in 1983. The Treasurer, Paul Keating, developed an option to broaden the indirect tax base with a Treasury proposal known as 'Option C'. It was not a value-added tax or a multi-stage tax; it was a broad-based retail tax. It was put to the National Taxation Summit in 1985. The secretary of the ACTU, Bill Kelty, led the opposition to it and forced Prime Minister Hawke to distance himself from it. It collapsed.

As a barrister in the 1980s I acted in litigation for the Commissioner of Taxation and for taxpayers. I thought Option C was a good idea if the revenue raised could be used to take some of the weight off the income tax system. The narrow and inefficient wholesale tax was riddled with exemptions. My view was, and is, that it is better to have lower income taxes, fewer transaction taxes and a broad-based tax on consumption. Some in the Liberal Party opposed Option C on the grounds that it would raise a lot of revenue that the Government would keep while refusing to lower income tax—the quid pro quo of the whole idea. Some on the right—more libertarian than Liberal—argued that a Government should be kept poor so that it cannot afford to interfere with freedom. Some 'supply-siders' argued that the way to raise more revenue was to cut tax. Tax cuts, they say, will stimulate the economy and pay for themselves. Ronald Reagan took this approach in the early 1980s. George W Bush tried it in the early 2000s. Neither managed to balance the US Budget.

Depressing as it sounds, balancing a Budget means generating revenue and restraining expenditure. Tax is a necessary evil. If taxing is to be done, it should be done effectively. As the seventeenth-century French finance Minister Jean-Baptiste Colbert put it: 'The art of taxation is to pluck the goose with a minimum of fuss.'

A goods and services tax (GST), or value added tax (VAT), is different from a straight retail tax, which applies at the end point of sale to a consumer. A VAT or GST involves a tax at each stage of production, distribution, wholesaling and retail. A business is liable to remit tax on a sale but gets a credit for the tax it has paid on a purchase. This system of input credits means that the net tax applies only to the overall value-added component. Applying the tax at every stage makes it harder to avoid. The input credit system prevents the tax cascading. The full liability applies only at the final consumption.

Australia's wholesale sales tax (WST) was introduced in 1930. At that time economic output was weighted much more towards goods than towards services. Since then, as in most modern economies, in Australia the production of services has grown much faster than the production of goods. There were various rates of WST: 10 per cent, 20 per cent and 30 per cent. Because the base of the tax was shrinking in proportion to the economy, the revenue this tax raised was also shrinking in proportion to the economy.

In 1993 the Coalition went to the federal election under John Hewson with a policy of sweeping away the WST and replacing it with a 15 per cent GST. Labor campaigned against the GST and won the election. No sooner had it won than it increased all the rates of wholesale sales tax—to 12 per cent, 22 per cent and 32 per cent—in an effort to maintain the revenue from this base. In its last Budget, in 1995, Labor was still trying to extend the wholesale sales tax to hardware and building materials.

Hewson's GST was a 15 per cent tax on all goods and just about all services except education and health (the normal exceptions).

Other indirect taxes were to be abolished, including WST, payroll tax, petrol excise and tariffs. When the Coalition got into political trouble, Hewson launched Fightback II (in December 1992), which narrowed the GST base by excluding food. That was politically popular, but it dramatically increased the complexity of the tax, as was made clear in a notorious *A Current Affair* interview with Michael Willesee:

WILLESEE: If I buy a birthday cake from a cake shop and GST is in place do I pay more or less for that birthday cake?

HEWSON: Well, it will depend whether cakes today in that shop are subject to sales tax or they're not, firstly. And they may have a sales tax on them. Let's assume that they don't have a sales tax on them, then that birthday cake is going to be sales tax free. And of course it would be exempt; there would be no GST on it under our system. One with a sales tax on it today would attract a GST and then the difference would be the difference between the two taxes whatever the sales tax rate is on birthday cakes, how it's decorated, because there will be sales tax perhaps on some of the decorations as well, and of course the price will reflect that accordingly. But the key point is that the average Australian will have more money in their pocket.

WILLESEE: Just on the birthday cake—because I'm trying to pick up a simple example—you tell us in what you've published that the cost of cake goes down, the cost of confectionery goes up, there's icing and maybe ice cream, and then there is candles on top.

HEWSON: That's right, now that's the difficulty, that's what I'm addressing in the question. To give you an accurate answer I need to know exactly what type of cake to give a detailed answer. I mean, if it's just a cake from the cake shop that is not presently subject to sales tax, it will not attract a GST. If it is from a shop that falls under sales tax and it's decorated with candles as you say, that attracts sales tax. Then of course we scrap the sales tax.

WILLESEE: If the answer to a birthday cake is so complex—
you do have an overall problem with GST, don't you?

Hewson proposed to exempt food from GST. Food was defined as
'food purchased for home consumption but excluding foods currently
subject to wholesale sales tax'. In other words, if it attracted wholesale
sales tax, it would also have the GST. Plainly Hewson did not know
whether a birthday cake was subject to wholesale sales tax. The WST
was complicated and riddled with exemptions; that is why we wanted
to sweep it away. But Hewson ended up making it the base for the
GST on food. To know GST you still had to know the WST base. The
Government was incorporating the complexity of the old system into
the new and all in the cause of simplifying the tax system!

I learned a big lesson from this campaign. Keeping the base
broad meant keeping the tax simple. Keeping the design simple meant
keeping the answers to questions simple. Mastering the answers was
critical to explaining the policy. Hewson's failure to master the detail
killed him in the last days of the 1993 campaign. It made me paranoid
about getting on top of the detail of GST when we revisited the issue
in 1997.

Shortly after my appointment as Treasurer, in 1996, the Treasury
asked me to set aside several hours for a full briefing, with slide show,
on the tax system. When I arrived at the Treasury building, nearly
thirty people had assembled, many more than I expected. Ken Henry,
then the head of Tax Policy Division, led the briefing. He had become
a career Treasury officer after completing a PhD in New Zealand. A
stint in the office of Paul Keating as a liaison officer had exposed him
to the political process and he understood it well. One of his private
interests was rescuing injured wildlife—a softer side in a Treasury
number-cruncher. He was one of the coming men in the Treasury
Department.

After a few minutes it became obvious that the focus was on the
indirect tax base and WST. Henry had numerous tables and charts
designed to show that this base was shrinking, that the revenue from
it was shrinking, and that the system was not sustainable. The longer
he went on explaining this point, the more frustrated I became.

After the best part of an hour I interrupted. 'You are telling me that the wholesale sales tax system is broken,' I said. 'You do not need to persuade me about this. I spent the whole of the 1993 election campaign telling anyone who would listen that the WST system was broken and needed to be replaced with a GST. We lost. As I recall you were doing your best to help the then Government shoot down the GST. The fact that we still have the wholesale sales tax system is testament to your success.'

This was something of a showstopper. I was telling the Treasury that I knew the economic case. I knew it inside out. I knew it a lot better than those in the room—I had actually lost some skin on it. They might have intellectually supported a GST. I had done so in the court of public opinion. And lost, to our cost.

It taught me a lesson about the way the Treasury Department operated: it had its own view. In the Treasury, it had long been an article of faith, probably since the days of the Asprey Committee, that Australia should have a GST. But when the time came to serve the Government of the day in opposing the GST, Treasury did so. A good public servant will work for the Government of the day. Henry had been in favour of a broad-based consumption tax under Keating, but he worked against the GST when the Coalition put it forward. Public servants will work for good policy or bad policy; that is their obligation. It is up to the Government to set the policy and it is up to the Government to get it right.

The GST had been central to our defeat in the 'unlosable' election of 1993. Members lost their seats and many suffered big setbacks in their careers. No one in the Treasury suffered a setback over GST. They could be for it or against it and still get promoted, and in most cases they had done both. MPs account to the electorate. They are responsible for policy. They cannot hand this over to the public service. Nor should they.

The ferocious onslaught against GST in 1993 had made it an ogre, a pariah, a no-go issue after the 1993 election. When John Howard became Liberal Leader in May 1995, a journalist asked him about the GST. He replied: 'No, there's no way that a GST will ever be part of our policy.'

'Never ever?'

'Never ever. It's dead. It was killed by the voters at the last election.'

Our first Budget came down in August 1996. We then reverted to the practice, begun under the previous Government, of bringing down the Budget in May. The 1996 Budget presented a two-year program to tighten fiscal policy by 1.5 per cent of GDP and to balance the Budget. This meant the May 1997 Budget had very few new measures and, compared with the huge dimensions of our first Budget in 1996, very little excitement. The centrepiece of the 1997 Budget was a 15 per cent rebate against $3000 of tax on savings. The idea was to encourage saving.

The rebate was not means-tested. It was capped, but it was available to everyone. In fact, we had carefully discussed whether it should be means-tested. I had been against it. If the object was to boost savings, there was no point in means-testing out the people who were likely to increase their savings. Problems of administration would also make a means test complicated and expensive. Howard agreed with that decision. We asked Grahame Morris, Howard's political adviser, for his view. He agreed: no means test.

The day after the Budget, Labor Party frontbencher Michael Lee asked Howard in Question Time how he could pocket a tax rebate of up to $450 (15 per cent of $3000) on his savings when a person with smaller savings would get a far smaller rebate. This is an inescapable feature of cutting tax: people who pay more tax get more of that tax cut, at least in dollar terms. Howard answered: 'The savings rebate in the interests of simplicity has been made non-means-tested. I ought to tell the honourable gentlemen that I will not be claiming it—and it is up to you not to claim it. Are you going to make an equivalent promise?'

That killed the savings rebate. Howard was saying he would not claim it and was challenging others to do the same. How can you introduce a tax cut and challenge people not to take it up? We had deliberately introduced the rebate without a means test. If Howard thought it was wrong to claim it, why should others be allowed to do so? The next day the *Sydney Morning Herald* splashed the headline 'PM

Trips Up on Cashback Offer'. Its story read: 'The federal Government has marred the first day of its Budget sales pitch with the Prime Minister revealing he will not apply for the universal savings rebate which forms its centrepiece.'

After the Budget week I made it a practice to do a national tour to explain the Budget at public meetings and in the media. The Budget was on track to balance. Interest rates were falling. But at the end of the Budget week, it was clear we had not done well. Howard's faux pas was going to make it a hard sell. The net approval rate for my first Budget was 37 per cent. For the second it was 3 per cent.

That Thursday, at the end of the Budget week, Howard and I met to review the political situation. He was going to the bush to deal with native title problems. I was about to start my national tour. We were disappointed by the Budget's reception. We both knew that while we had fixed the outlays side of the Budget, the tax side was in dire need of reform. We had promised not to introduce a GST. Howard had gone so far as to say 'never ever'. We couldn't do anything about tax reform that term. But if we repeated the pledge not to introduce the GST, we would close off any hope for tax reform in the next term as well. Both of us knew something would have to be done sooner rather than later. We made a pact. Neither of us would rule out a GST again. I said: 'We should keep our options open. What is the point of getting into power if we're not going to do something?'

I flew down to Melbourne to do a post-Budget breakfast, and a post-Budget lunch with the Essendon Football Club. At the lunch I was asked about tax reform and GST. I kept the option open. I said: 'If we decide to do it in a future Parliament, I think the fair thing would be to tell people and seek votes accordingly.' I did not rule out a GST. My answer was miles away from 'never ever'. The next day the *Sydney Morning Herald* splashed the headline 'Costello's New Push for GST'. The door had been opened.

That day Howard was at Longreach in Queensland with Tim Fischer. Tim was stunned by the newspaper report and raised it with Howard. He thought I had gone off on a frolic of my own. But Howard could not complain. It was precisely the course we had agreed upon two days earlier. The next day Howard was interviewed on Channel 7's *Face to Face* program. When asked about GST he said: 'We made a commitment about this term of Government, quite a precise commitment, and I intend to honour that commitment, but if you're saying to me do I envisage the Australian taxation system remaining as it is for the next five or ten years, I'd have to say no.' He kept the door open.

A week later at a lunch in Brendan Nelson's electorate, Howard laid down three tests that any tax reform proposal would have to meet. It would have to generate more jobs, generate more exports and improve the living standards of the Australian people. Since we had argued in the 1993 campaign that the GST would do all of these things, it was pretty clear where this was going. On 16 June we had a meeting of the parliamentary party during a sitting in Canberra to discuss the issue. There was overwhelming support for tax reform but a range of views on how it should be progressed. It was nonsense to talk about tax reform without a GST. There remained considerable nervousness about the issue, but there was no turning back.

In August the High Court intervened. It decided that a number of the state indirect taxes were unconstitutional. This meant not only that the states could not collect them in the future but that collecting them in the past had been unlawful. The taxpayers were entitled to refunds. The states turned to the Commonwealth. We had anticipated the decision and had a plan to deal with it. The Commonwealth would enact laws to impose the taxes that the states had previously operated and hand the revenue over to them. Then we would put a 100 per cent tax on any reimbursement of previously paid state tax. If a person claimed back their state tax, the Commonwealth would tax it 100 per cent, recover it, and hand it right back to the states. It was cumbersome but effective.

This got the Commonwealth into the role of collecting state taxes, including petrol excise, as an agent for the states. The system could not be sustained on a long-term basis. The states' system of indirect tax had fallen apart and the Commonwealth's indirect tax system was not that far behind. What we needed now was a way to progress to a conclusion of the issue that dared not speak its name— tax reform.

The High Court decision became the trigger to announce that a taxation task force would accelerate the tax reform process. The task force comprised Treasury (Ken Henry), the Treasurer's Office (Nigel Bailey, my senior tax adviser), the Cabinet Policy Unit (David Stevens), the Department of Prime Minister and Cabinet (Dr Ian Watt, deputy secretary) and the Australian Taxation Office (Peter Simpson, second commissioner).

I chose Ken Henry to chair the task force; this would give him the chance to make up for the 1993 campaign against GST. The task force was moved out of the Treasury building and housed in another building in a safe room. Its members were given separate security passes. Only authorised people could access the room. They were not to talk to anybody outside their group. The contact for direction and report-back was directly between Henry and me: it was not to go through normal Treasury channels.

At the outset I decided that the rate for the GST should be 10 per cent. This was lower than the rate we had proposed in 1993 and would make the new tax easier to sell. Any rate lower than 10 per cent would not provide sufficient revenue to abolish other indirect taxes and cut income taxes. The abolition of other taxes was important if we were to achieve the economic benefits—less complexity and lower transaction costs. The reduction of income taxes was important because it took the weight off earnings and incentive.

The crucial thing was to keep the base as broad as possible. The broader the base, the greater the amount of revenue it would raise and the simpler it would be. The complexity in indirect tax comes from exemptions—from sorting out which sales are subject to tax and which are not.

Henry and his team constructed a model to assess the broader economic effect of the GST, particularly on inflation. This was absolutely critical. The GST would lead to a one-off increase in prices through the economy; we had to stop second-round effects on inflation. To protect pensioners and others on fixed income, it would be necessary to pay compensation to maintain their purchasing power. The higher the price effect, the higher the compensation and the lower the revenue available to abolish other indirect taxes and reduce income taxes. Henry and his team went over and over their model looking for behavioural effects and consequential factors that would affect the Consumer Price Index (CPI). The lower they made that, the more exciting the rest of the package became.

The GST would obviously fund the abolition of the Commonwealth WST. But the idea was not just to replace one tax with another; it was to introduce one broad tax that would replace a host of inefficient and narrow ones—transaction taxes like bank account debit tax and stamp duties on shares, which were inefficient and impeded rational allocation of resources. Since these were state taxes, part of the GST would have to be given to the states to reimburse them for their abolition.

A special premiers' conference was arranged for November 1997 to discuss the issue. I briefed it on the likely revenue that a GST would raise and the kinds of taxes that could be abolished. None of the state premiers wanted to go out on a limb and campaign for a GST. They were more interested in how revenue was going to be shared than how it was going to be raised. They were adamant that they should be given either a share of any revenue the GST raised or a share of Commonwealth taxes generally.

One of the difficulties we had had in our 1993 campaign was the argument that every country that had introduced a GST had subsequently increased it. Our opponents argued that introducing the GST was the thin end of the wedge. I searched for a mechanism that people could trust to stop any subsequent increase in the rate. We were trying to get the states to abolish many of their indirect taxes. This led me to the idea that we should give the states all of the GST revenue in return for the abolition of specified indirect taxes. Since it was their revenue, the rate of GST could be increased only with their unanimous consent and with the agreement of the Commonwealth, which would need to legislate it. There was a very low chance that you could ever get nine governments to agree unanimously on changes to the GST rate, especially as, at that time, Australia had never had just one political party in office at all levels of Government. I was convinced the public would see this as a strong mechanism against any increase in the rate, a mechanism to be policed by governments against each other. At the same time, giving all of the GST revenue to the states would give them a tax base that would grow with the economy. In the early years we would have to compensate them before the GST reached maturity, but after the first couple of years it would grow so strongly that they would have a windfall. The GST would grow more strongly than the inefficient and narrow taxes the states were abolishing. Every state would be better off with a revenue stream guaranteed to grow rather than continuing to rely on Commonwealth grants.

The next stage was to construct a model of the income tax system and of family benefits. The Tax Task Force built a model that could be carried in a laptop computer and displayed on a screen using the then new PowerPoint software. The model would allow the user to change income tax thresholds and rates and cost the different packages. The results could be projected on a screen with distributional tables showing who gained and who lost.

This was the first time I had ever used PowerPoint. It had never been used in the Cabinet room before. I used it to brief the Prime Minister and his office and then the entire Cabinet. Prior to that it would have been necessary to print various options, photocopy them and distribute them to all of the members of the Cabinet. If they asked for a different option, the process would have to be repeated. Now we could do it instantaneously on a screen in front of them. We had unlimited options, which could be produced immediately.

The final briefing of the Cabinet on the tax package took seven hours. For seven hours members peppered me with questions and asked for explanations. Using PowerPoint I was able to show them diagrams that illustrated how the GST worked. The diagrams showed costings and they illustrated our income tax thresholds and compared them with existing ones. As I walked out I asked one of my colleagues what he thought of the presentation. He told me: 'I didn't understand much of it. But I thought the coloured diagrams looked great!'

While I was buried in the modelling that was coming up from Ken Henry and his team, my office began preparing the public for the reform agenda. I wrote a document called 'In Need of Reform', which was distributed to households throughout Australia. We encouraged third-party advocacy groups to begin television advertising on the need for reform. The Business Council in particular was very helpful. I had no misapprehension about the political danger of GST: I had seen it defeat Keating in 1985 and the Coalition in 1993. Todd Davidson drew a cartoon of the decision to go with a GST before the 1998 election. It showed me dancing with a ghost disinterred from a grave. I looked as I felt: highly apprehensive.

There were points at which I felt things were touch and go. One day I was briefing Howard and his office. Everybody understood that the GST would apply to a set of golf clubs and everybody understood it would apply to the 'green fees' to play a round of golf. I remember trying to explain to our working group that it would also have to apply to a golf club membership fee. Otherwise, by becoming a member, golfers could avoid GST on their game which casuals would have to pay if they took a 'walk-up booking'. The prospect that GST could apply to golf club memberships certainly came as a surprise to the colleagues. Howard was a member of a golf club. His department head, Max Moore-Wilton, was incredulous: 'You mean you pay to join the club and you get taxed for the privilege?' Yes, I explained, this was precisely what I meant. He looked very queasy and began shaking his head.

Nigel Bailey was the point man for my office on the task force. He did an outstanding job. As we left the Cabinet room after this briefing he turned to me and said: 'Toothpaste, toothbrush, golf membership. You can see why Keating claimed it was a life-changing tax.'

Putting a GST on alcoholic products meant we had to change all the alcohol excise rates. This led into the complex minefield of alcohol taxation and unleashed huge arguments between South Australian winegrowers and winegrowers in other states about whether wine tax should be based on volume or value. We agonised about this as much as about any other issue. Volumetric tax favours premium wine. Ad valorem tax favours low-value wine. But it was not just wine that was affected. Spirits, beer, low-alcohol beer—all had to be adjusted.

Imposing a GST also necessitated changes to tobacco excise. I was not a smoker and not familiar with the prices that applied to different products. John Fahey, the Minister for Finance, was a lifetime smoker who later kicked the habit after a serious illness. I told our senior Ministers in a briefing that tax changes would lift the price of a packet of cigarettes to above $10. Howard exclaimed: 'Gee, when I gave up, they were $3 a packet.' John Fahey chimed in: 'When I started they cost one and sixpence!'

We were also dramatically changing and simplifying family benefits. Twelve family benefits were simplified into three. We increased rates, changed income tests and improved tapers. Improving tapers means that money is deducted from a benefit at a lower rate, as income rises, rather than a higher one. It lowers the effective marginal tax rate.

The process went extremely well. At the very end, just as we were preparing to go to the printers, Howard raised the idea of reducing the GST to 8 per cent. By doing so there would be no switch from direct to indirect taxation. He felt this would make it easier to sell our proposals to the welfare lobby. It would have. But it also would have meant no income tax cuts. This was the whole object of the tax reform: to lessen the burden on income taxes by broadening the indirect tax base.

When he raised it with me I almost had a seizure. We had been working on this program day and night for twelve months. We had carefully briefed the Prime Minister all the way through. We had done every sum on the basis of a 10 per cent GST. Now, within sight of the launch, he wanted to look at altering a fundamental component, which would require the adjustment of everything else—income taxes, family allowances, excises, state taxes that were to be abolished. I nearly lost it. I started telling him all the reasons why it could not be done. I started talking faster and faster. I could hear my voice rising. I could feel my face starting to flush. I was battling to control my temper. I would not agree. He asked me to go away and look at it. I went back to my office. I told my chief of staff, Phil Gaetjens, what had happened. He gave me some breathing exercises to try calm me down. Then he started ranting and raving. His voice began rising as he walked around the office shouting and cursing.

I had no intention of redoing the proposal. The launch date was set. Without Treasury's assistance there was no prospect of developing any alternative proposal. My staff and I decided to wait and keep our cool. We waited. When no alternative proposal was developed, the Prime Minister's office dropped the 8 per cent idea. Finally we had a policy.

I had set the launch date for 13 August 1998. My birthday was the next day. I had not had many nights off over the past year and I intended to have a night off for my birthday. The final policy was called 'Tax Reform: Not a New Tax, A New Tax System'. A 200-page document, it was packaged as 'ANTS'. It changed income tax, family payments, health insurance, pensions, Commonwealth–state financial relations, indirect taxes, state indirect taxes, business registration and withholding taxes. It had distributional tables and price effects across the whole economy. It was simply the largest tax reform in Australian history.

I decided we should conduct the launch like a Budget lockup. Journalists would be given the package to study, and then, inside the lockup, I would do a press conference to explain it. Howard also wanted to address the press conference. That was fair enough—he was the Prime Minister. It was agreed he would do an introduction before I unleashed my PowerPoint presentation on the assembled media.

As it turned out his brief introduction went for the best part of an hour. When he finished he left the room. I then opened my computer presentation and went through a detailed explanation. I had no doubt that this would be a hard sell. But the policy was out there.

We went into a media blitz. We had no time to waste. It was time to get on with the 1998 election. This was the chance to succeed where other Treasurers had failed. This was the chance to right the wrong of the 1993 election. This was a reform that would last for generations.

We lost a lot of skin in the election of October 1998 but we scraped home. It was the only time until then (and possibly since) that a party in the Western democratic world had won an election proposing to introduce a new tax. Our win rewrote the rule book. The fact that the reform was so broad and the Opposition so vehement meant that it dominated the election. There is no doubt that people were voting on this as a central issue. As a result, our victory gave us a mandate. I was keen to implement it as soon as we were returned after the election.

Our plan was to legislate the program by mid-1999. This would allow a year for business to get ready before the GST took effect on 1 July 2000. The Sydney Olympics were also to be held later that year. We wanted foreign tourists to pay the GST, just as Australians paid the European VAT. We also wanted the system properly bedded down before the next election, due in 2001.

The first part of the legislative package—A New Tax System (Goods and Services Tax) Bill 1998 and fourteen related bills—was introduced into the House of Representatives on 2 December 1998 and passed on 10 December 1998. The bills were introduced into the Senate on the same day as their passage through the House. The second package—A New Tax System (Commonwealth–state Financial Arrangements) Bill 1999 and eleven related bills—was introduced into the House of Representatives on 24 March 1999 and passed on 31 March 1999. These bills were also introduced to the Senate on the same day as their passage through the House. The total package comprised twenty-seven bills.

The bills forming the New Tax System hold the distinction of having received the most scrutiny of any legislation in the history of the Senate in this country. A record of four separate Senate committees undertook inquiries into the bills, investigating their effect on issues such as education, the environment and the arts. A select committee was set up to examine the economic effects. Labor went all out to defeat the tax reform. The Government did not have the chair on any of these committees, which all recommended that the package be defeated. The idea of the committees was to find every aggrieved lobby group and air every grievance in an attempt to create public opposition to the tax reform.

I established a war room in Parliament House and a 'Tax Unit'— comprising Phil Gaetjens (chairman), Dave Alexander, Richard King and Rob Jeremenko—whose job was to monitor every claim about the GST and reply to every falsehood. They had corridors of press clippings, economic analysis and industry submissions. They filed issues under various headings: 'Weird and wacky claims', 'Lies' and

'Outright lies'. They had continuous electronic media monitoring and reported to me all the lines that had to be replied to, corrected or repudiated.

Horror stories of businesses that had decided to close rather than make the effort to implement the GST were everywhere. The National Tax and Accountants Association president claimed the GST would cost jobs: 'Not less than 200000 employees will be lost in the first year'. 'Truck drivers could die from unwarranted pressure to cut costs on the back of the GST,' said the Australian Trucking Association. The left-wing Australia Institute issued a press release: 'At least sixty-five more people will die each year due to increased air pollution and traffic accidents if the Government's proposed changes to fuel prices in the GST package go ahead.' The Queensland Minister for Energy claimed that increases in electricity bills from GST 'will lead to cold showers and cold meals'. Reported seriously on radio, he said: 'Cold baked beans for lunch, cold fish and chips for dinner could become part of the Australian staple diet.'

The Government did not have a majority in the Senate. To secure passage of the legislation it would be necessary to get two extra votes. The former Labor senator Mal Colston had declared himself independent. He might vote for the legislation or at least abstain. We would then need to win the vote of at least one other (non-Government) senator. I began to focus on Senator Brian Harradine of Tasmania.

In the early part of 1999 I held meetings with Harradine, who had a list of policies he wanted included in the May Budget. Elected in 1975, he was a veteran of the Senate. He had begun his political career in the Australian Labor Party in Tasmania, where he had been secretary of the Trades and Labor Council. He was close to the anti-communist Democratic Labor Party, which had broken away from the ALP in the mid-1950s and become its bitter opponent. The federal executive of the ALP expelled him in 1968. He ran as an Independent for the Senate on a platform of conservative family issues and opposition to abortion. On most industrial relations issues he was still a Labor man. On economic issues he opposed Liberal market-oriented policies. Thanks to his decisive vote in the Senate, he had managed to extract enormous and disproportionate Commonwealth spending in the small state of Tasmania.

Although I did not agree with Harradine's economic ideas I had enormous respect for the man. I always found him pleasant to deal with. But he had a capacity to talk in an elliptical way. He would never name his precise demands when he was negotiating. Maybe he thought this was too grubby. He would talk of his general concerns, with the object of getting you to volunteer concessions that you thought he wanted. For example, he would talk about the need to help families more—in particular, large families. He would talk of the benefits then applying and agree that these were very good, as far as they went. If you asked him the direct question, 'Do you want them to go further?', he would never precisely answer or deign to specify the amount by which they should be increased. You were left with the impression that something should be done, but it was impossible to pin Harradine down on what or by how much.

In March 1999 Harradine raised with me his concern about a number of publications that received Commonwealth Government funding. One was a leaflet on homosexuality called 'Out There'. Another was a sex education booklet that described some sexual behaviour that he found offensive. As Treasurer I took little interest in publications from the Family and Community Services Department but I was definitely going to take a strong line against them if they offended Harradine. Our tax reform was essential for the future of the country. I was not going to let that go down for the sake of some departmental sex education.

I spoke to the Minister concerned, Michael Wooldridge, and asked him to do something. He told me that, although he personally had no objection to the material, he would help. I gave these assurances to Senator Harradine. He was happy. He then raised with me the question of additional funding for marriage and relationship education. I announced that in the Budget.

Our GST package included a major reform of family assistance by rationalising and improving payments. Senator Harradine was concerned about the eligibility of older but still dependent children to receive benefits. So in the Budget we announced that we would extend eligibility for family tax benefits to young people up to the age of twenty-one and, if they were receiving a youth allowance, top that up to the level of the family tax benefit. All the issues that Harradine had brought to my attention were covered off by the time of the Budget.

When I spoke to Senator Harradine on Budget night he seemed very satisfied. He acknowledged the work I had done and thanked me. 'There are no items I have overlooked?' I asked. He assured me I had covered all the items he was worried about. I did not ask him how he would vote on the tax package—nor would he have told me. This was his usual practice. It was partly strategic: by concealing his intentions until the last moment, he was always able to come back and extract a little extra.

The bills for the new tax system were still before the Senate when I left Australia at 9 a.m. on Friday 14 May 1999 to go to the APEC Finance Ministers' meeting in Langkawi, Malaysia. When the plane stopped in Singapore, the Australian High Commissioner informed me that Harradine had told the Senate that afternoon that he would vote against the GST! In a 20-minute speech on amendments to the excise rates Harradine announced his position on the whole New Tax System: 'The question that I have to ask myself is whether I am going to be a party to imposing an impersonal, indiscriminate tax on my children, my grandchildren and their children for generations to come. I cannot.' He went on: 'I apologise. I know my name will be mud but it has been mud before today, and it will be mud again later on.'

I had been busy attending to his demands on all sorts of other things but it made no difference. It was the principle of the thing he objected to! We were now faced with the complete defeat of the package. The composition of the Senate would change on 1 July. After that there was no chance of getting it through with the votes of Independents. Having laboured so long and so hard on the GST, I did not want to see all of that work and effort wasted. If we walked away from the package, it would not be the end of it. It would be an issue again at the next election. That would mean a third GST election. The GST had been on and off for twenty years. It was right and necessary. It would never go away unless we dealt with it once and for all. The only way to do that was to introduce it.

I had speaking engagements in Hong Kong after the Langkawi conference and did not get back to Australia until five days later. But I was in daily contact with Howard, with the Treasury and with my office to see what we could do, whom we could deal with and what compromises would be required. The Cabinet met in Longreach while I was still overseas. It had no stomach for a double dissolution on GST. With the Coalition having lost the 1993 election and nearly lost the 1998 election on the GST, the prospect of another election on GST had no appeal to me. It might even deliver the same result—a Coalition Government in the House of Representatives with a hostile Senate. I felt gutted. From mid-1997 I had hardly done anything other than work on this. We had been honest and up front about our policy. We had won an election on it. We had legislated the program through the House—and lost it by a vote in the Senate.

The day after I returned to Australia, Howard and I began negotiations in the Cabinet room in Melbourne with Senator Meg Lees, the Leader of the Australian Democrats, and Senator Andrew Murray, the Democrats' spokesman on economic matters. I had held talks with them back in March, when they had given me a list of their demands. It involved narrowing the base of the GST, reducing the income tax cuts, changing the compensation package, increasing fuel excises and renegotiating the agreement with the states. The list was so extensive that I had focussed on Harradine, but I never closed off the discussions with the Australian Democrats.

I was acutely aware that the greater the number of exemptions from the GST, the more complicated it would become. Exemptions might make it easier to pass the legislation but they would make it harder to implement. If the exemptions became too extensive there would be a point at which they would outweigh the usefulness of the GST. The whole appeal of GST was as a broad-based tax. If it became riddled with exemptions, it would be no better than the wholesale sales tax it was replacing. I was determined to fight for as few exemptions as possible.

In our negotiation with the Democrats I played bad cop while Howard played good cop. I argued strenuously against any exemptions and Howard was conciliatory. We negotiated for seven days. The deal we hammered out was eventually set down in a lengthy exchange of letters and summed up in the Prime Minister's press statement of 28 May 1999:

> All major elements of the original plan have been kept. The principal changes are the exclusion of basic food from the GST and restructuring of proposals concerning diesel fuel in response to the strongly put views of the Australian Democrats on environmental issues. The full measure of the income tax cuts for middle Australia has been preserved. The family benefits have been maintained in full. The special savings bonus for self-funded retirees will now be available from age fifty-five. Compensation arrangements have been strengthened. Generational reform of Commonwealth–state financial relations remains. The states will, as promised, receive the full proceeds of the GST. Benefits for rural and regional Australia have been preserved.

Howard recorded his appreciation of my work: 'At all stages during the reform process he has displayed a skilled and comprehensive understanding of the many complex issues in what has been described as by far the most detailed and extensive economic reform embraced in Australia for many decades.'

Lees stuck to the deal and voted for the reform in the Senate, even though she was under pressure from her party not to agree at all. Opposition inside the Democrats was led by Senator Natasha Stott-Despoja, who voted against it and used the issue to advance her own claims to leadership. She replaced Lees as Leader in April 2001. She herself stood down from the leadership in 2002. Her successor, Senator Andrew Bartlett, fell on bad times. By 2008 the Democrats had lost all of their Senate seats.

While the GST deal may have contributed to the Democrats decline, it was not the principal cause. They would have folded in any event. The party was a function of a particular and peculiar set of circumstances. Don Chipp, a former Liberal, had created it after Malcolm Fraser had dropped him from his ministry. Chipp represented a more moderate or small-'l' liberalism than Fraser at the time. His early Democrats were mostly genteel, progressive Liberals. As time went by, the membership was increasingly left-wing, focussing on environmental issues. The rise of the Greens, with a more hard-edged, leftist line on the environment, economic policy and foreign affairs, leached support away from the Democrats.

I pay respect to Lees for negotiating over the GST package. She was able to achieve many of her party's objectives, such as a higher tax on diesel transport; subsidies for alternative fuels and funding for the Australian Greenhouse office. But many in her party were more interested in symbolic politics than practical outcomes. The GST was a symbolic 'no-go' for the left. They said they were against it because it was regressive, applying equally to everyone regardless of income. So too is petrol excise or carbon tax, which they do not seem to mind. If you are concerned about the distributional impact of a broad-based consumption tax, the way to handle it is to compensate lower income earners with income support. This was a major part of our package. We could have negotiated over additional compensation.

The Greens had no interest whatsoever in negotiating over the GST. I asked their Leader, Senator Bob Brown: 'What about negotiating a few environmental wins?' He refused on principle. He had a hard-line economic policy on which he would not compromise, even for environmental objectives. His opposition was total and inflexible. The name of the Greens Party leads people to think that it is principally an environmental party. In fact, it has economic, tax and international relations policies on the far left of politics that it holds just as dear. It used the GST agreement to attack the Democrats and undermine them from the left. Eventually the Greens became the third party in the Senate.

The amendments to the GST required renegotiations with the states. Since food was now excluded from the GST, there would be less revenue for the states (which were to receive all the GST revenue in return for abolishing many of their taxes). The agreement was amended to alter and delay the states' timetable for abolishing their taxes in return for GST. Some had to go immediately, some later, and some on a date to be agreed. Later, when the GST revenues rose to more than was necessary to compensate the states for abolishing their taxes, they dragged their feet, wanting all the GST while delaying the abolition of their state taxes. Cooperation was not made easier by the fact that, when the GST agreement was first negotiated, the Coalition held Government in three states and two territories, but by the time it was implemented, the Coalition had lost office in Victoria, Western Australia, South Australia and the ACT.

As it turned out, the GST provided a very strong and growing source of revenue to Labor governments, which had opposed its introduction. It helped their re-election. It freed them from reliance on the annual Financial Assistance Grants which were always subject to the vagaries of the federal Budget. It gave them certainty. It should have breathed new life into federalism. The states had long made the complaint that they did not have a revenue base sufficient to manage their responsibilities. I had hoped that, by giving them one, they would take more ownership of the delivery of state services instead of always claiming that their problems were caused by a lack of funds from Canberra. This has not happened. The revamping of federal–state financial relations is the one area of the reform that turned out well below my expectations.

The bills were debated in the Senate for nearly sixty-nine hours—the third-longest debate in the history of the Senate—fifty-four minutes shorter than the second-longest, the Communist Party Dissolution Bill. They finally passed the Senate with amendments on 28 June and came back to the House for approval. When the legislative changes were back in the House of Representatives on 30 June 1999, a little-known Queensland Opposition backbencher, Kevin Rudd, told the Parliament:

> When the history of this Parliament, this nation and this century is written, 30 June 1999 will be recorded as a day of fundamental injustice—an injustice which is real, an injustice which is not simply conjured up by the fleeting rhetoric of politicians. It will be recorded as the day when the social compact that has governed this nation for the last 100 years was torn up. It will be recorded as the day when the nation's taxation system moved

from progressivity to regressivity. It will be recorded as the day when the Parliament of the country said to the poor of the country that they could all go and take a running jump.

Securing the legislation was just the first stage. Implementing the GST was always going to be much more difficult. It changed the taxation of all goods and services in the Australian economy. The prices of three billion products were to change all at the same time, around midnight on 30 June 2000. There were enormous practical problems. How exactly would the price on the shelves or on the product be changed? How could we stop the hoarding of products where prices would increase? How could we stop a buyers' strike over those items where prices would decrease? How could we stop businesses using the tax changes to increase profit margins? We were changing prices not just for some businesses but for every business and for every consumer in the country.

Before the system could work it was necessary for every business in Australia to register for GST and to obtain a new Australian Business Number (ABN). They would have to quote their ABN to every other business they dealt with so that the system of credits and rebates would work. The volume of these registrations was so great that there were long delays in issuing numbers. More than two million ABNs were issued.

The implementation of the GST also changed the company tax and income tax positions of business. Layered on top of this were changes to all excises, including fuel, wine, beer and tobacco. The system of deducting tax instalments and remitting company and income tax payments was also changed and modernised.

All of this would have been hard enough for businesses that kept good records. But many small businesses did not keep up-to-date records of sales and purchases. Some kept their invoices and receipts in a shoe box and took them to an accountant once a year. Some businesses would have to come into the tax system for the first time. Some small businesses were fearful about dealing with the Tax Office and asking for assistance. It would mean alerting the Tax Office to their existence and the possibility of back taxes. We had to assure them there would be moratoriums for any businesses that came forward during this period.

All the while our political opponents had been doing everything they could to defeat the legislation and to disrupt the implementation. There was no bipartisanship. Kim Beazley, Leader of the Opposition, boasted that Labor would 'surf into office on the back of GST'.

The Shadow Treasurer, Simon Crean, was a strong opponent. He was able to develop a line and relentlessly push it. He would not be diverted from his attack. He once brought a thermometer into Parliament and demanded to know what temperature was required for a chicken to be fresh (and thereby GST free) or cooked (and thereby subject to GST). These complexities arose from the changes forced by the Democrats. I dismissed it, rightly, as a stunt. 'Here is the would be heir to Curtin and Chifley who walks into Parliament brandishing thermometers … the chook that came to the dispatch box.'

Crean was a great negative campaigner but this gave him a poor public image when he became Leader and in the end it led to his demise before he had ever fought an election. He supported Mark Latham as a means of blocking the return of Kim Beazley whom, he felt, had not shown him the loyalty—at least not the kind of loyalty Crean had shown Beazley when he was Leader.

We needed an information campaign to assist the implementation. My staff, led by Tony Smith, auditioned advertising concepts. They arranged one day for Scott Whybin of Whybin TBWA Advertising to come to my office. Like most advertising executives he dressed in a style quite removed from the dark suits favoured by politicians. He did not say anything. He just put a set of earphones on my head and turned on a CD player. It played one of my favourite songs—'Unchain My Heart' by Joe Cocker. When the song finished, Scott took off the earphones and he said: 'That is your tax reform campaign.' I told him that I was not sure about the campaign but I sure liked the song. Scott took out some story boards that showed small businesses, buses, trucks, even a dog, bound in heavy metal chains, weighed down and then liberated by a new tax system. All the while Joe Cocker was singing in the background. It was a brilliant campaign. Kim Beazley's chief of staff was later to describe it as 'superbly effective'. It introduced a new generation to the music of Joe Cocker.

The Australian Tax Office was overwhelmed with demands for indicative rulings. Never having administered a GST before, it had no precedents to guide it. It had no staff with experience of GST. There was an enormous logjam as it tried to train staff. At one point the Commissioner of Taxation and I identified so many logjams in rulings over strata titles, hotels and rental units that, to break them up, I got him to come up to my office and I began to give indicative rulings myself. I was entitled to do this. I had decided the policy and knew how I wanted it to work. I was more qualified than anyone else to say how we intended it to affect particular transactions. Phil Lindsay, a tax specialist who had come into my office from the accounting firm KPMG to assist with implementation matters, was aghast at the thinness of the resources we were using to make these changes. He told me that in the private sector teams of accountants would ponder for months some of the issues that were being decided in my office in minutes.

Explaining and selling the GST around Australia had its problems. In March 2000 I agreed to address a Chamber of Commerce lunch in a place called Chambers Flat about 50 kilometres south of Brisbane. My subject was to be the GST. My driver had no idea how to get to the venue. He got lost and in the end he asked me to navigate. Since I had no idea where Chambers Flat was, I tried to navigate from a map of Brisbane and its surrounds. We were due at noon, which came and went. At 12.15 p.m. we still could not find the town. The organisers had assembled a class of school children to welcome me and to sing the national anthem when I arrived. As they stood in the stifling heat in front of the crowd, one of them fainted. My staff rang in to find out how far away we were. We still could not find the road. They rang back five minutes later to tell me a second child had fainted. By 12.30 p.m. we had still not located the venue. My staff called in again to say one of the kitchen staff had sliced a finger preparing the meal and an ambulance had arrived to take the poor fellow to the nearest hospital. It was after 1 p.m. I told them to start the meal—I would get there as soon as I could and, I hoped, before it finished. By the time we found the venue, the meal had finished, dessert was completed and the guests were drifting off. The poor children were being rehydrated at the back of the hall. I went out and thanked them for their attendance. We could not stay long as our next function was at Boonah. I hoped for better luck there.

Somewhere on the road from Chambers Flat to Boonah we spied a milk bar—isolated and looking a little run down. I asked my driver to stop and I went inside. The milk bar was deserted. A lady rustling around in a flat somewhere down the back came out and asked what I wanted. I ordered a sandwich.

'Will it be with GST or without?'

I was in the middle of nowhere, after a complete debacle at a function I could not find, starving, looking for a snack, and here was another GST joke.

'No GST unless you're registered with an Australian Business Number,' I told her.

'I got them forms out the back but me husband doesn't know how to fill them in.'

'Would you like some help?'

'You see if you can do it.'

She went out the back and returned with some paperwork. While she made a ham sandwich, I started filling in her registration form. When I had done as much as I could, I said: 'Show this to your husband when he gets home. There's only a signature required and then he can file it. I think he'll be quite happy.'

'I think he will be quite surprised,' she said. 'Things are pretty desperate if they've sent you all the way up here from Canberra to fill out them forms.'

The day before the GST took effect I was nervous. I did not know what would happen. Our opponents had predicted dire consequences. The media was at fever pitch. Since the GST would apply to football tickets for the first time, some journalists suggested that the crowds would boo me at the venues. Frenzy was promoting misunderstanding. Some claimed there would be an inflation explosion. Some claimed there would be a recession. The subject of petrol was especially sensitive.

The day that the GST started—1 July 2000—I went down to a deli in my own electorate, cameras in tow, to illustrate how it was business as normal. My deli performed beautifully in front of a wall of television cameras. They said they were totally prepared and there were no problems. When I asked them how they were recording sales and credits, it was clear they had no record-keeping system. There was no way they could produce an accurate Business Activity Statement. But they told the cameras they could. That was enough for me.

That day I had the chairman of the Australian Competition and Consumer Commission, Allan Fels, doing surveillance on prices and reporting any profit-taking. He was doing live broadcasts on the situation at petrol bowsers, like a war correspondent giving situation reports. He performed his media commitments superbly.

After the frenzy and the hype, it was a relief that the sun rose on a normal day. One of the cartoonists showed the sun coming up with 10 per cent taken out. One drew me as the cat that had taken the cream.

For years I had taken GST jokes on the chin. I could hardly move without someone making a reference to it somewhere, sometime. At the opening of a synagogue in my electorate where I was the guest of honour, the orthodox Rabbi Yrkowicz welcomed me and then turned to the congregation: 'GST must be in your hearts and in your heads. GST must guide your thoughts and your actions. GST must be part of this congregation.' Right on, I thought to myself. This was better than any sermon I had heard on the subject in a church. He then looked at the congregation: 'GST means Go Study Torah.'

People remember the scars of political life. For me the GST was one of the biggest. But I bear the legacy quite literally. I was having dental work done during the height of the GST debate. My dentist ordered a technician to make a gold crown. When the time came to fit it, the dentist polished it a bit and had a look inside. He let out a long laugh, then turned to me and said: 'If I ever have to identify you from dental records this should prove helpful.' He showed me the crown. The technician had carved the letters 'GST' inside.

8

SECOND TERM BLUES: 1998–2001

The Liberal Party's campaign director, Lynton Crosby, was pale and perspiring when I met him in the National Tally Room in Exhibition Park, Canberra, on the night of the 1998 election. I was due to go on television to discuss the results. I asked him how he thought we would go. He said the exit polls showed the Government would be defeated. 'Have you told Howard?' I asked. Lynton said Howard had assembled his family at Kirribilli House to give them the chilling news.

The first results from Tasmania showed that Warwick Smith, the Member for Bass, who had been defeated in the GST election of 1993 and re-elected in 1996, was in trouble. Smith was intelligent, affable and able. This would be the end of his parliamentary career. He had responsibility for aged care. In the 1996 Budget we had announced a system that allowed nursing homes to charge bonds to provide a source of capital to upgrade facilities and fund new places. The industry knew this was the best way to go. But the attack from Labor and some lobbyists had been ferocious. The Government had been forced to reverse the decision at that time. In a reshuffle, Warwick replaced Judi Moylan as Minister for Family Services. It did not help him in Bass in 1998.

As the results started coming in from the mainland states, we were losing seats all over. Russell Broadbent, who had lost Corinella in 1993 and been re-elected in McMillan in 1996, now lost again. But the swings were not uniform. We lost Chisholm, which Michael Wooldridge had vacated to run for Casey in Melbourne's outer east.

We lost Bendigo, where our member Bruce Reid was retiring, but we held McEwen with Fran Bailey. Labor made big gains in Queensland but we had a majority of 20 to start with. As the night wore on, it became clear that the Government had suffered a large swing but would hang on. Labor polled a majority of votes but not a majority of seats. The Government's majority was reduced to six. We snuck home.

I believe the main reason we crept over the line was our economic performance, in particular the reduction in mortgage interest rates, which by October 1998 were around 2.5 per cent lower than they had been in March 1996. Unemployment was still nearly 8 per cent and had hardly fallen because of tough expenditure cuts and particularly cut-backs in the Commonwealth public service. But the flip side was that the Budget was now in balance, contributing significantly to the reduction in interest rates.

John Howard gave his victory speech at 10.55 p.m. in the Wentworth Hotel, Sydney. Having made the point that the election was probably the first time a Western political party had fought an election championing a new tax, he pledged himself to Aboriginal reconciliation. ('I want to commit myself, very genuinely, to the cause of true reconciliation with the Aboriginal people of Australia.') This came as a shock to me and no doubt to just about everyone else who was listening. If you had taken bets on the issues Howard would mention in his 1998 victory speech it would have been long odds on Aboriginal reconciliation.

Relations with the Aboriginal leadership had been bad in our first term of Government. The low point had been in May 1997 when a number of Aboriginal activists turned their backs on Howard as he addressed the Reconciliation Council in Melbourne on the 'stolen generations'. A naturally upset Howard became agitated. As interjections mounted he began shouting to be heard. This had delivered awful images on television of the Prime Minister haranguing his largely Aboriginal audience. One of the Aboriginal leaders, Pat Dodson, and a former Liberal Minister, Ian Viner, resigned from the Reconciliation Council in protest against the Government's policies. There was no doubt whatsoever that relations should be improved. An opportunity to do so would come later in the term with the

Reconciliation Walk. But no one had been expecting that pledge from Howard on that election night in October 1998.

In that same speech Howard thanked me. For months I had taken questions on the GST. How does it apply to racehorse winnings? How does it apply to insurance payouts? How does it apply to a birthday cake? One wrong answer could derail the campaign, as it had with Hewson in 1993. As I said to Tony Smith, it is like sitting for a tax exam every day, taking on the trickiest questions and waiting to get found out. But in this exam 99 out of 100 was a fail. One error and the press would bring me down. 'If you can't explain it why should people vote for it?' had been the question thrown at Hewson in 1993.

Howard also thanked Jeff Kennett, the Victorian Premier. Kennett had enthusiastically embraced the arrangement by which all GST revenue was allocated to the states to cover assistance grants and the abolition of identified state taxes. It was a good deal for the states. In fact, all the premiers liked that aspect of the arrangement. But Kennett had played no role in the campaign. He had been a frequent critic of the Government in its first term, confidently predicting it would be a one-term Government. Howard and Kennett had enjoyed troubled relations since the publication of an intercepted phone call in 1987 in which Kennett had described Howard using a four-letter word and promised he would never support him. The reference in the speech to Kennett was probably a little insurance against another breakout from the volatile premier. No one could foresee that a year later he would suffer a shock defeat in Victoria.

One welcome feature of the election was the defeat of Pauline Hanson in the seat of Blair. This was a great relief to the National Party and vindicated the stand of Tim Fischer to oppose her party. One Nation was a threat to the National Party, particularly in Queensland, where whole branches had defected to it. It won almost a million votes in the election, with 8.4 per cent of first preferences votes. It outpolled the National Party but won no seats in the House of Representatives.

One Nation was particularly strong in rural areas which had been in long-term economic decline. Sugar farmers coping with low world prices inevitably had grievances about the new globalised export-oriented economy, which they felt was leaving them behind. People who owned guns were angered by the Government's decision to introduce tough laws against gun ownership. Many of them felt that they were not getting the sort of Government assistance they thought was directed to privileged minorities (privileged minorities would be anyone in receipt of Government payments—migrants, public servants, Aborigines). These were precisely the kind of people who had supported the Joh-for-PM crusade in 1987 and could be easily attracted to messianic politics. Pauline Hanson revelled in the role. She also seemed to have a lot of sex appeal for older men.

The more the journalists in the broadsheet press attacked her, the more this disaffected constituency admired her because she stuck to her guns. She was not put off by 'elite' opinion. She gave a voice to the way these people felt and she would not back down. Leftist students organised nasty and violent demonstrations, which were completely counterproductive. Protestors in torn T-shirts and Rastafarian dreadlocks hurling abuse at an immaculately coiffed middle-aged woman were never going to upset her political momentum. She needed them just as they needed her. In her they finally found the demon of Australian racism. In them she saw the lazy state-sponsored recipients of Government hand-outs who were dominating the airwaves and insulting decent hardworking folk who were not getting a fair go.

Part of Hanson's appeal was that she kept things simple. She didn't worry about statistics or facts. She insisted that Australia was being swamped by Asians. Simple, direct … and wrong. She also promoted what was known as the 'easy tax'—a 2 per cent tax on every transaction at every stage of production as an alternative to our GST. Our tax proposal had a series of credits to prevent tax cascading. Hers was simple and 'easy'—and would have been disastrous. Her sense of victimisation reached absurd heights when she videotaped a statement to be released if she were assassinated. It began with the words: 'If you are watching this I have been assassinated.' It was a new Joan of Arc speaking from the grave.

Some in the Coalition took the view that she merely represented the hardline conservative view of people who would normally vote for the Coalition, particularly for the National Party. They thought we should not alienate these people and risk losing their preferences by attacking her. My view was that she represented the far right, whose ambition was to discredit and undermine mainstream conservative political parties and, in time, replace them. Whatever Hanson may have thought or done, those who had muscled in to her cause, and influenced it, included people outside the mainstream Australian politics. The 'easy tax', for example, had been long championed by the Australian League of Rights, a notoriously anti-Semitic group. The gun ownership movement was associated with 'survivalist' groups in the United States and promoted the idea that Australia was in imminent danger of invasion and that the Government, by restricting gun ownership, was working hand-in-hand with foreign powers to disarm decent Australian patriots. Many of these gun lobby groups asserted that they had a constitutional right to bear arms. One problem for these people is that there is no constitutional right to bear arms in Australia. It was a dead giveaway that they were getting their party lines written in America, not here.

A whole network of far-right groups with doctrines on immigration, foreign affairs, gun ownership and Aboriginal rights gathered around Hanson. They found a political front-woman whom they could manipulate to advance their agenda. My view was that we had to take them on. The point was not to attack Hanson personally. It was to attack her policies in a logical and analytic way.

When she began her maiden speech in Parliament in September 1996, Hanson spoke as a simple 'businesswoman running a fish and chips shop' who had had her 'fair share of life's knocks'. She was against 'fat cats, bureaucrats and do-gooders'. But then she got to her crescendo. 'We are in danger,' she said, 'of being swamped by Asians.' This was false. If people genuinely believed it, it could lead to serious racial division in our country. When Howard observed that a new freedom of speech had come to Australia which allowed people to express views previously thought of as politically incorrect, it looked as if he was endorsing Hanson and her opinions. Free speech is welcome. The ending of political correctness is welcome. But a false claim about 'ethnic swamping' was unwelcome and something we had to expose as such.

Coalition ambivalence showed up in debates over the allocation of voting preferences in elections. In Australian federal elections, and in many of the states, a voter marks the preferred candidate and then rates the other candidates in order of preference. If Hanson were considered the leader of voters who would otherwise vote for the Coalition, she and her political movement would be rated above the Labor Party. If she were considered outside the mainstream of Australian political life, she would be rated below other mainstream political parties, including the Labor Party. The Coalition wrestled with this issue. It became a long-running debate between members within the parties. I wanted to go all-out to expose Hanson and her policies. We would have to make it clear we were not bargaining with her. It would mean putting her last on our ticket. The decision about preferences is usually made at a state level in the Liberal Party unless the federal leadership intervenes and demands an outcome. I could not determine that.

On the eve of the 1998 Budget, in a pre-Budget interview on Channel 9, I was asked directly about Liberal preferences. Laurie Oakes asked: 'Well, Jeff Kennett and Peter Collins have had the guts to say the Liberal Party should not direct preferences to Pauline Hanson; they should put Labor ahead of One Nation. Will you say the same?'

I replied: 'I can tell you, in relation to my own seat, where there is a One Nation candidate running against me, that candidate will be last, not because I have any love for the Labor Party but because I want to make it entirely clear that is not the future for Australia. The future of Australia is built on tolerance and respect and is built on developing a strong economy, not some idealised and wrong view of the past.'

After the interview I went straight to my office to begin writing the Budget speech, which had to go to the printers that night. Howard rang. He was angry. He said my statement would pre-empt the party's decision on One Nation preferences. I replied that I had every right to decide how preferences were going to be allocated in my seat and I had decided it. What's more I thought that all our candidates should do the same and the longer we let the issue run, the more damaging it would become. I was still writing the Budget speech. I should have been focussing on that. We spent more time that day arguing about Pauline Hanson than we did talking about the Budget. It shows how distracting the issue had become.

Some of my critics in the party muttered that it was easy for me to take on One Nation because it would not be a threat to me in my city electorate. But the idea that it could be placated and harnessed was completely mistaken. It would produce continuing and damaging controversy. It was wrong in principle and it would not succeed electorally.

Eventually the Coalition decided to put Hanson last on its voting card for the 1998 election. This enabled us to take on One Nation. The election marked the beginning of the end for Hanson and her party. If we had not made this decision, she and One Nation would have been more successful and the cancer eating into the conservative wing of the Coalition parties would not have been cut out.

The GST took effect on 1 July 2000. After all the predictions, the hype and the frenzy, the day itself was something of an anti-climax. Most businesses were required to remit the GST quarterly. The first return, on a Business Activity Statement, went well. The second was due (for the December quarter) early in the new year. It generated a lot more hostility, perhaps because of resentment at having to do the extra bookwork over the summer.

On 1 February 2001 the Beattie Labor Government was re-elected with a resounding victory that struck fear in the hearts of many Queensland federal members. On the swings in that election many of them were heading for defeat in the federal election due at the end of that year. Obviously the GST was proving difficult. There was more bad news to come. On 7 March the national accounts for the December quarter were released. They showed that the economy had contracted by 0.6 per cent. This was another consequence of the GST. So many consumers and investors had raced to beat the GST—particularly with housing and renovations—that there was a natural correction thereafter. It was our first negative quarter since the recession of 1991. The press was happy to announce that the economy was in recession. Technically a recession is two negative quarters. We were nearly at the end of the March quarter but would not know whether it was positive or negative until the figure was released in June.

On 8 March Melbourne's *Age* carried the banner headline: 'Recession Looms', with a particularly morose photo of me. There was no doubt about whom they were going to blame.

Obviously I did not want a recession—bad at any time but fatal in an election year. Clearly some fiscal stimulation was called for. Two days later we doubled the first home-owners' grant to $14 000 for new homes to give a kick-start to the housing industry.

The cost of petrol was also rising. We had cut petrol excise by 6.7 cents a litre as part of the GST package. Our plan was that the excise cut, together with other overall savings from the tax package that would amount to 1.5 cents per litre, would cancel out the GST and keep the price of petrol constant. Petrol prices had risen partly because world oil prices were rising and partly because of a decline in the value of the Australian dollar. As oil prices are fixed in US dollars, a falling exchange rate puts up prices in Australian dollars. In our work on the GST, we assumed that by taking taxes off exports we would improve the trade position and this should, all other things being equal, have put upward pressure on the exchange rate. But it was falling largely because the massive flow of investment into the United States, as part of the high-tech and dot-com boom, strengthened the US dollar. Our opponents blamed the GST for rising petrol prices. We had said the prices need not rise. They pointed to the fact that they had. This was, they said, a broken promise.

I drew up two alternatives to deal with this problem. The first was to cut the excise by 1.5 cents per litre—in effect to compensate for savings that the industry claimed hadn't materialised. The second was to abolish the indexation of petrol excise, which had been introduced in 1983. The leadership group met at the Lodge. I presented the two options. I preferred the immediate cut while leaving in place the longer term indexation arrangements. But I was happy with one or the other. The leadership group decided on both. They were announced the next day. Petrol excise has been frozen at that 2001 rate ever since.

On 14 March 2001, after finishing the Expenditure Review Committee meeting for the day, I went out to Portia's Chinese restaurant in Kingston, Canberra, to have dinner with my assistant Treasurer, Rod Kemp. While we were sitting at the table Phil Gaetjens rang from the office to tell me that the Australian dollar had just gone below US$0.50 for the first time ever. He rang again about half an hour later to say that journalists were baying for my blood. 'What do we tell them?' he asked. I gave him the standard answer: 'The Government does not set the level of the Australian dollar. In time it will reflect underlying fundamentals which are sound.' The next morning the *Sydney Morning Herald's* front page trumpeted the headline 'Australia Hits the Wall'.

Most Australians thought something must be desperately wrong with the economy if the exchange rate had fallen so low. Australia did not have many of the high-tech companies that were booming in the United States as part of what was now called 'the new economy'. By contrast, we had strong mining companies and a strong mining industry, which was derided as 'the old economy'. A particular line of attack on my economic management was that we had failed to encourage dot-com companies, had missed the technology boom and had therefore presided over the collapse of the currency. Many critics recommended that Australia quickly establish microchip manufacturing. Miners found it hard to raise capital or justify investment. The Labor Party at this point lacerated the Government for the weak exchange rate and its so-called reliance on mining. When, some years later, mining became immensely profitable and the high-tech bubble burst, it said we were riding the boom. If Labor had had its way we would have got out of mining just when it was about to take off and invested in technology just when it was about to collapse. Keeping out of the excesses of the dot-com boom served the Australian economy well. When the boom became bust, the United States went into recession but Australia continued to grow.

That was in the future. In early 2001, in the midst of these travails, we were fighting a by-election in the Brisbane seat of Ryan caused by the retirement of former Defence Minister John Moore. The outlook was grave. The national economic situation, the voters' resentment at the unnecessary by-election and the factionalism of the Liberal Party in Queensland all weakened our campaign. I spent a number of afternoons door-knocking in the electorate. I was generally well received but I suspect that the sight of the federal Treasurer standing on the doorstep ringing the doorbell was taken more as a sign of desperation than a case of democracy at work. On 17 March the seat fell to the Labor Party.

At the beginning of May, I was in Washington at meetings of the International Monetary Fund and the World Bank. My press secretary, Niki Savva, was woken in the middle of the night by staff back in Australia ringing to tell her that Laurie Oakes had published a confidential memo to John Howard from Shane Stone, the federal president of the Liberal Party. Niki was an experienced hand who commanded enormous respect in the press gallery. She kindly waited until 6 a.m. to wake me with the news and warn me it would be a bad day. The memo was intensely critical of the Coalition, with special venom directed at me. I had never heard of this memo. Stone had written it nearly three months previously, back in February, the day after the Queensland state election, after meeting with federal Liberal MPs to discuss the loss. According to the MPs, Stone said, the Government had been 'too tricky' on issues such as the GST on caravan parks, beer and fuel. 'We are seen as a mean Government.' He wrote that the MPs had said 'Our leadership is not listening'. There were repeated references to John Anderson and me. He concluded: 'However for you, PM, there is guilt by association.'

It was no secret that the federal Liberal MPs in Queensland had held a meeting the day after the state election. A number of the Senators and Members who attended the meeting told me about it. They said there was a lot of anger in the room at the state Coalition and the election loss. Our Queensland colleagues were worried about the federal implications of the defeat. They discussed a range of areas. The federal director of the Liberal Party, Lynton Crosby, had also called me about the federal implications of the Queensland state election.

It was not the first criticism that I had heard from MPs about the Government's fortunes and misfortunes in bedding down the GST. Through the latter part of 2000 and the early part of 2001 its implementation dominated party room meetings at which member after member would recount the problems of small business in particular. I would record each issue raised by each member and contact them during the week to try to iron out the difficulties. The party room meetings were open and forthright. Nobody could be under any illusion about the difficulties. There was no need for the MPs to convey their concerns through any third party. They were doing it directly and effectively themselves.

In March the Government cut fuel excise, abolished indexation, increased the first home-owners' grant and made changes to the Business Activity Statement. That was before I had heard of Shane Stone's document. I was appalled that it was written the way it was. I was also surprised that Howard had not told me about it or at least told me of the areas that criticised me. It was florid and colourful. A number of members who had attended the meeting disputed its accuracy. But it was too late for that. It was taken as the assessment of our own federal president.

The furore caused by the leaking of this memo produced some high farce. I had to fly home to Australia—a 28-hour flight—where journalists staked out the airport and camped outside my office. I did not want to say anything without knowing all the facts. I was taken out of the airport by a back exit. I had arranged for Stone to see me as soon as I got back. He was spirited into my office through a back door. He was very apologetic about the leak, maintaining he had only ever prepared one original of his memo, which he had given to John Howard. He insisted adamantly that even he did not have a copy. I pointed out to him that if he had not leaked the document, he was effectively saying that the leak came from the Prime Minister's office.

The next morning I had to fly to Canberra for a meeting of the federal executive of the Liberal Party. Journalists, cameramen and photographers were still staking out the airports in Melbourne and Canberra. On the same plane as me was the federal Treasurer of the Liberal Party, Ron Walker. A self-made businessman, Walker had been extremely successful. He liked to tell the story that he began his first business washing cars, with one of his early clients being the Lew family (whose son Solomon also became a successful businessman). While still in his twenties, Walker had been Lord Mayor of Melbourne. He was superbly connected throughout the business community of

Australia. Later, as chairman of the 2006 Commonwealth Games held in Melbourne, he wheedled a large sum of money out of me for the opening ceremony, including funds to drop a flying tram into the centre of the MCG on a cable. His association with the Commonwealth Games made him a well-known figure at Buckingham Palace. As a long-serving member of the federal executive of the Liberal Party, he outlasted many presidents and several federal directors. We walked to and from the boarding gate together, much to the delight of the press photographers.

The federal executive of the Liberal Party consists of honorary office bearers—president, vice president, treasurer, paid staff, federal director, deputy director, parliamentary leadership and the presidents of each of the state divisions. The party varies in culture and outlook from state to state. There are no organised national factions. Someone who is considered on the right in the Victorian Liberal Party may be very much on the left of the Queensland Liberal Party.

Not much was said at the executive meeting, just the known facts. Somebody had leaked a highly colourful memo and done a reasonably good job of damaging the Liberal Party in the lead-up to the Budget, due that week. The federal president had every right to communicate forthrightly to the Prime Minister but he should have done it face to face. Memos like this are bound to be leaked. The Labor Party and the journalists seized on the words *mean* and *tricky* that Stone had used. The Government's critics, especially, used them during the *Tampa* and 'children overboard' event. Their description of Howard as mean and tricky was not original. The Liberal Party's federal president was the first to use the terms.

John Howard set up an investigation into how the document was leaked. The head of the Department of the Prime Minister and Cabinet, Max Moore-Wilton, and Tony Nutt from his office were put in charge. They intended to fingerprint the only copy of the document. If this investigation ever happened I never heard about its findings. I was told subsequently, by someone who claimed to know, that the investigation established that the document had been photocopied in the Prime Minister's office. I have no interest in the findings of this inquiry. The only lasting damage to come out of the affair was the tag 'mean and tricky'. It was still being used against John Howard some seven years later.

On 22 May 2001 I delivered the Budget, which was particularly directed at providing additional compensation to older Australians for their perceived loss of purchasing power arising from the GST. This included a one-off $300 payment to pensioners and self-funded retirees. As I said: 'It will stimulate the economy, it's good policy, and pensioners deserve it.' The *Australian* presented the Budget under the headline 'The Cheque's in the Mail'.

The national accounts to be released on 6 June were now critical. If the March quarter showed negative growth, Australia would be officially in recession, as the media had already predicted. The Labor Party was eagerly anticipating the event, with Beazley declaring: 'There is no worldwide recession. Asia is fine. The US is fine. Europe is fine.' The implication was that Australia would be the only country in recession. As it turned out, the economy grew in the March quarter by 1.1 per cent. Beazley was wrong on both counts: Australia was growing, but the United States was not 'fine'—it was heading towards recession.

It had been a horror year, but the turn of the economy began the turn of the Liberal Party's fortunes. On 14 July there was a by-election in the Melbourne suburban seat of Aston. The sitting member, Peter Nugent, who had entered Parliament with me in 1990, had died suddenly of a heart attack. I had known Peter before either of us entered politics. We went in together. He was a small-'l' liberal. The party was naturally not prepared for a by-election. It chose as its candidate Chris Pearce, a businessman who did not have a long history in the party but who proved to be an extremely diligent worker and a conscientious member. He impressed me from the outset. He would later become my parliamentary secretary and was well respected in the business community.

It was not a good time to have a by-election. We had sustained a swing of 9.6 per cent in Ryan four months earlier. If Labor was going to win the 2001 election, it was certainly going to win Aston. Since it was in my home state and in my neighbourhood, I launched Chris Pearce's campaign and went back three or four times to campaign with him. On one occasion a pro-marijuana campaigner emptied a box of some suspicious leaves all over me in a shopping centre. We held the seat. The swing was 3.66 per cent, less than what is normal in a by-election. The Coalition Government was coming back. For years afterwards Chris Pearce would organise an annual dinner, on Bastille Day—the day of the by-election. He would call that dinner 'The Turning Point'. This was all before a ship named the *MV Tampa* sailed into Australian waters.

In the year to June 2000 there were 4175 unauthorised boat arrivals in Australia on seventy-four boats. The next year there were 4141 on fifty-four boats. In August 2001 alone there were 1212 arrivals on six boats. The people arranging the trade were increasing the capacity of the vessels they used as people smuggling became more sophisticated. Most of these boats came from Indonesian islands and headed for Christmas Island or Ashmore Reef—Australian territories in the Indian Ocean close to Indonesia. Once they set foot on Australian territory, arrivals could claim refugee status, entitling them to a hearing under Australian law and, if successful, to protection and entry to Australia. Sometimes the people smugglers would drop off their passengers and sail back to Indonesia. Sometimes they would deliberately wreck the boats, which were often leaky to begin with, near Australian territory. Most of the people landing at this time were fleeing Afghanistan or Iraq. Since Australia shares no border with either of these countries, they had travelled through several countries before arriving in Indonesia to board boats to take them to Australian territory. Some of them had flown on commercial flights into Indonesia, which was used as the transit point. They were not in fear of persecution in Indonesia but Australia was a much more attractive long-term destination. The going rate for a place on a boat to Australia was US$10 000. The Australian Government sought the cooperation of Indonesian authorities to crack down on the people smugglers and to collect intelligence that would help to close down the organisers.

Under the Hawke and Keating governments any person arriving without a visa or lawful entry document was put in 'detention', usually in abandoned army camps. (This was the policy of mandatory detention inherited, not invented, by the Coalition Government.) While in detention they could make their claim for refugee status. The claim itself would not take long to assess, but unsuccessful claimants could then appeal through the legal process, which could take years. The increase in the number of arrivals meant that detention facilities, poor enough in any event, were now thoroughly inadequate.

The worst part about this was the position of the children. When whole families were waiting for their cases to be heard, the children would also be kept in detention. It would not be humane to separate children from their parents, but releasing the whole family would risk the chance they would disappear into the community. There was no real prospect in an open country of rounding up people years later and no stomach for their deportation. Eventually, by reducing the number of arrivals and by opening facilities in nearby towns, the Government was able to get all children out of detention. But the traffic overwhelmed the resources and the legal system was too slow—we should have acted more quickly. The conditions were sub-standard.

In August 2001 the Norwegian-registered vessel the *MV Tampa*, which carried sea cargo to and from Australian and foreign ports, was on its way from Fremantle to Singapore. Alerted by Australian Search and Rescue, it located a rickety vessel in distress. The captain picked up 433 people from the vessel and then continued his voyage to Indonesia. But the passengers he had taken on board demanded that he turn his ship around and head for Christmas Island. They threatened they would jump overboard unless the captain turned around and headed for Australian territory.

Cabinet discussed the matter on the morning of 27 August 2001. Its view was that, since the people had been picked up and were being taken to the nearest port in Indonesia, the vessel should stay its course and that to allow it to turn around and enter Australian waters was to let those on board hijack the vessel. This would be a great victory for the people smugglers. The Government advised the ship's captain and the Norwegian Government that the ship did not have permission to enter Australian territorial waters or to land in Australia. If medical assistance was required, it would be provided, but the *Tampa* should not enter Australian waters. At first the captain appeared to accept this instruction, but he then changed his mind and headed for Christmas Island.

The National Security Committee met in the Cabinet room in Canberra to discuss this issue on the afternoon of 27 August. Those present included the Prime Minister, the Deputy Prime Minister, the Treasurer, the Minister for Defence, the Minister for Foreign Affairs and the attorney-general. Also in attendance were the Chief of the Defence Force and the heads of the Office of National Assessments, the Department of Foreign Affairs, the Department of Defence, ASIO and the Department of the Prime Minister and Cabinet. Information was still sketchy but the committee was of the clear view that the ship should not enter our waters and that if necessary it should be boarded and turned around.

The committee met again the next day. It authorised the Australian Defence Force to prevent the *Tampa* from entering Australian waters. The Special Air Service boarded the ship, checked the health of the people it had taken on board (none of whom needed medical treatment) and redirected it to Indonesia.

The *Tampa* affair quickly became hotly contested in Australia, particularly when newspapers published photographs of those on board lined up on the deck of the *Tampa*. The Opposition did not suggest the ship be allowed to dock at Christmas Island. But there were many critics of the Government, including many journalists, who did. Some alleged that the Government had engineered or manufactured this issue for electoral gain, a charge made against John Howard for many years. As one present at the meeting of the National Security Committee and who supported its decision, I have no doubt it was the only decision that could have been responsibly made. To have allowed the ship into Australia, when it had been turned around on the demands of the passengers taken on board, would have been to give a clear signal that Australia had an open-door policy, provided enough pressure was applied to a ship's captain or indeed to the Government.

Australia conducts an offshore refugee resettlement program directed to those in the greatest need. We take in, per capita, more refugees than almost any country in the world. Our policy is to help those most in need. Unauthorised boat arrivals cannot be screened to ensure that they have legitimate claims to refugee status. Most do, but not all. Those people who do obtain refugee status in this way take places in the refugee program that otherwise would have been given to people who may have waited far longer or could not afford to pay the people smugglers.

The stand-off was resolved when agreement was reached for those rescued by the *Tampa* to be sent to New Zealand and Nauru for processing. This became known as the Pacific Solution. They would be assessed for refugee status under international law supervised by the International Organisation for Migration. Most would eventually gain refugee status.

The controversy sent a clear message to people smugglers and their unfortunate clients that Australia would enforce its border controls. The Government then excised Christmas Island and Ashmore Reef from the Australian territorial zone in which refugee status could be claimed. This meant that claimants could not invoke the Australian legal system by landing there, although they would still have rights under international covenants. The number of unauthorised boat arrivals began to fall to almost negligible levels. I would be surprised if a future Government reverses these measures and puts Christmas Island and Ashmore Reef back into the territorial zone.

Although the political tide had already turned at the Aston by-election, there was one further event before the 2001 election that overshadowed even the *Tampa*. On 11 September 2001, hijacked planes flew into the twin towers in New York and the Pentagon in Washington. The terrorist attacks in the United States, and the Australian Government's decision to send troops to Afghanistan, put national security firmly on the agenda at the election on 10 November 2001.

But as the campaign wore on, domestic issues came to the fore again. We were at last over the nightmare of the GST. Labor ran on a policy of 'rolling back' the GST, but after so much effort to implement it, the prospect of changing it all back again did not have much appeal to business. I think by this time the country was exhausted with GST. The economy was growing again and unemployment was starting to fall. The Government won a net of four seats from the Labor Party.

Beazley was unlucky. If he had come to the Labor leadership in 2006 rather than 1996, he would have had a better chance of becoming

Prime Minister. A second-generation MP, he had a good feel for the ALP organisation. He was also a good debater in the House. Critics said he was too wordy, too long-winded, but in fact he was much better than any of his successors to date. Beazley was in the wrong electoral cycle.

Issues that exploded during the election smouldered on after voting day. Labor continued to claim that it had been cheated of victory by lies told in the controversy over SIEV 4 (Suspected Illegal Entry Vessel 4). On the eve of the election, Peter Reith, the Minister for Defence, had released pictures of asylum-seekers in the water off Ashmore Reef who had been rescued from the SIEV 4 by Royal Australian Navy personnel. Reith maintained the pictures confirmed advice he had been given that children were thrown overboard. This advice came from the commander of Northern Command, who reported that a child had been thrown overboard. This was passed on to the head of Strategic Command, who was on an interdepartmental committee known as the People Smuggling Taskforce. This task force reported to Ministers, who relied on its reports to brief the media.

When I heard about the matter, from media reports, it was not unexpected. I had sat through many meetings of the National Security Committee in which we had been told that asylum-seekers had threatened to throw children overboard. We had been told to expect it to happen. I now thought to myself, with horror, that it had finally occurred. I am sure other Ministers thought the same.

The Defence Force later concluded that the children were in the water not because they had been thrown overboard but because their boat had sunk. The passengers had repeatedly sabotaged the engine and the steering, hoping it would force the navy to rescue them and take them onshore. When the boat sank, the navy rescued them. To sabotage a boat in the open sea and sink it with children onboard has the same outcome as putting children overboard. Either way, the person is creating, and intending to create, a life-threatening situation which will lead to a rescue.

There is no question that the Ministers honestly passed on the information they were given in the initial report. Subsequently, there were people in the chain of command who cast doubt on that original report. The Chief of the Defence Force (CDF), Admiral Chris Barrie, reported to his Minister, Peter Reith, that there were doubts about the accuracy of the initial report, but he did not change his advice. He said he adhered to the initial report. The Minister relied on the advice of the CDF, which changed only after the election, once Admiral Barrie's successor investigated and reported differently.

Labor held various inquiries to try to prove their case and attack the credibility of Reith and more particularly of Howard. The question was whether the Prime Minister should have corrected the initial report on the eve of the election and whether he had enough information to do so. At the time of the election it was not at all clear what the facts were. There was a great deal of confusion. Labor was unable to establish that the Prime Minister had been advised that the initial report was wrong. It could not show that he had intentionally misled the public. Of course, this did not stop them from endlessly alleging that he had.

I believe the SIEV 4 case had no effect on the election at all. Whether children were thrown overboard or whether they were loaded onto a vessel that was then sabotaged and sunk was not a big vote-turner. The Government had taken a strong stand on border protection and the Opposition supported it. The Opposition tried to have it both ways. They would claim they were as tough on border protection as the Government, then, when the critics of the Government claimed the policy was heartless, they would nod and wink and agree with that too.

But there was more. In 2005 the Melbourne Theatre Company performed a new play called *Two Brothers*. It was written by a successful playwright, Hannie Rayson, who was supported by the Australia Council, a publicly funded organisation. As federal Treasurer I allocated funds to the Australia Council and other arts bodies. It is evidence of Australia's liberal democracy that some of those funds ended up with Rayson to help her write a play that vilified the Government and demonised me. The play is agitprop about good and evil. Evil is personified by the brother who is a senior Minister in the federal Government. He is also a liar and an adulterer, whose wife is a dizzy snobbish blonde and whose dead child was a drug addict. The playwright claimed that I was the inspiration for the character. In the play the Minister orders the navy to let hundreds of illegal asylum-seekers drown rather than rescue them at sea. It turns out the Minister is a mass murderer too.

The play was an obvious reference to the tragic events concerning SIEV X. In October 2001 this boat sank, killing more than 350 passengers. Those on board had paid people smugglers to sail to Australian territories. Some of them got off the vessel when they saw how unsafe it was. The precise location of the sinking is not known but it is thought to have been in Indonesian waters. No Australian agency was aware the vessel was in trouble until after the disaster had occurred. No Australian agency knew it had set sail, its point of departure or its whereabouts until after it sank.

It was a terrible tragedy. The nearest Australian ship is thought to have been 150 nautical miles away. No aerial surveillance ever sighted the vessel. The suggestion that the Royal Australian Navy would knowingly let hundreds of people drown at sea is shocking and a disgraceful allegation. Members of the RAN were prepared to risk their own lives to rescue survivors of sinking vessels, diving into the sea themselves when necessary.

No one drowned on any boat located by the RAN. It is possible that there were other boats—unknown to us even now—that sank. Closing down the people-smuggling trade saved the lives of hundreds, probably thousands, of people who otherwise would have boarded unseaworthy boats that would have been lost and sunk without trace in the vast expanse of the Indian Ocean.

The premise of the play *Two Brothers* was that the Howard Government was responsible for the SIEV X tragedy. No Australian Minister ever gave or would give the sort of order on which the play is based. I am pleased to say the play was a great flop. My daughter Madeleine was taken with her secondary school class to see it. One can imagine the lesson in class the next day: 'Your father is a mass murderer. Discuss.'

Senior Ministers, particularly Philip Ruddock, had to put up with this kind of calumny over and over again. Ruddock was on the small-'l' liberal side of the Liberal Party. He had been one of the few who had crossed the floor to vote with Labor when it moved a motion in the House on immigration that was designed to attack Howard for his 1988 views. As Minister for Immigration his job was to administer a system that had become exceptionally legalistic. As a lawyer he saw it as his responsibility to act in a dispassionate way and not be swayed by public opinion, enthusiasm or passions. This technique worked well when he was being cross-examined in interviews. He would patiently, and at great length, explain the situation and try to cool the temperature. It sometimes gave the impression that he was cold and clinical. But he was under enormous pressure during this period, with demonstrations aimed at his home and family. The demonstrators failed to understand that the more they targeted him, the less likely he was to change his position on any of the issues. He would have considered it a personal failing to do so.

When Ministers were introduced at the campaign launch in Sydney in 2001, Ruddock received the greatest ovation. This was because he had become a special hate-object for journalists and critics on the left. As far as the Liberal audience was concerned, he had not bowed to this pressure and had shown great strength of character. He became something of a darling in the Liberal Party at the time.

If the policy of border protection is so bad, a Labor Government will reverse it, return the Indian Ocean territories to the migration zone and give boats from Indonesia free access to Australian waters. I doubt that this will happen. I also doubt that Hannie Rayson or other playwrights and artists will vilify the members of those governments who continue the policy. This issue was used as a battering ram by left-wing opponents of the Government. Once the Howard Government lost office, they seemed to lose interest in the policy.

Each time you have to take a controversial decision in politics, you lose some shine. It was happening to Howard. So each election gets a little bit harder. We had now won three and were into our third term. Howard would turn sixty-four this term—the age at which he said he would consider his future. With the defeat of Labor and its policy of rolling back the GST, the problem of a new tax system had been finally laid to rest. I could look forward to the next election without that becoming an issue again.

9

MELTDOWN:
THE ASIAN FINANCIAL CRISIS

In the aftermath of World War II the victorious powers established key global institutions to promote order and resolve disputes. They designed the United Nations and its instrumentalities, negotiated the General Agreement on Tariff and Trade (GATT), later to give birth to the World Trade Organization (WTO), and established the International Monetary Fund (IMF) and World Bank. The conference that created the IMF and the World Bank was held in 1944 in Bretton Woods, New Hampshire. These two institutions are often described as 'the Bretton Woods institutions'.

The task of the IMF was to help countries keep exchange rates stable and fixed to the US dollar (the world's reserve currency), which in turn was fixed to gold. The idea was that this would prevent countries engaging in competitive devaluations to take export markets from each other and would promote trade and economic growth. Economic growth and rising living standards were seen as essential to avoid a recurrence of the events that had led to grievances, confrontations and war. The Fund would make loans or advance liquidity to countries with balance of payment problems. By drawing on loans from the Fund to supplement their reserves they would be able to maintain their fixed exchange rate.

The World Bank originally helped with the reconstruction of Europe after World War II but increasingly moved on to promote development in Asia, Africa and newly emerging states. Principally its activity involves lending funds at rates lower than could be obtained from the private sector.

By convention the president of the World Bank is an American and the managing director of the IMF is a European. The countries of the Soviet bloc did not join the IMF until after the fall of the Berlin Wall and the dissolution of the Soviet Union. Nearly all countries today are members, with a few exceptions (such as North Korea and Cuba).

In 1971 the United States decided to move its dollar off the gold standard. Other countries then moved gradually off the US peg and allowed their currencies to float. In Australia the currency was 'managed' for some time and in 1983 the Hawke Labor Government allowed the Australian dollar to float.

Advances in technology and the rapid movement of capital swept away the old system of fixed exchange rates. We learned in Australia in the 1980s that it would take massive reserves to defend a fixed exchange rate and even then it was unlikely to work. In the late 1990s countries in Asia would learn the same.

As the world of fixed exchange rates passed, the original mission of the IMF also passed. The IMF continued to provide various funds to assist member countries through economic shocks, but it altered its role to focus more on giving advice and technical assistance, reporting on countries' economic performance and attempting to promote transparency of economic policy.

Every country in the IMF appoints a governor to the Fund who can attend and speak at the annual meetings. The countries are not equal. They are allocated a shareholding or quota to reflect their shares of global GDP. With the rise of new economic powers, particularly in Asia, the composition of global GDP, as between sovereign states, has altered. These changes have not been reflected fully in the shares or quota that countries hold in the IMF. As a consequence the institution is 'overweight' in European influence and 'underweight' in Asian influence.

Each of the major shareholders has a seat on the 24-member executive board and is represented by a full-time executive director. The board meets several times a week to run the Fund. Twice a year Ministers or central bank governors from the countries making up the board meet to 'oversee' the direction of the executive board. Some countries appoint their central bank governor to the Fund. In the case of Australia, it is the Treasurer who serves as the governor on the Fund.

When I first joined the small group of governors overseeing the executive board, it was called the Interim Committee. After twenty-five years it decided to become permanent and was styled the IMF Committee (IMFC). Just like the managing director, the chair of this committee is usually a European. In 1999 the Chancellor of the Exchequer, Gordon Brown, became the chairman of the IMFC—a position he held until he became Prime Minister of the United Kingdom. At that time I was the only Finance Minister to have served in office longer than he did. Brown was an effective chairman and pushed the IMF to focus on transparency and surveillance. He also had a keen interest in development—mostly a province for the World Bank—and on occasion brought the IMF governors together with the World Bank governors to engage on issues such as aid or debt relief. This was useful as the IMF governors tended to be central bankers or Finance Ministers responsible for raising revenue and the governors of the World Bank tended to be Aid Ministers, who spent it. The Finance Ministers had a better grip on the kind of economic policy that would spur development and raise living standards. The Australian Treasurer is also a governor on the World Bank.

Following World War II, official debt—issued by sovereign governments—was a much larger part of the global economy than it is today. Most of the Allied countries had issued war bonds to finance the war effort. The private sector was a lot less sophisticated. Nowadays, private sector borrowing and lending dwarfs government borrowing and lending. Lenders can move money by electronic transfer much faster than in previous generations. Currencies are traded the same way and the volume of the currency trade has risen enormously. There will be a currency market in action somewhere in the world at any given time, giving immediate quotes on cross-rates, which move instantaneously on the release of significant news or data. Financial instruments have become much more sophisticated, with derivatives being traded to hedge a currency, interest rate movements or stocks.

The transactions of borrowing and lending, payments and currency conversion move seamlessly across national borders. It is all a feature of globalisation.

The consequence is that the capacity of the IMF to influence the global economy is much less than it used to be. Some think that the IMF is some kind of international lender of last resort, that when a country runs out of money it can always turn to the IMF for a loan. But the resources of the IMF are not great and are certainly not enough for it to finance a country. In any event, it would be extremely hazardous for there to be an international organisation always available and willing to bail out a country from the effect of irresponsible policies. Other countries would soon get sick of funding an organisation that relieved countries of the consequences of their own bad policy.

Nor is the IMF an international receiver that can step in and provide an orderly workout for countries that get into trouble. There is no global or international rule for insolvency. Nation states deal with these issues under their own domestic laws, which determine who gets what in the event of insolvency.

The IMF may be able to use its position as the world's most representative financial institution to negotiate international cooperation when a country suffers financial difficulty of such a dimension that it threatens other countries or the global situation. It also has staff who are used to dealing with the problems of different countries. It has certain lines of liquidity that can be used. But in a financial crisis its intervention will work only if other creditors, lenders and investors have confidence that its program will ease a difficult adjustment and address the underlying causes of instability.

The IMF headquarters are in Washington, not far from the White House, and the United States has the largest shareholding, or quota— three times that of any other single country and sufficient to veto any change to the Articles of Agreement. This means that the United States has very significant influence. With a heavy concentration of Europeans on its executive board, the Fund also naturally focuses on issues of urgency or importance to Europe.

Through the early 1990s the Association of South-East Asian Nations (ASEAN) region was characterised by strong economic growth, fiscal policy, foreign investment and high savings rates. Addressing a conference on macroeconomic issues facing ASEAN in Jakarta in November 1996, the managing director of the IMF, Michel Camdessus, said:

> I frequently have the opportunity to discuss the challenges of economic management with your counterparts in other IMF member countries. I don't think I will be divulging any confidences if I tell you that these discussions often centre on how their countries can attain the economic results that ASEAN countries are already achieving—that is, high and sustainable rates of growth ...
>
> I point to the policies that your countries have pursued. In particular, I emphasise the role that prudent fiscal policy has played in bringing about macroeconomic stability. Singapore, of course, has been running large fiscal surpluses for many years. But Thailand has also been in budgetary surplus for some time, and most countries in the region, including—strikingly—the Philippines and Vietnam, have been moving in this direction.
>
> I also point to your high domestic saving rates, your success in attracting foreign saving, and your efforts to ensure that your countries' current account deficits are driven by export-oriented investment, rather than consumption; and are driven by the private sector, rather than Government spending.

He sounded a note of warning:

> Large net private capital inflows have tended to raise aggregate expenditures, increase inflationary pressures and widen current account deficits in all major recipient countries. Yet, part of these inflows—especially those of a short-term nature—can be suddenly reversed, either because of changes in market sentiment about the recipient country, contagion effects or changing financial market conditions in other countries.

No one was worrying too much about that at the end of 1996. In the first part of the 1990s Thailand's economy was growing year after year at around 8 per cent. But in May 1997 the Thai baht came under pressure. Defending an exchange rate which was fixed to the US dollar, the Bank of Thailand seriously depleted its reserves. Thailand was forced to move to a managed float of its currency. When this failed to stabilise the situation it requested support from the IMF.

The Reserve Bank of Australia had provided some technical assistance to the Bank of Thailand in this period. The flight of capital and the plunge in the Thai baht were not only affecting Thailand but battering confidence in other ASEAN countries. On 11 August 1997 I announced that Australia would participate in an international financing package sponsored by the IMF and designed to stabilise the situation in Thailand. Using our reserves, we would do a currency swap of US$1 billion with the Bank of Thailand to add to Thailand's foreign reserves. Our contribution was contingent upon the Thai authorities reaching agreement with the IMF on an appropriate policy package to deal with the weakness in the Thai economy. This was done on 20 August 1997 when the IMF approved financial support of about US$4 billion as part of a program of macro-economic adjustment and financial sector reform.

Our concern was first focussed on Thailand, but the instability that first surfaced there was spreading to other ASEAN countries. I heard stories of dealers and investors who did not know that there was a difference between the Thai baht, the Malaysian ringgit, and the Indonesian rupiah, and who simply decided to exit all their positions in South-East Asia. Just as they had rushed into South-East Asia looking for good returns, now they were rushing out—even faster. They assumed that all the countries of South-East Asia were more or less the same. If enough people thought that way and acted that way all the countries would experience the same instability. Contagion was beginning to take hold.

In September 1997 the Annual Meeting of the IMF was held in Hong Kong to coincide with the handover of Hong Kong from Britain to China. The Chinese premier, Li Peng, opened the meeting. This was a fascinating moment—the leader of a communist state presiding at capitalism's annual get-together. In this surreal environment, many thought that the Asian miracle was experiencing only minor hiccups and that business would soon get back to normal. But in the margins of the meeting I found that regional Ministers were alarmed that the crisis was spreading so rapidly.

The second-largest shareholder in the Fund and the largest economy in the region was Japan. Eisuke Sakakibara, the Vice Minister for International Affairs in the Japanese Ministry of Finance, approached me in Hong Kong with a proposal to establish an Asian Monetary Fund, focussed on Asia, which would provide liquidity and support for countries hit by the financial contagion in the region—a kind of Asian IMF. Sakakibara was highly respected. He was proposing a fund of US$100 billion. Japan would contribute the largest amount but was looking for other regional countries to make up the pool. Since most of the ASEAN countries were in financial stress this left few other possible contributors. Australia was one. Japan was looking for critical Australian support. Trying to raise US$100 billion and set up a new institution in the middle of a financial crisis is a tall order. I told him that the Australian Government might be able to assist with a few billion but not tens of billions of dollars. At the time we were actively cutting expenditures in an attempt to balance our Budget. That was an important part of our strategy to withstand the regional instability.

There were few other countries with deep enough reserves to contribute tens of billions. China was one—but China was unlikely to help fund the Japanese initiative. My view was that the only way to harness the kind of liquidity required to deal with the developing crisis would be to get international assistance from the global institutions. As a global fund the IMF had the most significant funds available. Now was the time to activate them. The existing institutions had a lot more in expertise and personnel than any start-up institution would have for a considerable time. In a crisis, time is valuable.

Our hope in August was that by a strong show of support for Thailand the crisis could be contained. But throughout the region equity markets plummeted, currencies crashed, capital took flight and what began as a financial crisis was soon affecting the real economy. Interest rates spiralled, confidence crashed, countries staggered into recession.

In late October 1997 the Indonesian Government made a request for financial assistance from the IMF. The IMF and other multilateral agencies proposed a program to target expenditures, the money supply, a longer term withdrawal of subsidies and improvements to the financial system. On 1 November I announced that Australia would provide supplementary financing up to US$1 billion to Indonesia as part of this package. Bilateral commitments amounted to $18 billion in a total package of $36 billion. The funding was enormous. By December Korea became the focus of the storm. Korea was the eleventh-largest economy in the world. Battered by the financial crisis and capital flight, it was fast running out of foreign reserves.

All through the late 1980s and early 1990s the Australian Labor Government had made it a diplomatic objective to have Australia recognised as part of Asia. It hoped Australia could hitch itself to the high-growth Asian economies, attract the levels of investment that were pouring into the region and—instead of being left behind—begin to match the Asian growth miracle. But in 1997, with international capital pouring out of the region, the Asian miracle was collapsing and it was not so desirable to be viewed as part of Asia.

Australia was under pressure. If countries that had higher growth rates and better savings than ours were collapsing, how could Australia expect to be untouched? Even if the contagion could be confined to (non-Australian) Asia, so much of our trade was in the region that an economic collapse by our export partners would inevitably bring on recession in Australia.

Having stepped up to assist Thailand and Indonesia, I believed we had no alternative but to do the same for Korea, our second-largest export destination. We had a lot at stake in stabilising the region. On 3 December I announced that Australia would be willing to make US$1 billion available to Korea, as part of an international financial effort to build Korean reserves.

I desperately hoped that the announcement of these programs would stabilise the situation. At this stage Australia's reserves were not substantial. The crisis was affecting countries that had started with larger reserves than we held. Now we were pledging some of our reserves. I did not want to be like the life-saver who swims out to the rescue and then needs to be rescued himself.

The deterioration of the situation in Korea attracted the attention of the United States. Korea was not just a large economy; it was the most militarised peninsula in the world, with a fragile ceasefire in place defended by a US Military shield. There was a dictatorship in the North that could well be tempted by the prospect of economic collapse in the South. From an Australian perspective, all three countries—Thailand, Indonesia and Korea—were of direct and immediate importance. Indonesia, our nearest neighbour, was of particular concern.

On 4 December the IMF announced financial support of US$34 billion as part of a program to stabilise Korea. Bilateral donors pledged that, if needed, they would provide an additional $20 billion as a second line of defence. The IMF estimated that Korea's usable reserves, which were around US$11 billion at the beginning of December and around US$8.5 billion a few weeks later, would be US$4.5 billion by the end of the month. Korea was quickly running out of reserves. There was television footage showing Koreans queuing to donate gold jewellery to the Government to help cover the situation.

The sizes of the packages were escalating as the crisis was escalating. But it was not enough. After the announcement of the 4 December Korea package, the Korean won kept falling—another 40 per cent in the next two weeks. With no improvement the rate of diminishing reserves would be exhausted by the end of the month.

The international banks now realised that, if they withdrew credit from Korean institutions, they would not get their money back. The only way to stabilise the situation and have the prospect of recovering their money was for the banks collectively to rollover their loans in the hope that this would bring confidence back to the country. But any one bank would not forgo its rights if it thought the others would go ahead and get priority over whatever was left. A move by any one bank would trigger the default anyway. Under the auspices of the New York Federal Reserve (the most important bank regulator in the United States), the major international banks met and agreed to a coordinated rollover of short-term debt. I contacted the Australian banks to get their agreement to join in.

The IMF began working on an intensified program that involved increasing interest cash rates to 30 per cent and lifting the interest rate cap to 40 per cent. In support of a stronger program the IMF proposed accelerated credit, including bilateral credit from countries such as Australia, which had pledged to help. Negotiations in Washington went late into Christmas Eve. By the time they concluded it was Christmas Day in Australia. I monitored the negotiations and agreed to activate our bilateral support. It was a bad Christmas. I spent Christmas Day in my office working on, and announcing, the activation of our financial assistance. If Korea went down I was sure that other countries would follow. I could not be sure what would happen in Australia. The next few weeks would tell whether it was enough. It would be a white-knuckle ride.

The November program for Indonesia had not worked. By January confidence in Indonesia was collapsing. The rupiah, which had traded around 2400 to the US dollar in the first six months of 1997, was around 6000 when the November program was announced. By January it was 8000. At-call interest rates were around 40 per cent.

On 15 January, President Suharto of Indonesia signed a new letter of intent for a new program, in a ceremony broadcast on television and attended by Michael Camdessus. The object of Camdessus' visit was to get Suharto's personal commitment to the program and to show, on television, that he had given it.

Like most other IMF programs, the November program had had macroeconomic targets and also included some structural adjustment to eliminate subsidies. But the January program was different. It proposed to remove tax privileges for the car project and credit for the aeroplane project, end the monopoly of the state-owned Bureau of Logistics (BULOG) over the import and distribution of sugar and wheat flour, eliminate the Clove Marketing Board, abolish all restrictive marketing arrangements and fully deregulate the domestic trade in all agricultural products.

Withdrawing privileges for the car and aeroplane projects was designed to withdraw the privileges of the President's family and cronies. The object was to restore confidence by reducing corruption. But some of the proposals, however admirable, like fully deregulating agriculture, were barely practised in developed countries like the United States and Europe. How Indonesia was going to fully deregulate domestic trade in agriculture within a few months was something of a mystery.

The Indonesian economic collapse was meanwhile provoking rising prices, food shortages, riots and deaths. The prospect of the country of 220 million people immediately to the north of Australia suffering mass starvation weighed heavily on my mind. This could be a humanitarian disaster. It could lead to mass evacuation, which would destabilise the region. It was uncertain how the political instability would work out. In fact, it ended Suharto's presidency. (The last change of regime in Indonesia—the one that brought Suharto to power—had been accompanied by killings estimated to amount to hundreds of thousands.)

My view was that Indonesia had to follow a program that would gain the confidence of the international community. It had no real choice but to cooperate with the IMF and the other lenders (including the World Bank, the Asian Development Bank and bilateral donors), which could provide the liquidity essential for the stabilisation of the currency and foreign capital. But I also took the view that some aspects of the IMF program were beyond the capacity of the Government and irrelevant to the urgency of the situation. Ending the Clove Marketing Board, for example, would be a structural reform, but in a country on the brink of hyper-inflation and suffering food shortages, the Clove Board was not the problem.

The January program failed to halt the collapse of the rupiah. All of the Budget targets were out of reach almost as soon as they were made. With the economic situation deteriorating so badly there was no way the structural reform would ever be enacted. The question became whether Indonesia should receive financial support in any event. Support is always made on certain conditions, known as 'conditionality'. The conditionality of the Indonesian package was far in excess of that for any of the others. It was clear many of the conditions would not be met. In that case should the country still receive support on humanitarian grounds or in the interest of regional stability or should it be left to suffer the consequences of the collapse of its economy?

My father Russell with my mother Anne, Janet, Tim and me (at right). Our world was the Blackburn neighbourhood, the state school and the Baptist church.

At Monash University in the 1970s I built a coalition of liberal, conservative, right-wing Labor and Jewish students to overcome the Left's control of the campus. (© Newspix/News Ltd)

After three years as a solicitor, I started at the Bar in 1984. I focussed on commercial and taxation law, but was soon swept up in industrial law.

With Michael Kroger, my friend from student days, after injunctions were granted in the Dollar Sweets case. Behind me is Fred Stauder, a hero of small business who established a milestone in Australian industrial history.

Above: *The Press dubbed it 'The Dream Team', but Alexander Downer's stint as Opposition Leader, with me as Deputy Leader, lasted only a few months in 1994.* (© *Fairfax Photos*)

Left: *In January 1995 John Howard replaced Downer as Opposition Leader. In December 1994 Howard had asked me not to contest the leadership, saying, 'I only want one term'. Here we are, jubilant and confident, with Tanya Costello and Janette Howard.* (© *Newspix/News Ltd*)

On the eve of the 1996 election the Labor Treasurer Ralph Willis released two
forged letters that claimed the Coalition had secret plans to cut grants to the states
for schools, hospitals, buses and trains. Willis apologised when it was shown they
were forgeries. (© Bill Leak)

The 1996 Budget was one of the best received in Australian
history. The public knew that the Government had inherited
a huge financial deficit and was doing something about it.

Left: *Dancing with death: a skeleton labelled GST has been recovered from the coffin in which it lay buried. (© Todd Davidson)*

Below: *Critics thundered that the GST would mean the end of the world. But the cartoonist Nicholson observed that the sun still rose on the morning after the GST. (© Peter Nicholson)*

The Howard Cabinet decided not to join the Reconciliation Walk over the Sydney Harbour Bridge in May 2000. But Tanya and I led many Victorian Liberals in the December walk in Melbourne. (© Newspix/News Ltd)

I have enormous admiration for British institutions and for the Queen, but I voted for a republic in the 1999 referendum. I believe Australia will gradually loosen its connections with the Crown. (© Auspic)

The 2004 Boxing Day tsunami killed hundreds of thousands and displaced more. At this school in Aceh 410 students out of 540 were killed. Australia provided $1 billion in aid. (© Fairfax photos)

The Treasurer and the rock star during the November 2006 G-20 meeting in Melbourne. No doubt about who was more popular.

In 2003 John Howard decided to continue as Coalition Leader and Prime Minister. Some journalists wanted me to challenge him or to resign as Treasurer. I knuckled down to work for the Government's re-election. (© Alan Moir)

The cartoonists loved my baby bonus and the slogan: one for Mum, one for Dad and one for the country. (© Mark Knight/Herald Sun)

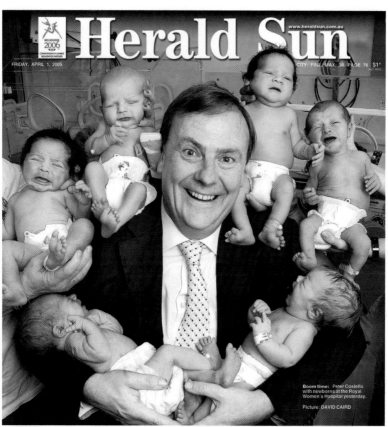

Herald Sun

www.heraldsun.com.au

FRIDAY, APRIL 1, 2005
CITY: FINE. MAX: 30. PAGE 76. $1*

Boom time: Peter Costello with newborns at the Royal Women's Hospital yesterday.
Picture: DAVID CAIRD

BABY BOOM

Kate Jones and Jason Frenkel

Victoria: the place to breed

VICTORIA is in the grip of a baby boom, spurred on by the $3000 baby bonus.

Australians have received $440 million in baby bonus grants, almost a quarter of which went to Victorian families.

Hospitals are reporting a boost in birth rates of up to 10 per cent

— nine months after the bonus was announced.

Victoria's fertility rate is expected to keep rising. A record number of mums are booked into maternity wards in coming months.

Treasurer Peter Costello said during a visit to the Royal Wom-

en's Hospital yesterday that he was as proud as any new dad.

"I feel proud to have brought the maternity payment to birth — it wasn't as painful as most childbirths, but it was my little bit of labour," Mr Costello told the *Herald Sun.*

He said the baby bonus would increase to $4000 in July 2006 in a further effort to lift the birth rate.

"I wouldn't hold off waiting for the $4000 — get going!" he said. "The more babies the better."

Victoria's surging fertility rate matches an overall increase across

Australia. Births at most Melbourne maternity wards are up.

Frankston Hospital expects to deliver 2001 babies by the end of the year — 30 per cent more than in 2003.

Births at the Royal Women's Hospital — one of Melbourne's biggest maternity hospitals — soared 10 per cent in February, compared with February 2004.

Continued Page 2

Continued Page 2

MAIN GAME: YOUR No.1 FOOTY LIFTOUT – STARTS P41

The photographers loved the slogan too. David Caird won a Walkley Award with this picture.

Above: *The May 2005 Budget announced tax cuts on low-, middle- and high-income earners. Asking a Liberal whether he would like to lower taxes is like asking a farmer whether he would like rain. (© Newspix/ News Ltd)*

Left: The Australian *was not the only newspaper to welcome the 2005 Budget.*

The Daily Telegraph *greeted the 2005 Budget with tax cuts and measures to move people from welfare to work.*
(© Newspix/News Ltd)

The Defence Department used to dominate its Ministers and would not disclose details of its financial plans to the Expenditure Review Committee of Cabinet. I fought this practice and won.
(© Newspix/News Ltd)

Channelling Peter Garrett, the rock star and Labor Member for Kingsford Smith in the House of Representatives. (© Newspix/News Ltd)

In October 2005 the world's leading central bankers and finance ministers met in Beijing, where I was seated next to the Chinese President Hu Jin Tao. When President Hu's opening speech received only polite applause, I stood up and led a standing ovation by the capitalist world's bankers for him.

At the APEC meeting in September 2007, Cabinet ministers worked in parallel universes. They met the APEC leaders to discuss the future of the world and then caballed at the Quay West hotel to discuss the future of John Howard. I was convinced that Howard would not resign. (© Auspic)

Cartoonist Patrick Cook doubts John Howard will ever resign as Prime Minister. (© Patrick Cook)

Ron Walker, a self-made businessman, was the honorary treasurer of the Liberal Party and a highly successful fundraiser.

The 2007 election campaign was a choice between the economic management team of Howard–Vaile–Costello or a roll of the dice on Rudd–Gillard–Swan. (© Newspix/News Ltd)

The toughest question in the 2007 election campaign came from 5-year-old Rourke Sheridan: 'Who made cactuses?' (© Fairfax Photos)

At a press conference on the Sunday morning after the electoral defeat. Life will mooch on. (© Newspix / News Ltd)

With Tanya, Madeleine, Phoebe and Sebastian.

The Australian Treasury supported the IMF program and took the view that conditionality should be strictly adhered to. I had other advisers, such as the Deputy Governor of the Reserve Bank, Stephen Grenville, an old Indonesia hand, who believed that it was more important to stabilise the economy first, forget the structural reforms and possibly even apply a fiscal stimulus to aid recovery rather than tighten the fiscal policy and risk contracting the economy further.

I do not think it is credible, in an economic crisis where there is a flight of foreign capital, to take expansionary measures. A Government must take measures that will restore confidence. My view was that Indonesia's best hope was to cooperate with the IMF to restore confidence in the country, but that the IMF also had to be careful that its prescriptions did not make the situation worse. In my view not enough thought had been given to sequencing of reforms, to the capacity of the Indonesians to implement them or to separating essential measures from the merely desirable.

I put this view strongly to IMF Managing Director Michel Camdessus when I called him in February 1998. He said he was under immense pressure from the major shareholders of the Fund, who thought Suharto was stalling to protect himself and his family. 'You are at the extreme left,' Camdessus told me. 'The G-7 is at the right.' The G-7 comprises the US, French, German and British economies—the major developed economies.

I took this matter up with other members of the G-7, calling the US Secretary to the Treasury, Bob Rubin, about it on 12 March, and later that month I wrote to the chairman of the IMF committee, Gordon Brown. I also raised it at the spring meeting of the IMF in April 1998.

The United States had been absolutely focussed on Korea for strategic reasons. But there was no such strategic issue, as the United States saw it, in Indonesia. Nor was there a powerful Indonesian constituency or lobby in the United States. So the United States was not at all disposed to revisit the IMF program.

I regarded myself as a friend of Indonesia throughout this crisis, not defending the corruption and cronyism of the regime but urging a sensible economic program. But there was little sympathy for

Indonesia in Washington. On 14 April the US deputy secretary to the Treasury, Lawrence (Larry) Summers, claimed at a meeting with me in Washington that Australia was fuelling Indonesia's resistance to taking hard medicine. This was nonsense. We were encouraging Indonesia to take the medicine. But we wanted to make sure the medicine would treat the illness. We were urging the program to be redrawn. We wanted a program that would work. Larry is highly intelligent and articulate. Our conversation was what would be called, in diplomatic circles, open and forthright. Ted Evans told me afterwards that he had never witnessed a meeting like it. There was give and take on both sides.

The January program had failed. The question was whether it would be revised or whether Indonesia would be left to collapse. Eventually all the parties recognised that this was not an option for a country with the fourth-largest population in the world. Throughout April work continued to refocus on reforming the financial sector and setting more achievable fiscal targets. It was a sensible revision and one that Australia had lobbied for. But that was no guarantee of success. The critical issue was to restore confidence in the country and its Government by an achievable program of economic reform. On 21 May, President Suharto stood down and passed the presidency to his vice president, BJ Habibie. The rupiah continued its dive, at one stage falling to 16 000 to the US dollar—about one-seventh its pre-crisis value.

In May the IMF approved the disbursement of US$1 billion in loans. In June it settled a further agreement with the new Government. But recovery was slow and very painful. In 1997 the Indonesian economy contracted by 13 per cent. Foreign investment collapsed. It would take a decade to revert the levels of foreign investment back again to pre-crisis levels. Meanwhile millions would be thrown back into poverty.

Of the countries affected by the financial crisis in the late 1990s Indonesia suffered the most significant economic setback. Korea rebounded strongly. Thailand was beset by political troubles but it has enjoyed economic growth again. The situation stabilised in the other 'Asian Tigers'. But they lost the lustre they had in the 1980s and the early 1990s.

The controversy over the Asian financial collapse and the IMF response to it led the IMF in 2003 to conduct an evaluation of its role in Indonesia, Korea and Brazil. It concluded, of Indonesia: 'In retrospect, the extensive structural conditionality in the January 1998 program became a distraction from taking much needed action on bank and corporate debt restructuring, which was missing from the January program.'

This is as close to an admission of error as one could expect from an international institution. It recommended: 'A crisis should not be used as an opportunity to force long outstanding reforms, however desirable they may be in areas that are not critical to the resolution of the crisis.' This was my view at the time.

Does the international community have a right, in return for providing financial support, to dictate terms for reform? My answer is that the international community should look to action that secures the financial system against threats to stability and prevent the contagion spreading to other countries. It must have an eye to the humanitarian situation. It cannot allow itself to be used to prop up corruption. But it cannot prescribe domestic political or economic policies. This is an area of sovereignty for the country and its people to resolve.

Much and all as we disagreed with Indonesia's agricultural policy we could no more use the IMF to dismantle it than we could use the IMF to dismantle the European agricultural policy. The IMF should intervene with a program to deal with underlying economic problems. Without such a program there will be no confidence. But it is not equipped to be some kind of supra-national regulator. Nor should it be. The intelligent staff of the IMF are not elected officials. They do not account to the people of the country. They are not experienced in leading public opinion or gaining public support for a reform program. They will not have to live with the consequences. They may well have good ideas, but only the national leadership has the ability and responsibility to see through a reform program.

Australia was the only country, other than Japan, to offer assistance to all three countries that entered an IMF program—Thailand, Korea and Indonesia. In order to provide the financing for Korea and Indonesia, it was necessary to establish a Commonwealth legislative framework, which I did with the International Monetary Agreements Amendment Bill 1998. This authorises the Australian federal Treasurer, upon request by the IMF, to provide financial assistance by currency swaps or loans to support a country in an adjustment program. It frees Australia from the need to use reserves. The Parliament, in certain situations specified in legislation, has authorised the Government to be able to intervene and to do so with a loan—fully reported and transparent—if it considers that necessary.

The events of 1997 and the slowness of the IMF's response to them did become the focus of some concern, perhaps even resentment, in Asia. Countries in the region felt the IMF did not act with the same urgency as it had at other times in Latin America (important to the United States) or Turkey (important to the European Union). They felt this was a consequence of the structure of the IMF—a structure which represented the economic order in the post-World War II era but not the economic global order as changed by the dynamic and growing Asian countries.

In April 1998, on the initiative of US President Clinton, a special meeting of Finance Ministers and central bank governors was convened to discuss the Asian financial crisis and the international financial system. The idea was to gather a representative group that would give more voice to the emerging economies. The group was known as the Willard Group, after meetings to coordinate it were held at the Willard Hotel. The number of countries at this meeting, and a subsequent meeting chaired by Clinton himself, varied. But eventually membership was fixed to include the G-7, China, Russia and some other economies systemically important to the international financial system.

The group became the G-20, comprising nineteen countries plus the European Union (EU). It held its first meeting in Berlin in December 1999 in the newly refurbished Reichstag and was chaired by the German Finance Minister, Hans Eichel. Australia was a member of this group along with Indonesia and Korea (the crisis-affected countries of Asia), Mexico, Brazil and Argentina (the crisis-affected countries of Central and South America), Turkey (another crisis-affected economy), India, Saudi Arabia and South Africa. Its objective has been to reform international financial arrangements to provide stability and ensure effective cooperative arrangements to respond to crises. In my mind this included reform of the IMF—giving a greater voice to Asia and focussing that institution more on the Asian region.

Reforming international institutions is hard. They tend to become dominated by full-time staff. The Members or Ministers are dispersed in national capitals and principally occupied by domestic problems. They are unable to devote their full energies to international challenges. It takes some time to become familiar with the issues and to make progress with colleagues of like mind. The turnover of Ministers means that very few are around long enough to see through changes. In my time as Australian Treasurer I dealt with five US Treasury secretaries and eight Japanese Finance Ministers. Ministers turn over but the international bureaucracy continues and tends to dominate the management and direction of these institutions.

My view is that the G-20 is an important international institution. It is small enough to allow real participation from the Finance Ministers and central bankers around the one table. It represents two-thirds of the world's population and around 90 per cent of gross global national product.

In 2005 the G-20 met in Beijing. It was opened by President Hu Jintao in the Great Hall of the People. As I was the incoming chairman for the next year I sat beside the President on the stage. Assembled before us were the G-20 Finance Ministers and the world's most important central bankers from the US Fed, the Bank of England and the European Central Bank.

When Hu finished there was polite applause. This, I thought to myself, is not how the President is used to being received. I got on my feet to give him a standing ovation. Slowly the rest of the audience followed. So, as an Australian Liberal Government Treasurer I led the world's central bankers in an ovation to the communist leader in the Great Hall of the People! I thought back to the student communists I had clashed with at Monash University in the late 1970s. They would be shocked, but I can't help thinking their side has changed more than mine.

In November 2006 I chaired the G-20 meeting in Melbourne. We were trying to focus the G-20 on its central purpose of reforming international financial arrangements promoting cooperation and stability. Some success had been made in this area, and to its credit the IMF recognised the role played by the G-20 in doing so. We were also focussed on resource issues. Emergence of new global giants and their demand for energy and minerals has led to rapid escalation in commodity prices. We wanted to engage the developing and developed world over the issue of energy security. In past generations the scramble for resources proved a source of disputation and conflict. We also focussed the G-20 on the great demographic changes that will affect not just countries but regions and our world as well as the financial flows around the globe between savers and borrowers.

The president of the World Bank attended these meetings, as did the managing director of the IMF. But the meeting of the G-20 is not a World Bank or aid donors' meeting. It is a summit for dealing with and improving arrangements to help with financial crises.

International organisations must be careful about 'mission creep'. The wider the agenda, the more shallow the attention given to each particular issue. Other countries sought to raise issues like North Korea's nuclear program, the Doha Round of trade negotiations, and other matters of international concern. But if different international organisations set up for a particular purpose become the focus for general issues of concern they become less likely to get measurable achievements in the areas for which they have been created.

The rock star Bono appeared in Melbourne at this time to promote overseas aid. He came to visit me. As he was leaving my office, my staff lined up to have their pictures taken with him. I had had visits from Foreign Ministers, Prime Ministers and Presidents in that office. The staff never lined up for photos with them! It showed me where rock stars stand in the popularity stakes relative to political leaders.

Unfortunately the G-20 conference in Melbourne was subjected to violent demonstrations. This puzzled me. The G-20 was set up to bring developed and developing countries together and to give developing countries, particularly crisis-affected countries, a say in international financial arrangements. The demonstrators were of extreme left views. They were hostile to capitalism. But if they had thought for a moment, they would have realised that this was a representative body trying to give a voice to the developing world in international financial arrangements. In this forum poor nations like Indonesia were able to put their proposals on the international financial system directly to the major industrial nations of the G-7.

There is a class of demonstrators that is opposed to globalisation. They are hostile to any organisation with the word *world* in its title. They like protesting outside meetings of the *World* Bank, *World* Trade Organization and *World* Economic Forum. The demonstrators successfully disrupted the WTO Summit in Seattle in 1999, giving anti-globalisation campaigns a big head of steam. In 2001 I gave a speech about globalisation to the Sydney Institute (see Appendix 7) in which I tried to answer what I perceived to be their criticisms. Anti-globalisation demonstrators use the world-wide web to communicate with each other and organise global coverage of their demonstrations. One of the Melbourne newspapers advertised the website where protestors could find information on how to protest, connect with each other and get organised for the militant demonstrations. The protesters would have been pleased that their violence had international coverage. It showed that they were not letting down global comrades in their protests against global forums. At one stage the Victorian Police mounted a horse-charge down a main street of Melbourne's CDB to try to break the lines of demonstrators. Some of the assembled Finance Ministers and central bankers were surprised to see such a thing. I told them that Melbourne was the horse-racing capital of Australia and that horse racing up Collins Street was not unusual on a Saturday afternoon!

But the work inside these forums is much more important than the demonstrations outside. We live in an interconnected world. Financial ripples in one country can affect countries on the other side of the world. Just how connected we are was demonstrated in 1998 when the Russian Government defaulted on sovereign bonds. The shock waves around the world brought down one of the world's best known hedge funds, Long Term Capital Management, which had to be bailed out by the US Federal Reserve.

All through the Asian financial crisis, the view of the US Treasury was that insolvent banks could not be propped up by Government bail-outs. Yet in cooperation with the private sector, US authorities went to the rescue of a hedge fund on the grounds that the knock-on consequences for the financial system would have been unacceptable. There are clearly two different perspectives here. One is dispassionate advice to other countries about how to deal with a problem and the other is urgent action a country will take to protect its own financial system. The sub-prime lending actions of the US market have since created ripples of instability affecting banks and other financial institutions around the world.

Globalisation—that is, the ability to connect buyers, sellers, lenders and borrowers around the world across national borders with instantaneous transactions facilitated by technological advances—means that financial systems and economies are more interdependent than ever before. Once we would talk of a regional economy as an area in a state or around a provincial city. Now we are more likely to use the term to refer to a number of countries in a particular part of the globe.

Can this acceleration of trade and commerce brought on by technological advance be reversed? Of course not. A few countries have tried to cut themselves and their economies off from these developments. To the extent that they have succeeded they are backward. Harnessing these forces is critical to economic growth and to rising living standards. But the power of these forces requires as many adjustment mechanisms as possible. The international capital flows have been described as a transmission line of 30 000 volts. A country that is connected to this power will need a strong distribution system—that is, a financial system that is well-regulated and well-capitalised, with various safety mechanisms allowing the charge to be dispersed.

A flexible exchange rate is another adjustment mechanism to move in response to these capital flows. Flexible product, service and labour markets will also be best placed to respond to the constant economic changes and competition coming from buyers, sellers and producers all around the world.

Some of the Ministers who understand this best are those who have, in their own lifetimes, experienced a shift from a command economy to a market economy. As they have seen production quotas swept aside and prices fixed by the state abolished, they have seen a market flourish. They understand that restrictions in particular areas are likely to reduce flexibility and increase risk to the whole. At our G-20 meeting in Melbourne in November 2006, our colleague Alexy Kudrin, the Russian Finance Minister, paused to pay tribute to someone he described as a great man, who had passed away that day—Milton Friedman. Kudrin had grown up under communism, yet he openly acknowledged the debt he owed to Friedman. It was a moving and historic moment.

10

WAR AND TERRORISM:
THE THIRD TERM

The Asian economic crisis of the late 1990s set in train momentous political changes in Indonesia. With his economy collapsing in January 1998, President Suharto looked for help from the International Monetary Fund. The IMF agreed to make the necessary loans—provided Suharto agreed to a wide-ranging program of economic reforms. On 15 January he signed up, in a ceremony broadcast live on television. It showed the managing director of the IMF, Michel Camdessus, small, dapper and elegant, standing, with his arms crossed, over the ageing and heavy-set Suharto as he signed. It was enormously damaging to Suharto's authority. The senior leader of South-East Asia who had exercised unquestioned rule for thirty years was seen to be at the mercy of international finance. His presidency was doomed. In May, Suharto stood down in favour of his Vice-President, BJ Habibie.

This development gave the Australian Government the opportunity to reopen discussions with Indonesia on the future of the troubled and unstable East Timor—a largely Catholic entity in Muslim Indonesia. The Australian public generally sympathised with the East Timorese, who had supported Australian troops in World War II. The Whitlam Government had approved Indonesia's annexing of East Timor after a military invasion in 1975. In the course of this invasion the Indonesian military killed, some say murdered, five Australian journalists. The relatives of these newsmen, and their supporters, naturally kept the episode and their memory alive. The Indonesian military also put down, brutally, the periodic demonstrations in Dili.

The Australian Government asked President Habibie to agree to an act of self-determination. To the great surprise of most observers, Habibie agreed. The Indonesian Government proposed a referendum to choose either special autonomy for East Timor within Indonesia or its separation and independence. On 5 May 1999 the United Nations, Indonesia and Portugal (the former colonial ruler) agreed on a UN-supervised referendum to be held on 30 August 1999. The East Timorese rejected autonomy by a 78.5 per cent vote. This amounted to a vote for independence. Almost immediately pro-Indonesian militia began violently to disrupt any movement to implement separation from Indonesia.

Here was war breaking out on Australia's border. Twenty-five years earlier Australia had stood by and let the Indonesian military resolve the situation. Now, given the refusal of the East Timorese to accept Indonesian rule, the overwhelming vote for independence in the UN ballot and public sympathy and support for East Timor, it was clear that Australia would have to intervene.

The Australian Government began to assemble a force that could take control in East Timor and disarm the militias. The force, under the command of General Peter Cosgrove, had international support. The Australian Defence Force (ADF) was always confident we had the capacity to disarm the militias. The important point was to avoid confrontation with any elements of the Indonesian military, who were sympathetic to and supportive of the militias. Such a confrontation could escalate to war with our nearest neighbour.

On 15 September the UN Security Council (Resolution 1264) authorised a multinational force, which became known as INTERFET—the International Force in East Timor. Australian troops landed on 20 September 1999. As a member of the National Security Committee of Cabinet, I was participating for the first time in a decision to send a major Australian combat force into action. At the peak of INTERFET, twenty-three countries contributed 11 000 troops. Australia contributed around 5700 personnel. It was the largest Australian military deployment since the Vietnam War. The

ADF planning was first-class. I was surprised to find that the United States considered itself so stretched that it could not put any combat troops on the ground. It was able to assist with intelligence and theatre surveillance, but Australia was required to execute the landing relying on its resources alone.

The INTERFET operation was a great success. By 23 February 2000 the UN Transitional Administration in East Timor (UNTAET) had taken over management of the force. East Timor became an independent sovereign state in May 2002.

This experience led the Government to make two significant decisions concerning our defence. The first was to purchase airborne warfare air command (A-WAC) capabilities. This was to give us the capacity for theatre surveillance. We would not have to rely on allies for that in the future. The second was to purchase C-17 heavy lift capacity. The ADF had the capacity to make amphibious landings, but it needed additional theatre and lift capacity.

In our Budget for 1999–2000, brought down in May, we had not anticipated a military operation on the scale required. On 23 November 1999 I announced that a levy would be introduced from 1 July 2000—0.5 per cent for incomes over $50 000 and 1.0 per cent over $100 000—to raise $900 million to cover the cost of the deployment. However, by the time of the 2000–01 Budget, brought down on 9 May 2000, I announced that we would scrap the levy. People still talk about the East Timor Levy. In fact, it was scrapped before it ever began to apply. There was no hostility at all to the levy. There was enormous support for East Timor's independence and great pride in the Australian role—and especially the military role—in achieving it. Many Australians would have liked to pay a contribution. But we were able to fund the engagement from general revenue and still have a Budget surplus.

The troubles in East Timor were far from over. In 2006 there was an outbreak of rioting caused by rivalry between the political factions and their surrogates in the military and police. It required the return of a large contingent of Australian troops and police. Australian forces sought to isolate and neutralise the leader of the rebel group, Major Reinado. Later in 2008 he was killed in a shootout during an apparent coup attempt against the Government of Prime Minister Xanana Gusmao and President Ramos Horta. East Timor is not yet able to sustain itself as an independent country without outside assistance. There is still a very significant deployment of Australian military personnel and police in the country.

On September 11, 2001, I was in Melbourne grappling with the collapse of Australia's second domestic airline—Ansett. John Howard was in Washington, preparing for an address to the United States Congress. He rang me on the morning of September 11 (Washington time) to talk about the financial assistance the Ansett receivers were seeking to keep flights in the air. It was the major political issue on our minds at the time. He was on his morning walk. Shortly afterwards and not too far away a plane crashed into the Pentagon.

I saw the second attack on the World Trade Center live on late-night television (Australian time). It seemed possible that the first crash was an accident, but when there was a second, it was clear something horrendous had happened. The telephone starting ringing immediately—colleagues rang in to ask whether I had any news on the subject, wondering who was responsible and where it would lead. Our security agencies were scrambling for information by contacting our allies and related agencies overseas. It was not clear who was responsible, although right from the outset the principal suspect was the international terrorist network al-Qaeda.

I received a brief report that night and was told that our agencies would liaise throughout the night with counterparts overseas. The National Security Committee would meet in the morning to review the intelligence and decide on any response to be taken. At first light I left for Canberra, where the agencies, principally ASIO, the Federal Police and the aviation authorities, briefed the committee. We were worried that civilian aircraft in Australia could be hijacked. The agencies were trying to account for every aircraft then in Australian air space. The committee decided on immediate steps to secure Australian flights and airports against any attack.

Howard's address to the US Congress was postponed. He was taken to a safe location and then lent the Vice-President's plane, *Air*

Force II, to fly back to Australia. No one was yet absolutely sure who was responsible and whether there would be further attacks and where they might be. Howard rang me from *Air Force II* on his way back to Australia to discuss the nature of a military response that would be likely to get at the terrorists who had organised the attacks and to disrupt their safe havens. There was no question in my mind that Australia had to be part of any international effort. Howard told me that he intended to invoke the ANZUS alliance. I said he was absolutely right to do so.

At its first sitting soon after the atrocity of September 11, 2001, in which nearly 3000 people, including ten Australians, were killed, the House of Representatives passed a motion to express its horror at the attacks and its condolences to the loved ones of those killed. The House declared that the attacks were an attack on the United States of America within the meaning of Articles IV and V of the ANZUS Treaty. Article IV provides that 'an armed attack in the Pacific Area on any of the Parties would be dangerous to its peace and safety and declares that it would act to meet the common danger'. Article V provides that an armed attack on the metropolitan territory of a party is an attack for the purposes of Article IV.

The House also endorsed 'the commitment of the Australian Government to support within Australia's capabilities United States-led action against those responsible for these tragic attacks'. There was no need to call a division. The motion had unanimous support and members stood in their places for a minute's silence.

In October 2001 the Australian Government announced the deployment to Afghanistan of Australian Special Forces, with air and naval support, as part of the international Coalition to end the Taliban rule in Afghanistan and to strike at terrorist training bases. The international Coalition, together with local Afghan opposition forces, proved extremely effective. By December the Taliban was defeated and a new interim Government sworn in. The last Taliban stronghold to surrender was Kandahar. One of the defenders of Kandahar was an Australian, David Hicks, who was captured by the Northern Alliance and turned over to US forces.

The reconstruction of Afghanistan involved a long commitment. Australian troops are still fighting in Oruzgan Province. These commitments, together with measures to enhance counter-terrorism in the wake of September 11, 2001, meant that the Budget for the year ended 30 June 2002 dipped narrowly into deficit—0.1 per cent of GDP. It was the only deficit I introduced after we balanced the Budget in 1997.

The terrorist acts of September 11 will be a defining event of our age. People will always remember where they were when they heard the news, and how they felt. The fact that John Howard was in Washington did, in my view, make the events even more cathartic for him. It cemented and personalised his relationship with US President George W Bush. The horror of that terrorist attack dominated our thinking about the response to terror and the need to take no chance that something similar—or worse—could be allowed to happen in Australia.

Even though Australians were killed in the terrorist attacks of September 11 those attacks were directed at the United States.

On 12 October 2002, a bomb ripped apart a bar and a club in Kuta, Bali, killing eighty-eight Australians and, in total, more than two hundred people. With Australian sporting teams taking end-of-season trips to Bali there were some communities that had suffered multiple fatalities. The injured were flown back to Australian hospitals for medical treatment. In my own electorate, a young mother who had gone to Bali for a birthday celebration was killed. I tried to console her grief-stricken husband and child. The Bali bombings brought home to me the human suffering caused by an act of deliberate terrorism. She was an innocent. She was not engaged in politics or Government or anything else that could have offended the militants who undertook the callous killing. The bombers may not have targeted Australians exclusively (many Indonesians also died), but they and the organisers knew and intended that the principal victims would be Australians. It was not an attack on Australian soil, but for Australia it was the equivalent of the al-Qaeda attack on the World Trade Center in New York. If we had had any previous doubts, now we knew that terrorists wanted to kill us too.

Australian forensic teams provided enormous assistance to the Indonesian police in tracking down the bombers, and three were eventually found guilty. They were connected to the militant Islamic group Jemaah Islamiyah. We had received no intelligence that there would be an attack in Bali. But Australian authorities had been urging Indonesian action against this group for some time. For Australia, terrorism moved beyond the abstract and general; it became real and personal.

In a broadcast on Al-Jazeera television in November 2002, Osama bin Laden claimed that the Bali explosions 'were carried out by the zealous sons of Islam in defence of their religion'. He also said: 'We warned Australia before not to join in Afghanistan and in its despicable effort to separate East Timor. It ignored the warning until it woke up to the sounds of explosions in Bali.'

In other words al-Qaeda linked the Bali bombing to Australia's role in supporting independence for East Timor, done in accordance with a UN-supervised ballot. Prior to 1975 East Timor had never been part of Indonesia, having been a Portuguese colony, not Dutch. The East Timorese were not Muslim; they were predominantly Christian. The Indonesian Government accepted the independence of East Timor. We did not use force against Indonesia, only against lawless militias. But terrorists do not worry about such details.

Osama bin Laden also claimed that the Bali bombings were a response to Australia's engagement in Afghanistan, which was authorised by the United Nations and under the ANZUS alliance. It ousted the Taliban and disrupted terrorist bases that gave sanctuary to al-Qaeda.

The attacks in the United States in September 2001 and in Bali in October 2002 prompted Australia to significantly boost its national security and intelligence resources. In the 2007–08 Budget I reported that the Government had committed an additional $10.4 billion to security for the ten years from 2001 to 2010–11. We also massively upgraded our defence capability following our experience in East Timor.

In the wake of September 11 there were anthrax scares in the United States. We had some in Australia as well. In 2002 a letter was received in my Parliament House office that contained organic matter. It was opened by the receptionist on the front desk. Suspicious, she reported it to security, which closed down the Ministerial Wing of Parliament House and brought in a decontamination unit to the Prime Minister's Courtyard. All of my Canberra staff were required to go through a decontamination shower—first in their clothes and then without them in the open-air courtyard on a freezing Canberra afternoon. Fortunately, when analysed, the material was shown to be not harmful, although it did contain some bacteria.

From 2001 the first call in each of our Budgets was national security and defence. We established new tactical assault capacity and a Chemical, Biological, Radiological and Nuclear Response Regiment, as well as increasing personnel for the Australian Federal Police and Sky Marshall units. When you are seeking to defend against an attack that can come in any place against any innocent citizen it is hard to assess where to stop. Some had criticised the Australian Government for not giving adequate warnings against travel to Bali. Our general approach after September 11 and Bali was to err, if at all, on the side of doing too much rather than too little. When attacks have died down it is easy to say there is an over-reaction. But if innocent citizens are killed I would rather know it was in spite of a security over-reaction and not because of an under-whelming response. This is the way our Government thought when it came to deal with the issue of Iraq.

The National Security Committee began meeting more frequently. As each new terrorist attack occurred—for example, the Madrid bombing of 2004—it analysed how it had occurred and sought to identify any weaknesses in the Australian system that new terrorist techniques might exploit.

The bombing in the London underground of 7 July 2005, which killed fifty-two civilians including an Australian, opened a new area of concern. The four young men who apparently carried it out had lived all or most of their lives in Britain and appeared quite assimilated into British life. They did not enter Britain with the purpose of committing a terrorist act. They were British; they were home-grown.

If this could happen in Britain, it was possible in Australia. Some of our fellow citizens, apparently well adjusted to Australian life, could be radicalised and turned to terrorism. Ours is a nation of diverse ethnic backgrounds. It gives freedom to all religions. It respects different customs in dress, culture and language. It maintains a decent tolerance. But these freedoms can be respected only within a framework of tolerance accepted by all. There are some people who are not prepared to respect this framework of tolerance. In the name of religion or politics they are prepared to take away the rights and freedoms of others, even to murder them. The terrorist who does not respect the freedom of others, and the rights of the innocent, lives outside the rules of a civilised society.

In an attempt to make this point in the context of endorsing freedom and tolerance, on 23 February 2006 in Sydney I gave a speech entitled 'Worth Promoting, Worth Defending—Australian Citizenship: What It Means and How to Nurture It'. My belief is that the best framework within which to protect rights and liberty is the Western legal framework. Obviously, terrorists do not respect that framework. It is important to defend the framework against its opponents and to show how alternative views may undermine it. Here is what I said:

> We have a compact to live under a democratic legislature and obey the laws it makes. In doing this the rights and liberties of all are protected. Those who are outside this compact threaten the rights and liberties of others. They should be refused citizenship if they apply for it. Where they have it they should be stripped of it if they are dual citizens and have some other country that recognises them as citizens.
>
> The refusal to acknowledge the rule of law as laid down by democratic institutions also stabs at the heart of the Australian compact.

I cited a Muslim cleric in Australia who claimed: 'There are two laws. There is an Australian law and there is an Islamic law.' I argued that 'There is one law ... the law enacted by the Parliament under the Australian Constitution. If you can't accept that, then you don't accept the fundamentals of what Australia is and what it stands for. There are countries that apply religious or sharia law—Saudi Arabia and Iran come to mind. If a person wants to live under sharia law these are countries where they might feel at ease. But not Australia.'

This simple speech was considered controversial by some and applauded by others. It was reported around the world and quoted in the *Washington Post* and *The Times* in London. In Australia some (wrongly) condemned it as being anti-Muslim. But there was enormous public support. One of the current affairs programs in Australia conducted a poll on my suggestion that dual citizens who wanted to live under sharia law should do so in a country that practised it, not in Australia. More than 36 000 people took part. An emphatic 98 per cent of callers supported it. There had never been a bigger margin on any subject, according to the program.

In May 2007, I received a letter from Mrs Maureen Santora of Long Island City, New York. She wrote:

> I am an American who spent this past January and part of February in your beautiful country. It was the trip of my dreams. I am also the mother of firefighter Christopher A Santora, who lost his life on September 11, 2001. I appreciated your words more than you know. My only wish is that America and England will 'hear' your message and follow your leadership. We in the 'western' world can not allow any group to take over our beliefs of freedom and tolerance. If the members of any group are unhappy with our rules, then they should find another place to reside. Thank you for your words of wisdom. May the world hear your message and your voice of justice. Thank you again, Maureen Santora.

At the time, Australian David Hicks was in Guantanamo Bay in Cuba awaiting trial before a military commission. Eventually he pleaded guilty and was repatriated to Australia, where he completed his sentence. Melbourne's St Paul's Anglican Cathedral displayed a banner demanding 'Justice for David Hicks'. Hicks had gone back into Afghanistan after September 2001 to volunteer for service with al-Qaeda. He had trained for terrorist attacks. He was lucky he was not killed when he took up a position against Coalition troops that liberated Afghanistan from the Taliban. He got out alive. For his role in training for terrorism he served five years in custody. Christopher Santora had signed up to save lives and trained for that purpose. In trying to save the lives of others, he lost his own. It was a most monstrous injustice. I would have been more impressed had the cathedral hung a banner demanding 'Justice for Christopher Santora'.

The loss of life and the damage in New York and Washington, when trained and coordinated terrorists were able to use civilian aircraft, raised the question of the damage that trained and coordinated terrorists could achieve if they had weapons of mass destruction—chemical, biological or nuclear.

After the defeat of Saddam Hussein's invasion of Kuwait in the first Gulf War, of 1990, no-fly zones were maintained against the Iraqi military to protect the Kurdish minority in the north and to prevent further incursions into Kuwait in the south. The UN Security Council Resolution 687 of April 1991 required Iraq to destroy, under international supervision, 'all chemical and biological weapons and all related subsystems and components and all research, development, support and manufacturing facilities related thereto'. The resolution also required the destruction, removal or rendering harmless of ballistic missiles with a range greater than 150 kilometres.

Over the course of the following decade, Iraq had taken every opportunity to delay, confuse and frustrate the work of the UN inspectors. In light of the events of September 2001, the possibility that Iraq could still have its weapons of mass destruction and, worse, make them available to terrorists, began to look like a clear danger to international security.

To enforce Resolution 687, the United Nations set up a Special Commission (UNSCOM) to take possession of and destroy Iraq's weapons of mass destruction and to assist the International Atomic Energy Agency (IAEA) to monitor and prohibit the development of nuclear weapons, materials or facilities in Iraq. On 31 October 1998, Iraq announced it would cease all forms of interaction with UNSCOM and its chairman and end all of UNSCOM's activities in Iraq, including monitoring. There was no doubt that Iraq had had chemical weapons. It had used them against its Kurdish population in 1988, killing 5000 and injuring 10 000. It also had the capability of creating biological weapons and it had been seeking a nuclear capability. UNSCOM had never been able to take possession of and destroy such weapons. Nor was it able to confirm that Iraq's capacity had been dismantled.

On 8 November 2002, UN Security Resolution 1441 declared that 'Iraq has been and remains in material breach of its obligations under relevant resolutions, including Resolution 687 (1991), in particular through Iraq's failure to cooperate with United Nations Inspectors and the IAEA and to complete the actions required under … Resolution 687'. The Resolution went on to afford Iraq a final opportunity to comply, and to that end set up an enhanced inspection regime with the aim of bringing to full and verified completion the disarmament process. The process established the United Nations Monitoring, Verification and Inspection Commission (UNMOVIC) and provided that any false statements or omissions or failures by Iraq to comply with and cooperate fully in the implementation of the resolution would constitute further material breach of Iraq's obligations. The resolution recalled that the Security Council had repeatedly warned Iraq that it would face 'serious consequences' as a result of its continued violation and obligations.

While the cat-and-mouse game between Iraq and UNMOVIC was played out over the Christmas period of 2002, serious planning was also under way for military action against Iraq—in other words, for military forces to locate and destroy any stockpile of weapons of mass destruction or the capacity to produce them. The UNMOVIC head, Dr Hans Blix, reported that Iraq was unable to account for 6500 chemical bombs and about 1000 tonnes of chemical agents, including VX nerve gas. He found strong indications that Iraq had produced more anthrax than it had previously declared and that some of it had been retained. In particular, Iraq had not declared 650 kilograms of bacterial growth, enough to produce 5000 litres of concentrated anthrax. There was no indication from Iraq that it would comply with the UN resolutions requiring the identification and destruction of those weapons of mass destruction.

After the Coalition forces defeated Saddam Hussein and his regime, no weapons of mass destruction were ever located. This means that at some period the regime destroyed its weapons or stocks of agents or dispersed them in some form or other. If Saddam Hussein had disclosed this action and accounted for it to the inspectors early enough, and if he had fully cooperated, he may well have saved his regime. But he refused to cooperate and he deliberately let it be thought that he possessed the weapons. It may be that he did not want to disclose to his own people, to his ethnic minorities or to real or imagined foreign enemies that he had disposed of the weapons. He may have made the assessment that if his enemies knew he did not possess this capability, they would have mounted insurrections against him. In the end this led to his overthrow by international forces. It was a poor judgement—one of the great miscalculations of our time.

Throughout 2002, the Australian Government's National Security Committee reviewed the progress of weapons inspections in Iraq and considered whether Australia might take part in any military action. On 10 January 2003, when I was due to drive my family on a holiday to the plains in western Victoria, I was called back to a National Security Committee meeting in Canberra. We decided to 'forward base' Australian forces to prepare for any military action that might take place in Iraq. The forces would be substantial—land, sea and air. My view was that we would probably go to war. Saddam Hussein gave us no reason to believe that he would undergo any sudden and dramatic change of heart.

After that meeting I flew back in a light plane to join my family, who had driven up to Victoria's Wimmera district. The afternoon sun produced a golden glow on the wheat crops. As I looked out at that beautiful and tranquil scene I reflected on the probability that Australian troops would shortly go into battle, that some would lose their lives and that others would sustain serious injuries. The decision weighed heavily on me. I did not talk about it with my family, or anyone outside the committee; it was obviously highly sensitive. I had supported decisions to send Australian forces into combat in East Timor and Afghanistan, but the danger and the probability of casualties in Iraq were much higher. How quiet and peaceful the Australian wheat fields looked compared with what would soon be unleashed in a time zone seven hours behind us.

I have heard people claim that political leaders go to war lightly or without due regard for the servicemen and -women in the direct line of fire. I have to say that this was never my experience. I found these meetings of the National Security Committee sombre. The Ministers were sombre. The chiefs of the forces were sombre. We always considered the likely casualties and deaths. We knew that we would have to explain our decisions to grieving spouses or parents. Our decisions were never made for domestic political advantage. All of the advice coming to the National Security Committee was that Iraq still possessed weapons of mass destruction and the capability of producing more. While we expected Australian casualties, we also knew that if weapons of mass destruction were used against our own citizens or allies, there would be even more casualties. After a decision is made and the consequences are known, it is easy to step back and second-guess. But at the time when the outcome is unknown, there is always an alternative to be considered—in this case the concern that one day weapons of mass destruction could be used against Australians or their allies.

The Labor Opposition in Australia did not support the dispatch of Australian troops to Iraq. They did not claim that there were no weapons of mass destruction. As their Foreign Affairs spokesman, Kevin Rudd, stated on September 2002: 'There is no debate or dispute as to whether Saddam Hussein possesses weapons of mass destruction. He does.' The basis of their opposition was that any action against Saddam Hussein should be taken only by a force authorised under Article 42 of the UN Charter by the Security Council. This amounted to saying that Australia's engagement, and indeed the Coalition's engagement, would be conditional on the agreement of all of the members of the Security Council who possessed a veto. The French were clearly prepared to exercise a right of veto and, according to this logic, the French would have the final say as to whether the Coalition, including Australia, would go to war in Iraq.

I pointed out in the House of Representatives on 18 March 2003 that there had been no UN authorisation of military action against the Serbs in Kosovo in 1999. This had been done to halt ethnic cleansing and homicidal atrocities. The NATO countries could have stood by while Russia vetoed any action in the UN. The Australian Labor Party had not argued they should. In the case of Iraq, Australia could have stood by if a further resolution was vetoed, but as I said in the House of Representatives, 'You are effectively saying to any one of the five powers that they have the right to veto your policy at a particular point. Not all of them; any single one of them. It is effectively saying the French could veto Australia's foreign policy. Suppose Australia wanted to take a strong stand against some area of French interest. Would we hand over to the French the right to veto that? I do not believe so.'

In any event the Security Council had already found Iraq to be in breach of Resolution 687 and had repeatedly warned it of the 'serious consequences' of its continued violations. In my view the Opposition was looking for a way to placate its anti-war constituency by hiding behind a process issue. It could have argued that the Coalition should not go to war in Iraq because there were no weapons of mass destruction or because these weapons were once there but had been disarmed. But it had no doubt they were there. If you are convinced there are weapons of mass destruction and that the regime will not disarm them then you have to decide whether to do something about it or not. The Security Council had warned Iraq what would happen. Saddam Hussein assumed no one had the will to make it happen.

On the night of 17 March 2003, the full Cabinet authorised Australian military action as part of the international Coalition in Iraq. The meeting lasted about three hours. There were no officials and no note-takers. At the end of the meeting the Cabinet recorded a formal decision to go to war. It is not necessary under the Australian system for Parliament to authorise military action. Only the Parliament can authorise *funding* for military action, as it does for everything else, but a decision to deploy troops is an executive act made by the Government. Our military advice was that the Iraqi regime would be defeated, although there would be significant casualties among the Coalition and others. There was discussion in the Cabinet about what form a post-Saddam regime would take and the work that would have to be done to secure it. Given the fact that the Opposition would not support this action I wanted Parliament to debate the matter, and suggested that we should move a resolution so that we could vote positively for action rather than vote negatively on any Labor resolution to oppose it.

On 18 March 2003, the Prime Minister moved that the House of Representatives 'endorse the Government's decision to commit Australian Defence Force elements in the region to the international Coalition of military forces prepared to enforce Iraq's compliance with its international obligations under successive resolutions of United Nations Security Council'. He was greeted by cries of 'Shame!' After three days of parliamentary debate the motion passed on party lines.

The war began on 20 March 2003, Baghdad time. The Coalition was the United States, the United Kingdom and Australia. Australian Special Air Service forces were among the first into Iraq, securing the west of the country against potential missile launches. During the war our National Security Committee met daily, receiving reports from the defence forces and defence intelligence. Australian deployments made bombing raids over Iraq and the Australian Navy shelled Iraqi targets. On 9 April US forces took control of Baghdad.

The Australian Government's decision was that Australian troops would take part in the active combat where support was most needed. We hoped that once the military campaign had been successful, other countries would join the occupation of Iraq and we could scale down our commitment. Other countries did contribute after the defeat of Saddam Hussein but never to the extent that would cover all the operational needs. As a result, Australia continued its commitment, principally in the south of Iraq. Australian forces were very highly regarded. They achieved all of their objectives. Their contribution was significant militarily and important to our allies. The Labor Party, which had opposed the war from the outset, also opposed Australia's contribution to the stabilisation of Iraq.

The Government's decision had been based squarely on Iraq's failure to account for weapons of mass destruction. We did not join the Coalition to bring about regime change. I had no sympathy for Saddam Hussein, whom I considered one of the most vicious dictators of our time. Iraq and the Iraqi people are much better off without him, but we did not go to war to depose him. Our purpose was to destroy weapons of mass destruction or the capacity for such. The decision to go to war had the unanimous support of the Cabinet and the National Security Committee. There was hardly any opposition inside the Liberal Party. The Labor Opposition argued against the engagement only on procedural grounds. It demanded a new resolution from the UN Security Council. If there had been such a resolution, the Opposition would have supported war to destroy weapons of mass destruction, which it also believed existed. It did not dispute the essential case, which was based on Saddam Hussein's refusal to verify the destruction of his weapons of mass destruction.

The Leader of the Opposition who guided Labor's response was Simon Crean. He was replaced by Mark Latham in December 2003. Latham promised that if he was elected at the October 2004 election he would have Australian troops home by Christmas. The Iraq War was never popular in Australia, but Latham's promise was seen as ill considered. He played to anti-US sentiment but looked risky on great matters of national security. The war was not the major issue in the 2004 election; it turned on Latham's character and experience.

Our third term of office had opened in the aftermath of the events of September 11. During the 2004 election campaign there was a terrorist attack on the Australian Embassy in Jakarta. The principal focus of the Government during this term was national security and defence. Defence and security personnel were deployed in East Timor, Afghanistan and Iraq. In July 2003 we also landed troops in the Solomon Islands under the Regional Assistance Mission to the Solomon Islands (RAMSI). The tempo of the commitment was high and we were engaged in a huge build-up of defence capability. Although Australian elections principally turn on domestic and economic issues, foreign affairs and defence issues were now to the fore as never before.

11

FROM MABO TO MAL: INDIGENOUS AUSTRALIA

There were no Aboriginal children at my primary school in the early 1960s. At my secondary school, Carey Grammar, there was a program to award a scholarship to an Aboriginal student. Many of the students worked hard to raise money for this scholarship. In my time the scholarship was awarded to an outstanding sportsman who was very popular. There was a lot of goodwill towards him in the school and towards Aboriginal people in general. I cannot remember any overt discrimination. But there were few Aboriginal people living in suburban neighbourhoods of outer Melbourne. Most Australians who live in the capital cities of the country have little contact with indigenous people.

In the mid-1960s my aunt Frances Northrop moved to Alice Springs. She was my mother's eldest sister and had suffered a partial paralysis on her right side as a result of a difficult birth. It was a setback she was able to overcome, completing her education and, later, training in theology. After graduating with a Licentiate in Theology (ThL), she became a deaconess in the Church of England, originally doing chaplaincy work at the Children's Hospital in Melbourne. As a child I was hospitalised with a number of ailments and she was the chaplain who visited me. Initially, she was asked to go to Alice Springs to do parish work in the Church of England diocese, but after two years she joined the Department of Native Affairs, later the Department of Aboriginal Affairs, in which she spent the rest of her working life focussing on Aboriginal welfare. She was awarded a medal in the Order of Australia for her services.

On visits down south she would often talk to us about her work and explain some of the problems she encountered. When I was twenty I visited her and saw something of Alice Springs and the work she was doing there. It was my first real exposure to the problems afflicting Aboriginal people. As part of her work Frances would visit the camps, some on the outskirts of Alice Springs and some farther away like the missions and the pastoral stations, to check on the welfare of people who were mostly living in humpies. I went with her on a number of these visits. She would identify any children who needed medical care. She would also deal with the victims of crime, mostly the result of alcohol abuse. Some of the places we visited were confronting. She would often be called to give evidence at trials and bail hearings.

In Alice Springs, Frances shared a house with another deaconess of the Church of England—Sister Eileen Heath, a legendary figure in the Northern Territory. Through Frances I got to know Sister Eileen quite well. She was almost part of the family. She was also a big part of many families in the Territory. Generations of indigenous leaders would speak fondly and warmly of Sister Eileen and Sister Fran.

Born in 1905, Sister Eileen is still alive, living in retirement in Perth as I write in 2008. She began working with Aboriginal people at the Moore River Native Settlement in Western Australia in 1935. At the end of World War II, she was asked to run a hostel for 'half-caste' girls in Alice Springs. Many children who had been evacuated south after the bombing of Darwin in 1942 were now returning to the Northern Territory. The plan was to take over a rest home a short distance south of Alice Springs, which had been used as a recreation centre for servicewomen during the war. After arriving in Alice Springs, Sister Eileen decided to open the property as a hostel for children who came in to attend school in Alice Springs, to provide training for the girls in domestic science and some training for boys in farm and mechanical skills. It was not a school. She named the hostel 'St Mary's'.

Under Sister Eileen's management the hostel soon grew, taking in nearly seventy children varying in ages from five to sixteen. Many of the parents paid a contribution to the living costs. It was at this hostel that the film-maker Charles Chauvel discovered Rosie Kunoth, who starred in the film *Jedda*, a story of the difficulty faced by a young Aboriginal woman in modern (white) Australia.

Sister Eileen was enormously competent and forceful in a polite, softly spoken way. This brought her into conflict with the church hierarchy. At the end of 1955 the church decided that the hostel needed to be run by a man. It gave Sister Eileen notice that she would be replaced by a church army captain from New South Wales. There was an uproar in Alice Springs. Paul Hasluck, the Minister for Territories, offered her a job in the welfare branch of his department, looking after Aboriginal families. She worked in this area until her official retirement and long after that she continued to help various welfare organisations. She worked for nearly thirty years for the Prisoners' Aid Association and ended up on the Parole Board of the Northern Territory.

Both Frances and Eileen, single women, devoted their whole working lives to Aboriginal welfare. Even in the late 1970s, when I first accompanied them on their rounds, it was obvious that alcohol was a major problem for the Aboriginal people in and around Alice Springs. The violence associated with alcohol and the breakup of families were devastating communities. Aboriginal people were living in poverty. The best efforts in building housing were failures. Frequently, families would move out of the new houses and live in nearby humpies.

Years later St Mary's was to become the focus of allegations about the 'stolen generations' of Aboriginal children, particularly those of mixed descent, who had been taken from their parents and housed in Government institutions or, more often, in church missions. St Mary's was alleged to be one of these institutions.

At the time children who were not of 'full blood' were thought to be especially at risk. In many cases it was the station owners, or European men employed to work on the stations, who fathered these children. There was a widespread fear that they would not be accepted as tribal members because they had been fathered outside the tribes.

The policy of the Minister responsible in the 1950s, Paul Hasluck, was assimilation. This was more humane than previous policies based on the idea that indigenous people belonged to a dying race that should be 'protected'—that is, restricted to certain areas or reservations and subject to intrusive controls. Assimilation meant preparing Aboriginal children to participate in Western society by educating them and training them in skills that would lead to employment. It did not include any emphasis on preserving Aboriginal culture. Sister Eileen was a supporter of the assimilation policy, although she was careful to ensure that it was a matter of choice and not compulsion: 'It depended on the people themselves, on how far they wanted to be assimilated,' she said.

In 2000 a test case was brought on behalf of two members of the 'stolen generations'—Lorna Cubillo and Peter Gunner—to claim damages against the Australian Government for having taken them from their parents and for their treatment in supervised care. Peter Gunner had been born at a pastoral station called Utopia, not far from Alice Springs. A patrol officer placed him in St Mary's hostel in 1956. Although Eileen had already left St Mary's by then, in 2000 she was called as a witness to give evidence of the circumstances in which children were taken into St Mary's and the conditions at the hostel. The judge found that Gunner had been removed from Utopia station with the consent of his mother, who wanted him to be given a Western education.

Sister Eileen was ninety-two years of age when she gave her evidence in the court. The judge found as follows: 'She was a most remarkable witness. Quite apart from her dedication to the well-being of the Aboriginal people, to which she has devoted most of her working life, her recollections of her work and her clarity of thought and expression were most impressive. She was an exceptional witness and I accept all aspects of her evidence without qualification.'

Sister Eileen's evidence was that no child admitted to St Mary's could be truly described as a stolen child. She acknowledged that it was important for children to be bonded to their family and she maintained that that was her view in the 1950s. She said that in most of the cases children brought to St Mary's were brought with the mother's consent. She advocated, and had advocated, removing part-Aboriginal children from remote locations without schools so that they could receive an education. But she also stated: 'If the mother did not consent, the child should not be taken unless there were very serious reasons why the child should be removed for neglect or violence ...' At that time this also would have been the case for white children in dysfunctional families.

Since the judge found as fact that Mr Gunner had been taken to St Mary's with his mother's consent, he determined that he had not been 'stolen'. This does not mean that no Aboriginal children had been taken against the will of their parents. There would have been many children at risk who were taken against their parents' will. In many cases it was done for the protection of the child. There also would have been many cases of children thought to be at risk who were removed when it was not necessary or not warranted in the circumstances.

Knowing the dedication and selfless work of Sister Eileen, it is impossible for me to believe that she was part of a program to steal children away from their parents or to take them without consideration of their welfare or without considering the wishes of their parents. Many of the people involved in this period are now dead. We are fortunate that Eileen was still so clear of mind when these matters were litigated so that she could shed light on these cases.

Attitudes have changed. Today authorities place more emphasis on the importance of children staying with their parents—in both white and Aboriginal communities—than in years gone by. The pendulum has swung. But sometimes authorities are criticised for not intervening early enough, even when there are repeated incidents of neglect.

In 1995 the Human Rights and Equal Opportunity Commission (HREOC) began an inquiry into the separation of Aboriginal children from their families. Its report, *Bringing Them Home*, was published in 1997. It tells harrowing stories of children taken from their families. It is hard to imagine the trauma this would cause a young child. It would scar them for life. The report gave people who had been hurt or damaged by their experiences the opportunity to tell their stories. It helped the wider community understand what they had been through.

Some of those separated from their parents might have found good foster homes. But some children were maltreated in some institutions, just as there were orphanages where white children were maltreated.

We are only now becoming aware of the level of the problems that existed in some government and some church institutions.

But not every child separated from their parents was 'stolen'—as the Gunner case shows. Some were removed for their own protection. Without investigating the circumstances of each person, case by case, it is impossible to settle an exhaustive list of who was wronged. Attempts to generalise about every person in a particular area or a particular generation are wrong. Wild claims about genocide or attempted genocide are ridiculous.

In my view we should sensitively acknowledge the deep hurt and suffering of children who were wrongly taken from their parents. Children who were maltreated while in care are entitled to compensation. But it is important to be careful about the facts and neither diminish nor overstate them. This is an emotional issue, especially for the people who have suffered so much.

The federal Government was responsible for the administration of Aboriginal affairs in the Northern Territory, but the policies in the states were conceived and implemented by state Governments. When the *Bringing Them Home* report was released in 1997 each state Government moved to make amends. At the time all the state Governments except in New South Wales were Coalition Governments. Their responses varied.

Premier Kennett in Victoria proposed that 'this House apologises to the Aboriginal people on behalf of all Victorians for the past policies under which Aboriginal children were removed from their families and expresses deep regret at the hurt and distress this has caused'. In Queensland the Parliament expressed 'sincere regret' for the hurt suffered by those Aboriginal people 'who in the past were unjustifiably removed from their families'. The Western Australian Parliament observed a minute's silence. The South Australian Parliament expressed sincere regret 'at the forced separation of some Aboriginal children from their families' and said it 'apologises to these Aboriginal people for these past actions'. The Parliament of Tasmania also responded in much the same terms.

In New South Wales the Legislative Assembly said it 'apologises unreservedly to the Aboriginal people of Australia for the systematic separation of generations of Aboriginal children from their parents, families and communities'. When a Labor Government was elected in Queensland in 1999 it moved that the House 'apologises … on behalf of all Queenslanders for the past policies under which indigenous children were forcibly separated'. When Labor was elected in the Northern Territory in 2001 it too moved an apology.

Comparison of these formulations reveals two significant differences. The first is the extent to which they describe forced removal as taking place. In New South Wales it was described as 'systematic separation of generations'. In Victoria it was described as 'past policies under which Aboriginal children were removed from their families'. In South Australia it was described as 'forced separation of some Aboriginal children'.

The second area of difference is the expression of remorse. In New South Wales, Victoria, South Australia and Tasmania the resolution was that the Parliament 'apologises' to the Aboriginal people. When the Queensland Government changed in 1999, a new resolution was passed in the Parliament which went beyond expressing 'sincere regret' and provided that the House 'apologises to Aboriginal and Torres Strait Islander people'. In Western Australia the Labor Opposition proposed that the House 'apologises'.

On 26 May 1997 John Howard opened the Reconciliation Convention in Melbourne. Foreshadowing the HREOC report *Bringing Them Home*, he said: 'Personally, I feel deep sorrow for those of my fellow Australians who suffered injustices under the practices of past generations towards indigenous people.' He went on to say: 'Australians of this generation should not be required to accept guilt and blame for past actions and policies over which they had no control.'

This is undoubtedly the case. Australians descended from convicts are not guilty of the crimes of their ancestors. Nor can a person be blamed for the act of someone they do not know and over whom they have no control. Nobody would suggest otherwise. Howard did express 'sorrow' and he did acknowledge 'the pain and trauma' of people who suffered under those policies. The word he did not use was 'apology'. Some of the audience stood up and turned their backs on him. As interjections increased in number and volume, he raised his voice and his speech took a haranguing tone. This prompted further interjections and catcalls. Old wounds were re-opened.

No one thought Howard or any other member of the 1997 Government had personally removed children from their families or instituted a policy to do so. I do not believe anyone in the audience expected or wanted the current political leaders to take personal blame for events of the past. They wanted an acknowledgement that they had been wronged by Government policy. Since the leaders who had instituted and administered the policy were all long out of office or long dead, they wanted the people who could speak in the name of the Government to acknowledge this past wrong and apologise for it.

From that moment on, the use of the word 'apology' became the overriding issue. Howard could and did use all sorts of other words. He expressed 'sorrow', but that was not enough. His critics wanted to hear him say the word 'sorry'. When he said he was sorry about the suffering that members of the 'stolen generations' had experienced, that too was not enough. His critics wanted him to say 'sorry' for the policies and the conduct of them. Even in the 2007 election campaign he was still on the back foot trying to explain how you could be sorry about something but not say 'sorry' for it.

The whole issue was symbolic. The form of words would not have improved the health or housing or education of one single Aboriginal man, woman or child. But a lot of politics is symbolic. People find these arguments more accessible than arguments about the level of resources or the design of programs to administer health, housing or education.

Technically, a person who has not caused or contributed to an act cannot be held responsible for it. In that sense they cannot even apologise for it. But in everyday life we apologise for a whole host of things we may not have actually done. 'I am sorry if you misheard me' is a polite expression designed to promote better understanding. Jeff Kennett in Victoria, Dean Brown in South Australia and Tony Rundle in Tasmania all apologised to Aboriginal people on behalf of their Governments. I do not think anyone thought this meant that they or their Governments were complicit in stealing children. They dealt with the issue and moved on. The federal Government may have been technically correct but symbolically it lost. It was unable to either resolve the issue or move beyond it.

There were some who did not want to move on. They saw this issue as a great battering ram against either the Coalition Government or Howard, or both. Early action may have diffused the issue and resolved it. As it continued, positions on both sides became entrenched.

An apology was eventually given. It was one of the first acts of the new Labor Government elected in 2007. The Opposition supported it. The press acclaimed the Prime Minister, Kevin Rudd, who delivered the apology. If the argument was that an apology should be avoided because it would give rise to legal liability, then that liability has arisen anyway. But I do not think it could be used to establish any general liability. While the apology will not improve the conditions of a single child, by getting the symbolism right the previous Government could have saved a lot of energy for the policies that will deliver better education or better health to Aborigines or lift Aboriginal children out of poverty.

If, in the past, Aboriginal children were removed from their families in circumstances where it was unjustified and unwarranted, in more modern times the authorities have swung the other way and are almost scared to intervene and remove Aboriginal children who are at risk. It is tragic but true that even today there are many Aboriginal children at risk of violence and sexual abuse. For a while it was almost taboo to talk about these problems. It would have led to charges of racism or to accusations of belittling the suffering of those who were, or who believed they were, stolen. It took the courage of the Crown Prosecutor for Central Australia, Nanette Rogers, to break this silence, in 2006. Her stories of the horrific crimes committed against innocent children led to an investigation into sexual abuse and violence in the Northern Territory. The results were released in June 2007 in a report called *Little Children Are Sacred*. The cases documented in that report are horrendous.

We now realise that by refusing to talk about these issues we were not protecting Aboriginal people. We were protecting violent predators (who happened to be Aboriginal) at the expense of innocent children (who were also Aboriginal). These are always delicate and sensitive issues. Authorities not wanting to be accused of creating another 'stolen generation' may have been too slow to intervene. The children suffered, not because they were removed but because they were not removed.

As Treasurer I last visited Alice Springs in 2005. The conditions were worse, in my view, than they had been when I first visited twenty-five years earlier. In the meantime the Government had introduced massive welfare programs. In 1989 it had established the Aboriginal and Torres Strait Islander Commission (ATSIC) in an effort to hand autonomy of decision-making to Aboriginal people. It had received numerous reports from the Human Rights Commission and spent tens of billions of dollars. But overall there had been little significant progress. Its frustration with this lack of progress led the federal Government to abolish ATSIC in 2004.

Members of ATSIC had been elected by a nation-wide ballot of Aboriginal people. All Aboriginal funding went directly to the commission, which was in charge of distributing it. The commission was highly politicised and highly factionalised. There were financial irregularities. The final blow came when the chairman of the commission faced allegations of rape, brought by an Aboriginal woman, over events that occurred many years before. ATSIC was paralysed and the public had no confidence in it. Nor did I.

When the Government abolished ATSIC, it did not cut Aboriginal funding; indeed, we increased it in successive Budgets. We decided that spending on Aboriginal health would be done through the Health Department, and spending on Aboriginal education through the Department of Employment, Education and Training. This process is known as 'mainstreaming'—that is, attempting to deliver services to the Aboriginal community in the same way they are delivered to the non-indigenous community. Since the problems are greater, the services are much greater per head of population.

The release of *Little Children Are Sacred* showed that something had to be done urgently about law and order in the Northern Territory. The Territory Government was responsible but was plainly failing to address a dire situation. Many of the outlying communities had no local police. A sex offender could quite often go days, weeks or months without any prospect of arrest. Sentences of sex offenders were often lenient. Authorities were reluctant to take children at risk out of their communities for fear that they too would be accused of inappropriately removing children. The brutality of the cases and the ages of the victims shocked Australia.

Dealing with this horrific situation, the Government announced a federal intervention in the Northern Territory. It was unprecedented. The public overwhelmingly supported this. Newspoll in July 2007 showed approval for federal intervention at 61 per cent and disapproval at 23 per cent—nearly three to one. One feature of separatism that had gone too far and worked to the detriment of Aboriginal people was the permit system. Under this system it was necessary for outsiders to get a permit to go into an Aboriginal community. In some cases the offenders or their sympathisers had corrupted the community leaders, who would refuse permits to visitors who might have uncovered abuses. This left the victims almost as prisoners of the perpetrators.

It was astounding that the Australian press, normally vociferous in demanding access to all areas, had been so silent about a system that banned them from particular parts of the country. The federal intervention ended this system in the larger townships and road corridors leading to them.

The intervention also introduced restrictions on the sale of alcohol. It banned possession of X-rated pornography. It introduced quarantining of welfare payments so that income support could not be used for alcohol or substance abuse. It increased the police presence. The army was also sent in to help. Funding for these measures was well in excess of half a billion dollars.

The Minister responsible, Mal Brough, should be given a lot of the credit. Although he did not identify himself as indigenous, his sister did. The fact that he had this background gave him confidence to take on the issue and to stare down opponents who in the name of autonomy or self-determination opposed white intervention in black communities. Unfortunately Mal Brough lost his seat in the 2007 election.

After the issue of an apology to the 'stolen generations', the next symbolic issue our Government was to face in Aboriginal affairs was the Reconciliation Walk. Here I was determined to get the symbolism right.

The Council for Reconciliation was established in 1991 to promote reconciliation. It organised Corroboree 2000 at the Sydney Opera House, at which it launched its final proposals, known as the Roadmap for Reconciliation. Government and indigenous leaders attended the corroboree on 27 May, the date of the 1967 referendum that gave the Commonwealth powers to make laws for Aboriginal people. Members of the public were invited to show support by walking across the Sydney Harbour Bridge the next day.

As Prime Minister, John Howard was invited to address the proceedings in the Sydney Opera House. On this occasion there was no controversy over the 'stolen generations' but there were interjections and some heckling. The draft document on reconciliation did not call for a treaty between Australians, something that I oppose and a majority of Australians would oppose. But it included proposals to enhance Aboriginal rights, to step up economic development and to address disadvantage. The proposal for a walk across the Harbour Bridge to demonstrate support for reconciliation captured the public imagination. Hundreds of thousands of people took part.

In the lead-up to these events there was intense press and public interest in how many people would participate and, in particular, whether Government Ministers would do so. It is not a big thing to go on a walk across the Harbour Bridge. Again, it would not lift a single Aboriginal child out of poverty. But in my view the country genuinely wanted reconciliation. There is and was so much goodwill for indigenous people in the broader community. A demonstration of that goodwill would give them pride and confidence. An acceptance by the indigenous people of that statement of goodwill would in turn encourage continuing efforts by non-indigenous Australians to work to address Aboriginal disadvantage.

Members and leaders of the New South Wales state Government agreed to join in the Reconciliation Walk. Some members of the Howard Government also wanted to participate. I was one. Howard raised the issue in Cabinet. He said that if some Ministers were to take part and others refused to do so, this would signal division inside the Government and it would be used by opponents against those who declined to take part. I could see this argument and I could see the advantage of a common position. I argued that, if the Cabinet wanted to take a common position, it should walk together as a show of Cabinet solidarity in favour of the cause of reconciliation. That would be enormously symbolic. I described it as a 'knockout statement'. It would remove all the bad blood that had emerged in the events of 1997. The Cabinet kicked the issue around. There was some support. But Howard and the majority of the Cabinet were against taking part in the march. Their idea of a common position was that none of us should participate.

In this climate, if Howard refused to take part in the walk while I did, it would be huge news and be seen as a leadership split. My decision could be taken as a political ploy rather than a genuine desire to promote reconciliation. I did not want to overshadow the march in this way. I did not want to be accused of using the event to push my own agenda. I decided that I would not participate in the Sydney walk but that when the equivalent walk was organised in Melbourne, I would take part. By that stage the temperature would have cooled and Ministers from other states would always be able to say they were not in Melbourne on that particular day.

A reconciliation walk in Melbourne was organised for 1 December. I contacted all of my Victorian Liberal colleagues and suggested that, as a statement of commitment to reconciliation, we walk together. Most of the Victorian federal MPs and the state leader of the Opposition joined me and Tanya in this march. There was wide media coverage and our decision was contrasted with Howard's. But I do not believe my involvement detracted from the reconciliation issue or the march itself.

I walked alongside the chairman of ATSIC and with a number of the Aboriginal leaders. They were glad of my support. I was proud to be there. Apart from a small group of socialist activists who hurled abuse, at one point spitting on us, the reaction of the thousands of people in the Melbourne march was overwhelmingly positive.

I support reconciliation. It may be said to be entirely symbolic, but a lot of issues in this area are. To me it is a commitment to work for better outcomes. Many of the people who marched would have no personal involvement with indigenous problems and would not come across Aboriginal people in their day-to-day lives, but they had a genuine desire to make things better. The Coalition has every reason to reflect this view and to advance it.

A key to economic development for Aboriginal people will be the use of land. In 1992 the High Court, in the Mabo case, determined the existence of native title, something that previously had not been known in Australian law. The basis of the court's finding was that native title existed in the Murray Islands in the Torres Strait where there had been cultivation of land. There have been different kinds of land use by different native peoples. Rather than have these individually determined by the common law, the previous Labor Government passed the *Native Title Act 1993*, which prescribed a process for claiming native title.

At the time it was said, and widely understood, that the issue of a pastoral lease would extinguish native title. But in the Wik Case, handed down in 1996, the High Court found by narrow majority that the pastoral lease and native title could coexist. Naturally, those holding pastoral leases wanted clarification of their rights, and indigenous people were determined to resist any attempt to restrict their access to land that they might be entitled to under the High Court finding.

The decision in the Wik Case put incredible pressure on the National Party. It represented most of those areas where pastoral leases were issued. It was also the time of the rural revolt encouraged by One Nation. (The Coalition's strong stand against gun ownership had been controversial in many of these areas.) After painstaking work the Government developed a 10-point plan to deal with the Wik decision. Any legislation required majority support in the Senate, which the Government did not have. The amendments therefore seemed to involve an endless round of negotiations and were highly technical. Most of the detail was lost on the public, who again tended to treat the issue as a purely symbolic one—either you were for the pastoralists or you were for indigenous people. In reality, you could be for both and attempt to negotiate a sensible mechanism for dealing with land. But these issues required enormous attention to complex detail.

In the end the introduction of native title and the response to the Wik decision did not realise the aspirations or fears promoted by either side of the argument. The hope of indigenous people was that native title rights would change their economic situation. There have been cases where the legislation has enabled them to negotiate better royalty regimes than otherwise might have been the case. But it has done little to raise the living standards or develop economic security for indigenous people generally.

On the other side of the argument, the establishment of native title has not destroyed either the mining or the pastoral industries in Australia, although it may well have made exploration less attractive. The tortured negotiations involved in settling royalty rights may have delayed some developments, but plainly the mining industry in Australia is still very successful, as are the great pastoral industries.

The bigger problem for indigenous people is that their land rights are generally held communally: the clan or the tribe, not an individual, is entitled to the land. In English common law the ownership of the land brings with it rights to sell, lease, mortgage—to use that land in a variety of economic ways. This has been the foundation of much of the economic development in Western civilisation. If we were unable to buy and sell land but were restricted to using it for agriculture, each one of us as peasant farmers would be considerably poorer than we are now. It is the bundle of rights over land that enables individuals to deal with the land and gives them the opportunity to use it for a variety of purposes. In a free market system, land is put to its most valuable use (subject to environmental and other public interest constraints) and wealth is created.

I can understand why native title has always been understood in a communal sense. Aboriginal people had not developed a system of land title or transfer. But to restrict the use of the land they own in this way impedes their capacity for economic development and progress. If people of Asian or European descent were told that they were not able to buy, sell, mortgage or otherwise use their own land, there would be an uproar.

Aboriginal housing is also held in a corporation or public trust. Various Governments operate Government-owned housing which is rented out to low-income earners. But giving people title to their own houses gives them more pride and respect and brings them into economic life where they can buy and sell and engage in self-improvement. Again, Aboriginal people do not have this opportunity. We should not be so surprised if the housing stock is run down when people do not own it and have no way of capturing the benefit of improvements, renovation or good upkeep.

The same principles apply to income support—whether for indigenous or non-indigenous people. Income support is absolutely essential to keep hundreds of thousands of Australians in housing and to provide food and care for the young and elderly. But it is much better for a person to enter mainstream economic life and derive income from employment than to receive Government benefits. By entering the workforce they will invariably earn more money, but they will also earn self-respect and independence. They will come into social contact with other workers and learn values and skills such as reliability. With employment comes better health and a higher standard of living.

But indigenous people face an additional burden. Those living in remote communities have no chance of meaningful employment. There are not nearly enough jobs to make these communities economically viable or self-sustaining. This was brought home to me in a tour of Far North Queensland which I undertook with Noel Pearson. Pearson is an outstanding indigenous leader. He is frank and honest and is not intimidated by political correctness. He became a vocal critic of Government welfare when he saw how it was undermining independence and self-respect in Aboriginal communities. As we toured North Queensland in our light aircraft in 2005, Noel was reading a book during the flights. It was FA Hayek's *Road to Serfdom*. How things have changed.

Indigenous people in the north of Australia once led nomadic lives, hunting and gathering. When the mission stations or the pastoral stations were established, they tended to camp in or around them. They would be given some level of medical care, and maybe some education.

Rations would be available where needed. But outside the cattle stations there was no real economic base to sustain employment.

When equal wages came into effect in the cattle industry, many Aboriginal stockmen lost work. There was no longer an economic base for the Aboriginal settlements on the pastoral stations. In the 1960s and 1970s Government took over income support. Any person of working age who is unable to find a job is entitled to unemployment benefits. In many of these settlements without jobs, whole communities survive on income support.

Young people grow up without seeing anyone in meaningful employment. They realise they either have to leave the community to work or, if they stay, live on income support for much of their lives. It is very hard to convince young people to get an education if they have no real expectation of finding gainful employment. To get a job in Australia you must be able to speak some English. To grow up in a community that speaks a tribal language without good English is another disadvantage.

The saddest thing for me when visiting Aurukun in North Queensland in 2005 was to hear grandmothers tell the stories of how they have to raise their grandchildren because their parents have abandoned them or engage in substance abuse. Many of the grandmothers were raised at a time when the missions ran the communities. They told me they learned better English and better literacy under the missionaries than their children who were raised at a time when the Government had taken over responsibility for Aboriginal affairs and introduced welfare. This must be one of the few areas of Australia where educational standards of people schooled in the 1970s and 1980s are lower than those of people schooled in the 1940s and 1950s. These communities have huge problems with alcohol and drugs. They do not have retail stores. There is not that much to buy. But one of the products that always seems to be available for purchase is alcohol.

I was very impressed by the Family Income Management (FIM) scheme, designed to help Aboriginal people with savings. They could arrange for part of their income to be protected by being set aside for living expenses. They could also use direct debit savings for items they needed, perhaps furniture or whitegoods. Once they had met the savings target, the item would be ordered in from a catalogue. They would have the satisfaction of seeing a return from their saving effort.

Most people would agree on the importance of employment, self-respect, saving, achievement and community pride. These values are no less important for indigenous people than for whites. But the economic base in remote communities does not sustain employment and economic improvement.

Aboriginal people who live in towns or the major metropolitan centres have been much more successful in health, education and income than those in remote communities. You can hardly fail to notice the very high proportion of indigenous players in the various football codes, especially the Australian Football League (AFL). These talented footballers are highly paid. Their success has given them great pride and set a good example for young indigenous people. Whenever you visit a community, however remote, in northern Australia, it is common for a football to be pulled out and for kids to start a game. The AFL has done a great job in encouraging indigenous players. These players do not make the grade because of any special preference; the clubs recruit them on the basis of talent. They are in a highly competitive league that wants the most talented players. It so happens that a disproportionate number are indigenous.

Not every child has exceptional sporting skills. Most of us have to content ourselves with other things in life. Experience has taught us that in Aboriginal affairs separatism is not the answer and welfare is not the answer. But engaging indigenous people in the economic mainstream, giving them the opportunity to join it, educating them in a way that will help them join it, are all fundamental to solving the problems of low life expectancy, bad health and disadvantage generally. There is a lot of goodwill among Australians. With the right leadership they will work towards that solution.

12

LEADERSHIP:
FROM MEMO TO MADNESS

In the long-running struggle between John Howard and Andrew Peacock over the Liberal Leadership, I was a Howard man. I was pleased when he became Leader of the parliamentary Liberal Party in 1985. I thought it an important step forward because it meant a stronger focus on economic policy and a change in our approach to industrial relations.

But four days after I was pre-selected for Higgins, in May 1989, the party room dumped Howard as Leader and re-installed Peacock. I thought it had treated him unfairly. It did not help that the main plotters of the Peacock coup appeared on the ABC's *Four Corners* to boast about their exploits, including the way they told lies to deny they were planning the coup. During the subsequent 1990 election campaign, Labor was able to successfully exploit the divisions. It took great pleasure in quoting the anti-Howard plotters—Wilson Tuckey, Peter Shack and Christopher Puplick—from the *Four Corners* program. Bob Hawke repeated over and over again: 'If you can't govern yourselves, you can't govern the country.' He managed to pull off an election victory at a time when home mortgage interest rates were 17 per cent and the economy was sliding into recession.

During my first term in Parliament I had regular contact with Howard. In 1993 after Hewson lost the 'unlosable' election, Howard stood again for the leadership. There were three candidates: Hewson,

Howard and Bruce Reid (the Member for Bendigo). Hewson defeated Howard. After the ballot Howard stood up, congratulated Hewson and thanked his supporters. Bruce Reid then stood up and congratulated Hewson. He too thanked his supporters for voting for him. Bruce had got only one vote. We assumed he had voted for himself. There was speculation as to why he was thanking his supporters!

By this stage Howard had fought the 1987 election, lost the leadership in 1989, been passed over for leadership in 1990 and been defeated for the leadership in 1993. In all of these contests I had been in Howard's corner. I voted for him in 1993 because I thought we needed someone with more experience, both of politics and of the Liberal Party, than Hewson could bring to the job.

I nominated for the Deputy Leader in the ballot. Others in it included Peter Reith, who was Hewson's deputy from 1990 to 1993, and Alexander Downer. Howard did not want to alienate anyone by supporting a particular candidate. There were seven in the field. The ballot was exhaustive and the last two candidates were Michael Wooldridge and me. Wooldridge won.

Reith's defeat caused enormous problems for Hewson. Reith rightly assumed that Hewson had not supported him. He had been Hewson's loyal Deputy Leader all through the Fightback! experience. When Fightback! went down Hewson survived and Reith got the axe. Reith was not going to take that lying down. 'I was born to plot!' he boasted. He used to say: 'I still have the field marshall's baton in my knapsack.' Once we were flying home together from a regional Cabinet meeting on a light plane which was bouncing around in the bad weather. Three or four Ministers were looking at each other with queasy expressions. Someone weakly joked that the plane might crash and our remains be lost. I said we were lucky to have Reith on the flight. If our bodies were burned beyond recognition the crash investigators would find a metal baton in the wreckage. This, they would know, indicated the remains of Peter Reith.

Reith was an able contributor in the party room and later in the Cabinet room. He had a view on most subjects and developed it with great force. He was one of the 'dries' who supported smaller Government and lower taxes. I found him a great ally. The press liked to portray a rivalry between us—sometimes describing us as P1 and P2. When Howard became Leader, he encouraged the press in this. He liked to have competition among those he saw as potential successors. I never felt Reith was a rival.

When Hewson's leadership began to fall apart in 1994 I supported Alexander Downer for the leadership. After I put a ticket together I rang Howard to tell him the news. It was a difficult conversation. He wanted to run for the leadership but it was plain he did not have the necessary support. I told him so. After consulting over the weekend he realised I was right. He decided to support Downer and me. The leadership had moved on. I thought his leadership aspirations were at an end. How wrong you can be!

The critical turning point was Peacock's announcement in September 1994 that he would leave Parliament. Almost immediately a very excited Howard was on the phone to me.

'Have you heard the news? Do you realise what this means?'

'There will be a by-election in Kooyong?'

'No! The veto's been lifted!'

Howard, who had never stopped dreaming and scheming about a return to the leadership, got a completely new lease of life. He was back in the game. He knew that the Downer leadership, however new, was already ebbing away. He relentlessly promoted his credentials to colleagues and the press. 'I have a telephone,' he told me, 'and I know how to use it.' He also prided himself on his long-term policy commitments, which he had pursued throughout his career. (One was to back the single-income family, which he thought was discriminated against because the mother had chosen to stay at home and raise children.) He described himself as a 'cricket tragic'. He was a Geoffrey Boycott, determined to stay at the crease, strong on defensive technique, more determined to graft singles than to take risks by trying to hit the ball to the boundary or over the fence. An insatiable consumer of press and radio commentary and suspicious of print journalists, he used talk-back radio to reach the public directly. His family was also fully engaged in the political project. Later, as Prime Minister, he would often quote his 'focus group of one at Kirribilli' who reported what was being said on Sydney radio when we were in Canberra.

During the 2007 campaign his youngest son came back from the United States to be an adviser. For my part I always tried to separate politics from family life. I did not discuss politics with my family. For me, on the rare occasions when I was home alone with them, they were always a refuge from politics.

Late on Monday 5 December 1994 John Howard and Ian McLachlan came to my office, the Deputy Leader's office in Parliament House. There was to be a party meeting the next morning, the last for the year. If there was going to be a spill against Downer, it had to happen then. After that meeting Parliament would break for the Christmas recess. There would be no further meetings until the end of January. I told them there was no chance of a spill. The party had no stomach to depose Downer, who had only been elected in May.

We had a long talk about Downer's troubles. Howard wanted to convince me, in the event of a spill, to stand aside so that he could take the leadership unopposed. He said: 'If Downer resigns and you stand aside, I only want one term. Then I would stand aside in the next term to let you have a go.' He had, he said, had a long career as Treasurer, but this would be his crowning achievement. The offer was completely unsolicited. I did not ask for it; Howard volunteered it. McLachlan was there to support Howard. He had come to try to convince me not to nominate for the leadership. His view was that I would have my opportunity after Howard. McLachlan was not there as a supporter of mine; he was there on behalf of Howard. As I predicted, there was no spill the next morning.

McLachlan later brought the meeting up in conversations. 'That is a very, very significant undertaking that Howard made to you.'

'You bet it is. You should make a note of it.'

'I will.'

As I write in Chapter 4, in December 1994, Howard, Downer and I talked over the situation in Adelaide and agreed that, failing an improvement in the popularity polls, Downer would stand down on Australia Day.

On Australia Day 1995 Downer stood down. I did not nominate for the leadership. There was no ballot, no division. Howard was elected unopposed. In March 1996 he led the Coalition to a landslide victory over the Keating Government. A big part of our success was due to the fact that Downer had stood down graciously, that I had stood aside and that Howard had become Leader by acclamation. It showed the electorate we had got our act together. Howard did not look, as he had in the past, like a divisive figure. He looked like a Leader who could unify the Liberal Party. He and Downer subsequently became friends and confidants, bonded in due course by the Iraq War, for which Downer was chief spokesman, and their opposition to a republic (despite Downer's youthful republicanism).

The first term of the Coalition Government ran from March 1996 to October 1998. If Howard had observed the undertaking he gave at the 'McLachlan meeting', he would have stood aside some time in the year 2000—halfway through the second term, before the election due at the end of 2001.

The year 2000 was an extremely difficult one. The Government had gone to the election of 3 October 1998 with a policy of introducing a 10 per cent GST as part of a major tax reform. This was the centre-piece. Our objective was to have the new tax system operating by the financial year beginning 1 July 2000, and if we missed this date we would have to postpone the start date to the next financial year, three or four months from the next election.

We did not have a majority in the Senate. We had to negotiate the legislation with minor parties. These negotiations were difficult and the points on which we were forced to concede made the implementation of the GST—which was always going to be hard—a nightmare. A change of leadership in the midst of the implementation of the GST was out of the question. Howard would have looked as if he was walking out on this very difficult tax reform. I had lived, breathed and obsessed about tax reform continuously from May 1997. No one else was up to speed on the policy. I wanted to bring it home; no one else could. To complicate it all, many commentators were predicting a recession in 2001. Consumers were spending strongly before the start-up date, hoping to beat any price rises. But demand would fall away in the quarters following the introduction.

As we were struggling with implementing the GST in 2000, Philip Clarke interviewed the Prime Minister on Radio 2BL on 26 July. Howard said:

> As far as my own political future is concerned, I have said before that if the party wants me to lead it to another election, which will be at the end of next year, I am happy to do so. After that, obviously one has to recognise I'll then be in my sixty-third or sixty-fourth year, and you start to ask yourself and that's fair enough. And nothing is forever. And I don't have the view that I am so indispensable and so important and so vital that, you know, the Liberal Party will be bereft without me. That is an arrogant view. By the same token, I have good, I have very good, health and I am applying myself to the job very effectively and I am enjoying it.

In this interview Howard volunteered the idea that he would retire after the next election, due in 2001—in our third term. I understood him now to be saying that, instead of serving one and a half terms, as he had indicated in the McLachlan meeting, he would run for re-election and serve two and a half terms before retiring mid-term to give his successor time to consolidate before the 2004 election. Weighed down with the GST, I was in no position to force the issue, nor did I want to. I thought we would be lucky to get through the GST and win the 2001 election. If we won it, I would take up the question of leadership with Howard midway through the next term.

On 30 January 2001 John Moore stood down as Minister for Defence. He resigned from Parliament, causing a by-election in the seat of Ryan. We were in a parlous position: the economy had turned down, petrol prices were rising and bedding down the GST was proving extremely difficult. Although Ryan was a safe seat we did not need a by-election anywhere.

Howard told the Cabinet: 'You have seen that I haven't given a commitment to serve through the next term. I do genuinely intend, when I get to sixty-four, to consider what I am going to do. I am enjoying the job and I feel fit. But I will give it a lot of thought when I turn sixty-four. Some people thought what I said [to Philip Clarke] was a good idea. Some might have thought it wasn't a good idea. But it has been done and I am not undoing it. It was nothing more or less than an honest statement and I am not going to lie on these issues. I am no good at that.'

Nobody else in the Cabinet at that time knew about our meeting in 1994. McLachlan had left Parliament at the 1998 election. I understood Howard to be saying that the transition had been pushed back to the middle of 2003.

The Government lost the Ryan by-election on 17 March 2001 (with a swing against it of 9.7 per cent) but we won the general election on 10 November 2001. Howard and I did not discuss the leadership again in 2002. His sixty-fourth birthday was in July. I did not want to push him before then. It would not be helpful. I thought he should be given time to consider his position carefully. On 25 February 2003 he told me that he had not yet made up his mind but he wanted to give his successor time to establish himself before the 2004 election. The time to go, he said, would be around December or January. If he made an announcement some time before he retired, he believed he would become a lame duck. His intention was to announce his retirement when he was ready and immediately call a party meeting to elect a successor. He said he had discussed the issue with his family and their view was mixed.

'I would prefer the announcement in July,' I said. 'This is the timetable you set and it is the one I have been working to.'

'If Iraq goes well, the party would see me as a vote-winner and want me to stay on,' Howard said. 'But if Iraq goes badly, it would want me to go.'

'This amounts to saying that, if things go bad, you will hand over the mess to your successor with only eleven months to go. The time to go is when you are on top.'

'This is not just about you. We have to consider our colleagues and the party. I was fifty-six when I became Prime Minister and you are only forty-six.'

'But you engaged in a lot of work undermining Peacock. I have been very loyal to you. One of the reasons why the party is doing so well is that there is no one working against you and no undermining.'

A few months later, on 2 June 2003, Howard invited me around to his office. There had been speculation in the media that he would announce his retirement to the assembled delegates at the Federal Convention of the Liberal Party on 8 June in Canberra. He told me that he did not intend, and never had intended, to make an announcement on his future at the Federal Convention. He had given this matter a lot of thought, he said. 'It may not suit you personally, but I am still fit. I am still interested in the job. The feeling of our colleagues is that I should stay on. They think I represent the best chance of our winning at the next election.' He then read a form of words which he proposed to give out before the convention. He did not want to be a prisoner of his birthday, he said. 'I wish I had never made that statement about my sixty-fourth birthday.'

I told him: 'Now is the time to do the transition—when we are strong. We will get another term and set ourselves up for another. Labor will be stronger in the election of 2007 because they will get rid of both Kim Beazley and Simon Crean and find a new Leader.' Howard thought Beazley was Labor's best bet. He expected to run against him in the 2004 election, but if things went, as he put it, 'duck-shaped', he could still go before the election, he said. His situation, he said, was totally different from that of Hawke, who had been behind in the polls when Keating replaced him.

'One of the reasons why Hawke was behind in the polls,' I said, 'was that Keating was actively undermining him. I have never done that to you. Our colleagues would always prefer the status quo because that would mean they would not have to make a hard decision. I am putting my argument to you on the basis of what is in the long-term interests of the party. I am not putting it to you on the basis of my own interests, although naturally I am interested. I believe it is in the long-term interests of the party that there be a new leadership in the Liberal Party. It will allow us to fight and win the 2004 election.' He said that when he had made his statement about considering his position on his sixty-fourth birthday, he had been thinking of the 2001 election, not the 2004 election.

The next day he issued a press statement in the words he had read to me: 'I have given a lot of thought to my future. The Liberal Party has been very loyal and generous to me. I will always put it first. While ever it remains in the party's best interests and my colleagues want me to I would be honoured to continue as Leader.'

This provoked pandemonium in the press gallery. Howard refused to do interviews. Swarms of journalists wanted my response. I thought the best thing to do was to hold an 'all-in' press conference. If I had tried to speak to them one by one, it would have taken me a month. I went to the Blue Room and said: 'I will continue to serve the party as Deputy Leader and the country as Treasurer.' I then invited questions. The first came from Matt Price: 'Were you disappointed?'

'Well, it wasn't my happiest day.'

This was an understatement. Some of the media reported that I was sulking. Journalists always see winners as 'triumphant' and losers as 'sulking'.

Michelle Grattan wanted more. 'When did Mr Howard tell you of this decision?'

'Yesterday.'

'How?'

'In words.'

'How did you receive them?'

'Words which I heard through my ears.'

'Paint the picture.'

'The sun had risen, there was rain coming down, it was in words and it was heard through my ears. It was comprehended by my brain.'

The final question was: 'Do you think that your relationship with the Prime Minister will enter a new phase from now on?'

'Look, we have worked together competently and professionally. I think it has been a very big part of the success of the Government. I think it has given the Government a lot of stability and I think the strong economic management has been the foundation for everything else that the Government has done. I continue to want to work competently and professionally towards the objectives of good Government in Australia. I want to see Australia be everything it can possibly be. I want to see it prosperous and strong and secure and tolerant. Thanks very much.'

Some of the journalists would have liked me to resign as Treasurer. They would have been delighted if I had issued a leadership challenge. But I did not contemplate this. By resigning I would have looked as if I could not handle a turn of events that did not go my way. A few reversals in a career are not a tragedy. The party room would not vote Howard out unless things got much worse. The Liberal Party has never voted out an incumbent Prime Minister unless you include John Gorton, who voted himself out after a period of enormous destabilisation, principally from Malcolm Fraser. If I copped this on the chin and redoubled my efforts to help win the 2004 election, I thought my colleagues would recognise my loyalty to the party in the next term.

One Monday night a few weeks later Joe Hockey invited me around for drinks in his ministerial office. Hockey is always good company. He suffered from the fact that he was seen as being on the left of the New South Wales Liberal Party at a time when Howard and the right were in the ascendancy. This put him on the wrong side of issues such as the republic. He began a weekly appearance with Kevin Rudd on Channel 7's *Sunrise* program, which Rudd skilfully used to boost his profile. The affable Hockey may have helped Rudd's rise by appearing to make him more human, less ambitious and driven. I opened Hockey's campaign in the 2007 election. He could generate enormous support from friends and donors. He had performed well as a Minister. He will be among the next generation of Liberal leaders, along with Christopher Pyne and Tony Smith.

Hockey had Ross Cameron, Christopher Pyne and Tony Abbott in his office. They had been out to dinner together. Howard loyalist Abbott made a point of telling me how much the party had respected the decision I had made. It was, he said, the right thing to do. 'If we win the next election Howard will stand down,' he said.

'I expected him to stand down after the last one, Tony. How do you know he won't try to go again if he wins the election?'

'No, mate, this is his last election. That's clear. He'll do what's right for the party.'

'And if he tries to go again? Will the party tell him to go?'

'He won't need to be told. He'll do the right thing.'

'And if he doesn't?'

'A few of us will go and see him. He'll do the right thing.'

'Are you prepared to go and see him?'

'If necessary, but it won't come to that.'

As it turned out Beazley did not lead Labor to the 2004 election. Labor had a new experiment—Mark Latham—who proved of great assistance to the Coalition in the 2004 election. In April 2005, well after the election, I addressed the Australia–New Zealand Leadership Forum at Government House in Melbourne. The subject was 'Trans-Tasman Economic Cooperation'. I left the forum to head off to a Docklands restaurant, Livebait, for a dinner with four journalists from the *Age*: Jason Koutsoukis, Michael Gordon, Shaun Carney and Misha Schubert. The idea was to try to improve relations with a paper that was highly critical of the Government. On the way to the restaurant I took a telephone call from Dennis Shanahan, political editor of the *Australian* and a Howard intimate. Two News Limited journalists, Steve Lewis and Malcolm Farr, had, Shanahan told me, interviewed Howard in Athens. They had asked him about the next election, due in 2007. (By now Beazley had returned to the Labor leadership after the 2004 election.) Howard said he had beaten Beazley twice in the past. When asked if he could beat him a third time, he shot back: 'Yes, I would hope to try.'

Shanahan told me that this would be a front-page splash in the *Australian* the following day. It would report that Howard had declared that he would stay for yet another election, in 2007. The next day's headline was 'Howard Issues Challenge to Deputy'. Shanahan wrote: 'It's on. The Liberal leadership challenge has begun. But it is not Peter Costello challenging John Howard. Rather it is John Howard fronting up to Peter Costello.' The media labelled Howard's statement the 'Athens Declaration'.

Soon after this conversation, and while I was in the Docklands restaurant, Howard rang me from Athens. I left the table to take the call on my mobile. I told Howard I could not understand why he had raised this matter. I had been expecting a handover the following year.

He said that he had not changed his position, that he did not want to have a ballot over the leadership and that the party did not want to deal with the matter now. I told him that the press was going to make his interview a big story. He said he had not made any declaration that he was running for another term and that he should have given a different answer to the question.

Back at the table the journalists knew I had taken a call about something important. I told them it was Howard, that the papers were running a big story the next day but that Howard has assured me there was nothing in it. The dinner was an off-the-record affair, but when it finished around 10 p.m. Jason Koutsoukis went to the *Age* office and gave the paper the story that Howard had called me in the restaurant. The *Age* was able to splash a version of it as a spoiler the next day. Since it was off the record Koutsoukis should not have done it. None of the other journalists did. Koutsoukis later sent me a bottle of French wine to apologise.

The leadership issue was now raging again. I had already agreed to do the weekend television interviews. I could not cancel them but I knew they would be difficult. I always felt uncomfortable answering questions about the leadership. I did not want to disclose what had passed between Howard and me in 1994 and I did not want to say anything to deny it. I would try to evade questions about a handover but my answers ended up looking just that—evasive. Every time I talked about the leadership it looked as if that was the focus of my attention when in fact I was working night and day on being Treasurer. I was not trying to undermine the Leader and did not want to be seen in that way.

Howard was an expert at manoeuvring over the leadership. He had had a great deal of experience in his fights with Andrew Peacock. He naturally took advantage of the fact that, in the Liberal Party, the cult of leadership is very strong. The incumbent, particularly if he is the Prime Minister, holds all the aces.

When Howard returned to Australia we had a meeting in Sydney on 2 May 2005. He told me that the party would want a change before the next election: 'We had a talk about this before the last election. I made that clear then that I do not want a ballot. Why do you think

I went to the last election without giving a commitment to serve the full term?' We agreed the new Leader would need time. His view was that it should be somewhere between twelve and fifteen months before an election. I told him a new Leader would need eighteen months to two years. That would mean between Christmas and the first half of 2006.

I set out my views in my interview with *Meet the Press* on Channel 10 on Sunday 1 May 2005. (The interview had been arranged some weeks earlier—to discuss the forthcoming May Budget.) Paul Bongiorno chaired the panel. The guest journalists were Michelle Grattan of the *Age* and Glenn Milne of the *Australian*. My idea was to dampen speculation about the leadership. I began by emphasising that Howard had made it clear he was not 'throwing down the gauntlet'. It was in the interests of the Liberal Party that there be a smooth transition in leadership without a destabilising ballot.

Paul Bongiorno said: 'Mr Howard seems to have had form on this trip.' (He screened Howard's response to the recent election of 78-year-old Pope Benedict XVI. Howard had said: 'I think patience is a great virtue, not only in politics and the church but also in personal life.') Bongiorno continued: 'The journalists present clearly thought that was a message for you. Are you patient?'

I said I did not think the comment was about me and again tried to talk about the Budget. Grattan took up the leadership issue: 'Why don't you just go to John Howard tomorrow and say: "John, this is causing a lot of problems. What are your intentions?"'

That was precisely what I intended to do the next day. But to say so would have unleashed a frenzy in the press gallery. I was doing everything I could to hose down the story. I referred to Howard's formula that he would continue to serve as Leader for as long as the party wanted him to. The Prime Minister had made his position clear. 'He has a formulation. You know what that formulation is.'

Grattan's retort was: 'But Mr Costello, this is nonsense. His formulation is lack of clarity. That is the whole point.'

'Well, Michelle, you'll have to take that up with him.'

'Why don't you take it up with him?'

Later Milne pursued the theme further: 'Let me indulge myself with one more hypothetical. I've listened to Paul [Bongiorno] ask you a question about ruling out a challenge. I've listened to Michelle ask you a question about ruling out a challenge. For a third time, will you rule out any challenge to John Howard this term?'

'Glenn, you're obviously trying for a headline. The headline you ought to write out of what I am saying is "Treasurer Focusses on the Issues at Hand and Refuses to Add to Speculation on Anything". That ought to be the headline. If anybody puts another headline on Monday's papers, it's a misrepresentation.'

Grattan also asked me about any feedback I might have had. I said that I told anyone and everyone who got in touch with me that I was getting on with the Budget. During this period there were members who contacted me to tell me they wanted Howard out and a change of leadership. I had no doubt there were members wanting Howard to stay who would also have contacted him. No one wanting him to stay contacted me. No one wanting him to go would have contacted him. The only people who spoke on camera would be those wanting him to stay. It is a low-risk operation to endorse the existing Leader.

Members elected in 1996 tended to be in the latter camp. Politicians elected for the first time in a big swing naturally identify with the Leader who achieved that swing. This is the case in every Parliament. The unexpectedly large swing in 1996 had brought in a number of people who had been pre-selected in seats we did not expect to win. The seats were either marginal or held by Labor. They had only ever known one Leader, John Howard. They had no experience of the Liberal Party under a different leadership. For many of them the Liberal Party was the Howard Party.

Some had only recently joined the Liberal Party before they were pre-selected for the 1996 election. An example is Jackie Kelly, who unexpectedly won the seat of Lindsay in western Sydney. Under the Constitution a person cannot nominate for election if he or she holds an 'office of profit under the Crown'. As an officer of the RAAF she should have stood down before nominating. She was probably loath to stand down given that she was not expected to win. She did so some weeks later. When the High Court invalidated her election, a by-election was called. She was now qualified to nominate and won the seat again with a larger margin. Jackie became a great Howard favourite. She was always good for a colourful quote. On 16 May 2000 she told the *Daily Telegraph* in Sydney that she did not want Howard to retire: 'I am happy for him to go until he is eighty or 100.' Later that month the *Weekend Australian* quoted her saying that she might stand down in Lindsay if Howard retired. As it happened Howard decided he would stay and she stood down from her seat anyway. (Many of the class of 1996 stood down in the 2007 election and several of the others lost their seats.)

Early in July 2006 I was standing in a field in a jungle plantation in the Solomon Islands. We had just finished the Pacific Forum Finance Ministers' Conference in Honiara. I was discussing Australian aid to the Solomons with a group of journalists. Malcolm Farr of the *Daily Telegraph*—the journalist who, with Steve Lewis, had elicited the 'Athens Declaration' in April—suddenly interjected. He wasn't in the slightest interested in aid to the Solomons: 'Can I just ask you just a plain simple question? Is there an understanding between you and Mr Howard as to his departure?'

I tried, for as long as I could, to parry the questioning with non-answers. This is how the 'conference' developed:

COSTELLO: Look, these things have worked in the interests of the Australian people and the Liberal Party and the people concerned, and there is no point in speculating on it.

FARR: That sounds a little bit like a Liberal Party policy of new paternalism. I mean, don't voters have a right to know what is going on? If you are saying it will work in their interests, don't they have a right to know what the plan is?

COSTELLO: Well, voters get the right to vote, that is the critical thing, and they will get the right to vote on who they want to run the country.

FARR: And you won't be telling them any time soon whether there will be a leadership transition before the next election?

COSTELLO: And they will have plenty of information at the time of the election.

JOURNALIST: The answer to Malcolm's question was a 'No,' though, was it?

COSTELLO: I can't remember the question.

JOURNALIST: Is there an understanding …

COSTELLO: The answer to Malcolm's question was my answer to Malcolm's question.

FARR: So there is no Kirribilli Agreement?

COSTELLO: So don't speculate. I am not going to speculate on these things.

FARR: But there is [*sic*] no secret arrangements or secret deals that we are not aware of; there has been no arrangement, no deal?

COSTELLO: For I think about the fifth time, I am not going to speculate on these things and I am certainly not going to speculate on these things in the jungles of the Solomon Islands.

FARR: Why not?

On the following Saturday, 8 July 2006, back in Melbourne, my political adviser, David Alexander, rang to say that Milne intended to publish a story in the *Sunday Telegraph* on the McLachlan meeting of 1994. This was the call I had been dreading.

Over the years there had been speculation about this agreement, deal, arrangement or whatever. Milne was the first journalist to discover that McLachlan had been a witness. I tried to get out of him who had given him this information. He said that he had it from a senior businessman. Milne had contacted McLachlan, who did not deny the story. He intended to run it the next day. Out of courtesy, he said, he was putting it to me. I told him that I would not confirm it.

For me this story was a disaster. The events had taken place twelve years before and plainly the undertaking had not been honoured. If the story were to come out now, it would look as if I was demanding the leadership on this basis. Howard would easily turn that to his advantage. He would say I was taking the decision out of the hands of the party room and treating the members with disrespect. This was not my position at all. I believed that a transition was in the interests of the Liberal Party and would set us up with the best chance of winning the 2007 election. Just as an orderly transition from Downer to Howard had ushered in the return of the Coalition and four election victories, an orderly transition and renewal of the party could set us up for 2007 and the election after that. I also knew that the very fact that this was Milne's story would be used to insinuate that I was its source, since I had been friendly with Milne over the years. I was not going to confirm the story, but I could not deny it.

Later that day McLachlan rang me and confirmed that Milne had put the story to him and that he had not denied it. He had been thinking about it all day, he said, and had come to the conclusion that he should tell the truth. 'It won't help me,' I told him. 'This will not help me in the slightest.' By this stage I knew the story would run anyway. There was no hope of stopping it. I asked McLachlan how many people he had told about the undertaking. He said he had told numbers of people. One of those in the know was Nick Minchin.

McLachlan had recorded the undertaking between Howard and me on a note that he kept in his wallet. I found out later that he had taken the note out of his wallet and read it to a group of former Ministers of the Howard Government who met together annually for lunch under the name 'South Wing'. The South Wing of Parliament House is the ministerial wing of the complex. People at this lunch included Tim Fischer and Alex Somlyay. It was held at the Union Club in Sydney. When the note became public Somlyay confirmed on radio that McLachlan had shown it to him. I now realised how many people knew of the note. The mystery was not that this had got out but that it had been kept confidential for so long.

McLachlan told me he had lived with it for years and he now thought the public should know the truth. He told me that Howard had also told the South Australian businessman Bob Day, a former

President of the Housing Industry Association, about his undertaking to serve one-and-a-half terms and to hand over the leadership.

Apparently Howard had confided in Day at the fundraising dinner at the Adelaide Hilton on 13 December 1994—the night we settled the transition from Downer to Howard in later discussions at the Adelaide Club (which I describe in Chapter 4). According to Day's note of the conversation Howard said: 'This is how it will go. I will take over leadership and if we win the next election then midway through our second term I will step aside and hand over to Peter Costello.'

In 2003 Day expressed frustration to McLachlan that Howard had not stood down when he had said he would. McLachlan thereby became aware that Howard had disclosed the undertaking to Day in 1994.

McLachlan told me he had gone to Howard when he resigned from Parliament in 1998 and told him: 'I'm going. You have one thing to do in the next term. You ought to give Peter a go.' That had not happened before the 2001 election. It had not happened before the 2004 election. He had told me previously that he was carrying this note around in his wallet, but I had never asked to see it or to know precisely what was written in it. I had never read it. I knew what had happened in the meeting and I did not need a note to refresh my memory. I am sure it was the same with Howard. He knew what he had said. He never denied it. His position was that, whatever he had said, it did not amount to a 'deal'. It is a sterile argument whether there was an undertaking, an understanding, an arrangement, an agreement or a deal. What was said was said. There is *no* dispute about it. People can interpret it for themselves.

I did not try to enforce Howard's undertaking. My view was always that there should be an orderly transition in the interests of the Liberal Party and the country. It should have happened before the 2004 election but when that did not occur it was even more important before the 2007 election. If the note had any significance, it showed that, rather than agitating for the leadership, I had been extraordinarily patient. I ended the conversation by telling McLachlan: 'You do what you think is right.'

Milne's story was sensational. Some reporters concluded that I must have given it to him. I did not. He picked it up by old-fashioned journalistic work. He had told me his original source was not McLachlan but a businessman in whom McLachlan had confided. Milne has never disclosed the source. One of the people who knew was the prominent businessman Robert Champion de Crespigny.

Inevitably, I was deluged with media inquiries on the Sunday. I made no statement. I made no statement on the Monday either, until I heard Howard had done an interview at the Sydney Opera House in which he had said: 'The situation is very simple. There was no deal made. There were lots of discussions at that time, including one in which Mr McLachlan was present. That did not involve the conclusion of a deal.'

The press took this to mean he was denying McLachlan's account. McLachlan, for better or worse, had told the truth. He should not have had his honesty questioned. The press was now in a fever. I had been the other person there: what did I have to say? The only way to deal with this matter was to call a press conference and take all questions.

I did this on Monday 10 July 2006. I confirmed what had happened. The journalists wanted to know whether this meant that Howard had lied. I was determined not to make any allegations at all against Howard, and I did not. I repeated what had been said at the meeting. There was no other course. It is not real life to pretend that you could say nothing. Journalists were camped outside my home and office. You either confirm the truth or attempt to deny it. I could not deny it. It had happened. I tried to emphasise the fact that it had not, and would not, stop me working for the Government and the Australian people.

COSTELLO: Well, there has been a lot in the papers the last couple of days, and I have never spoken about these events before, but since others have, the public is entitled to know the full truth. What happened was that Mr McLachlan and Mr Howard sought a meeting with me. The meeting took place on the 5th of December 1994. There were only three of us there. Mr Howard asked me not to nominate for the Liberal

Party leadership because he did not want a vote in the party room. He told me that he intended to do one and a half terms as Prime Minister and then would hand over. I did not seek that undertaking; he volunteered it and I took him at his word. Obviously that did not happen. I didn't stand on my digs; I continued to work for the Government to the best of my ability in the interests of the Australian public. And whilst this country can be improved, whilst there are still things to be done to make it better, I intend to give it every ounce of energy that I have. I did not ask Mr McLachlan to relate these matters but his account is entirely accurate.

JOURNALIST: Was there any equivocation in that deal at all?

COSTELLO: That was precisely what happened. They are the full facts of what happened. I have told you entirely what happened.

JOURNALIST: Was it a suggestion or a deal?

COSTELLO: I have told you the full details of what happened.

JOURNALIST: So there was no wriggle room at all for Mr Howard?

COSTELLO: That is what happened. I have a very clear recollection of the event. You can interpret them as you like but that is the full truth of what happened … and I can't say any more. That is precisely what happened. The public is entitled to know the full truth and that is what happened.

JOURNALIST: Will this create open hostility between you and the Prime Minister?

COSTELLO: No, it is not a matter of that. I did not raise these matters. I have been besieged by journalists that want to know what happened. There were three of us. All three of us have now given our recollections of what happened.

As far as I am concerned that is what happened. And as I said, what happened was that I went on working for the Government and the Australian people—that is why I have never spoken about that from that day to this. I have never spoken about this to anybody and I wouldn't have if Mr McLachlan and Mr Howard hadn't already got on the public record in relation to this matter.

JOURNALIST: Has the Prime Minister lied?

COSTELLO: Look, I am telling you what happened. I am not making any allegations against anybody. I am telling you what happened and, look, you can interpret whatever you like; that is what happened and people are entitled to know what happened and so I will tell you what happened. As I said, I thought the responsible thing to do was to work for the Australian people and the Government and that is what I am doing … working for the Australian people, and I will continue to work for the Australian people as part of the Government. Whilst there are things that can be done to improve Australia, I intend to dedicate myself to doing them.

JOURNALIST: Does that include serving as Treasurer, under Mr Howard, to the next election?

COSTELLO: Well … that is the question I already answered for you, which is this: whilst there are things to be done to improve Australia and whilst I can serve the Australian people, I will continue to do it.

JOURNALIST: Will you serve as Prime Minister before the next election?

COSTELLO: I have already answered my intention. I will continue to serve the Australian people and whilst there are things to be done that can make the Australian nation stronger and better and more prosperous and be the proud country that I want it to be, I will continue to do that. Thank you.

The next day the Cabinet met in Sydney. There was mayhem on Phillip Street outside the building where the Cabinet met. I had to push through a huge media pack. The press was spoiling for a fight. Earlier that morning Howard had said: 'Now all of these things did happen twelve years ago and in the end, I repeat what I said yesterday, that the leadership of the Liberal Party is not my plaything. It's not Mr Costello's plaything. It is the unique gift of the 100 men and women of the federal parliamentary Liberal Party and any member of the parliamentary Liberal Party who forgets that is indulging in hubris and arrogance.'

This was a bit rich. As already stated, I had not sought an undertaking about the leadership in 1994; he had given it freely. The whole idea in 1994 was to prevent a divisive contest going to the 100 men and women of the parliamentary Liberal Party. Howard had not described it as 'hubris and arrogance' then. He had not described an orderly transition as treating the leadership as a 'plaything'. It had been a sensible arrangement to allow him to become Leader unopposed and subsequently Prime Minister.

I knew the story was not going to help me. But I was not prepared to suffer both a damaging story and aspersions on my integrity. I was not going to deny the truth or to turn and twist trying to evade it. I said to the assembled press: 'My parents always told me: If you have done nothing wrong you have got nothing to fear by telling the truth.' I had done nothing wrong. I had not leaked the story. I told the truth.

I had a meeting with Howard after the Cabinet meeting on 11 July. The Howard office had been scouring the record to find instances when I had denied there was ever a deal. They were feeding this material to journalists—quotes from newspapers, interviews, television footage, radio broadcasts over the past twelve years. But they could not find any killer quote. They could not challenge my integrity. I was telling the truth. Until 10 July 2006, whenever questions touched on the subject I had taken pains to avoid answering them and had tried to bat away interest in the subject. I had wanted to protect Howard and the party.

I reminded Howard that I had been very patient and that, far from disclosing the agreement or insisting that he adhere to it, I had continued working for him and for the party. He reminded me that there had been lots of discussions. 'I have no doubt I was giving you the impression I wouldn't stay long. But I didn't think we would be as successful as we have been.' He asked me who Milne's businessman was. I told him I did not know. I reminded him that I had not asked for his undertaking, that he had offered it. I reserved my right to ensure that the historical record was accurate. Tony Abbott rang me two days after the Cabinet meeting to tell me that he was a great supporter of both Howard and me and that Howard had told him that I was entitled to feel a bit thwarted.

In the following week the Whips, on behalf of Howard, began working on lists of numbers in case there was a leadership ballot. I did a careful analysis of the Liberal Party room myself. My assessment was that a little more than a third of the 110 members in the party room would vote for a change in leadership, maybe a few more. Those solidly against change were mostly the class of 1996. They made up more than a quarter of the party room. I could have sought a party room ballot, but my assessment was that Howard had a majority. If I challenged him and lost, I would have to go to the backbench, which would weaken the Government. Some counselled that I *should* weaken the Government because eventually that would lead to a second spill and a leadership change. But I did not want to weaken the Government eighteen months out from the election. I wanted our party to retain Government. After twelve years of loyal service to the party as its longest serving Deputy Leader, it was not my intention to try to tear it down. Some called it a weakness; I saw it as loyalty. During the period in which I was Deputy Leader we had not lost an election. I always believed the best hope of renewing the Liberal Party would be a sensible, mature transition—like the one I had organised for Howard in 1994 which set up the party for the 1996 election. Ten years later I wanted to do the same again.

On Sunday night, 30 July 2006, Howard rang me at home to tell me that he was going to announce that he would continue as Leader to the next election. I told him that this was the wrong decision and that he would find it extraordinarily hard to win a fifth term in 2007. Nobody would believe that he would serve out a full term if he was re-elected at the age of sixty-eight. Labor was claiming we had no long-term agenda because Howard, our Leader, had no long-term plans to stay. The party would be weakened by the fact that everyone would expect the Leader to stand down after the election. The best possible thing to do would be to allow a smooth transition before the election.

I had already told Howard this at our meeting on 11 July. On both occasions I spoke to him directly and clearly so that there could be no misunderstanding. I never raised my voice. I was not emotional. I appealed to reason. The principal point was that he was in danger of leading the party to defeat in 2007, which would be bad for it, bad for Australia and bad for him. He then read me a letter which he was circulating the next day to all colleagues:

> In recent weeks I have taken a variety of soundings within the parliamentary party to ascertain its feelings on the leadership issue.
>
> My position has been that I would remain Leader of the Liberal Party for so long as that was the party's wish, and that it was in the party's best interests that I did so.
>
> My soundings tell me that the strong view of the party is that the current leadership team, with me as Leader and Peter Costello as Deputy Leader, should remain in place through to the next election.
>
> My purpose in writing is to inform you, in advance of a public announcement, that I will commit to leading the party to the next election. I remain enthusiastic and keen to ensure that the Coalition achieves a fifth electoral victory. I spoke to Peter Costello yesterday to advise him of my feelings.
>
> Leadership of the party is a great honour, of which I remain profoundly conscious. It is, moreover, the unique gift of the party room.
>
> Just as the party now wants me to continue as Leader I accept that it has a perfect right to change its mind if it judges that to be to the party's benefit. If that were to occur, I would not ignore the party's shift in sentiment.
>
> Please believe me when I say that the next election will be hard to win. We must, therefore, go to it with our best people in the right places.

A crucial element will be Peter Costello's contribution, not only as Deputy Leader but also as Treasurer, where his work over the past decade has been so important to our success.

I have thought it desirable to resolve my position regarding the leadership in advance of Parliament returning on the 8th of August. Hence this letter ...

I carefully considered his announcement and his appeal to me to remain as Deputy Leader and Treasurer. I also considered what would happen if I refused to accept his decision. The instability might lead to change or it might not. It would certainly make a tough election even harder. If Howard were forced to go against his will, he would not make it easy for his successor. He would not go quietly. With Howard out and about, publicly justifying his position, any successor would be fighting on two fronts in the campaign.

The next day I rang Howard to tell him I would stay on. I put out this statement:

John Howard informed me last night that he intends to fight the next election. I am glad that the issue has now been settled. It allows us all to plan accordingly.

I have spoken to many members of the public and colleagues and it is clear that most people do not support a leadership transition at the current time.

I am committed to serving in the Parliament for the long haul. I am committed to the long-term interests of the Liberal Party and the nation.

The Government has had significant political achievements but there are enormous political challenges ahead. It is clear to me that the party wants me to continue to work, as I have in the past, with all of my energy as Deputy Leader and Treasurer.

As Deputy Leader and Treasurer I will work for the re-election of the Coalition Government, for the election of all our candidates and for the re-election of John Howard as Prime Minister.

Working as Treasurer is a tremendous honour and responsibility. We face many economic challenges.

Australia is a one-trillion-dollar economy. We need disciplined and responsible decisions to build for our future.

I look forward to fighting the next election with total energy and commitment and beyond that to work to address the nation's great challenges for the next decade and beyond.

After the 2007 election some suggested that John Howard had intended to step down in December 2006. Of course, if he had wanted to, he could have done so. He could have stood down on any day he chose. But if, at any time, he was intending to stand down in December 2006, he never communicated that to me. If he had intended to do that I would have expected him to tell me. He knew if he stood down I would be elected Leader. The fact that he told me no such thing tells me he did not intend to go. He did not want to lock himself into any timetable for departure.

By December 2006 Labor had a new Leader, Kevin Rudd. Howard would not have stood down then because he would have taken the same view that he took later, during the week of APEC, that he could not be seen to run from a fight. This was his stated view, even after the Cabinet concluded he should go in September 2007.

Although Howard had at various times suggested he might go— in 1994 at the McLachlan meeting, in 2000 when he spoke about his sixty-fourth birthday, in 2003 in the lead-up to his birthday, in the aftermath of the 'Athens Declaration', during the Quay West debates in September 2007—the fact remained that when it came to the crunch he always decided against it. There was always a reason why he had to stay. Even during the 2007 election he said he would have to stay in the fifth term to put a new preamble in the Constitution and to campaign for it in a referendum.

There is another overriding reason why Howard would not have gone in December 2006. By that stage APEC was well advanced. The program was prepared—the entertainment and the outfits (always a big thing at APEC meetings) had been chosen. Mrs Howard was involved. The summit was to take place in Howard's home town, Sydney, where he had established his official residence at Kirribilli House. It would be the largest diplomatic event ever held in Australia. President Bush, President Hu Jintao of China, President Putin of Russia and the leaders of seventeen other nations were due to attend. Neither John nor Janette Howard would want this high-level summit to be hosted by anyone else in their city at their Kirribilli residence.

Before the APEC summit started, Howard rang me from Sydney. (I was in Canberra to do a press conference on the June quarter National Accounts.) 'We have two sets of numbers today,' he said, 'one good and one catastrophic.' The good one was the national accounts showing that the economy had grown 0.9 per cent in the June quarter and 4.3 per cent through the year. The bad one was the Newspoll showing that Labor had opened up an 18-point lead on the two-party preferred vote. Rudd had also widened his margin over Howard as preferred Prime Minister. Normally an incumbent Prime Minister leads as preferred Prime Minister because he carries the prestige of the job. In the lead-up to the 1996 election, Keating was the preferred Prime Minister even though the Coalition won. There were no reassuring words that I could think of. It was just another poll in a long line of polls that showed we were going to lose. In my view the public had made up its mind that it wanted a change of leadership. At my press conference on the national accounts I was soon asked: 'Treasurer, can you explain why these strong economic figures are not translating into strong support for the Government in the opinion polls?'

That afternoon I greeted President Hu at a full ceremonial welcome in Canberra. I then flew to Sydney. Shortly after I arrived at my hotel, Alexander Downer rang to say he had spoken with Howard and had told him he could not win the election. The only hope was a change in leadership. According to Downer, Howard had responded that if that was the view of his senior colleagues, they should tell him. Downer told me he was going to canvass their views.

On Wednesday morning senior Ministers met with US President George Bush at the Commonwealth Offices in Phillip Street, Sydney. This was to be the first of three meetings with the leaders of the largest APEC countries. On each occasion there would be one-on-one talks between Howard and the visiting leader. They would then come into the Cabinet room, where three or four senior Ministers from each side would join the discussion. On the Wednesday we met President Bush, Thursday President Hu, Friday President Putin. The meetings were followed up each day with a meal: on Wednesday a private dinner with President Bush at Kirribilli, on Thursday a public lunch at the Sofitel for President Hu, on Friday a public lunch for President Putin at the Opera House.

On the Wednesday, after I had finished my meeting with Bush, Tony Abbott rang to tell me that Janet Albrechtsen, a long-time pro-Howard journalist, was going to write a 'Howard Must Go' column in the *Australian*. Abbott had tried to persuade her not to write it. He had also consulted Nick Minchin, who told him that he had been promoting a leadership change for eighteen months but he was now of the view that it was too late. Abbott thought a change might give us a chance to win. He asked me whether I was prepared to take the leadership. I told him it should have been done in the middle of 2006. He asked me what my attitude would be if Howard left voluntarily: Would I accept the leadership at such a late stage? I said that, in the unlikely event of that happening, I would do my best by the party and try to win the election. 'Of course I will take the leadership', I told him.

That evening the Prime Minister, Deputy Prime Minister Mark Vaile, Defence Minister Brendan Nelson and I had a private dinner with President Bush at Kirribilli House. The President was in good form. We discussed world affairs, particularly al-Qaeda, Iraq and Iran. We also talked about the developing sub-prime crisis in the United States. There we were, discussing the state of the world, when behind the scenes Howard was canvassing his departure. He said nothing about it to me.

The next morning we met with President Hu. At the lunch afterwards Kevin Rudd upstaged Howard by delivering his speech in Mandarin. Howard was subdued. He had other things on his mind. That afternoon a business forum began at the Sydney Opera House. Then another dinner and another business reception at the Overseas Passenger Terminal at Circular Quay. At the dinner Downer rounded up the other Ministers present (apart from me) and asked them to go back to his hotel when the dinner finished. He did not tell me he was organising this meeting.

He assembled Ruddock, Nelson, Hockey and Macfarlane, along with Julie Bishop, Malcolm Turnbull, Kevin Andrews and Chris Ellison, in his apartment at the Quay West hotel to discuss the leadership. Next morning, four of them rang me to report the essence of the conversation—that the Coalition was likely to lose the election under Howard and that it would be best for him to go. Downer was to tell Howard their view. There were different levels of enthusiasm for a change. Several were eager, believing it would give us the chance of winning; some were more pessimistic and thought that at best it would minimise losses. No one was against it. All agreed that a 'no change' scenario meant defeat because the public had stopped listening to Howard. Downer told me that day that Howard might call to say: 'It's yours, mate.'

On Friday, Bush gave an address at the Opera House, which the senior Ministers attended. Then we went back to Phillip Street for the meeting with President Putin. There we were again—Howard, Downer, Putin and me. Yet the Cabinet had decided the night before to ask the Prime Minster to go. The talks went on as if nothing had happened. We were in parallel universes—face-to-face meetings with world leaders and meetings at night to canvass Howard's departure. For four days I saw Howard several times a day. He never raised the issue with me. Downer had become the link between Howard and his colleagues. I delivered a speech on the regional economy at the Opera House that afternoon. Then I went home. That night Downer went to Kirribilli House to report to Howard that his Cabinet wanted him to go.

On Saturday 8 September, Downer rang to tell me that the Prime Minister was digging in. According to Downer, although Howard had previously promised to stay only as long as the party wanted him, he was now saying he would stay unless the party told him to go. He wanted the party to take responsibility for any change. He would not voluntarily stand down. This would look bad for him and his family. Downer told me that Janette Howard was present when he met Howard at Kirribilli House to report back on his soundings of the view inside Cabinet.

It was clear that Howard would not relinquish the leadership voluntarily. Over the years we had discussed his possible exit on many occassions but it had never come to anything. I was surprised that he had raised it now, because it was bound to leak. You cannot hold a meeting of nine Cabinet Ministers to discuss whether the Prime Minister should go and then expect it not to leak. By now I had received calls from Ministers who were not even there. Mal Brough had not been at the Quay West meeting but he called me on the week-end to discuss it. He knew all about it. Others called me on the Saturday. Some were sure Howard would go. They included Turnbull, who was strongly agitating for it. Some wanted to talk about port-folios they would have in a reshuffle. Others wanted to talk about the policy changes I would put in place for the election. Downer, who had been deputed to negotiate with Howard, went cold once Howard began to dig in. Abbott, who had been in favour of the change on the Wednesday afternoon, changed his mind on the Wednesday night.

The discussions at Quay West on Thursday also canvassed the po-sition of the Deputy Leader. Downer did not want a ballot. He thought that he was the natural deputy. Others, including Turnbull, thought they should be considered. But the idea prevailed that a ballot would be divisive and that Downer should take that position unopposed. Brough was insisting that there be a ballot.

On the night of Saturday 8 September, most of the Ministers were at the Opera House for the APEC 'cultural event', the final event of the meeting. Hugh Jackman hosted it. It included a number of singers and dancers exhibiting different kinds of music. The world leaders sat in the front row while the Ministers sat further back. Afterwards there was another dinner and a spectacular fireworks display on Sydney Harbour. Tanya and I hosted the US Secretary of State, Condoleezza Rice. Before the event started a number of the Ministers took me aside to tell me again that Howard must go. Nelson and I had a long conversation on the forecourt of the Opera House, which was seen but not heard by several journalists. I had been through this whole saga so many times—many more times than they had. I was a better judge of the likely outcome. There would always be some condition that would stop any change.

Yet the thing was still alive when we returned to Canberra on Monday 10 September for an address to the Parliament by the Canadian Prime Minister, Stephen Harper. Downer told me that Howard was willing to see Ministers individually if it was their view that he should go. This produced a flurry of telephone calls between the Ministers to see who would, and who would not, go in and deliver such a message.

Howard decided he had better send a message of his own. On the current affairs program *Today Tonight* he said: 'I've talked about my position with my own family at length last night.'

Anna Coren asked: 'What did you say to your family?'

'They want me to continue to contribute. They support what I'm doing. I mean, I have lived through politics with my children all of their lives ... And we're very close and they're supportive. They give me a lot of counsel and advice. And I want to stay on because there are things I want to do for the Australian people.'

The interview outraged Howard's Ministers. He had asked their advice and they had told him he should go. Now he was saying he had consulted his family and they had told him to stay. The family's advice was more important. All the talk about how he would stay 'for as long as that is the party's wish' had gone. Now he would stay for as long as his family wanted him to.

In the *Today Tonight* interview there was no mention of the meeting of Ministers and no suggestion that they had given the Prime Minister a message. The dance between Howard and his Ministers— the week of madness—had not yet reached the ears of the press. But on Tuesday the press got some idea of what was going on. There were media reports that two Ministers had told Howard to go. One of these must have been Downer since he was the one who delivered the Cabinet view to Howard at Kirribilli House. When the story broke, Downer went on television to pledge his full support for Howard and to say that there would be no change.

On Tuesday, Canadian Prime Minister Stephen Harper delivered his address to Parliament. Later that day Howard called a number of Ministers around to his office. He told some to come in while others were still present. He asked them whether they wanted him to go.

Apart from Hockey and Brough, they found it difficult to tell him to his face what they had decided at Quay West. Every Minister in the Cabinet, with the exception of me, the Deputy Leader (who was elected by the party), was there by the appointment of the Prime Minister. They had enjoyed promotion to the Cabinet from him. They felt vulnerable. They were concerned that the branch members might turn on them if they were seen to push him out. He made it clear to them that he would place the responsibility on his Cabinet Ministers.

We now had the worst of all possible worlds. It was known that most of Howard's Cabinet wanted him to go. The election was two months away. The Ministers felt they had been trapped into expressing a view and then had it thrown back at them. Some of the media's reporting suggested their behaviour had been treacherous. But all they had done was to give their opinion when asked. Downer was not going to take on Howard and Howard was not going to voluntarily stand down. He would make any departure messy. The debacle had to be ended.

I went to see Howard early on the morning of Wednesday 12 September. I told him that his Ministers were extremely angry. They were being portrayed as disloyal for giving him a view when he had asked for it. Some, like Mal Brough, were threatening to resign. If Howard wanted to stop the fallout he should make it entirely clear to the public that nobody had been disloyal to him or to the party. He should make it clear that he had started the whole thing.

I also told him that, if he was going to stay on, he should make clear precisely when he intended to go No one believed that, if re-elected, he would stay for a full term. The formula he had previously laid down—that he would stay as long as his party wanted him—was in shreds. His senior colleagues did not want him to stay. He would not be able to use this formula to get through another federal election campaign. He was shocked. He now realised how bad things were. He told me he would carefully consider his position. He said that he had told Downer he would not fall on his sword, but that Downer had misrepresented his position to the Ministers and had led them to believe that he might go voluntarily. I asked Howard: 'If your position

was that you wouldn't go voluntarily, why did you ask their opinion?'
There was no answer.

At the party room meeting that day, Howard stood up and stated
that he had decided to stay on. He said that it was not unusual for
there to be continuing discussions on his future. It was not wrong
or treacherous or disloyal to talk about the future of the party or
the future of its leadership. He said I had not done anything disloyal
and he had had extreme loyalty from the leadership group. There
should be no rancour and no anger over the events of the past few
days. All the discussions had happened with his full knowledge and
blessing and he did not mind anything that people came to tell him.
He said that although the published polls were bad, he wanted to
stay on until he had implemented all the things he had taken to the
election. After the election there should be an orderly transition and
he should be succeeded by 'Peter, the man on my left' (he was speaking
geographically). He opened up the party room for discussion.

In this surreal atmosphere—where the Prime Minister had just
admitted that a majority of his Cabinet had, at his invitation, advised
him to leave and that for the first time he would not serve out the
full term if re-elected—members of the party stood up to talk. The
matters they talked about were dental care, the Wheat Board, the
hydrogen car, disability funding, veterans' affairs and the drought. By
the end of the party meeting, nobody had mentioned the elephant in
the room. Nobody had mentioned the events of the week. One of the
most chilling moments was when Cameron Thompson, the Member
for Blair, claimed that the opinion pollsters had been spooked and
were falsely reporting public opinion. We had reached a new stage
of unreality.

That night Howard went on the ABC's *7.30 Report*. Apparently
none of the press had picked up that he had told the party room that he
would stand down in the next term. Kerry O'Brien, the interviewer,
appeared to miss it until well into the interview, when Howard said:
'I would expect well into my term, and after all those things have
been implemented and battened down, I would probably ... certainly
form the view well into my term that it makes sense for me to retire,
and in those circumstances, I would expect, although it would be a

matter for the party to determine if Peter would take over.' This was the reason he did the interview—to get it out that he was, for the first time, announcing that he would retire in the next term. But it was so hard for him to say it. Even when he did say it, it came out as: 'probably ... certainly'.

Some continued agitating for a change, even if it required a party-room ballot. Andrew Robb, a former federal director of the Liberal Party, told me that after Howard's announcement that he would not serve out the next term, his situation had become untenable. Robb said he was going to deliver this message to Howard. On the following Sunday night he called on him at the Lodge. Howard was courteous but unmoved. The Cabinet was afraid that if Howard was forced out, he would turn on them. We were well behind in the polls. Fighting Labor while fighting allegations from Howard about disloyalty would be an impossible task. I told Robb the Ministers had no stomach for a ballot. Judging from the mood of the party room on 12 September, the leadership had become unmentionable. Howard had started the whole episode and Howard had ended it. It began on Tuesday 4 September and ended on Wednesday 12 September. The week of madness. If he had wanted to go, he could have. Maybe for a while he thought he would.

Shortly before the disastrous federal election of 2007, Howard hosted a lunch at Kirribilli House for the News Limited journalists Dennis Shanahan, Terry McCrann, Andrew Bolt and Piers Akerman. It was clear we were going to lose the election. These journalists had been Howard supporters (although Bolt had written that Howard should go). Those who have spoken to me about the lunch describe it as a farewell to the Government, maybe a farewell to Kirribilli House. Inevitably the talk turned to the election. Howard had pledged that if we won the election he would step down well into the term. He was sixty-eight and going for a fifth term.

'If you win, all bets are off,' one of the journalists told him. 'If you win, people will say that you have to stay.'

Could this be serious? Could it be that his supporters were not just thinking of the fifth term and 2007 but a sixth term and 2010? Before the 2001 election Howard thought it would be his last. But when he won, his friends and supporters urged him to stay on for the 2004 election. He was a proven vote-winner. Before the 2004 election he thought it would be his last. When he won again, his supporters urged him to stay for the 2007 election. If he had won it, I have no doubt they would have said that, as a winner, he had to stay for the 2010 election.

The logic was that if Howard won, he should stay. Only if he lost could it be said that he should have gone. But losing would throw the party out of office. Then we would know there should have been a change of leadership. But it would be too late to make a change. The party was at a dead-end.

The public resolved the issue and it did so emphatically—voting out the Government and voting out Howard in his own seat of Bennelong.

Leadership is not only about winning; it is also about departing. The only Liberal Leader who understood that he had to settle the time of his departure, for the sake of the party, was Sir Robert Menzies. He was not just the *leader* of the party, he was its founder. He had every right to stay around. By standing down, he showed extraordinary leadership. When he did it, he set up the party for a win at the next election and the next after that. Unlike Menzies, Howard never managed a transition. He did not accomplish generational change.

After the best economic record of any Australian Government and after an Age of Prosperity from a golden era of continuous economic growth, the Coalition was defeated in the spring of 2007. We lost because we failed to renew. We mismanaged generational change. We did not arrange the leadership transition. The electorate did it for us.

13

BRINGING HOME THE BACON:
THE FOURTH TERM

After the 2004 election only six Ministers of the original fifteen in the 1996 Cabinet were still serving. Three of us—Howard, Downer and I—would see out the whole term, until the election defeat on 24 November 2007. The other three—John Anderson (Deputy Prime Minister), Robert Hill (leader in the Senate) and Amanda Vanstone—would retire during the term.

Robert Hill was the longest serving party leader in the Senate. He had been elected Senate Leader in 1990 while we were in Opposition and had been leader of the Government in the Senate since the 1996 election. He served as Minister for the Environment and Minister for Defence. He retired from the Senate in January 2006 to take up an appointment as ambassador to the United Nations in New York. Hill was a moderate from South Australia, attuned to the nuances of party opinion and skilled in balancing competing interests in the party and in the Senate.

Amanda Vanstone had been in the original Cabinet as Minister for Employment, Education, Training and Youth Affairs. She was dropped from Cabinet and appointed Minister for Justice in the reshuffle of October 1997. David Kemp took over her portfolio and came into Cabinet in her place. In January 2001 Vanstone came back into Cabinet as Minister for Family and Communities Services to replace the retiring Jocelyn Newman. In January 2007 Vanstone retired from Parliament to become ambassador to Italy. A bon vivant, she cut a colourful figure in Australian politics, more interested in the bigger picture than in the detail of administration.

John Anderson, the Leader of the National Party, was in the original Cabinet as Deputy Leader of the National Party and Minister for Primary Industries. When Tim Fischer stood down from the leadership of the National Party in July 1999, Anderson became Leader. In our second term, he served as Minister for Transport until he stood down from the leadership in July 2005. Health problems were making parliamentary life difficult for him. He had also been through the tragedy of losing a baby. He had toyed with the idea of retiring in September 2003 and told his deputy, Mark Vaile, that he was going. But he decided to stay on to implement our water reforms, which he felt passionately about. After one false start at retirement, he reached an understanding with Mark Vaile that he would stand down during the 2004–07 term. He wanted to ensure a smooth transition to Vaile as Leader.

Mark Vaile's situation in 2003 mirrored my own. John Howard had first signalled that he would consider retirement before the 2004 election but then decided to stay. When it became known that John Anderson was staying, Vaile contacted me from Mexico, where he was attending a meeting of the World Trade Organization. He asked for copies of the transcript of the press conference I had given when Howard decided to stay in June 2003. He asked me for advice on how to handle the announcement. He wanted to respond in the same terms. We joked about our similar situation.

I got on well with both Anderson and Vaile. Anderson was a personal friend. He is a decent man with a strong Christian faith that had propelled him into politics. When he stood down from the leadership in June 2005, I told the House of Representatives:

> I know the burden it was on John to have the demographics and the economics moving against him almost continuously throughout the period of his leadership of the National Party.
>
> I often wondered whether it was taking a toll on his health, because he agonised so deeply about those particular issues, and maybe it did.

As a consequence of that, I think we can say that he did truly give to his country not just his talents, his intellect, his commitment and his loyalty but also his health in many important respects. We admire you, and we pay tribute to you, John, and to your family ...

As Minister for Trade, Mark Vaile supported opening up and liberalising trading relations—always a sensitive issue for the National Party. In fact, he spent months in intense negotiations to conclude the US Free Trade Agreement in 2004. There were occasions when it looked as if it would fall apart, but he kept at it. One of the problems was foreign investment. During these troubling negotiations he rang me from Washington several times to discuss the concessions the Americans wanted and the concessions we could make. I wanted the Free Trade Agreement but I also wanted to protect Australia's fundamental interests. He pursued these matters vigorously and we got the outcome we wanted. The US Trade Representative Bob Zoellick complained to Vaile that he was facing a tag team: 'Sometimes you, sometimes Costello, sometimes someone else. Who am I dealing with here?' On some of the sticky issues there was direct contact between Prime Minister Howard and President Bush. It was exhausting work. Vaile deserves great credit for the way in which he ultimately pulled it off.

Neither Anderson nor Vaile had their jobs made easier by the election of National Party Senator Barnaby Joyce in 2004. Joyce was a maverick, elected on a populist rural platform. He believed that the hope of the National Party lay in distinguishing itself from the Liberal Party. Since the Government had a majority of one in the Senate, Joyce was able to grandstand on practically every issue. He felt no loyalty to the Coalition. He wanted to share the Coalition's record of achievement in economic management but he also wanted to oppose the measures necessary to deliver those results. The more he demanded, the higher his profile became. He quickly became one of the best known Senators in Australia. He was so well known that he was referred to simply by his first name: Barnaby. With all this coverage he became seen as more energetic and successful than other members of the National Party, who played in the team and received nothing like the coverage. He made the life of the National Party Leader a misery and undermined his authority in the party and in the broader community they represented.

There are no big differences between the Liberal Party and the National Party. But there are big differences inside the National Party, especially the National Party in Queensland, where there is a Coalitionist wing, represented by Senator Ron Boswell, and a populist wing, represented by Barnaby. Most of Barnaby's supporters are the people who had supported the Joh-for-PM campaign.

Bob Katter, the Member for Kennedy, had also been elected a National Party member from Queensland but became so independent that he left it. Barnaby is an independent inside the National Party and Bob an independent outside it. They fight over the same constituency. Pauline Hanson's One Nation also appealed to this constituency. Barnaby, Bob, Pauline—it was a three-horse race in the Queensland Derby.

After the 2004 election, the Cabinet had no new faces. This was partly because two retiring Cabinet Ministers had stood down in July before the election—David Kemp and Daryl Williams. We knew John Anderson would be standing down during the term and many (including me) expected John Howard to do likewise. That would give us the chance for a real reshuffle. But as the term wore on there was no leadership change. Howard attempted to put a fresh face on the Government in other ways.

In January 2006 Robert Hill's appointment overseas allowed Brendan Nelson to be appointed to Defence and Julie Bishop to come into the Cabinet in the Education portfolio. Kay Patterson also decided to stand down and Mal Brough was brought in to Family and Community Services. Brough also became Minister Assisting the Prime Minister for Indigenous Affairs, which Amanda Vanstone as the Immigration Minister had previously handled. Malcolm Turnbull became parliamentary secretary to the Prime Minister.

There was another attempt to freshen up the Government a year later when Vanstone accepted her diplomatic appointment. Kevin Andrews replaced her and this allowed Joe Hockey to move into the sensitive portfolio of Employment and Workplace Relations. Ian Campbell was moved sideways out of Environment to Hockey's former portfolio of Human Services. Turnbull, still in his first term, was promoted again, this time to Campbell's portfolio of Environment, and given the responsibility for water resources.

These reshuffles brought talented people such as Bishop and Turnbull into the Cabinet. They also gave younger members the opportunity to become Ministers or parliamentary secretaries—people such as Christopher Pyne and Tony Smith, people we need to nurture as the future of the party. Pyne established a reputation as an articulate and forceful debater. He obtained a regular role on the ABC's *Lateline* program and was the first to take some of the shine off Latham in debates against him. He had an enormous work ethic. On the night of the 2001 election he saw me on camera making a speech, and rang my mobile phone with some suggestions on what I might say. The phone began ringing while I was being broadcast live on national television. I answered and asked him to call back. How I could speak to the nation and him simultaneously is beyond me. Unless he thought I should hold the phone to the microphone!

Our new ministry performed well but it did not succeed in making the Government look fresh or new. The face of the Government was still Howard. To a lesser degree it was Downer and me. No amount of reshuffling at the lower ranks could give the impression that this was a new Government. It was still the Howard Government, in office since 1996 and now in its fourth term. In 2007 it would be seeking a fifth. Kevin Rudd was to exploit this during the election campaign. He claimed to represent 'New Leadership, Fresh Ideas'.

By 2004 I had brought down nine Budgets with seven surpluses. We were well on our way to eliminating Commonwealth debt. The net debt of the Commonwealth had grown to $96 billion by the time the Keating Government was voted out. I made it a policy goal to eliminate it. This would save eight or nine billion dollars in interest payments each year, putting the Budget in a structural surplus.

But as we came within sight of this goal, the financial markets began to get cranky. With no debt, the Commonwealth would not need to issue Treasury bonds (the instrument for borrowing). These were widely traded because they were rated AAA. They provided a good benchmark for other interest rates. Bonds issued by semi-Government instrumentalities or private companies which had lower credit ratings would be priced at a margin over the Commonwealth bond rate. Without that rate the issuers, investors and traders would find pricing more difficult. After struggling with debt all these years, and being on the brink of eliminating it, the financial markets made it clear to me that they liked having debt and wanted to keep it.

There was no technical problem in eliminating debt and closing the Treasury bond market. In the late 1990s the United States had balanced its Budget and looked like it was on a path to eliminate its debt. The US Federal Reserve looked at the issue of retiring all US Treasury bonds and the effect that this would have on financial markets. I discussed the issue with Alan Greenspan on a number of occasions. The Fed concluded there was no insurmountable problem in retiring all US debt and operating without US Treasury bonds. The private market would have to adjust its way of pricing but it could be done without any great disruption. I took the same view. The Australian markets could still operate in a smooth and efficient way in such circumstances.

But as time wore on a key difference emerged between our situation and that in the United States. We continued to run Budget surpluses and stayed on track to eliminate debt. The United States went back into deficit and began running up its debt again. By 2007 its debt to GDP ratio was nearly 50 per cent. In our terms, that would have meant around $500 billion debt! The question of operating without Treasury bonds never became a practical prospect for the Americans. I joked with Greenspan: 'You sure figured out a way to deal with the problem of eliminating debt!'

In 2002 I initiated a public review of the Commonwealth Government Securities (CGS) market. It concluded that closing the market would lead to slightly higher interest rates arising from higher costs associated with managing interest rate risk without a Treasury bond futures market. It was not a big problem. But it was not worth having a fight about it with the financial institutions and the superannuation funds. Accordingly, I announced in the 2003–04

Budget that we would maintain sufficient CGS on issue to support the Treasury bond futures market: around $50 billion.

This meant that we would issue bonds to the value of around $50 billion, even though we did not need the money. What we needed was to keep a market of bonds. If you borrow money you do not intend to spend, you have to do something with it. We were starting to build large deposits at the Reserve Bank. The Government was borrowing money to put on deposit at the Reserve Bank. It was paying interest on the bonds and receiving interest on the deposits.

For this reason I announced during the 2004 election campaign that the Commonwealth would establish a 'Future Fund', which was the way of marrying twin objectives—keeping the bond market alive while eliminating net debt. Our large surplus balances held at the Reserve Bank would be invested by an arm's-length entity in a way that would generate returns but not manipulate or unsettle the market.

Investing these sums would give a better return than merely holding them on deposit. A Government with a good credit rating is able to borrow money at low interest rates. If it invested this money and generated a return greater than the cost of borrowing, it would begin generating profit. You could also lose the money if you invested in assets that fell in price. But by investing the money wisely it should be possible to obtain a greater return than the cost of the funds. On a long-term basis it should not be difficult to exceed the long-term bond rate. Taken to its logical extreme, this process could enable the Government to become an investment business. But a Government is not an investment business, and we were not doing this as a money-making scheme. It was important to separate it from Government, put it under the control of people who were above reproach and focus it on a particular investment objective.

That objective was a long-term liability that no previous Government had been prepared to deal with—unfunded Commonwealth superannuation. Historically, Commonwealth public servants were in a superannuation scheme that promised them a certain percentage of their pre-retirement income for life. These are known as 'defined benefit schemes'. A public servant who retired at fifty-five would therefore get a pension for twenty, thirty or more years. The payment of this pension would be taken out of consolidated revenue—that is, future tax receipts.

What effectively happened was that public servants employed in one generation were having part of the costs (the wage component) met by the taxes of that generation and another part of the costs (retirement benefits) met by the taxes of future generations. Past generations had thrown the retirement costs of their public servants onto our generation and we were throwing the retirement costs of our public servants onto future generations of taxpayers. If the cost of public servants were to be fully paid at the time of employment, it would be necessary not only to fund their wages but also to fund their retirement costs by setting aside the money to pay those benefits as and when they fell due in the future. This is what is meant by fully funded superannuation.

The accrued liability of the Commonwealth under the public service defined benefit scheme was not just the costs of public service pensions in the ten years we had been in office but the costs accrued by previous Governments. My plan was to fully fund existing public servants and, as well, to fully fund the retirement costs of all past public servants. We would therefore fund the present and the past—effectively accepting a double burden in this generation in order to relieve future generations. This is an important point. It was not just a plan to fund costs accruing under our Government but also to catch up and fund the liabilities of all previous Commonwealth Governments.

This fitted in very well with our Intergenerational Report, which had shown that demographic changes would open up huge gaps between revenues and expenses for future generations. By funding one of the future costs—the retirement benefits of today's public servants—it would alleviate pressure on future generations. It was my determination not just to eliminate net debt but then to go further and fully fund past and current superannuation liabilities as well. The Future Fund would be the vehicle to do this.

On 21 April 2006, as far as we can tell accurately to a day, we eliminated debt in net terms. I named the date 'Debt-Free Day' and declared:

From tomorrow our Government will no longer be a net borrower. In fact from tomorrow we will start to save, to save for some of the big challenges of the future ...

When we become debt-free tomorrow it will not be the first time. The Commonwealth was debt-free for a short period in the early 1970s, more than thirty years ago.

The Commonwealth began borrowing to finance the First World War. Borrowing stayed high through the Depression years. Commonwealth borrowing peaked in the mid-1940s as a result of the cost of financing the Second World War effort.

Through the long post-war expansion under the Coalition Government, Government debt was progressively reduced and, in net terms, eliminated at the start of the 1970s. It was the Whitlam Government, and the series of events it set in train, that sent us back into borrowing. Net borrowing started at a low level in the mid-1970s then debt peaked under the Keating Government at $96 billion or 18.5 per cent of GDP ... Government interest payments amount to $8.4 billion per annum, or around 1.5 per cent of GDP ... Next year we are forecasting net interest payments of $0.3 billion.

This means every year, year after year, the taxpayer is saving billions in debt-servicing costs. Today, 1.5 per cent of GDP devoted to interest payments would be $14 billion. The reduction of these costs is one of the reasons why Commonwealth spending has fallen and is now the second lowest in the OECD.

And what now that the debt is paid off? Let me disappoint some people and say that now is not the time to let our hair down and make whoopee ...

We are a party of low tax and to keep tax low we have to keep spending down. We have the second-lowest spending (proportionate to the economy) in the developed world and the eighth-lowest tax burden. If we can be wise about spending we can, as we have in years past, return money to taxpayers by lowering the tax burden.

Although they are the most important responsibility, our responsibility is not just to today's taxpayers. Our responsibility extends to the taxpayers of tomorrow, the future of our country, the ones we expect to carry us when our generation is in its old and declining years.

By early 2006 we had also established the Future Fund as an independent statutory fund administered by a board of guardians. We made the first deposit to the fund out of accumulated surpluses up to 30 June 2005. We made the second deposit out of the Budget surplus for June 2006. We deposited the first instalment received as payment for the issue of shares under T3—the third float of Telstra shares—and allocated the proceeds of the second instalment to the fund as well. We deposited the remaining shares the Government held in Telstra in the fund. We made a further deposit from the surplus in the financial year ending June 2007. This meant that by August 2007 the fund had been allocated more than $60 billion. By accumulating earnings on these funds, it would have sufficient assets to meet the Commonwealth's unfunded superannuation liabilities by 2020—expected to be $140 billion. No further contributions would be required. From 2020 no payments from consolidated revenue would be required. Future generations would be relieved of that cost in its entirety.

The Treasury developed a measure called 'net worth', which measured the Commonwealth's financial position after taking into account its net debt and financial liabilities. In 1996, net debt was nearly 20 per cent of GDP, while the Commonwealth's unfunded superannuation liabilities were 16.3 per cent of GDP. The Mid-Year Economic Review released in October 2007 showed that net worth after gross debt on issue and superannuation liabilities had turned positive. The Commonwealth Government was fully provisioned for its liabilities.

From 1996 we had turned the Budget from deficit to surplus, put in place our debt-reduction strategy and eliminated net debt, had our credit rating on foreign currency bonds upgraded twice to AAA level, weathered the Asian financial and economic collapse, drought, SARS, terrorism, the US recession of 2001 and a serious devaluation. All through this time international events had worked against us but we had stuck to the plan. Unlike the region, unlike the United States, we had avoided recession. The hard work had paid off. If we had not done all of this, world events would have brought us down.

From around 2003 the global events that had been moving against us started moving back in our favour. We did not know it at the time. We did not know what the magnitude would be. Only now, as we look back, can we pick that time as a turning point.

In the Budget delivered in May 2003, the Government forecast an increase in the terms of trade of 1.75 per cent. In fact, the terms of trade increased by 7 per cent. In the Budget brought down in May 2004 we forecast an increase in the terms of trade of 4.5 per cent. In fact, the terms of trade grew another 10 per cent. We forecast strong growth in the Budget of May 2005—12.25 per cent. The growth did not meet the forecast but it wasn't far off—around 10.9 per cent.

What took Treasury and all economic analysts by surprise in 2003 was the start of a huge increase in the prices of mineral commodities, which has continued.

The terms of trade measure the prices a country receives for its exports against the prices it pays for its imports. For a good part of the twentieth century Australia's terms of trade declined because we received low prices for wool and paid high prices for imported industrial goods. But our terms of trade peaked in 1950–51, during the wool boom arising from the Korean War. During the boom farmers were getting a pound (£) for a pound (lb). There had been another peak in 1974, led by strong rises in prices for minerals. By 2006, our terms of trade were around the 1974 peak and in 2007 they were higher.

The substantial lift in the terms of trade was not just the result of an increase in commodity prices. Many people miss the fact that there had also been a decrease in the prices of industrial goods, largely the result of mass production moving to East Asia and in particular China. China was churning out manufactured goods at cheaper and cheaper prices—and was consuming more energy and more steel to do so. Australia was well placed to provide raw materials for both. So it was not just that our export prices were rising but also that a substantial component of import prices was falling. Our terms of trade were improving on both sides of the ledger. For much of the developed world, the rise of China led to downward, anti-inflationary pressure on prices of manufactured goods.

As these price rises took effect, mining companies started looking at new investment to lift capacity. We went through a huge investment surge as producers prepared expansion of mine capacity and transport infrastructure to lift production to meet new demand. Many projects that were not viable on historical prices also became commercial once prices rose strongly. This brought a whole lot of new projects to viability and again encouraged new investment. But the lead times are long and it takes a great deal of time to expand a mine's capacity. There is a need to expand not just the capacity of the mine itself but the road and rail links and the port infrastructure.

The Commonwealth has never run the commercial ports in Australia. The ports in Western Australia that are used to export iron ore are owned and operated by the exporters themselves. The iron ore exporters have vertical integration. This means that they can invest and lift capacity at their own discretion, investing as they see fit. The main coal export ports on the east coast are, however, multi-user ports and in some cases are owned by third parties. Many different and competing companies use the same port. Some ports were set up by state Governments and then sold to the private sector—for example, Dalrymple Bay near Mackay in Queensland.

When a port is owned by the private sector and used by other companies the port owner will want to lift handling charges to boost profit. The exporters will want to keep them down to minimise costs. The port is a natural monopoly because an exporter can hardly move the rail line to another part of the coast. The exporter has to use the port to which their rail line is connected. Arguments about prices charged to users in these cases of infrastructure monopoly could be either agreed (unlikely) or arbitrated by a competition regulator. The port owner would not invest unless they were satisfied that the prices they could charge to users would provide an adequate return on their investment.

In Australia, arguments over an acceptable rate of return and pricing led to chronic delays in investment, which led to restricted capacity. The ports became a bottleneck. One of the things that concerned me enormously during this price surge was that quite often ships would queue for weeks, sometimes months, outside the coal loading ports in New South Wales and Queensland, waiting to pick up deliveries. The sight of thirty to forty ships queued up outside a port at a time when we were enjoying record coal prices was enormously frustrating.

But fixing the problems in the ports would be only the beginning of the solution. There were also bottlenecks in the rail lines. The west-coast producers owned their rail lines and could invest in increased capacities. In Queensland the rail line was owned by a state government corporation and was a multi-user facility. Again delays in investment meant that there were bottlenecks in production.

The lift in the terms of trade caught markets and the companies by surprise. New construction to lift mine capacity takes time. Problems of regulation also made these delays worse on the east coast. At my instigation the Commonwealth offered to take over access and pricing regulation of ports from the states. The offer was rejected by the state Governments. It was frustrating to see infrastructure bottlenecks caused by regulatory problems that hampered our economic advantage, and even more frustrating to have offers to take control and deal with these problems rejected by state Governments who wished to hang on to their historical powers. In my view, if the Commonwealth is to take responsibility for the national economy (which it should), it should have full jurisdiction over all areas (including critical export infrastructure) that govern it.

Mining does not employ a large proportion of the labour force. It is a capital-intensive industry. But the investment surge meant that tradesmen were in great demand to build more plant and more capacity. The Government invested record amounts in trades training, but the level of the investment surge meant that there were still shortages in this area. We continued to increase spending in successive Budgets.

An investment surge and a demand for skilled labour can put pressure on wages in other parts of the economy, as employers have to compete to keep employees otherwise attracted by large wage offers in the booming industries. A lift in the terms of trade generally works out in an inflationary way. For example, during previous peaks in terms of trade in 1951–52 inflation peaked at 22 per cent, and in 1974 at 16 per cent.

We could not hope to contain inflation on a terms of trade surge without a flexible industrial relations system. In an award-based system, an award variation flows through to all the employees covered by the award. It applies to those working for very profitable companies and those working for less profitable companies. Under collective bargaining unions can use a settlement in one area as a precedent for wage outcomes in other areas. If the wage rises in the mining industry had been transmitted through the whole labour force, as happened under the award system in those periods, we would have had inflation as we had in those periods. But the option of individual statutory agreements—Australian Workplace Agreements (AWAs)—meant that large salaries could be paid to those working in profitable sectors without a general flow-on. The mining industry was the most prolific user of AWAs to attract and keep labour. An AWA can be quarantined. It is a testament to the improved industrial relations climate that, in this terms of trade surge, inflation was held to 3 per cent, rather than the 15 or 20 per cent of previous times.

The increase in commodity prices was, of course, not all beneficial for Australia. One of the commodities that rocketed in price was oil, of which Australia is a net importer. This produced inflationary pressures in the economy. Since oil prices are set in the international market a Government cannot control domestic price rises in petrol and diesel. Because transport is a large component of the cost of business, it feeds into inflation. It is critical to stop prices feeding back into wages and creating second-round effects. This is why decentralised industrial relations are so critical. It is why the Government focussed on labour-market reform and promoted the option of individual AWAs.

By 2007 the economy was enjoying the eleventh straight year of growth under the Coalition and the sixteenth year of growth since the recession of 1991. Continuous growth led to high employment and kept bank profitability high. Mortgage and loan defaults were low. Strong consumer demand was good for all businesses. The profit share of the economy reached 28.1 per cent in the 2007 March quarter—an all time record. Company profitability surged and, although we cut company tax, we collected more of this tax on a lower tax rate. The Government's major tax reform had taken effect from 1 July 2000, which involved reform of the indirect tax system, income tax, Commonwealth–state relations and family assistance.

In September 1999 we announced changes to the business tax system to halve the rate of capital gains tax from 1 October 1999 and company tax from July 2000. This was known as 'The New Business Tax System'. Coming up to the May 2003 Budget I decided that we should also have another round of income tax cuts. We were getting on top of our economic problems. We had first stabilised, then reduced, and were now on track to eliminate net debt. By cutting tax we would ensure that the tax burden as a proportion of GDP did not rise. I saw it as an important opportunity to heighten economic incentives. It was what I had come into politics to do: to balance the Budget and to cut taxes.

In the May 2003 Budget I announced an increase in the thresholds for the various marginal rates of income tax. It took the press by surprise. We had had a major round of tax reform and tax cuts three years earlier. What was more, 2003 was not an election year and the conventional thinking of the press was that a Government would cut tax only when an election was imminent.

The effect of these tax cuts was not large and I did not bill them as such. To me the principle was important. I explained that if a Government can fund its expenses and still deliver a surplus to pay off debt, then it should try as far as possible to cut the tax burden for individual tax payers. The Budget changes meant that a taxpayer on $45 000 would receive a tax cut of $208 and a taxpayer of $55 000, a tax cut of $448.

The day after the Budget, Amanda Vanstone, the Minister for Family and Community Services, was interviewed about welfare reviews. In an effort to explain and justify the importance of welfare compliance, she said: 'If I can put it in this perspective, you know we were mentioning earlier it's a third of Government outlays that we spend. And, on a one-on-one basis if someone says to me, look, couldn't people just have $5 more? And you meet people in very impecunious circumstances and your heart just opens up and of course you want to give them $5 more. Five dollars, hell, what would it buy you? A sandwich and a milkshake if you're lucky ... on a human basis that's what you want to do. But then you add up the range of people we're giving benefits to, and the last assessment I had is that if we give everybody on either welfare or getting family tax assessment $5 more a week, it's $10 billion in the forward estimates period.'

What Vanstone was saying was that she would, if she could, give $5 more to each person on welfare, even though it would buy only a sandwich and a milkshake. She was pointing out that collectively the cost of doing so was prohibitive. What we had done in the Budget was to give tax cuts—some only $5 per week—which would help all taxpayers, at a cost of $10.7 billion. But it was the colourful phrase 'a sandwich and a milkshake' that stuck in the public mind. The Opposition used this phrase cleverly to suggest that all the Government had done was to provide a 'a sandwich and a milkshake'—a derisory tax cut. If we had not cut taxes no one would have complained. No one would have complained that they were missing out on a sandwich and a milkshake. We had taken everybody by surprise and cut taxes. Then we were criticised for not cutting tax enough.

The way I saw it, the increases in thresholds were like indexing tax thresholds but better. If wages rise to keep pace with inflation they may not increase in real terms. But the higher nominal wage may put some part of the same real income in a higher tax bracket under a progressive income tax system. This is known as 'bracket creep'. It is argued that to stop it, tax thresholds should be indexed to inflation. The movement in the thresholds would not be great in a climate of low inflation. But they would prevent a Government getting a windfall of revenue out of inflation. The 2003 increases in thresholds were greater than indexation. They not only protected taxpayers against bracket creep; they provided real tax cuts.

Although I felt the Government did not get as much credit as it should have, I was sure that the principle was right—to fund expenses, deliver a surplus and if possible make a return to taxpayers, who, after all, were paying the taxes in the first place. I decided that, if I could, I would go further in the next Budget. This was becoming feasible as we were now on top of debt and interest savings were delivering a recurrent improvement in the Budget position. As the economy kept growing, more people started finding work, which also aided tax collections. Improvements in the terms of trade lifted company tax receipts. We could either bank larger surpluses or return some of the benefits to the public by way of tax cuts. If we did not cut tax there would be a great pressure to allocate rising tax receipts to new expenditure. In economic terms, lowering the tax burden and heightening incentives to work generally provides a better boost to an economy than new programs of Government expenditure.

In the 2004 Budget I raised the marginal tax thresholds more aggressively. I announced a two-stage program over two years to take the threshold for the top marginal tax rate from $62501 to $70000 and then $80000. The sensitive 30 per cent rate, which was the rate applicable to most wage earners, would continue to apply past $52000 to $58000 and then $63000. This would ensure that 80 per cent of taxpayers faced a top tax rate of 30 per cent or less. This had been the effect of our tax reform under the new tax system. We had never made the promise that we would always keep 80 per cent of taxpayers on a top rate of 30 per cent or less; we had just promised that the reforms from 1 July 2000 would produce this outcome. From time to time tax rates would have to be adjusted to return to that benchmark. The program that I laid down in the 2004 Budget was to ensure that we would not dip below that measure in each of the four years of the forward estimates. What started off as a high point for the tax system was built in as a guaranteed floor. In the 2004 Budget I also announced a new Baby Bonus of $3000 and a new annual lump sum payment of $600 per child to each family eligible for the Family Tax Benefit.

We had the election in October 2004. Labor came out with a policy that guaranteed to deliver the second round of my Budget tax cuts. It also proposed a working tax bonus and a new family payment, part of which was to be funded by the abolition of the $600 annual bonus paid to families in receipt of the Family Tax Benefit. Labor published tables showing families would be better off, on a fortnightly basis, with these changes, but the tables left out the annual $600 bonus, which Labor planned to abolish. Taking into account the annual bonus, many families would have been worse off under Labor's policy. The dodgy tables were an attempt to be too clever by half, and I discovered the trick the day the policy was announced.

The Labor Leader, Mark Latham, claimed that his policy would help families and 'ease the squeeze'. I pointed out that his tables had been carefully drawn to exclude the $600 payment. Taking that into account, I said, he was trying to 'hoax the folks' because so many families would be worse off.

Latham was erratic. He had had a chequered career as a mayor in a Sydney suburban council. In a celebrated incident he had broken the arm of a taxi driver. As a Labor frontbencher he had taken parliamentary abuse to a new level. But when he was elected Leader, Labor enjoyed a surge in support, striking fear into the heart of Howard and the Government. A believer in the theory of triangulation, he wanted to move the political debate to new issues such as reading to children. He was interested in economic theory and had written a book called *Civilising Global Capital*. I spent an hour or so trying to read this book but found it impenetrable. I have never met anyone who has read it. Because it was so dense it was taken as evidence that he had considered these matters.

Yet Latham ran a reasonable campaign in 2004. He was widely judged the winner of the televised debate with Howard. He was let down badly by Wayne Swan, who had thought up the policy that involved abolishing annual family payments of $600. Swan defended the policy on the grounds that the $600 bonus 'was not real' and therefore its abolition made no difference. We ruthlessly exploited this ridiculous claim. I was to say over and over again that the annual bonus 'looks like money, smells like money, spends like money but according to Labor isn't real'. People knew Swan's claim was nonsense. They got those payments. They spent them. They knew they were real all right.

Swan seldom packed a punch. He was not a major player in the Opposition. He was active ferreting around for an angle to get up on news reports. But he was policy-light. Later, as shadow Treasurer, he adopted the tactic of not asking me questions in Parliament so that he could stay outside the fray. A dedicated Beazley man, he was one of the group described by Latham as 'the roosters'.

The Coalition did not have a good campaign in 2004 but it won seats from the Labor Party because the public was worried about Latham's erratic personality. Some Liberals misread the result. They thought the Liberal Party was on a new upward trajectory. On 7 December 2004 (after the election) at the last joint party meeting of the year, Howard claimed we had had one of the best years since the Coalition had been formed. He said: '1963 was a re-affirmation of the ascendancy of the Coalition', and rated the 2004 victory alongside it. What he was saying was that we had been through the trough (compared with Menzies' near loss in 1961). After 1963 the Coalition went on to win a huge majority in 1966 and another victory after that.

A note of triumphalism was starting to creep in. After all, this was his fourth election victory. But I thought this misread the outcome; in my view Latham's failings masked the fact that the electorate was already becoming fatigued with the Coalition and Howard. We won because Labor made a critical error with its choice of Leader. If it corrected that error, the Coalition's problems would be laid bare in 2007.

We were now into our fourth term. It is conventional wisdom that in the first Budget after an election there is no point in cutting tax. The idea is that tax cuts should be held back for election years, and 'nasties' introduced in the first year of a three-year term. But I thought that by cutting tax in the first Budget after the election we would surprise the cynics and reinforce our credentials as the party of low tax.

In the 2005 Budget I announced the establishment of the Future Fund (an election promise). I announced that earnings would accumulate in the fund. These earnings otherwise would have been treated as revenue to the Commonwealth. They would have gone on the bottom line and been added to the surplus. By quarantining earnings in the Fund and not taking them into the Budget we began reporting lower Budget surpluses than otherwise would have been the case.

In the Budget speech of 10 May 2005, I announced that we would cut the lowest marginal tax rate from 17 per cent to 15 per cent. This was aimed at delivering tax cuts to lower paid earners. I also announced that in two steps we would take the threshold for the top marginal tax rate first to $95 000 and then to $125 000 from

1 July 2006. Increases in other thresholds would ensure that 80 per cent of taxpayers faced a top marginal tax rate of 30 per cent or less over the whole of the forward estimates. The increase in the threshold for the top rate meant that a person would have to earn more than double the average production wage (a means of comparing earnings on an international basis) to go on to the top rate. This threshold had previously cut in at a lower rate than the OECD average. Now we would do better than that average. The *Australian* newspaper described the Budget as 'Bringing Home the Bacon'.

My view was that the top marginal tax rate of 47 per cent (plus the Medicare levy of 1.25 per cent) was too high and cut in too low. Cutting the top rate would make our tax system more competitive. But it came with a political problem. Cutting the top rate of tax by 1 per cent would produce a tax cut of $1000 for a person on $100 000, of $10 000 for a person on $1 million and of $100 000 for a person with an income of $10 million. There were such people, and the press gleefully reported who they were, generally in the context of criticising corporate salaries.

Increasing the thresholds for the top rates would deliver a tax cut to all these people but the tax cut would be the same amount for everyone earning over the top threshold. In this case the tax cut would be $4502 for everyone earning more than $125 000. The top rate would apply to only 3 per cent of taxpayers in 2006. It would make the top bracket irrelevant to nearly all Australians and minimise the disincentive that it provided. It would be easier to sell a change of threshold that capped the tax cut for higher income earners than a change of rate that would produce deeper and deeper tax cuts for higher and higher income earners.

The Budget process began each year in November, six months before the finished product was to be delivered. The Ministers would lodge their proposals. The senior Ministers in the Government would weed out a large portion of these proposals and allow the remainder to be worked up for presentation to the Expenditure Review Committee (ERC) of Cabinet.

The ERC would begin meeting in February and go through March until April, when the Revenue Committee would meet to look at any technical tax measures. With all these decisions taken, the Treasury would start to lock in the economic forecasts and try to draw a bottom line.

In the last two weeks before the May Budget I would work on the Budget alone in a safe room in the Treasury Building. Officials would run their programs at night to produce a running update of where the Budget bottom line was going.

I decided that our Budget surplus should be at least 1 per cent—for macroeconomic reasons and to continue our investment in the Future Fund, which would first eliminate net debt and then fund outstanding superannuation. The remaining monies could be used to cut taxes. Before each of the four Budgets from 2003–04, I prepared a proposal for income tax rates and thresholds that would deliver tax cuts. In the last fortnight I would outline them to John Howard. With his agreement that became the final decision. They were not discussed with any other Ministers. Ministers would be briefed on the nature of the tax cut on the Budget day, but the precise details would be known to only the Prime Minister and me.

Howard was nervous about the politics of being seen to cut tax for high income earners. To avoid this I worked up the changes to the threshold rather than the rate. Our Budget was again paying bonuses to carers; we were investing large sums in our Welfare to Work package, which would eventually produce savings but in the short term involved additional expenditures. Expenditures on national security were also rising but we had the capacity to deliver a tax cut of this dimension.

Labor denounced the 2005 Budget, claiming that the increase in tax thresholds favoured 'high income earners'. In his reply to the Budget, Beazley said:

> Tonight I am drawing a line in the sand for John Howard on Australian values and the sort of country we want to be, a line between us and this Government, which says someone earning $500 000 a year deserves ten times the tax cut of an Australian earning $50 000 a year ... The Treasurer got a big cheer from the Liberal Party backbench on Tuesday night when he announced a whopping big tax cut on their super, and he got a huge cheer

when he announced that these same politicians would be exempt from the top income tax rate. He was offering them a massive tax cut. Here was the Treasurer, using the nation's public finances to gain the support of his colleagues for a tilt at the leadership. It makes no sense to skew tax cuts towards those who have already enjoyed the greatest gains from our recent prosperity.

Beazley's remark about 'a whopping big tax cut on super' was a reference to the Budget decision to abolish the superannuation surcharge. I introduced this measure in my first Budget in 1996 to get higher income earners to share the burden of closing the Budget deficit. The superannuation surcharge proved extraordinarily complicated to administer. It was particularly difficult for people in defined benefit schemes. State Supreme Court judges had successfully obtained a decision from the High Court that the surcharge could not apply to them on constitutional grounds. But the surcharge could and did apply to Federal Court judges. I was thoroughly sick of trying to administer it. Now that the Budget was in surplus, it was no longer required. In previous Budgets I had cut the rate. This time I decided we would abolish it. Labor had opposed the introduction of the superannuation surcharge in 1996. When we abolished it in 2005, Labor opposed that too!

Beazley's crack about Coalition politicians cheering for being exempt from the top income tax rate was a reference to the fact that MPs' salaries were lower than the threshold where the top marginal tax rate would cut in, at $125 000. MPs were not in the top 3 per cent of income earners and therefore MPs would not come into the top tax bracket. It was obvious that Beazley's stand was an attempt to reconnect with lower income earners. Labor was still suffering from its proposed abolition of the annual bonus payment for the Family Tax Benefit. They had a lot of ground to make up. An attack on 'the rich' in defence of 'the poor' seemed one way to do it.

The Australian Democrats and the Greens joined Labor in opposing these tax cuts. Together they would be able to defeat the legislation in the Senate. But I was confident we would ultimately legislate the tax plan because the composition of the Senate would change on 1 July 2005. Counting on Barnaby Joyce (not always a certain proposition), we would be able to pass legislation when the Senate resumed in August. The difficulty was that the tax cuts were due to apply from the start of the financial year. It would be too complicated to have the old tax rates applying from 1 July and the new tax rates applying some time from August. My GST experience had taught me that any complexity in the tax system was blamed on the Government, regardless of who was responsible for causing it.

I wanted to stare down the Labor Party. It was full of bravado on Budget night, proclaiming how it would stand up for ordinary people. It proposed less tax relief for upper income earners. But in my view this was the most uncompetitive part of the tax system. It was important to deal with that as well as to give tax relief to lower income earners.

I had an inkling of just how nervous Labor was the day after the Budget. It is traditional on that day for the shadow Treasurer to take the major debate in the House on a 'Matter of Public Importance'. This gives the Opposition the opportunity to explain its line of attack. I expected that Wayne Swan would take this debate. Since the Labor Party was making a great stand on the issue, it would be a good opportunity for him to explain Labor's reasons and rally the troops. But to my utter disbelief he squibbed the debate, leaving it to the shadow assistant Treasurer, Joel Fitzgibbon. Joel was not a heavy hitter. I was further astonished when, in the first Question Time after the Budget, Labor did not ask me a single question. I had never seen such a feeble response.

As I travelled around the country to sell the Budget, it became clear that Labor was getting no traction from opposing our tax cuts. But a back-down would be dangerous for Beazley's leadership. Since Labor would not crack on the legislation, I had to solve the problem of how employers would be able to pass on the tax cuts from 1 July.

I discussed it with the Commissioner of Taxation. He agreed he could issue a new schedule detailing the deductions employers should make from 1 July, as if the tax legislation had passed, as long as I could assure him it would eventually pass. Employers could then operate under the new tax scales, even though they had not been legislated. They would deduct less tax and thereby pass on the benefits of the tax cuts. Subsequent legislation would validate their position. This seemed like a good solution. But then we realised that these schedules themselves would need to be tabled in Parliament. If the Opposition voted to disallow the schedules they would be struck down. The law would then require higher tax rates to continue on 1 July. The only valid schedules would also direct employers to deduct higher amounts.

One thing that Labor would not crack on was the tax legislation. But would they go a step further and disallow the schedules? As we began the lead-up to 30 June I began to pressure them. By disallowing the schedules they would be denying Australians their tax cuts, even though they knew the cuts would be validated by August. It would be a useless and empty gesture. Few Australians would thank them. But Labor had drawn a line in the sand! How far would it go? Day by day it refused to show its hand. When we reached the end of the Budget session, Labor had not moved a motion for disallowance. The schedules stood. The tax cuts flowed on the 1 July. Labor never explained why it squibbed it. By 10 August we got the legislation through the new Senate, which validated our position. It was a hard fight but one well worth winning.

I did not anticipate that the next shots would be fired from our own side.

Pushing out the thresholds delivered tax cuts but capped the amount for upper income earners. In the aftermath of the Budget, journalists and others naturally asked me why the Government had moved thresholds rather than rates. I explained how a rate cut delivered larger tax cuts the higher the income. That is why I decided on the capped proposal. Even that was attacked for favouring 'the rich'.

The *Australian* newspaper was agitating for larger tax cuts. Journalists wrote story after story on the issue and no amount of explanation could get a fair hearing. The then editor, Michael Stutchbury, was manic on the issue. He promoted the idea that a ginger group of backbenchers was agitating for major tax reform. The members of this so-called 'ginger group' were any MPs rung by any reporter on any given day who made sympathetic noises about cutting taxes. I knew all of the Coalition MPs who had an interest in tax. I knew those who were named as members of the ginger group very well. There was no organised group and certainly no common view on what they would like to do. Like most Liberals, including me, they were just in favour of lower taxes.

The newly elected Member for Wentworth, Malcolm Turnbull, saw an opening on the issue, particularly the campaign to cut the upper tax rates. Even before we had legislated the tax cuts in the Budget, he suggested that the top marginal rate should be cut to 40 per cent. I was sympathetic to cutting the top rates but before 1 July 2005 we had never had a majority in the Senate. Without that, there was no chance to cut upper tax rates. The fact that we could not legislate higher thresholds indicated how far beyond our capacity it was to cut the top rate. And it only applied to 3 per cent of income earners. The remaining 97 per cent were very important in political terms. It would be a serious mistake to forget them. Turnbull's views were music to Stutchbury's ears and he excitedly promoted them.

The noise was still at a low level. It went up in volume in late August when Howard, in an interview on the ABC's *Lateline*, said he thought the top marginal tax rate was too high. This surprised me. We had carefully discussed the strategy of moving thresholds rather than rates. Howard had been very nervous about doing even that. Now he was suggesting a change to rates which would produce much larger tax cuts for much higher income earners. To use a bushfire analogy, the issue jumped containment lines. Turnbull released a spreadsheet which modelled 274 different combinations of rates and thresholds. He did not promote any particular one but he gave the impression that whatever we had done, it wasn't enough.

We had just cut tax for the third year in a row. Labor had opposed us. We had used an ingenious device to deliver the tax cuts. We had the Opposition on the back foot. All of a sudden our own side began agitating discontent on the outcome. It turned the critical focus from the Opposition onto the Government.

The press sensed a difference between Howard and me and were only too happy to play it back as a leadership issue. Turnbull's intervention also allowed them to play him into the leadership issue. When Kerry O'Brien, on the *7.30 Report*, asked me whether Howard and I were at one on this issue, I said:

> Asking me whether I'd like to lower tax rates—asking a Liberal whether he'd like to lower tax rates—is like asking a farmer whether he'd like rain. The answer is yes ... and if we could make it lower, of course, yes of course, I'd love to see it lower. I wouldn't just restrict myself to the top rate, by the way. I'd say of all the rates, of course, we'd like to see all rates as low as is consistent with good Budget policy, lower interest rates and decent expenditures.

We had just had a smashing win on tax. We had tax cuts in place from 1 July. Comments by Howard and Turnbull undermined our political position. Our own side was suggesting we had not gone far enough. I explained to Turnbull that the best way to cut tax further was to restrain expenditure. The extent to which we could do this would be the extent to which we could increase tax relief. He understood this point and agreed with it as a backbencher. Later in that term, when he became a Minister in charge of expenditure programs, he produced an array of them. It is a common story. Each Minister is convinced of the importance of his or her own departmental programs. Sometimes they are right. But if each of them had his or her own way, Commonwealth spending would be limitless. Taxes would be much higher. Ministers in spending portfolios usually win plaudits for expenditure. The Treasurer carries the can on taxes.

The change in the Senate opened the way to deal with upper tax rates in the next Budget. They were not competitive. To get around the political obstacles I had tried to deal with the problem by making fewer and fewer people subject to them. But now I decided to face the issue head-on. Since the Prime Minister was on the record saying the top rate was too high, he could hardly oppose a proposal to cut it. The difficulty was that all sorts of figures got bandied around about how Australia's upper rates of tax compared with those of other countries. Very few people had a clear idea of where other nations applied their tax rates. People would always cite US tax rates, but in the United States there are not just federal income taxes, there are state income taxes as well. It is only by comparing all taxes over all levels of Government that you get a clear grip on where Australia's income tax rates stand in comparison with overseas practice. I set up an independent study to make an international comparison. The study was undertaken in early 2006 by Dick Warburton, the chairman of the Board of Taxation, and Peter Hendy from the Australian Chamber of Commerce and Industry. The document is extremely useful. It is the most exhaustive and rigorous comparison ever produced in Australia.

It is not easy to do these benchmarking exercises because the data from different countries are not always collected on a comparable basis. But the report showed that Australia had a low overall tax burden compared with other developed economies—the eighth lowest in the OECD. The threshold for our top marginal rates was slightly lower than the OECD average as a result of the tax cuts in 2003, 2004 and 2005. But our top two marginal tax rates were slightly higher than the average of the developed nations, by around 2 percentage points. This provided the data to benchmark our tax system and the empirical case to cut top marginal tax rates—or at least to bring them into line with the average of the developed economies.

In the 2006 Budget I announced we would cut each of the top tax rates by 2 per cent. This would give us rates of 15, 30, 40 and 45 per cent. I increased thresholds to guarantee that 80 per cent of taxpayers would have a top marginal tax rate of 30 per cent. Previously 3 per cent of taxpayers had been affected by the top marginal tax rate. The 2006 Budget lifted the top threshold so that it applied to only 2 per cent of taxpayers.

The scale I prepared for the 2006 Budget was originally intended to lift the thresholds for the two top rates of tax to $100000 and $200000. This would mean a person would only go on the second top rate on income over $100000 and the top rate for each dollar over $200000.

On the Wednesday before the Budget I outlined these thresholds to John Howard. He was adamantly opposed to them. He said it would look like the tax cuts were being skewed to the rich. I told him that we could afford it, that it was costed, that I had taken criticism over the

2005 Budget for not going far enough. I said that now was the time to deal with the issue—which was the most uncompetitive part of the tax system—before we got into an election year.

He would not budge. I got angry. We were at the end of the Budget process. I had conducted nearly all of the ERC. I was locked up in the Treasury. I was working under enormous pressure. The Budget had to be put to bed. I had not expected Howard to oppose my proposals. We had a heated argument. I had to compromise on an agreement to lift the thresholds to $75 000 and $150 000—not as good as $100 000 and $200 000, but an improvement nonetheless.

I had a big victory in another area—a plan to simplify and streamline superannuation. The taxation of superannuation in Australia was a monstrously complicated affair made even worse by a decision of the Labor Government in 1988 to pull forward revenue by taxing contributions into a superannuation fund as well as earnings in a superannuation fund. This meant there were three points of taxation: on contributions, earnings and end benefits. There were also complicated rules as to how much could be contributed and how much could be taken out at different preferential tax rates. Over the years I despaired of this system and decided that the only way to maintain confidence and simplify the situation was to abolish one point of taxation. With the Treasury I had worked up a plan to abolish the tax on end benefits so that a person over sixty taking superannuation from a taxed fund would not be subject to tax on their benefits—no tax on an income stream and no tax on a lump sum. It was a dramatic simplification. I had held the plan for more than a year but had done nothing with it because we did not have the fiscal room to pay for it. The plan became more expensive because I added to it a change to the assets test for pensioners to allow those reliant on the age pension to keep a larger sum without clawback. This was to show fairness to those without superannuation as well.

As the bottom line improved in the lead-up to the Budget I saw the opportunity to announce the plan. I raised it with Howard the week before the Budget. Superannuation is a complicated area and there are few people in Parliament on top of it. While he didn't fully grasp the detail, he didn't demur. I explained that we would propose it in the Budget and give ourselves a year to consult before the changes took place. If it ran into problems, I told him, we would then still have the option to drop it before we were irrevocably committed. By announcing it I would get it in the forward estimates. Again, using the improved Budget position to cut tax was a pre-emptive strike against further expenditure.

In fact we did not run into problems. A year later we implemented it. It was the largest reform to superannuation tax ever undertaken.

To his credit Howard went along with the plan even though he had little notice of it. It was one of those things that became possible only at the last minute as the bottom line came into focus and we got the head room to do it.

Beazley was not about to repeat the mistake he had made the year before. He did not oppose our 2006 tax cuts even though they delivered far larger benefits to higher income earners than the ones he opposed in the 2005 Budget. He had obviously decided that his previous response had been a mistake. He changed the focus of his attack. In his Budget reply, he said: 'I support the modest overdue tax relief that middle Australian families received in the Budget. They will need every cent of it … no tax cut can make up for your losing your penalty rates. No tax cut can make up for your being unfairly dismissed.'

It was clear that Labor had decided to draw another line in the sand. But it was not on tax, as Beazley had promised in 2005. It was on industrial relations.

In the Budget of 2007, again I lifted the tax thresholds, this time aggressively at the lower end as well as the upper. We were enshrining some new basic principles in the tax system—that 80 per cent of Australians should be on the top tax rate of 30 per cent or less, that only 2 per cent of Australians should be on the top marginal tax rate, and that low income earners should not come into the tax system at all. I returned to my 2006 proposal of lifting the threshold for the top rate to $200 000. Howard agreed to $180 000. I was at least getting closer.

By 2007 we had cut tax in five successive Budgets. Taking into account the changes from 1 July 2007, a person earning $30 000 had

had tax reduced by around 54 per cent since 1999. In 1996 the top marginal tax rate applied from $50 000. If that had been indexed, the threshold would have moved to $68 000 by 2008. We had lifted it to $180 000 and cut the rate from 47 per cent to 45 per cent.

Labor did not oppose our 2007 Budget tax cuts. From 2005 onwards they were silent on the issue. I had one more tax plan—the one I released on the first day of the 2007 election campaign. This was the one that would bring down the top rate and entrench a competitive system with benchmarks for those in each bracket. When the election came, Labor had no tax policy. As it turned out, they did not need one; they adopted nine-tenths of the Coalition policy.

The four-year cost of the tax cuts announced in the 2003 Budget amounted to $10.7 billion; in 2004, $14.7 billion; in 2005, $21.7 billion; in 2006, $36.7 billion; and in 2007, $31.5 billion. On each occasion I cut tax by the maximum amount available, after expenses, which would leave the Budget in surplus by at least 1 per cent. Each year revenue estimates were revised upwards, principally because the terms of trade were better than expected. Each year I pushed the Treasury to give me its best estimate, the reasonable upside, so that we could maximise reductions in income tax. Each year they claimed they had done so. Each year I acted on it. Each year from 2003 to 2007 their estimates were exceeded.

Even now the projections in the Budget are very conservative because we built in an assumption that the terms of trade would return to historical levels in the projection period. If they do not—that is, if they stay at current levels—revenue estimates will significantly exceed those currently in the Budget. When Labor came to office they inherited built-in Budget surpluses well in excess of 1 per cent of GDP, with the likelihood of revision upwards.

It is all very well to say that in 2003 we had $100 billion available for tax cuts over the period to 2011. In 2003 we did not. No one knew where things would be five, six, seven or eight years later. In 2003 no one suggested the outcomes that occurred. As revenue exceeded our forecasts on the upside, we adopted the practice of returning the dividend to taxpayers. We did not need larger surpluses. Lowering tax rates was increasing work incentives, adding to the labour supply and keeping the economy strong. We had the longest period of economic growth of any Government in Australian history. It was the right thing to do. The taxpayers were entitled to share in the benefits of a strong economy. By 2007 we had no net debt and we had superannuation fully funded.

Our stated object was a Budget surplus of at least 1 per cent, but in fact the outcomes were always greater. They were even higher if you include the bottom-line earnings from the Future Fund. Earnings on the fund were quarantined inside the fund. We altered our reporting systems to take them out of the cash balance. The historical tables in the Budget papers show the earnings from the Future Fund quite separately. If you add them back in, they significantly raise the reported surplus.

In economic terms these earnings can rightly be considered a component of the underlying cash surplus, which measures whether the Government is putting money into the economy or taking it out. Future Fund earnings are not spent; they are saved. They have the same economic effect on the economy as the cash surplus, which is also saved. In economic terms (which matter for the purposes of monetary policy), the Budget surpluses are higher than we were officially reporting. The 2007–08 mid-year review reported an underlying cash surplus of 1.6 per cent of GDP for 2006–07. Including the earnings of the Future Fund made it closer to 1.8 per cent.

We put Australia in a much stronger fiscal position than the United States, the United Kingdom or any of the G-7 countries. Unlike them, we have eliminated debt in net terms. We took the opportunity to make the tax system more competitive—and not just the tax system: during this period we reduced the taper rates on benefits. (A taper rate is the rate at which a benefit is clawed back for each additional dollar of income.) Together with Welfare to Work changes, improved taper rates increased work incentives. It was no accident that by 2007 unemployment was at a 30-year low. This was on a record participation rate of 65.3 per cent. When I became Treasurer the participation rate was 63.4 per cent and the scourge of the economy was unemployment, at around 8.5 per cent. We halved the unemployment rate while increasing participation rates to record levels!

After a decade of our economic management a new phrase entered the lexicon in Australia. It was a phrase Australians had not heard for a very long time: labour shortage. We were at or close to full employment.

Economic growth, low inflation, low interest rates, employment growth, privatisation and share ownership contributed to a huge accumulation of household worth. In net terms—that is, after allowing for debt—household wealth tripled from 1996 to 2007 from around $1.7 trillion to more than $5 trillion. Rising real incomes were enjoyed by the lowest income households as well as higher ones. This was an Age of Prosperity: the longest period of economic growth ever experienced by Australia.

14

GOING CACTUS:
THE 2007 ELECTION

Ashburton Primary School was an unlikely place in which to
field the toughest question of the 2007 election. Two weeks
into the campaign I was in my own electorate to open a new
playground that our Government had funded under the 'Investing
in Our Schools' program. After I had addressed the school assembly,
a representative from each year was chosen to ask me a question. It
started with Grade 6 and went down to the beginners' class. The
questions were about computers, my family, my job, the kinds of
subjects that primary students are interested in. It was the last question
that caught me out. Rourke Sheridan, five years old, walked to the
microphone and, in a confident voice in front of the whole school
(and, unknowingly, the nation's television, radio and print media),
said: 'Hello, Mr Peter Costello. My name is Rourke and I want to
know who made cactuses.'

The children squealed with delight. I was dumbfounded. Rourke
was on every television news bulletin that night and his photograph
was splashed across all the broadsheets the next day. Who made cactuses? 'That, Rourke, is one of the great questions of life,' I told him.
The *Sydney Morning Herald* ran with the headline: 'Are You Cactus,
Mr Costello?' The Quill Award for the best news photograph of the
year in 2008 was judged to be 'Costello and the Cactus Question'.

Why did the Coalition go cactus in 2007?

Kevin Rudd was elected Leader of the Labor Party in December 2006. As the shadow Minister for Foreign Affairs he had energetically prosecuted a case against the Government over AWB Limited. AWB Limited had paid kickbacks to the regime of Saddam Hussein in breach of UN sanctions. Rudd claimed that the Government had known of these kickbacks, or been warned about them, and had failed to act on the warnings. In fact, the Government was furious with AWB Limited for its behaviour. It was a private company with a statutory monopoly on the export of wheat. The Government did not control the company. It had no shares in it and did not appoint directors. Many of us thought the AWB should not have the monopoly anyway. I had long wanted to end it. The fact that this company enjoyed special privileges under statute was bad enough. For it to behave in this way infuriated us. The Government established a royal commission to investigate who had been responsible for these kickbacks. Other countries had companies that had breached UN sanctions. None did what we did to investigate those involved and to bring them to justice.

The royal commission completely undermined Rudd's allegations. But he repeated over and over again that there had been twenty, thirty, forty or more warnings—whatever the figure of the day was. It was a rhetorical device that insinuated Government involvement. After calling all the witnesses and considering all the evidence, the royal commission dismissed any suggestion that Ministers had been warned and it exonerated them.

Apart from this episode Rudd had not attracted much notice in the Parliament. He was not a good speaker in the House. As the Foreign Affairs spokesman he was not part of the main game, which is invariably domestic issues. But from the time Beazley returned to the Labor leadership in January 2005, Beazley trailed Howard as preferred Prime Minister—usually by a margin of two to one. Howard and I discussed whether or not Beazley would lead Labor to the 2007 election. Howard thought he would. He was confident Labor would not choose Rudd. 'Rudd is too long-winded, too academic. He's a bigger windbag than Beazley. He won't cut it with the voters,' he said.

I agreed that Rudd had little appeal. His main previous experience had been as a Queensland public servant. Before he became Leader he did not have strong support in the polls.

I was confident that Labor would not elect Julia Gillard. She was far too left-wing and the right-wing power brokers would never allow it. Nor would it choose Wayne Swan, who was underperforming as shadow Treasurer. I tended to Howard's view. But when he made his 'Athens Declaration' that he could beat Beazley again, I told him that Beazley might not last as the Leader to beat. 'Labor may go for someone younger and fresher. We may not be up against Beazley. They did it in 2004. They could do it again.'

An election does not turn on the preferred Prime Minister but on the two-party preferred vote. Keating led Howard as preferred Prime Minister through November, December, January and February before the Coalition won on 2 March 1996. We won the two-party preferred vote—the one that counted.

Although Beazley trailed Howard as preferred Prime Minister, the Beazley Labor Party was leading the Coalition in the polls. According to Newspoll, Labor was in front of the Coalition by August 2006 and stayed ahead in every poll until the election. ACNielsen also recorded Labor as leading the Coalition in two-party preferred terms from April 2006 to November 2007.

The public still did not know Rudd. But after he was elected Leader he immediately polled better than Beazley as preferred Prime Minister. By February he had passed Howard. Some Liberals were confident that he was enjoying a long honeymoon but that, when it ended, the Coalition would wear down Rudd's lead. We did not. Rudd remained preferred Prime Minister until the election. An incumbent Prime Minister will usually do better in these polls than the Leader of the Opposition because he or she has the gravitas of the office. (Remember Keating in 1996.) The fact that Rudd remained preferred Prime Minister continuously throughout 2007 showed that the public had formed its view. It wanted a change. It wanted a new Prime Minister.

A Government that has been in office for a long time can run out of ideas. We had been in office for more than a decade. We had made some big reforms but we were not yet out of ideas. In 2007 we announced more and bigger new policies than in nearly any other year. They started with the $10 billion National Plan for Water Security, announced on the eve of Australia Day, principally to address water use in the Murray–Darling Basin. I had advocated a national control for the cross-border water system for some time and was glad to see the Prime Minister announce it. It was a vast improvement on the National Water Initiative that we had announced in 2004, which itself was an improvement on the Water Agreement of 1994. The Department of the Prime Minister and Cabinet drew up the plan. It was big and it was bold.

In February 2007 the Minister for Ageing, Santo Santoro, announced a $1.5-billion package of reforms, 'Securing the Future of Aged Care for Australians', to improve quality choice and affordability in aged care. In March, Brendan Nelson announced $6.6 billion over thirteen years to acquire twenty-four Super Hornet aircraft. In May I brought down a Budget in which I announced the Higher Education Endowment Fund, improved vocational training, the second AusLink program, measures to encourage the use of solar power and deal with carbon emissions, and a new round of tax cuts. It was the best received Budget I had ever delivered, with a net positive rating of 48. The last Keating Budget before Labor lost in 1996 had a negative rating of −4. (The rating measures those who think the Budget is good for the economy less those who think it is bad.)

In June the Prime Minister and Mal Brough announced our response to the national emergency confronting Aboriginal children in the Northern Territory. This was based on the recommendations of the report *Little Children Are Sacred* and involved federal intervention, including troops and police, with massive public support. A week later the Government announced an additional $1.8 billion package of disability assistance which funded accommodation services and proposed a new payment for each child under the age of sixteen with a disability.

In August, Howard announced a Commonwealth take-over of the Mersey Hospital in north-west Tasmania and I announced the establishment of a Health and Medical Investment Fund (HMIF) of

$2.5 billion, with the income from the investment to be used for high-technology medical equipment.

In September the Minister for Veterans' Affairs, Bruce Billson, announced the improved indexation for disability pensions for veterans. In October, Howard announced the commitment of $4.4 billion over ten years for a second infantry battalion.

There was, in other words, no shortage of announcements throughout 2007. But we never drew level with Labor in polling. In some polls we were twenty points behind. On 16 July, Cabinet kicked around a number of policy proposals, some small, some dramatic, some good, some silly. But they were not the answer because policy was not the problem. 'We've got policy coming out our ears,' I said to the Cabinet. 'The problem is, no one is listening.' The electorate was tired of the Government and of John Howard. The same thing had happened to Keating and his Government before the 1996 election.

The way to freshen the Government and seize back the attention of the electorate is to have a new Leader who can deliver a fresh message to the public. This was the argument I had put in 2006. But that opportunity had passed. It would therefore be even more important to raise doubts about the Opposition, to get the media to focus on Rudd and to ask the question about his capacity, especially since he had no ministerial experience.

Rudd had been subject to very little critical scrutiny, and when he had faced scrutiny he had not been entirely truthful. The Western Australian Labor Government had banned any dealings by its Ministers with Brian Burke, a former premier of Western Australia and by this time a lobbyist, who had served time in prison. His influence over the Western Australian Labor Party was enormous. The Corruption and Crime Commission in Western Australia had investigated him and secret recordings showed that, despite the ban, Burke had extensive contacts with some Ministers in the state Government. When this came to light the Premier, Alan Carpenter, sacked them.

Rudd had also had dealings with Burke, who had the capacity to sway votes in the Labor caucus in any leadership bid. When these dealings became public, Rudd was less than open. He came up with unbelievable accounts of how he had had accidental meetings with

Burke when he happened to be in Western Australia, including on one occasion when he tagged along with a colleague to a restaurant where, to his great surprise, Burke was hosting a dinner. What is more, it turned out, to his surprise, that Burke had invited people to the dinner to meet Rudd. And at this accidental meeting Rudd had found himself to be the guest speaker.

I told the House of Representatives that anyone who dealt with Burke would be morally and politically compromised by the association. Burke would use such contacts to his own advantage. My words were borne out almost immediately but in an unexpected way. When Burke was challenged over his dealings with Rudd he went on the offensive. Far from just dealing with Rudd, Burke let it be known that he had had a meeting with Senator Ian Campbell, our Minister for the Environment. Campbell was not looking for favours from Burke or votes from federal Labor members. As a Minister he had granted Burke a meeting. But Burke used the contact to embarrass Campbell and the Coalition. Howard took the view that there would be no point trying to distinguish the Campbell case from the Rudd case, although they were clearly distinguishable. He asked Campbell to resign. Campbell did. It was a travesty of justice. Campbell had been my parliamentary secretary. He was a fine Minister and friend. Rudd paid no penalty for his association with Burke. Campbell lost his job. Campbell left the Parliament shortly afterwards.

It also turned out that Rudd was less than open when his office was involved in a plan to move the Anzac Day dawn service at Long Tan in Vietnam forward by several hours so that it could be shown live on Australian television. Rudd claimed that nothing had been confirmed and that his office had not been involved. Emails showed this was not the case. The press knew how sensitive Rudd was on this issue because of the way he abused the journalists who exposed the story. Then there was Rudd's visit to a lap-dancing nightclub in New York called Scores. He said he had been too drunk to remember what had happened at the club, although he had rung his wife to apologise about the incident the next day.

All these issues raised questions over the credibility and honesty of the new Leader of the Opposition. The press would pursue questions of character if it wanted to, as had been clear in its pursuit of the 'children overboard' issue. But it did not want to damage Rudd. It gave him the benefit of the doubt. The Canberra press gallery wanted a change of Government and was not about to derail the change that it saw coming. These incidents did not affect Rudd's approval rating. Some even thought they humanised Rudd or showed his ability to withstand scrutiny on difficult and unsavoury issues.

In August the *Daily Telegraph* published a leaked report from the Liberal Party's pollsters, Crosby Textor. I had not seen this report. From time to time, as Deputy Leader, I would be told the numbers in the party's quantitative polling, but I was not given written reports or shown the research on swinging voters questioned in focus groups. As far as I know the only people who ever received these reports were the federal director, Brian Loughnane, and John Howard. Whoever leaked it may have been trying to get the message to a wider audience.

The report said: 'Kevin Rudd is [a] markedly stronger option than previous leaders ... and attractive in some ways because he is strong and competent in many ways so just like John Howard, but younger.'

On Howard it said:

There is significant disillusionment with the Liberals on the issue of broken promises and dishonesty. Some voters have reframed 'experience' to 'cleverness'. With the arrival of a younger leadership alternative the age and energy of the Government has been thrown into question, raising questions about whether they are listening or getting arrogant, complacent and reactive.

The arrival of a younger and fresher Labor Leader made the age of the Liberal Leader and the longevity of the Government significant and negative factors. Beazley was not the threat to Howard that Rudd proved to be because he had been around for a long time and had already lost two elections. Even with Beazley, Labor was in a winning position. But under Rudd the Government's weakness on renewal and generational change was laid bare. Labor used issues such as the environment, Kyoto and climate change to highlight this difference. They became symbols of how the Government and Howard were out of touch, old or stale and how Labor would provide new leadership or fresh thinking.

Almost as soon as the 2007 Budget was delivered Treasury began revising its revenue forecasts upwards. It was plain that expenditure on some programs was slipping behind schedule and that expenses would be lower than Budget forecasts. This provided room for some of the policy announcements we made during 2007.

Under the Charter of Budget Honesty a pre-election statement on the Budget position would be issued. This legislation was designed to prevent an incumbent Government overstating the financial position. The Pre-Election Economic and Fiscal Outlook (PEFO) in 2007 would not show a position worse than the Government reported in the Budget. It would show the position was much stronger.

I knew that a pre-election statement showing a much stronger bottom line than we had budgeted for would provide room for both sides of politics to announce new policies and engage in new expenditures. It was important to get this increased money off the table, where it would be spent, and back to the people who had paid it—the taxpayers.

From August I began working on a new tax plan, which we could announce during the campaign. It would restrict expenditures by our side as well as by Labor. The Labor Party would be faced with the choice of either endorsing our tax plan or using the funds for new expenditures. If Labor chose the latter we would fight the election on tax cuts. If it chose the former we would have the advantage of delivering a significant tax plan—our issue—and getting bipartisan support for something in the national interest.

The tax plan that I drew up had two features. The first was to raise the upper limit for the lowest tax rate and increase the Low Income Tax Offset (LITO), which would move us to a system in which low income earners paid no tax until they earned more than $20 000. The second feature of the plan was to cut the top marginal tax rate, in stages, from 45 to 40 per cent and the second-top rate from 40 to 35 per cent. We had already been moving to benchmarks of what percentage of taxpayers would be on each marginal tax rate. Our new plan laid down new benchmarks—45 per cent of taxpayers on a rate of 15 per cent or less; 85 per cent of taxpayers on a rate of 30 per cent or less; 98 per cent of taxpayers on a rate of 35 per cent or less. The goal was to meet these benchmarks in five years' time (in 2012–13). The beauty of it was that the benchmarks would require the thresholds to be adjusted to keep these percentages constant. We would lock in the tax reform against inflation and wage increases. If wages increased, the thresholds would have to move to keep the same percentage of taxpayers at the required rate. To me this was the culmination of all the work we had done in cutting tax between 2003 and 2007.

The timing of our implementation of this plan and the exact thresholds would depend on the amount of money that could be reserved for tax cuts. I drew up three options. After consulting with Howard, I settled on option three, which was then modified seven times with each different option given a letter: 3a, b, c, d, e, f and g. We finally settled on option 3g. It was a long and painstaking negotiation. Two other major proposals would require significant funding if they were adopted as election commitments: one was a rebate on educational costs paid by parents; the other was an increase in pension entitlements.

Back in July I had been working up a package on housing affordability. With a long period of economic growth and low unemployment, house prices had been growing strongly. This is good for anyone who owns, or is paying off, a house, but it makes the price of entry much higher for first-time buyers. Demand for housing was strong and no one would want to crash the demand side. But supply was limited by restrictive land release policies implemented by state Governments and by taxes and charges on land release and transfer.

I was promoting measures to deal with the supply problem, but I also worked up a plan for tax-free savings accounts for young people, which they could draw on after the age of eighteen. The idea was that they could save tax-free for a deposit on a home. A further inducement to encourage young people to save for housing was to enable another person to put money in the account and claim a tax deduction of $1000 per annum. A parent or a grandparent could utilise a $1000 deduction to add monies to a child's savings account, which could help the child get a start in the housing market. The amounts would accumulate with the interest being tax-free. The child would be eligible to draw on it from the age of eighteen to buy a home. A child could maintain the account after eighteen and put their own savings into it and claim a tax deduction for each $1000 of contributions. If the account was not drawn for housing purposes, it would be rolled into a person's superannuation at the age of forty.

I had a vision of every young Australian with a tax-free savings account. Once each child had such an account, the Government could distribute any Budget surplus not required for investment directly into these savings accounts, which would be preserved for young people to buy a house or otherwise roll into superannuation. The surplus could be distributed to individuals but could not be drawn down until the age of eighteen and could be spent only on a house or eventually retirement income through superannuation. We had so many other policy announcements that we decided to hold back on this one until the launch of the election campaign.

Howard wanted to spend as much as possible on the education rebate. The idea was to rebate a percentage of the cost of educating a child, including school fees, up to a certain limit. Mal Brough, the Minister responsible for pensions, wanted to increase the aged pension, particularly that of single aged pensioners. I wanted to preserve as much of the financial resources as possible in order to cut taxes. We had robust discussions on how much would be allocated to each of these proposals.

Howard formed a small group to settle election policy. It consisted of himself, Downer, Minchin, Brough, Vaile and me. We discussed these various proposals throughout much of August and September. We also regularly debated them over dinner at the Lodge. The Prime Minister's economic adviser, Nigel Bailey, supported tax cuts, as did the Cabinet secretary, Peter Conran. In the end we decided to go with a tax policy. The actual detail was settled directly between Howard and me. We decided to announce it on the first day of the election campaign.

There was a good reason to announce it early in the campaign: it would not be possible to announce a major tax cut of $34 billion without explaining how it would be funded. In fact, it would be funded by an improved Budget position. But this meant we would have to announce the improved Budget position to explain how we were funding the tax cuts. The way to do this was with a mid-year Budget review. That had to be done before Treasury released its pre-election PEFO update, which, under the Charter of Budget Honesty, was due out ten days after the issue of the writs. So the tax cuts had to come out, at the latest, ten days after the issue of the writs.

At a joint press conference with Howard on the first real day of the election campaign, Monday 5 October, I released the mid-year review, which showed a major revision upwards of the bottom line, and the policy to cut taxes by $34 billion, which brought it back down again. The bottom line was still stronger but much closer to where we had expected it to be at Budget time. No one other than our offices had any idea it was coming until the press conference started. It took the press and the Labor Party completely by surprise. It was designed as a policy of shock and awe!

It soon became apparent that Labor had no tax policy and certainly nothing to match our announcement. Our campaign got off to a flying start. It was the best first week we could have hoped for. By the end of the week Rudd and Labor had copied the policy. They adopted the same threshold increases introduced in the same years with the same low income tax offset—identical. Out of our $34 billion policy, 91.5 per cent of Labor's response was the same. The only detail Rudd did not match was our proposal to shave the top tax rate of 45 per cent over three years down to 42 per cent and the second-top rate of 40 per cent over three years down to 37 per cent. This was an instalment to reduce the rates to 40 and 35 per cent by 2012–13 in the following Parliament. Rudd baulked at this. He said upper income earners did not need a tax cut. But to cover his bets he said that in the next Parliament (2010–13), he would cut to a top rate of 40 per cent (our policy).

I had started cutting those top rates in 2006 and I had wanted to implement a timetable that would finish the task. My policy would have cut the top two rates in the next Parliament, from 2009. There would be another instalment in 2010. Rudd's twist was to leave all the work to the Parliament after that—not before 2011. The risk is that it will never now be implemented. There will always be a political reason not to act. If we could have locked in bipartisan support, the rates would now be legislated to fall. It could have been done and it was all financed. It is a matter of great regret to me that I did not get the legislation in place that would have cut those rates. Rudd copied 91.5 per cent of the plan. I wish he had copied the remaining 8.5 per cent as well.

The Coalition won the first week of the campaign but it was the only week of the campaign we won. On the Sunday night at the end of the first week, the televised Leaders' Debate took place. It was widely believed that Beazley had won the Leaders' Debate in 2001 and that Latham had won it in 2004. But Rudd was weak on domestic policy and had had a bad week playing catch-up on tax. The debate took place before a live audience in the Great Hall of Parliament House. It was overshadowed by silly arguments about whether Channel 9 could use an audience to score the debate on a running basis with a device known as 'the worm'. Members of the selected audience were asked to watch the debate and move a dial to indicate their response. This fed into a line on the television screen that moved up when the audience liked what they were hearing and moved down when they did not. The worm was notoriously unreliable because it depended entirely upon who was chosen to be in the studio to work the dials. The methodology used to select the audience was problematic. The worm was a classic example of 'Garbage in, Garbage out'. An unrepresentative sample would give an unrepresentative result. I did not see the worm because I was in the audience at the debate. I thought Howard did well. But the worm killed him: it judged Rudd to be the winner of the debate. The debate contrasted a new leader against an old one, a fresh face against an old one, and played directly back to the Labor Party's strength.

In the second week we announced our proposal to lift the utilities allowance for aged pensioners to $500 per annum. This was the outcome of our discussions on assistance to aged pensioners. Mal Brough wanted to go further and was afraid that Rudd would trump us. But Rudd was unprepared for this announcement and eventually decided to copy it too. Labor won the second week because the press judged Rudd to be the winner of the Leaders' Debate.

The third week opened badly for the Government. A weekend newspaper reported that, according to 'Government sources', Malcolm Turnbull wanted to ratify the Kyoto Protocol but Cabinet had decided against it. Of course, the Cabinet had discussed the idea of ratifying the Kyoto Protocol many times, ever since it had been negotiated in 1997. Robert Hill had done a sterling job at the Conference in negotiating a target for Australia that frankly looked impossible at the outset. At the time I was surprised that, after investing so much effort in getting such a good outcome, we did not ratify it. The reason was that the protocol, by leaving out huge emitters in the developing world, was going to have little impact on global climate change. The protocol was flawed by the fact that it covered only the developed world.

Nonetheless, it was our policy to meet our target. What is more, we were one of the few countries that would do it. I had come to the view that since we were pledged to meet the target we should ratify the protocol even though it would not make any difference in the global scheme of things. John Howard's view was that it would look last minute and desperate for him to change his position. I think he was right. He had held out on the issue so long that it would not have been credible for him to change. It was something we could have done with a fresh leader; that would have allowed us to change direction. When I was preparing announcements on the APEC weekend in the light of Howard's possible retirement I included this as one of our major changes.

Rudd used the issue of Kyoto like he used the issue of broadband. It wasn't the detail of the policy that he appealed to. He used the issue as an illustration—an example of how he was modern and in touch and how Howard was tired and out of touch. Turnbull was in a tough fight in Wentworth, a seat considered to be very sensitive to environmental issues. He was under attack from the high-profile Geoffrey Cousins, a former advertising guru and an adviser to Howard who wanted to block a pulp mill in Tasmania. It may have been thought that if it was known that Turnbull supported the ratification of the Kyoto Protocol, it would help him in Wentworth. But there was no chance that the

Coalition could support it while Howard was the Leader. We had been through all that many times before. The story was counterproductive because it switched the campaign to environmental issues, where Labor had a strong lead. More than likely it reminded those concerned about global warming not that they should vote for Turnbull but that they should vote against the Liberal–National parties.

In the middle of the week Tony Abbott was to debate Labor's shadow Minister for Health, Nicola Roxon, at the National Press Club in Canberra. He came to Melbourne for an announcement by John Howard on health in the marginal seat of Deakin. I was there too. (By coincidence the announcement was at a medical clinic where my mother was a patient. As we walked around the clinic that day another lady introduced herself to me. It was my first primary school teacher— Miss Harle—the one who had promoted me to Grade 2 some forty-five years earlier; it was a thrill to see her.) The announcement that day was not our major health policy; it was on funding for practice nurses. Howard spoke, I spoke, and Abbott made some brief remarks. He was to have only a minor role.

Howard was in full campaign mode, shaking hands and talking to staff. This meant that the announcement started later than expected. By the time it was over and Abbott arrived back in Canberra, the debate at the Press Club was nearly half over. By turning up late he looked as though he did not respect the shadow Minister or the press. Roxon had a go at him. He responded sotto voce but the boom microphone picked up his words. He told Roxon that her complaints were 'bullshit'. Already that day Abbott had been forced to apologise for comments he had made about an anti-asbestos campaigner who was seeking to have new pharmaceuticals listed for subsidies under the Commonwealth Pharmaceutical Benefit Scheme. Bernie Banton, who was suffering from asbestosis and mesothelioma, had developed a high profile in his fight against the manufacturing company that had used asbestos—James Hardie. It was wrong—and bad politics—to attack him. He died shortly afterwards. Luckily, by the end of the week, Peter Garrett, the shadow Minister for the Environment, told a journalist that, regardless of the policy Labor announced, 'once we get in we will just change it all'. It made Labor look like it had a secret agenda. This gaffe got us back in the game, but Labor still won the third week.

The fourth week of the campaign was dominated by an interest rate rise of 0.25 per cent, announced by the Reserve Bank the day after the Melbourne Cup. The Bank had never before lifted interest rates during an election campaign. Before I became Treasurer, it was the practice for the Treasurer to announce interest rate changes—and no Treasurer would announce a rate rise during a campaign. The fact that the RBA made its announcement in the feverish last weeks of an election campaign demonstrated, once and for all, its independence. The Labor Party seized on the rate rise to attack the Prime Minister's claims about keeping interest rates low. Home mortgage rates were still lower than at any time under the previous Labor Government but it was a propaganda win for Labor on the issue of credibility. Howard said to the borrowers of Australia: 'I'm sorry.'

The next day Howard and I held a joint press conference on the issue of economic management. Dennis Shanahan from the *Australian* asked Howard: 'If you're not responsible for the interest rate rise, why did you apologise for it?' It was a lure to draw him back into the controversy over the 'stolen generations'. Howard knew it: 'Well, I said that I was sorry they'd occurred. I don't think I actually used the word *apology*. I think there is a difference between the two things. I think we've been through that debate before, haven't we, in the context of something? Just speaking as an individual, of course I'm sorry when interest rates go up ...' It derailed the press conference. The night before, the press reported that Howard had apologised for the rate rise. Now they said he refused to apologise.

It was not all to Labor's advantage. The interest rate rise put economic management back at the centre of the campaign. This was the one area in which the Coalition led Labor right through the campaign. As preferred Treasurer I was leading my opponent by more than two to one. The only time the Coalition got close to Labor on a two-party preferred basis was that night—the night of the rate rise. With interest rates rising, people began to think about the economy and who they wanted to manage it. They were unsure about Rudd and they did not want Swan. Politically, the interest rate rise had a mixed effect. Labor won the fourth week of the campaign although it was a split decision.

The two party launches dominated the fifth week. The centre-piece of our launch was to be the education rebate, the home savings accounts and an initiative to bring forward child-care rebates to reduce fees paid for child care. We wanted to focus squarely on economic management. As Deputy Leader I gave the first speech. I was followed by the Nationals Leader, Mark Vaile, and then John Howard as the Liberal Leader. In my speech I said:

> If the experience of the last eleven years has taught me anything, it has taught me there is no clear sailing in economic management. Just when you think you have passed a difficult period or a new challenge, there is one waiting around the corner …
>
> Today we have further challenges: all-time world-record oil prices; a one-in-100-year drought that lingers on and on and on; the collapse of the sub-prime US lending market, which is now having reverberations around the world. And all of these things will buffet global inflation, they will buffet our economy, they will buffet exchange rates, they will affect growth and job opportunities. They will require careful management on the Budget, on tax, on structural policy, on industrial relations, on competitiveness, on investment. And on 24 November the Australian public will have the choice of the experienced economic Howard–Vaile–Costello management team or a roll of the dice on Rudd–Gillard–Swan.
>
> My charge against the Rudd–Gillard–Swan collection is not just that they don't have the experience but, because they haven't had the experience, they haven't thought through the policy. They haven't thought through what is really required to manage this economy …
>
> Like the bulls of Pamplona they are stampeding to declare themselves economic conservatives.
>
> They would have you believe there were never reds under the beds, just economic conservatives—poor misunderstood economic conservatives, yearning to be free.

Howard had adopted the practice of writing his speaking points on a few sheets of paper but delivering his speech without a prepared text. In 2001 this had worked beautifully when he had come up with the line: 'We will decide who comes to this country and the circumstances in which they come.' It was memorable and it electrified the audience. It also energised the voting public. But there are risks with an unprepared text. No one else has had the opportunity to assess the phraseology. You could hit or you could miss. The technique did not serve him well at the launch of 2007. He dealt well with the policies but the rhetoric was askew. He personalised the voters' choice. Rudd was the preferred Prime Minister. If the election became a question of whether the public wanted him or Howard to be Prime Minister, Rudd would win. We wanted to make it a contest between the skill and experience of the two teams. But Howard emphasised his own position. He said:

> I want to tell you why I want to be Prime Minister of this country again ... I want to be Prime Minister again so that we can build an even stronger and greater Australia. ... I want to be Prime Minister again to carry forward my principles and those of the Coalition on education. ... I want to be Prime Minister again so that we can achieve a lasting recognition in our Constitution of the first Australians ... I've tried ... to express to my fellow Australians ... why it is I would like to be Prime Minister of this great country again.

All this simply reminded people that he had already been Prime Minister for eleven and a half years and he wanted to go around again. But it was not clear for how long he wanted to be Prime Minister again, since he had said he intended to step down during the next term. Mark Textor, the party's pollster, went into meltdown. '*Me, me, me, me, me.* He is completely off message.' The voters' choice was supposed to emphasise the choice between an experienced team, which people could trust to look after their mortgages and jobs, and the inexperienced and unknown alternative of Labor.

Since Rudd had run out of policy, he tried to make a virtue of this in his election launch by claiming he would underspend the

Coalition. This could not be tested because he had not released all his policies or allowed time for independent bodies to cost them. But it was a clever pitch. His weakness was economic management and he pitched himself as more conservative than the Government. Labor won the fifth week.

Howard suffered two particular handicaps during the campaign. He did not have a wide circle of advisers. He trusted only a small group, some of whom had left his service. His most trusted confidant had been Grahame Morris, his senior adviser and briefly chief of staff. Morris was so loyal that during one earlier controversy he had advised Howard to sack him, which Howard did (although he continued as a commentator on Howard's behalf). Also in Howard's circle was Max Moore-Wilton, secretary of the Department of Prime Minister and Cabinet and a 'can-do' bureaucrat who delighted in the nickname 'Max the Axe' (he prided himself on crashing through bureaucratic obstacles). He had left Howard's service in 2002. Arthur Sinodinos, who had succeeded Morris as chief of staff, was another of the circle. He had moved on in 2006. These resignations had been heavy blows to Howard, who was unable to fully reprise his trust in new and more junior staff.

Bennelong also proved a dreadful distraction throughout the 2007 campaign; Howard knew he was in trouble in his own seat. He spent several Sundays in the lead-up to the election campaigning there. This meant that the Sunday evening news bulletins carried a Bennelong story that also featured Howard's opponent, the well-known television presenter Maxine McKew. Weekend television news programs are the most watched news programs in Australia. With Howard campaigning in his own seat, the weekend news reported that he might not even get re-elected to Parliament. Only once previously had a Prime Minister lost his own seat. It was a big story and it helped McKew. It undermined our effort to convince the electorate that Howard was needed to steer the country. He was having trouble convincing his own constituents.

On 15 November 2007 the party's pollster prepared a note based on research on how we should frame our message in the final week of the campaign. Because it involved me I was shown a copy. It read:

1. Peter Costello must play a greater role in the last week not only to leverage the economy but also to deal with the succession issue: including 'seeing through' John Howard's more favourable promises and policies.

2. The Prime Minister must avoid references to only himself rather than his team when talking about the next term as many switch voters believe that many of 'his' promises won't be enacted as he will not personally be there to see them through (even on the economy).

3. Union influence and chaos, higher interest rates, slower jobs growth and raiding superannuation remain the potential consequences of a Labor victory.

In order to deal with the succession issues and to leverage up the economy, Howard and I decided to do a joint interview on the current affairs program *Today Tonight* in the last week. It was difficult. The idea was to explain how after all these years there was a plan for an orderly succession and continuity. There was a fine line because we did not want the interview to focus on Howard's intention not to see out the term for which he was seeking re-election. The fact that we are of such different heights made the seating arrangement look peculiar.

On the Wednesday I had a long-standing engagement to debate Julia Gillard on ABC Radio National's morning program. It was to be held in front of television cameras in Melbourne's Federation Square. Gillard turned up halfway through the half-hour allotted for debate. She was, she said, held up in traffic. It was the same offence that Tony Abbott had committed earlier in the campaign. But it rated only a passing mention on the evening news bulletins. The press was not going to give any of the Labor stumbles the sort of coverage they gave to a Coalition setback.

After the debate, or non-debate as it turned out, I flew to Sydney to speak at a lunch with John Howard at the Wentworth Hotel. I met him in his Phillip Street office first. There was no staff with him. He was alone with his son Richard. He looked crushed. Howard told me that party workers had distributed a bogus leaflet in the seat of Lindsay. The state director, he said, was handling the issue and had expelled those involved.

We walked down to the hotel together. I was happy with the luncheon, where there was strong support from the business community. But it did not matter. That evening the ABC's *Lateline* reported the bogus Lindsay leaflet. The next morning, the retiring member Jackie Kelly gave her version of the events on *AM*. We had no hope of getting our final message to the media after that. Kelly and the bogus Lindsay leaflet stole the last forty-eight hours of the campaign.

15

UNFINISHED BUSINESS

In 2006 the *Bulletin* magazine—then Australia's oldest—asked me to launch its special edition on the 100 most influential living Australians. The guest of honour was the man they judged the most influential Australian of all—Rupert Murdoch. It was an opportunity to talk up Australia's movers and shakers, including our artists, writers and poets.

I discussed five issues of public policy that bedevil Australia. One was lifting Aboriginal people into the mainstream of Australian life. The other four were federalism, water management, the ageing of the population and the transition to a republic. Anyone who could fix one or more of these problems, I said, would surely be on the list of the 100 most influential Australians by the year 2100.

Federalism has failed Australia. By federalism I mean the system of Government where powers are divided between different levels of Government which discharge separate responsibilities in designated areas. In theory federalism allows various governmental services to be provided by the level of Government closest to the people. This should strengthen Government accountability and improve service delivery. Federalism should be a check on power or tyranny. It divides power so that the different levels of Government check and balance each other.

But there is no clear delineation between the powers of the Commonwealth and the states. The public is unsure about who is responsible for which services. Accountability suffers. Even in those areas that are clearly state responsibilities, the states usually blame any failure on the fact that they have not been given enough funding by the Commonwealth.

To help overcome this problem I decided to allocate all revenue from the GST—a tax that grows with the growth of goods and services in the economy—to the states. I hoped that, with guaranteed 'growth' revenue, the states would be able to take full responsibility for their services and the public would insist on higher accountability. But it made no difference. The states took the revenue but showed no sign of changing their rhetoric, blaming all their problems on under-funding by Canberra.

One of the reasons that this has been a successful state strategy is that the media are mostly state-based. The main newspapers are centred on the states, as are the major radio talk-back programs. Most of the channels in the television networks also have state bureaux dedicated to covering the state premiers and state Governments.

If a state premier demands more money from Canberra, people think it is likely that someone outside the state will end up paying. If the Premier were to demand that his or her state's taxpayers pay more, the idea would become far less attractive. Any demand on faraway Canberra will usually get a sympathetic hearing.

Our Constitution will never be amended by referendum to abolish the states or state Governments. The only way of structurally improving the situation is for the states to impose their own taxes and fund services for which they are responsible, or for the Commonwealth to deliver those services either by taking them over or by funder-provider agreements. An example of the Commonwealth taking over state services was the Howard Government's decision to establish secondary technical schools because the states had vacated the field. An example of the funder-provider model is the set of Australian health care agreements that provide Commonwealth funding for public hospitals.

I do not support the states imposing their own taxes in place of Commonwealth ones. All of the evidence is that they tend to levy them either on particular industries and transactions which are distortional—such as the outrageously high insurance taxes—or at different rates, such as payroll tax, creating unproductive complexity for national businesses.

Through the course of the Howard Government the Commonwealth involved itself in areas that were formerly the responsibility of the states—and nearly always in a good cause. It reformed the state gun laws in response to the Port Arthur massacre. It tried to reform the Australian history curriculum in schools. Its industrial relations laws—upheld in the High Court on the basis of an expanded view of the Corporations power—led to the ever-widening jurisdiction of the national Government.

The Howard Government was a centralist, not a federalist, Government. I had reservations about this. The Government set out to improve outcomes, but the more the Commonwealth took on, the higher the level of what was expected of it. Conversely, the less the state Governments did, the lower the level of expectation on them.

One of the main areas in which the Commonwealth is increasingly involved is water management. This is a traditional and constitutional responsibility of state Governments. They established the water authorities whose responsibility it is to capture water and develop distribution systems for the major capital cities. Some of these are now private. State Governments also established authorities, or local Governments, to meet these responsibilities in smaller towns and regional communities. The Commonwealth Government has traditionally not been involved in collecting, distributing or retailing water, nor has it been involved in irrigation schemes that take water out of the major rivers and waterways. These have always been operated by state authorities. The Constitution provides expressly that the Commonwealth cannot abridge the right of a state or its residents to the reasonable use of rivers for conservation or irrigation.

The drought that persisted from the late 1980s along most of the east coast and in southern Australia led to widespread restrictions on the use of water in our major cities. Many irrigation farmers and property holders were also unable to get their full allocations of water. The failure of the states to invest in new reservoirs or dams or to capture and reuse storm water made the situation even worse. Having no responsibility for water, the Commonwealth did not have a water department or any regulatory powers. But it became involved under competition agreements. These were agreements between the Commonwealth and the states designed to foster reform, particularly in the states, through Commonwealth bonus payments known as 'competition payments'. Under one of the agreements in relation to water, some of the payments were contingent on a state moving to price water properly—according to volume—and to assess new reservoirs environmentally before construction.

The Commonwealth Treasurer, on advice from a Competition Council, was responsible for making competition payments. Some of the states dragged their feet. When this led to the suspension or withholding of their payments, they were quick to blame Canberra. They would claim that any penalties or deductions robbed the state of entitlements or would lead to reduction of services, for example, in health or other areas. Where states complied with the requirements—say, by increasing the price of water—this too would be blamed on the Commonwealth: the price of water was going up, they would say, because they were being forced to raise it under threat of financial penalty.

The administration of the Water Agreement was dispiriting, the progress slow and the reform a poor return on the payments. I wanted to use our competition payments for a far more direct outcome. At the very least the states should use some part of their payments to improve water conservation. If they did not, my view was that the Commonwealth should use the money to do it directly.

In addition, landowners were telling the deputy Prime Minister, John Anderson, that the states were undermining the security of water entitlements. This led the Commonwealth, in 2003, to put to the states a new National Water Initiative (NWI). It included $500 million for the allocation of water in the Murray–Darling basin. The agreement was formalised in 2004 and later backed up by the establishment of an Australian Water Fund comprising the competition payments and additional funds. This fund was allocated directly to water projects rather than, as in the case of competition payments, general revenue—which the states could use in any way they saw fit (including for projects unrelated to water). The NWI also involved an agreement about who would bear the cost of a reduction in a water entitlement. Essentially, the holders of the entitlement would bear the cost of the first 3 per cent reduction, with the state and Commonwealth Governments sharing the risk for reductions greater than that amount.

The major irrigation waterway in Australia—the Murray–Darling basin system—crosses four states. To accelerate implementation of the NWI and to deal with this basin in particular, John Howard announced a National Plan for Water Security on the eve of Australia Day in 2007. Essentially, the plan was to commit $6 billion over ten years to modernise irrigation infrastructure and increase the efficiency of water use. It provided another $3 billion over ten years to retire or relocate non-viable or inefficient irrigators, with the water entitlements given up and used to restore the health of the river. An integral part of this plan was that the Commonwealth would have oversight of water management in the Murray–Darling basin. By this stage the Commonwealth had been funding water reform for more than a decade. I had allocated a new injection of funds to the Murray–Darling basin starting in the 2006 Budget. But the states still had regulatory control of irrigation and water allocation.

The states had allocated more than the system could yield in an environmentally sustainable way. The only way to restore the Murray River to health was to get back some of these allocations. The prospect of retiring large numbers of people who used irrigation for their livelihood was low, but it was necessary to offer incentives if we were ever going to address this problem seriously. Dealing with inefficient wastage in irrigation was also a good policy.

I was not involved in developing the detail of this plan but I had been advocating that the Commonwealth take responsibility for water regulation in the Murray–Darling basin for some time. My threshold point was that the Commonwealth needed to get a referral of regulatory power over interstate waterways, which were beyond the ability of any one state to manage. I was pleased that we made the investment conditional on the states referring such powers. The plan was developed inside the Department of Prime Minister and Cabinet, and the Prime Minister announced it. At the same time he also announced that Malcolm Turnbull as Minister for Environment would add water resources to his portfolio, a responsibility he had previously carried as parliamentary secretary to the Prime Minister. By now the Commonwealth had a full department with responsibility for water resources and a full policy to deal with the issue.

The preparation of this policy produced some jurisdictional tensions in the public service. The Commonwealth had never had a Water Department before, and there was competition as to which branch of the public service would have responsibility for dealing with the issue. In a speech to Treasury officers in March 2007, Ken Henry talked about the general achievements of the Treasury Department in the past year—the principal one of which was the G-20 conference. He went on to say: 'Water has got away from us a bit in recent times, but it will come back with some quality Treasury input at some stage. It will have to. We are, at last, right at the centre of policy development in the climate change area.'

His reference to climate change was to Treasury's engagement in drawing up a policy on emissions trading. Australia generates its electricity predominantly from coal-fired power stations. If we are to significantly reduce carbon emissions we must move to other energy sources. Significant technological breakthroughs with clean coal and sequestration may help in the longer term. But, either way, restricting our carbon emissions is going to raise the cost of energy.

In my view the best way to allocate the cost of reducing carbon emissions is through a market-based or trading system. I took a submission to Cabinet in 2003 to establish an emissions trading system. The idea was complex and was much less well understood then than it is now. The resource companies were opposed to such a scheme at the time. The Cabinet did not approve the submission, preferring to invest in technology as the way to deal with the issue. As I mentioned earlier, technological breakthroughs may be a big part of solving the problem. But if we do not get those breakthroughs we will be left without a response.

Attitudes changed as the energy and resource companies realised they would come into trading systems in other parts of the world. They took the view that it was better to come into a well-designed system where they could manage risk and cost. As a result, in 2006 the Government did adopt the proposal of an emissions trading system and established a task force to draw it up. It reported in June 2007. The report was largely the work of Martin Parkinson, one of the executive directors in the Department of Treasury, who had been seconded to the task force for that purpose. (Labor rejected our proposal. It had commissioned Ross Garnaut to prepare its own proposal and demanded more onerous targets.) The 2006 task force was what Henry meant when he claimed Treasury was at the centre of policy development in climate change. Treasury had also been involved, through competition policy, in water policy for over a decade. The thrust of that policy and of the NWI was to build a market trading system for water entitlements. The problem was not designing such systems; it was getting the states to implement them.

The Henry speech was posted on the Treasury website. Labor seized on it and promised to bring Treasury to the centre of water policy. The implication was that in doing so, policy would somehow change. After Labor's election, presumably after considering Treasury advice, the new Government negotiated exactly the same policy that John Howard had proposed in 2007. The Victorian Government, which had originally held out against the agreement, accepted it after the election of the Rudd Government, on substantially the same terms. It claimed that by holding out it had secured some more money, but this was public 'spin' rather than real substance.

The problem with rural water management is not a lack of policy but a lack of implementation of policy by the level of Government that has the legislative authority in the area—the states. The states have not only over-allocated water entitlements, they have also failed to price water properly. This precious limited resource is so under-priced that there is massive wastage. If it is priced according to volume it will not be wasted, and further, in commercial uses it will go to the most productive enterprises. It is important to be able to trade water entitlements in a market to allow water to go to the highest value use.

In relation to urban water supply, there has simply been under-investment in capturing water, in recycling it and in desalination.

In some cases this is because state Governments have forced water authorities to pay dividends rather than use their operating income for new investment. Major new investment will be necessary to deal with the shortages currently being experienced. Desalination requires significant energy use and it will run into objections over carbon emissions. This is where nuclear energy comes in. There are a lot of reasons why nuclear energy should be considered in Australia but the key may be to link it with water. Nuclear energy firing desalination is a feasible way to deal with urban water shortages.

In 2002 I released Australia's first 'Intergenerational Report'. The objective was to project Government finances over forty years. This would alert us to long-term trends that would require action by the current generation. It would also allow us to measure, over time, progress in dealing with those long-term trends.

The Intergenerational Report had been prescribed by the Charter of Budget Honesty, which we had passed in our first term of Government. The charter requires a report every five years to ensure that the current generation does not pass undue burdens to future generations as a way of meeting current financial obligations. The report would therefore benchmark equity between the generations in the management of Commonwealth finances.

The Intergenerational Report of 2002 showed that, over forty years, a gap of 5 per cent of GDP would open up between expenses and revenues (if revenue remained constant to GDP). This gap could be filled by a massive increase in taxation, by the accumulation of unsustainable debt or by harsh and radical expenditure cuts.

The principal driver of the increase in expenditure would be health, which would increase in proportion to GDP. Medical advances prolonging life and improving its quality are becoming more sophisticated and more costly. An older population would be more likely to draw on these treatments at a greater rate. One of the principal areas is pharmaceuticals. A male aged between sixty-five and seventy-four will, on average, use pharmaceuticals eighteen times the value of a male aged between fifteen and twenty-four—and the proportion of seventy year olds in the population is growing much faster than the proportion of twenty year olds.

The Intergenerational Report led us to focus on issues such as the low level of participation by older men in the workforce. With the ageing of the population it is necessary to encourage older workers to stay connected with the workforce longer, if only for part-time work. It highlighted the declining fertility of the population. No one complains about increased life expectancy, but until the publication of the Intergenerational Report few Australian leaders had been complaining about declining fertility, which is a feature of all advanced industrial societies, although the rate varies—lower, for example, in the United Kingdom than in the United States.

My first attempt to deal with the issue of fertility involved the introduction of a 'Baby Bonus' in the 2002 Budget. This allowed women to spread their earnings over the years that they were out of the workforce with children. In this way they could access lower taxation rates and generate tax refunds which would help the family budget. If they did not pay tax, they were eligible for a payment. The Baby Bonus did not really take off until the 2004 Budget, in which I amalgamated it with an existing maternity allowance and raised it to a lump sum of $3000. This was designed to cover costs associated with the birth of a child—obstetrics, lost pay and incentives for immunisation—which would make it a universal benefit.

The bonus captured the public attention. My press conference on the afternoon of the 2004 Budget also helped. This was when I urged Australian families to have 'one child for Mum, one for Dad and one for the country'. (When a journalist told me he already had two children, I told him to 'go home and do your patriotic duty'.) 'One for Mum, one for Dad and one for the country' made international headlines. The British tabloids loved it. I was fielding requests for interviews from all over the world. As I was coming out of the conference I asked my press secretary, David Gazard, how he thought it had gone. He said: 'You will get a big run on that one. But you delivered it to the wrong audience. Parents should have lots of children. Breeding is good. But not for those people. They're journalists!'

Jokes about fertility and children were to recur for some time. One newspaper photographer won a Walkley Award for his picture of me with six just-born babies. I was stopped in Collins Street one day by a man who said: 'My wife and I took your advice. We already had two children but we had one for the country. That was six months ago. Would you mind coming around to pick it up?'

Strangely enough, in the wake of this focus on fertility and the Baby Bonus, Australia's fertility rate bottomed and began to pick up. We were the only country in the Western world that reversed a decline. I do not claim that the Baby Bonus did it.

No one in their right mind would have a child for the sake of a financial incentive. But I do believe that, in reminding people of the importance of population replacement, our focus on fertility made childbearing more acceptable in circles where it might have gone out of favour. Some educated women might have been made to feel that interrupting their careers for children was letting down the feminist cause or wasting career opportunities. To hear it said, at a high level of Government, that having children was important not just for its own sake but for the health of our society was a significant countervailing view. Women would often joke that they were having children 'for the country'. The focus on the ageing of the population, on demographic changes and on the importance of children helped them to be more confident about doing so.

We also took steps to cut the ever-spiralling cost of pharmaceuticals. These included the increased promotion of generic products and of alternatives to some commonly used pharmaceuticals such as statins (including diet and exercise).

A focus on participation in the workforce led to measures to encourage single mothers to rejoin it when their children entered secondary school and to other measures to curtail the exponential increase in disability pensions on the basis of musculo-skeletal conditions and psychological problems.

Reforms of superannuation included extending to the age of seventy-five the cut-off point for making contributions, a tax offset for mature-age workers, the abolition of the superannuation surcharge and eventually the abolition of all end-taxes on superannuation for those over sixty.

Enabling older Australians to take part of their income in tax-free superannuation meant that any part-time work would be taxed at much lower rates because the superannuation was kept out of the tax system. The second Intergenerational Report showed that by 2007 participation in the workforce was at all-time record levels in Australia.

In a speech in 2002 trying to explain the long-term drivers of economic growth, I referred to the law of 'three Ps'—population, participation and productivity. Our economic growth is driven by the proportion of the *population* of working age. The higher their level of *participation*, the higher the level of economic growth. The higher the *productivity* of those participating, the higher the economic growth. The law of the 'three Ps' became a paradigm that we could run over all policies to see whether they helped long-term economic growth. It became widely accepted by policy makers and in time the Opposition also came to accept this framework.

On 6 November 1999 Australians voted by a majority of 55 to 45 per cent against an amendment to the Constitution to make Australia a republic. The only state in which the vote was close was my home state of Victoria, which voted 49.84 per cent in favour of the republic. The 'Yes' vote in Victoria failed by fewer than 10 000 votes out of around three million.

There is no point being churlish about the vote: it was decisive. But it is a matter of regret to me that the referendum was defeated. It is something that the Liberal Party will come to regret. I am not anti-British. I have enormous admiration for British institutions, including the supremacy of Parliament, responsible Government, the rule of law and an independent judiciary. I also have enormous admiration for the Queen. She is truly one of the world's outstanding leaders. When she came to Australia for the centenary of Federation, she congratulated Australia on 100 years of successful, peaceful, federated Government and made the point that she had been Australia's monarch for nearly half of that time. I had presented nearly 10 per cent of Australia's Federal Budgets, but compared to the Queen I was hardly a starter.

The Queen is exceptionally well informed about Australian affairs. In 1997 when I launched a coin to celebrate the seventieth anniversary of the opening of Old Parliament House, the head of the Australian Mint (for which I was responsible) presented me with the commemorative coin and proudly told me this was the second one minted.

'Who has the first?' I asked.

'We thought we should send it to the lady who opened Old Parliament House in 1927.'

'She is still alive seventy years after the event?'

Of course she was. The Queen's mother had opened Australia's first Parliament House in 1927 as the then Duchess of York. Her family has had an extraordinary connection with our country.

But Australia has changed. Originally our Governors-General were British, being representatives of the Crown in Australia. When the first Australian Governor-General, Sir Isaac Isaacs, was appointed in 1931, it was controversial. Thereafter we reverted to British-born Governors-General, including the Royal Prince the Duke of Gloucester, appointed by Labor Prime Minister John Curtin. Labor appointed an Australian in 1947 but the Menzies Government reverted to British-born appointees until its appointment of Richard Casey in 1965. By this time Sir Robert Menzies realised that Australia had outgrown the policy of appointing British-born Governors-General.

In my view the Liberal Party should have effected another natural and sensible change—that the Governor-General represent not the Crown but the Australian people. This is the essence of a republic, the head of which is usually titled 'President'. When I attended a government primary school in the early 1960s we assembled every Monday morning to salute the flag and recite the oath: 'I love God and my country, I honour the flag, I serve the Queen and cheerfully obey my parents, teachers and the law.' We would then sing 'God Save the Queen'. In Australia today many schools recite different oaths. None refers to the Queen. The values now affirmed in schools include friendship, duty, loyalty. But not monarchy. This is not because of hostility to the Queen. It simply means that we have moved on.

The republic referendum was defeated not because the public was against the concept of a republic. It was defeated because a majority rejected the particular model put forward. If I had had my way, I would have proposed an even more minimalist model. I thought the key to success was to persuade conservative Australia to the cause and to do this by not substantially altering the way our system works.

The Australian Republican Movement (ARM) thought the key lay elsewhere. It worried about a minimalist republic because it wanted to keep more left-wing opinion on board. These were those who wanted more substantive changes. Some wanted a Bill of Rights and some wanted a directly elected president with executive powers. Others wanted a new system of Government that would open the corridors of power to them.

Supporters of the status quo and those who wanted more radical change voted against the proposal and defeated it. I was reluctant to support the proposal initially but by the time of the vote I had become more enthusiastic. Perhaps it is in the political nature to be unable to see an election or poll without wanting to be involved. The more seriously I thought about it, the more important I saw it would be in a symbolic sense, and the more important it was for a conservative opinion to embrace it. I will try to explain why.

It was the Liberal Party's idea to establish a people's convention to examine the question of whether Australia should become a republic. Alexander Downer had first adopted it when he was the Leader of the Opposition. When John Howard became Leader he recommitted to it. The proposal was that the Government would appoint half of the members of the convention and the public would elect the other half.

The momentum for a republic was picking up steam in the lead-up to the celebration of the centenary of Federation in 2001. It had been ALP policy since 1991 that Australia should become a republic on the centenary of Federation, 1 January 2001. Keating, in his policy speech for the 1993 election, had promised to develop a discussion paper to consider options for a republic—which he described as a 'Federal Republic of Australia'.

I remember watching this policy speech in my electorate office. He delivered it in Bankstown in front of a blue curtain apparently designed by Baz Luhrmann, the film director. The phrase 'Federal Republic of Australia' produced a guffaw among those of us watching.

It sounded so much like the Bundesrepublik—the Federal Republic of Germany—that it was hardly likely to excite the Australian imagination, not least because federalism did not excite the Australian imagination. Malcolm Turnbull chaired the committee appointed by Keating. It concluded that a head of State could be appointed by the Government, by a vote of Parliament or by public election.

The platform of the Liberal Party unambiguously defended constitutional monarchy. The membership was overwhelmingly against any republic. In 1993 I gave a speech on the subject which was quite ambivalent:

> For practical purposes, Australia is a republic with a nominal head of state appointed by hereditary. The purpose of the head of state is to appoint a person, on the recommendation of the Australian Government, to hold executive power for a specified term at the pleasure of the Government. By convention that person—the Governor-General—is an Australian ...
>
> The best way of developing a truly indigenous and appropriate form of Government is to let our system evolve building on its past strengths and correcting past mistakes.

I discussed what would happen if the states refused, under their own constitutions, to abolish the position of the Crown and the need to define the powers of a president who would be 'circumscribed neither by convention nor the possibility of easy removal'. I then concluded:

> Our current constitutional arrangements have created a stable, peaceful and democratic environment for tolerance to hold sway. To radically change an arrangement that has no discernable practical problem for arrangements that involve mammoth technical problems and a great deal of uncertainty does not appeal to me as much of an exchange.

If a republic involved mammoth technical problems and uncertainty, I would not support it. Like most Liberals I did not believe the republic was a first-order issue.

I was also suspicious of anything that Keating put on the agenda. But I could not say that I was opposed to the principle or would never support it. Our system will evolve and I believe that it will evolve in this direction. All of our constitutional development since 1901 has been towards loosening our connections with the Crown and asserting a separate identity from Britain.

Later a proposal was put forward by the former governor of Victoria, Richard McGarvie, which provided a mechanism for the appointment of a president on the recommendation of a Prime Minister. This became known as the McGarvie Model. The idea was to establish a Constitutional Council of retired Governors-General, presidents, governors and judges of the High Court, who, on the recommendation of a Prime Minister, would appoint the president. The president would hold all the powers currently conferred on the Governor-General under the Constitution. The constitutional arrangements would be unchanged. The only difference would be that the appointment, on the recommendation of the Government, would be done in Australia by a council of experienced and disinterested people of high standing rather than from Buckingham Palace by the Queen. This would be a small evolutionary step. I had known McGarvie for a long time. At one stage he had interviewed me for a job as his associate when he was on the Supreme Court in Victoria. He was a Labor man but a very sensible one. I considered this a very sensible proposal.

At the Constitutional Convention in 1998 I supported the McGarvie Model. But Neville Wran, a former New South Wales premier, killed it on the floor of the convention by cleverly enquiring about the proposed age limits for those to be on the council. McGarvie had proposed an age limit of sixty-five to seventy-nine. His idea was that appointees must have retired from their significant offices before they could act on the council. He was too much the earnest and accurate lawyer and governor to realise that Wran's question was a trap. He answered it honestly. Wran had a feel for the theatre of the moment and exploited it. The convention broke into laughter about the proposition that such an ageing Council of State should appoint a president. Now that the issue of the ageing of the population is better understood, it does not sound so silly. The best answer to the question would have been to point out that the Queen in all likelihood will be appointing Governors-General at a much older age than sixty-five or seventy-nine.

The McGarvie Model did surprisingly well at the convention. It was the second most preferred of four models that were put forward for voting. But the ARM model led the count all the way through and was the one chosen. The ARM campaigned and organised best in the election and it had more delegates on the floor of the convention than any other group.

When I rose to address the Constitutional Convention in Old Parliament House on 3 February 1998 I knew it would be, for me, a significant speech. I did not want to denigrate our past in order to argue for change. In my view 100 years of continuous constitutional development had given Australia a robust democracy. But we could build on that success. I knew that at this moment I would have to declare myself on the principle of whether we should amend our Constitution and move towards a republic or whether we should remain with the status quo.

I was also aware that although the pro-republican media would welcome any statement from me as the Deputy Leader of the Liberal Party in favour of a republic, the party itself—that is, the membership of the party—would not welcome it. The party membership was, and probably still is, substantially against any move to a republic. Howard was well in touch with the majority opinion of the Liberal Party membership, which was far more weighted towards his generation than mine. Most of my speech was an attempt to put my view in context and to address my preferred model. This is part of what I said:

> It is quite commonly said that all this argument is about is whether we want an Australian as a head of state. If that were all we wanted then one of the options to fix it would be an Australian monarchy. But in truth, the problem is more the concept of monarchy.

The temper of the times is democratic. We are uncomfortable with an office that appoints people by hereditary. In our society and in our time we prefer appointment for merit. The system works very well but the key concept behind it is bruising against reality.

So I am for change. I believe there is an unease at the centre of our constitutional arrangements … because the symbols which underlie them are running out of believability and this gnaws at their legitimacy.

I made a plea to the proponents of the republic not to overshoot. It was important to win over conservative Australia, and that meant the bulk of the Liberal Party's constituency:

I am not for change at any price. But I am someone who believes that in changing we should secure and safeguard what is best: that by directing change we will get a better outcome than by allowing pressure to build up and explode with implications far less benign. History and convention make such a change feasible and a workable constitutional improvement.

My argument was that sensible evolutionary change would, in the long term, best preserve our parliamentary democracy. Without modernisation, our institutions would fray and fracture, ending in unpredictable or unanticipated results. The Crown, the monarchy, was once a unifying symbol for Australians—or, to be more precise, for those who identified themselves as British, which included the colonials and their descendants. But after Federation, Australians began to see themselves differently. As the years passed, the Crown became less and less of a symbol of identity or unity. It is running out of believability as an Australian symbol. Visits by the Queen are seen more as a visit by a foreign head of state than by a monarch to whom Australians owe common allegiance. But we should not leave behind the important legacies that came with British settlement, such as parliamentary democracy and the Westminster system. They are not symbolic. They are substantive guarantees of our freedom and order. They are separable from the Crown.

There was some talk at the convention that Liberals who were constitutional monarchists would get behind the McGarvie option and vote for it. If it had become the preferred model it would have gone to the vote in the referendum. Tony Abbott made a last-ditch appeal to John Howard to vote for it; but Howard was against it. His view was that constitutional monarchists should not support a particular republic model because ultimately they were against all models. I believe that if the McGarvie Model had been adopted, the Liberal Party would have swung behind it and the chances of success in the referendum would have been greater. As it was, the ARM had its preferred model and sufficient numbers of delegates to adopt it. Some supporters of the McGarvie Model, like myself, supported the ARM model—not because I changed my mind but because I thought the model was workable and was consistent with my view on the overall principle. But there were Liberals who would have supported the McGarvie Model who campaigned for a 'No' vote.

The supporters of the ARM model were trying to balance a moderate republic against those who wanted a directly elected president. The more militant supporters of that option decided they would rather defeat the proposal than win a republic with a symbolic president. Together, those republicans and the constitutional monarchists formed a majority which defeated the referendum in every state and territory of the Commonwealth.

Some of my colleagues, like Peter Reith, declared themselves for a directly elected president and campaigned for a 'No' vote. In part, their argument was that, once the public defeated this proposal, shortly afterwards there would be another referendum on a new proposal for a directly elected president. I was against this form of tactical voting. Referenda on the same subject rarely happen twice and, I warned, it would be a decade at the very least before this one came back.

My own electorate of Higgins voted in favour of the proposal, as did John Howard's Bennelong. Most of the inner-suburban seats voted that way. Kim Beazley, the Labor Leader, did not get a majority for the republic in his electorate. Nor did Kevin Rudd. As a rule of thumb, the closer an electorate was to the GPO in a particular state, the higher the republican vote. Critics would say this shows that the republic is supported by inner-city 'elites'. I think the vote reflected small-'l' liberal opinion. The Liberal Party should represent this as well as conservative opinion. If it fails to do so, the people of that opinion will find a home with other political parties.

My support for the referendum may have had a significant influence in getting Coalition voters to support it. Around 40 per cent of the Liberal party room supported a 'Yes' vote, although many would not say so publicly because it would have offended party members and could have affected their pre-selection. It was even more difficult for members of the National Party in this regard.

The failure of the 1999 referendum was not a success for the Coalition. The issue will come back and it will be much more difficult for the Coalition to handle it from Opposition. Any future model is likely to involve more substantive changes than the last one. If the party had embraced evolutionary change, we could have led the issue and secured sensible constitutional change. By not doing so we risked a far less sensible constitutional outcome.

There was one other issue put to the referendum in November 1999. The convention recommended that a new preamble be inserted in the Constitution. It was not clear to me why. It was said at the convention to be a 'consequential matter'. This is nonsense. There is no reason why a change from constitutional monarchy to a republic would require a new preamble and certainly not in the terms recommended.

The convention recommended that the preamble make reference to 'Almighty God', the federal system, the rule of law, the original occupancy by Aboriginal peoples and Torres Strait Islanders, cultural diversity, the environment, and possibly other matters. It may be that this was to placate delegates who wanted a Bill of Rights. But for others, the insertion of such matters in the Constitution ran the risk of giving ammunition to judicial activists who would find all sorts of new, and hitherto unknown, constitutional rights in the new preamble.

I was always against the preamble. I didn't vote for it. Once you begin enumerating laudable or worthwhile sentiments it is very hard to stop. Leaving some out may suggest they are less important, or not important, or do not have the prestige that constitutional recognition brings. Some saw the preamble as a statement of 'the vision thing'. It is a different matter if a constitution arises out of historical circumstances that can be recorded in, for example, a Declaration of Independence. But to me this was an attempt to invent idealism long after the event.

The preamble referendum had no significant opponents. The poet Les Murray originally drew it up. John Howard made some changes, and further changes had to be negotiated to secure its passage through the Senate. The Aboriginal Senator Aden Ridgeway, of the Australian Democrats, was particularly involved in these discussions.

In the week before the referendum Howard held a press conference with Senator Ridgeway to make a joint appeal to the Australian people to vote in favour of the preamble, whatever their view on the main republic question. He said that the preamble would give the nation 'a way, as we go into the next century, of expressing what unites us rather than continuing a debate about what doesn't unite us'. I am not aware of anyone who campaigned against the preamble but it suffered a heavier defeat than the republic referendum, with 39.3 per cent voting for it compared with 45.1 per cent for the republic.

Some have said that, if Howard had campaigned for a 'Yes' vote on the republic, it would have been successful. I am not sure about that. His campaign on the preamble did not swing voters. Few referenda have been defeated by a margin as great as that suffered by the preamble question. Among those that were defeated was the 1988 referendum on longer parliamentary terms, fair elections, the recognition of Local Government and guarantees of civil rights. The Australian public may be suspicious of politicians, but it is also suspicious of Local Government and constitutional protections to be interpreted by judges.

In October 2007, before our election defeat, Howard returned to the issue of a new preamble, proposing a referendum that would see a new 'Statement of Reconciliation' incorporated into it. Recognition of Aboriginal and Torres Strait Islanders in a constitutional preamble had been overwhelmingly defeated in 1999. It was a strange issue to raise on the eve of the election. It did not excite public imagination and it played no part in the election campaign.

There is more unfinished business than the issues I raised at the *Bulletin* lunch. One is the state of the Liberal Party, which, at the time of writing, is in Opposition in all states and the Commonwealth. This requires a response in three main areas: philosophy, structure and leadership.

The Liberal Party was formed in the 1940s to promote the great principles of classic liberalism—individual freedom, individual rights, private property, free trade. But it is also the representative of conservative opinion in Australia. Robert Gordon Menzies created the party by welding together the many disparate organisations that shared these values.

The world's great democracies all have two-party systems representing centre-right and centre-left politics. The divide seems so natural that it is replicated across cultures and languages in the Western world. The Liberal Party should remember this. It is the guardian of the centre-right tradition and opinion in Australia. By all means the party should reach out to people of progressive opinion, just as it reaches out to blue-collar labour. But it will never defeat Labor by outflanking it from the left. Nor will it win Government if it swings too far to the right. Most state divisions are trying to strike an effective balance. But in New South Wales the left–right split has seriously weakened the party. Restoring the balance in that state remains a major issue of unfinished business. It will come only with a renewed awareness of the give-and-take in the centre-right tradition.

The structural problem of the party—the weakness of the organisation—is more radical and intractable. Membership of the Liberal Party consists of individuals and individualists. No companies or trade associations join it. There are no great internal centres of power. There are not even national factions. The party organisation is all voluntary. The office bearers are all part-time.

As a result the Members of Parliament exercise great sway in the organisation. They are the party's full-time political actors. Federal MPs liaise with each other, travel around the state divisions and try to or tend to exercise control of the organisation. No one does more than the federal parliamentary leader, especially if he (and there has not yet been a she) is also the Prime Minister. This is the way Menzies wanted it. It gives the leader enormous authority. But the Menzies model, which works well in Government, works against the Liberal Party in Opposition.

The party's lack of an extra-parliamentary apparatus weakens it in policy, personnel and finance. Out of Government the Labor Party falls back on its constituent unions to employ its activists, raise money and provide an important extra-parliamentary apparatus. The Liberal Party has no equivalent. It cannot rely on large corporations, which always want to be a friend of the Government of the day. When the party is out of office in all of the states as well as nationally, there are no shelters to look after promising activists and nurture future talent except for the various Opposition staff jobs.

A related weakness in the structure is exposed when the parliamentary leader takes the party off course: there are no strong centres of power to restrain the leader or redirect the party. This was the case with Fightback! After the defeat in the 'unlosable' election of 1993, rank-and-file party members had good reason to complain that they had not been listened to. They had reported the public's dissatisfaction to MPs but had largely been ignored.

The party organisation then re-asserted itself. It played a role in ending Hewson's leadership and bringing about the end of Downer's. It had more influence at the beginning of the Howard Government than it did later. As the years went by, influence and power drifted towards the Prime Minister's office. There is no point criticising the federal president for failing to check the leadership of the party. The Prime Minister essentially held the power to select the federal president.

When the Coalition was elected to Government in 1996 it was also in office in all the states and territories except New South Wales. Since 1996 Labor has won office in all the states and territories and in the Commonwealth. It began its march back to office at the state level, where it adopted a new model of Government. Its strategy has been to minimise risk in an effort to prolong its period in office. It avoided major reforms which could prove controversial. Above all, it rode the economic recovery put in place by the Coalition Government and, after the introduction of GST, the rising revenues it produced.

To avoid any criticism of its failure of nerve or of its achievement, it perfected the technique of dominating the 24-hour news cycle. There is a daily announcement, usually by the state premier, which the metropolitan stations cover on their evening news bulletins. It is often previewed in the state newspapers that morning. The whole object is to create an effect or illusion of action. The following day another announcement would be made, to dominate the next 24-hour news cycle. There is usually very little follow-up or critical analysis in the media because the media has been moved on to the next announcement. The unending array of statements and promotions—including sporting events and fashion, food or arts festivals—squeezes the Opposition out of the media and positions Labor as an active but safe party of Government.

Rudd is very familiar with the policy of dominating the 24-hour news cycle. He employed the technique well in the 2007 campaign, always avoiding critical examination of his announced policies by making new ones and filling the agenda in such a way as to feed the relentless demands of the media. But he will find it harder to avoid critical scrutiny over time and at the national level. It is not possible for a Prime Minister's press office to dominate the news outlets in a way that a state Government can with fewer, and more parochial, outlets. The national Government may have a wider range of announcements but they tend to be in more substantial areas where progress can be evaluated. A state premier may announce the clean-up of local parks and waterways to mark World Environmental Day. The Prime Minister may announce progress on an emissions trading system. It may be hard to evaluate the success of a clean-up of the waterways and parks, but an emissions trading system affecting all companies in the economy is complicated and technical. If there is no serious progress, or if the design turns out to be significantly flawed, there is likely to be some critical analysis. People expect more from the national Government.

Eventually people begin to tire of these ceaseless announcements, particularly if results do not match expectations. But Labor has also developed a second technique to deal with the problem of longevity in office. The idea is to change the public face of the Government, to have the premier stand aside in favour of a successor—as Premier Bob

Carr did for Morris Iemma, Premier Peter Beattie did for Anna Bligh, Premier Steve Bracks did for John Brumby and Premier Paul Lennon did for David Bartlett. The same could be said in Western Australia, although Premier Gallop cited depression when he stood aside for Alan Carpenter.

An orderly and smooth transition allows the outgoing premier to carry off any baggage for under-performance or for political failings. The incoming Leader, generally elected unopposed, can then proclaim a fresh broom and a new Government. There is now a new face to fill the 24-hour news cycle. When these Governments go to the electorate, they are asking not for a second, third or fourth Labor term but for a first term of a new Government with a new premier.

The Liberal Party has a culture of the Leader rather than a culture of the party. With a few exceptions, such as RG Menzies and Henry Bolte, its leaders have been unable to time their departures to maximise the electoral fortunes of their party. Again, the ill-organised nature of the party membership has made it almost impossible for the party itself to insist that a Leader create such an opportunity. For many, the Prime Minister is the party and it makes no sense for the party to assert itself against the Prime Minister. The federal parliamentary Liberal Party has never voted an incumbent Prime Minister out of the leadership—not in the whole history of the party. The only time there has been a transition was when the Leader himself seized the initiative and brought it about—in the case of Menzies, who stood down for Holt, and in the case of Gorton, who voted himself out of office with the casting ballot.

The relationship of the party to the Leader—in particular, how to manage generational renewal—is perhaps the most salient of all the unfinished business of the Liberal Party. The window of opportunity is open to the new leaders, Brendan Nelson and Julie Bishop. Brendan Nelson came to the Liberal Party as an outsider but he has had time to get to know its culture. Although he was not a major player in the Howard Government, I was not surprised that he was elected Leader: he has kept close to his colleagues, taken the backbench seriously and actually listens when people talk to him. (He has the wonderful bedside manner of the practising doctor he once was.) He has the advantage of Malcolm Turnbull, who has been in Parliament for a much shorter period and has not established strong relations with his new colleagues. Time and experience may fix that. (Critics make much of Turnbull's personal wealth as evidence that he is not in touch with ordinary Australians. But he rightly points out that the wealth of the Rudd family exceeds his. Kevin Rudd is the richest Prime Minister Australia has had. Wealth is not a bar to office, provided it is not displayed ostentatiously.) Julie Bishop, the Deputy Leader, did not have John Howard's support when she won her seat against the Independent Allan Rocher, who had been Howard's numbers man. When Howard would not campaign for her she asked me, as Deputy Leader, for support and I gladly gave it. She was, after all, the Liberal candidate. She won the seat and incurred Howard's disfavour. She is highly educated, articulate, hard-working and determined—jogging to Parliament House early each morning to begin a long day's work.

After its election in 1996 the Coalition Government began the fight to balance the Budget, pay off debt and implement new arrangements for monetary policy. The Labor Party vigorously opposed it. The Labor Party vigorously opposed the Coalition's program of privatisation and tax reform.

As late as 2006 Kevin Rudd described Australia under the Howard Government as 'Brutopia'. 'Brutopia' is a fictional place described in Donald Duck cartoons as a hostile country aiming for world domination. Rudd was obviously trying to suggest that Australia was some kind of brutal utopia. He described the Coalition's Australia as 'an unrestrained market capitalism that sweeps all before it'.

But in the election year of 2007, Rudd made no further mention of 'Brutopia'. Even he could see that the results were in. The model had worked. Australia enjoyed an Age of Prosperity. He did a complete turnaround. He was not now interested in dismantling this 'Brutopia'. 'I am,' he said, 'an economic conservative.' Nothing could illustrate the triumph of the Liberal Party program more than the conga line of Labor MPs who queued up to declare: 'I, too, am an economic conservative.'

The legendary Prime Minister of Singapore, Lee Kuan Yew, once warned that Australia could become 'the white trash of Asia'. It was a mark of how confident the Asian economic tigers were of their growth and prospects in the 1980s and early 1990s and, by contrast, of the slipping status of Australia—an economy whose best days were generally considered to be behind it. The financial crisis and regional recession shook the confidence of the Asian Tigers. By contrast Australia's recovery gave it new confidence and status as the 1990s ended and we continued our longest run of economic growth ever through the best part of the first decade of the new century.

Early in 2007 I hosted a private dinner for Mr Lee, by that time Minister Mentor in the Singapore Government. I asked him if he remembered making the comment about 'the white trash of Asia'. 'How could I not when every time I meet an Australian I am reminded of it?' he said. I asked him: 'What is your view now?' He said simply: 'You have changed. Your country is a different place now.'

And it is. After nearly twelve years at the helm of economic policy I could see what a different country we had become. We had build an Age of Prosperity. No longer the laggard of the region, Australia had recovered its pride and confidence.

The greatest achievement of the Howard Government is its economic record. It is there for all to judge. In its last years it was helped by a very strong increase in the terms of trade, but the hard and important work had already been done. We balanced the Budget, eliminated net debt, reformed superannuation, established the independent monetary policy, liberated industrial relations, introduced the GST, cut capital gains and income taxes and built the Future Fund. Australia enjoyed continuous growth on low inflation and the best employment outcome in more than thirty years—during a period of great turbulence including a regional meltdown and an international recession.

The boom in the terms of trade brought challenges of its own, particularly managing inflation in an environment of full employment. Again, the Government was extraordinarily successful by historical standards.

There are some areas in which the Coalition could have done better. It could have moved earlier to remedy indigenous disadvantage. It could have solved the constitutional issues concerning a republic. It should have rebuffed the challenge from One Nation sooner.

On international issues the legacy will be more mixed. It is too early to say how events will work out in Iraq. There will be instability in that country for some time to come. But the current democratically elected Government is a great improvement on the tyranny of Saddam Hussein. There will also be instability in East Timor for some time, but no one says it would be better to return to the stability imposed by the Indonesian military. There is likely to be continuing instability in the Solomon Islands as well, but Australia's contribution was worthwhile. The future of Afghanistan remains uncertain, but the ongoing clearing of the Taliban and terrorist training strongholds from the country has improved security for Australians and the West. It has also ended a regime that repressed its own people, particularly women.

Australian relations with all its important regional partners were in a better condition when the Coalition left than when it entered office in 1996.

John Howard is the second-longest serving Prime Minister in Australian history. He deserves the accolades for leading his party to four election victories—the equal of Bob Hawke and second only to Menzies. His political legacy is soured by the fact that, when he was defeated, his party was left in Opposition in every state and Territory as well as nationally. The fact that his Government's economic achievement was so strong makes the defeat worse, not better. He is only the second Prime Minister to lose his own seat. But his record and the record of the Government he led rank him as second only to Menzies in the Liberal Party.

When I was first elected, there was a glass cabinet at the entrance to the House of Representatives in Canberra displaying an excerpt of an article written by Robert Menzies for the *New York Times* in 1948. It read as follows:

> I believe that politics is the most important and responsible civil activity to which a man may devote his character, his talents

and his energy. We must in our own interest elevate politics into statesmanship and statecraft. We must aim at a condition of affairs in which we shall no longer reserve the dignified name of statesman for a Churchill or a Roosevelt, but extend it to lesser men who give honourable and patriotic service in public affairs.

In my first term Dame Pattie Menzies sought me out. She asked about Tanya and my family. Then with a twinkle in her eye this grand old lady said to me, 'I am old and you are young. I do not know what your future holds. But with all my heart I wish you well, Big Feller!'

I was a junior MP just starting in Parliament. It was a gracious act for this veteran of public life to take an interest in me and it impressed on me the significance she gave to this 'most important and responsible civil activity'.

My eighteen years in Parliament—in Opposition and in Government—have confirmed me in the conviction, formed in my youth, that politics, for all its rough edges, is a civilised and civilising calling. Despite all the obloquy shovelled on the head of politicians, they are the men and women who work the machinery of our liberal, democratic way of life. They reflect public opinion—and at their best lead public opinion—and transmute it into laws that shape our society and our country. I have devoted myself in Parliament to liberalising our economy, to laying a basis for the prosperity of future generations, and to heightening the respect the world pays to, and owes, our country. I have discussed some of the unresolved problems that face us, especially addressing indigenous disadvantage and dealing with the structure of our federalism. We must deal with these to move forward as a free, fair and vibrant society. I have no doubt we can find the solutions that suit us, provided we do not succumb to the siren calls of demagogues, charlatans and ideologues.

The achievements of the past decade have laid an extraordinary foundation. Properly preserved and built on, we now have opportunities we never had before in Australia's history. The best years for our country are still in front of us.

APPENDICES

1   The Liberal Party and Its Future   339

2   The Life and Death of Harold Holt:
Biography by Tom Frame   343

3   The Spirit of the Volunteer:
Inaugural Sir Henry Bolte Lecture   347

4   Lone Pine Memorial: Gallipoli Peninsula, Turkey   352

5   National Day of Thanksgiving   354

6   Worth Promoting, Worth Defending:
Australian Citizenship   358

7   Challenges and Benefits of Globalisation   362

8   *The Bulletin's* Top 100 Most Influential Australians
Luncheon   366

9   Benchmarking Tax and Spending   371

10 Comparative Economic Statistics (Election 2007)   375

1 The Liberal Party and Its Future

*In October 1993, after our fourth straight federal election defeat, I gave
a speech to the Council for the National Interest, a conservative group in
Sydney. I argued that the Liberal Party should woo the blue-collar workers
that the Labor Party had deserted—people known in the United States
as 'Reagan Democrats'. A large number of them voted for the Coalition in
1996. In Australia they became known as 'Howard's Battlers'.*

The Liberal Party of Australia, which turns fifty in 1994, proved
a spectacular success in its first generation, holding Government
federally from 1949 to 1972.

... But in the last decade the Liberal Party has repeatedly lost
national elections. In its worst string of defeats ever, it has been out of
office since 1983.

Before the pundits become too apocalyptic about its future, one
should note that in the last year the Liberal Party has been elected to
Government in two states—Western Australia and Victoria. It is in
office in New South Wales. It is in office in Tasmania and it will come
to office in South Australia at the next election which is imminent.
Apart from Queensland, the Liberal Party will then be in Government
in every state of Australia.

Yet it is natural—not only natural but right—that this federal
electoral failure should lead to serious critical reflection. Plainly
something has gone wrong. If it is to win elections the Liberal Party
must become hungry for success.

... Although the Liberal Party lost by a nose in the 1993 election,
circumstances were such that it should have won by the straight. It
should not over-react to this defeat. But it should react.

In the wake of our most recent defeat, competing prescriptions
have been put forward for the future direction of the party. I will deal
with a number of them. The first prescription is to make the Liberal
Party more inclusive.

No one serious about electoral success would argue against
expanding the membership and support for the Liberal Party. We
should aim to include as many people as possible in our activities and
as our voters. We have room for many more.

... We should, of course, work hard at wooing ethnic communities. We can always work harder. But this is not to say we have
overlooked this in the past.

... It may be that at the peak level, ethnic leaders form closer
relations with those in Government rather than those out of
Government. Those in office are, after all, implementing policy and
directing funds—but this is a factor that will only be overcome by
success in winning elections. Success always brings its own rewards.
To blame the Coalition for not obtaining the favour that only office
permits is to blame it for losing elections, not for any stand-alone
failure.

The One Australia policy of John Howard circa 1988 was said to
alienate some ethnic groups, but even if this were true, it was a passing
policy and a lot has changed since then. In particular, since the advent
of Mr Keating's recession, both sides of politics now advocate lower
immigration levels.

... Let me state unequivocally, we value and want contribution,
involvement and support from those of all ethnic backgrounds ...

... I believe there is a group of blue-collar voters that is open to
switching from Labor. At a time when the Labor Party is increasingly
the preserve of academics, teachers, social workers, university-
educated union careerists and preoccupied with the concerns of
various 'liberation' movements—gay liberation, black liberation,
women's liberation—and environmentalism that will cost some of
these supporters their jobs, they must be coming to the realisation
that Labor is no longer their party.

These are the kinds of people who crossed over to the Republicans
in the Reagan elections, and became known in American terms as
'Reagan Democrats'.

I think Mr Keating must be aware that the ties of this group
are loosening. After launching his Women's Policy Statement during
the election campaign, including a promise to re-educate judges, he
made his promise to pay up to $30 per week to non-earning mothers
with dependent children in his 'Building on Strength' Statement of
24 February 1993. Which was the bigger vote winner? Who do you
think made the bigger electoral contribution: the Keating staff member,

Anne Summers, author of *Damned Whores and God's Police* and the Women's Policy Statement, or Annita Keating, full-time mother of four and exemplar of stable family life?

Labor is trying to straddle two constituencies with important political differences—the traditional blue-collar Labor vote and the new class, new Labor vote. Once Mr Keating derided this latter group as 'Balmain basket wavers'. Increasingly, he relies on them. As he deserts old ground in the quest for new ground, we should pay special attention to wooing the deserted ...

... In the last election Labor received around 4.75 million first-preference votes and the Coalition around 4.68 million first-preference votes. Obviously the Coalition attracts support from all occupation groups. But in terms of membership, electioneering and intensity of support ... small-business people, together with their families and those who identify with them, are the core supporters of the Liberal Party.

These people are always being squeezed by Government. Unlike big business, they cannot afford the shielding professions of accountants and lawyers to protect them against Government. They fall victim to complicated tax rules, training guarantee levies, ABS form filling, industrial awards, and they feel utterly exposed to union demands, with their back-up from a maze of tribunals, legislation, organisers and Government.

... These are, incidentally, the forgotten people. They are not organised; they do not spend their time extracting from Government because they are too busy attending to business and satiating Government's extraction from them. They are worried about their own future and the future for their children.

... The Liberal Party must always remember the forgotten people. But we must add to this base if we are to cross the electoral line and make it possible to practically aid these people. We have won a number of the policy arguments for them—even from out of office—for example, on freeing the rigid award system that shackles them and establishing enforceable remedies against unlawful trade union action. This has been of assistance. But there is no substitute for the ability to legislate, administer, tax, and spend or de-legislate, reduce tax or 'de-spend' as the case may be.

Consistent with our commitment to these forgotten people, we must enunciate the values that define them. But we must apply these values to issues that concern wider groups in the community. By addressing these issues, we can widen our constituency ...

On these issues (there are many more), the values of the Liberal Party—individual dignity, self-reliance, national sovereignty, personal liberty, a fair go—are highly relevant. These values resonate with those of the Australian people. There is an eager audience ready to listen to those who have the courage to address their concerns.

... Talking about values inspires controversy because people can understand them, they may resonate with them, or they may disagree with them. But they do become enfranchised by debates of this kind.

To put meat on the bones you have to engage in the specifics of tax–spend–legislate. An important part of the argument is in the detail. But this is the second layer of the argument. A large portion of the public never penetrates to this level. To communicate with them, you must communicate at the first level—'the vision thing', as George Bush termed it.

This means communicating the values that motivate a party's political approach to the issues of the day, and convincing voters this will improve their lot and improve the fortunes of those they care about. Since most Australians care about their country, it also means showing what this will do for the nation.

... A Government must always hold tax–spend–legislate subordinate to values. The organisation must always hold procedures–fundraising–meetings as subordinate to the vision. The vision is the rudder. The rest are the oars. Our members are far more interested in ideas than procedures. And we must give them a stake in ideas to sustain them through the long march of modern politics.

12 October 1993

2 The Life and Death of Harold Holt

*In August 2005 I had the opportunity to launch a biography of one
of my predecessors as Member for Higgins—Harold Holt. When the
founder of the Liberal Party, Sir Robert Menzies, stood down to allow
an orderly transition to Holt as Prime Minister, Holt took the Coalition
to an historic majority in the 1966 election. Holt's Prime Ministership
ended with his untimely death, which, unfortunately, has overshadowed
the history of his life and political career.*

I clearly remember 17 December 1967—the day Harold Holt disappeared in the surf off Portsea. It is my first clear memory of a political
event. I was ten years old. I was watching television in our family
home. Regular programming was interrupted and the announcement
was made that the Prime Minister was missing.

My reaction, like that of so many Australians, was one of shock.
How did the Prime Minister go missing? Will he be rescued? Will his
body be found? The days of fruitless searching ended with no answers
or explanations—just a sad realisation that it was over and he was lost.

All Australians shared in this sense of loss. Of course the loss
was much greater for Harold's family—and I would especially like
to acknowledge Sam, one of Harold's sons, who is with us today. The
riddle of the loss spawned its own industry of bizarre yarns and tales.
And it cut short a Prime Ministership that lasted less than twenty-
three months.

In the broad sweep of history we like to characterise a Prime
Minister by a major issue or event: Curtin—war, Chifley—bank
nationalisation, Menzies—our longest serving Prime Minister, Holt—
disappearance, Gorton—Commonwealth power, McMahon—1972
election defeat, etc. In that way of remembering history, the defining
event of the Holt Prime Ministership becomes not his life but his death.
In popular history it has come to overshadow his many achievements.

And the popular history of the Liberal Party is sometimes told as
moving from its apex under Sir Robert Menzies to decline through
Holt, Gorton and McMahon to inevitable defeat in 1972.

Of course, these are not the facts. After Menzies retired in 1966
the Coalition, under Holt, went on to win 82 out of 124 seats in the

federal election of November 1966, increasing its majority from 20 to 40. This was a swing of 4.3 per cent to the Coalition. The Coalition received 49.9 per cent of the first-preference vote. The two-party preferred result for the Coalition was 56.9 per cent, the highest level ever.

Of course, by that stage Arthur Calwell had led Labor to defeat in 1961 and 1963 and was saddling up for his third defeat as Leader. Calwell certainly helped the outcome in 1966. And at that stage Vietnam was not the political liability it was to become. But there is no doubt that the passing of the mantle from Menzies to Holt lifted support for the Liberal Party even though Sir Robert as the founder of the party was Australia's longest serving Prime Minister.

I was somewhat shocked to read a headline in the *Australian* on 5 August 2005 reading: 'Holt, the Real Whitlamite'. I think Harold Holt would have been shocked too. The idea that Whitlam, who would follow Holt, could somehow define his predecessor is absurd. And Holt's ministerial career was far more substantive than Whitlam's.

The headline misconstrued an article written by Tom Frame that was trying to make the point that an adoring press had over the years given a lot of credit to Whitlam for the achievements of Holt.

If the headline writer wanted to do an interplay between the two it should have read: 'Whitlam, a Real Holtite'. But I am sure this would have come as even more shocking news to Harold Holt.

What Tom Frame was arguing was that Holt set in train a whole lot of changes, modernising Australia—a focus on Asia, independence from Britain, independence of the currency, the ending of the White Australia Policy, Commonwealth leadership on Aboriginal affairs, and Commonwealth support for arts and culture.

Upon becoming Prime Minister, Holt resurrected proposals that had been rejected by Menzies to allow 'well-qualified' Asian immigrants access to family reunion and to reduce the qualifying period for non-Europeans to gain residency and citizenship from fifteen years to five—the same as applied to Europeans.

It was a fundamental blow against the White Australia Policy. And the White Australia Policy had been a cornerstone of Australian policy since Federation.

The White Australia Policy was bipartisan, although it was much more passionately supported by the Labor than by the Liberal Party. And although most would today think it was a policy of racial discrimination, in fact it was introduced and justified as an arm of economic policy.

The tariff was designed to protect Australian goods from cheap imports manufactured with cheap labour. The tariff was justified on the grounds that it protected 'European wage rates'. But if European wage rates could be threatened by 'non-European wage rates' offshore, how much more would they be undermined by non-European labour on-shore? The White Australia Policy was designed to keep out non-Europeans who would bring 'cheap labour' to Australia and thereby to protect union wage rates. The companies which paid arbitration rates were given tariff protection, and those white Australians who worked for those companies were given 'wage protection' from 'non-Europeans'. The White Australia Policy was considered integral to protecting wage rates.

As we now know, these were misconceived policies. And from the 1960s all were coming under pressure. The steps Holt took in relation to immigration recognised that Australia was modernising, and regardless of spurious economic argument, regardless of the strong public appeal of the White Australia Policy, a policy based on race was discrediting Australia in the eyes of a good part of the world.

Menzies was born in the nineteenth century and had lived all his life under the system of tariff, arbitration and White Australia. Holt, who was fourteen years younger, had done the same. The two shared a similar outlook. But when Holt became Prime Minister the Government had the opportunity to reconsider options that had previously been considered and rejected.

Options ruled out in earlier times were becoming possible, even necessary, as prevailing views began to change. The succession of Holt to the leadership of the Liberal Party allowed the party to reconsider these issues. In important respects Holt gave the Liberal Party an opening to modernise in response to changing social and economic factors at work in Australia.

… Holt was a moderniser in opening Australia to Asia and brought the Liberal Party and the Government with him.

It is interesting to wonder what might have happened if he had lived, and whether it would have led to an outcome different in 1972.

This is not to say that Holt did not have severe political challenges. Two issues that were eating away at his Government during 1967 were the controversy over the use of VIP flights and the *Voyager* disaster. Holt lost a by-election in the seat of Corio on the retirement of Sir Hubert Opperman, and the half Senate elections of 1967 reduced the Government vote.

There has been a great deal of speculation about the state of Holt's health as Christmas of 1967 approached. He was approaching sixty but he led an active life. There is no reason to suspect that he suffered any physical collapse when he entered the water on that fateful day.

Tom Frame deals well in debunking the more elaborate myths that came to be written and whispered in the years that were to follow.

The modern Liberal Party has produced six Prime Ministers now, book-ended by the longest serving and the second-longest serving Prime Ministers in Australian history. Holt deserves a position of honour in this company. A decent man and a tolerant man, he had a full and successful ministerial career. He was the first Member for Higgins. He is still widely admired in the electorate.

He took the reins of the Liberal Party after a long period of leadership in a smooth transition from its founder. He took the opportunity to modernise the party and set in train great changes which adapted Australia to a changing world. He took the Liberal Party to one of its greatest majorities. If he had lived longer he would have been able to continue the work. Perhaps, if he had, he could have saved the party from the events that led to the defeat of 1972 and its disastrous consequences.

But the personal tragedy of Christmas 1967 intervened. Nonetheless, the Liberal Party, the nation and especially the people in the electorate of Higgins owe him a great debt.

12 August 2005

3 The Spirit of the Volunteer

*Henry Bolte was the longest serving Premier of Victoria who came
from a simple farming background. In delivering a lecture in his honour
I reflected on the nature of community, the spirit of volunteerism and
how to build meaningful bonds between citizens. Some people call it
'social capital'.*

... Our living standards are higher than they have ever been; our
standard of housing, our cars, our domestic appliances, our health
services are better than they have been in previous decades; and our
economic abundance has increased. Yet many people feel they are
under more pressure than ever before; they feel they are working
harder than ever before and they miss the sense of community that
comes with a gentler pace of life.

Now some of this is nostalgia. Sometimes we tend to romanticise
the past.

Were people really happier without the automatic washing
machine when they hand-scrubbed their clothes or fed them through
the wringer? Were they happier when the standard working week was
forty-four hours, and men went to work at the factory on Saturday
morning and shops closed at lunch time, and the pub closed at 6 o'clock,
and they caught the train home to a two-bedroom house with a five-
person family?

No one would seriously argue that people would be happier if
they cut their incomes, moved into smaller homes, had their televisions
confiscated and the video and internet banned.

But there is this sense that if there was less home entertainment,
maybe less television, video, Gameboy, CD-ROM and internet then
the children might spend more time playing games outside with their
neighbours, and the parents in the street would know each other's
names and the sense of belongingness would increase.

What economic prosperity has brought us is choices. So many
choices that sometimes they are overwhelming. Once upon a time, you
could walk into a shop and order a cup of coffee. Now there is drink
in, take out, coffee, mocha, Colombian, cappucino, latte or double soy
chino. Will you take that with or without sugar, Equal or Nutrisweet?

One of the reasons the neighbourhood existed was that choices were more limited. Transport was limited. The neighbourhood was the geographic limits of how far children could go to play with each other or adults could walk to do the shopping. But with transport people can cross the metropolis or the state. They can choose their friends in a radius of 100 kilometres rather than 100 metres.

Of course, the advent of the internet means that people can cross the globe pursuing a particular interest and are no longer bounded by any geographic limits at all. The cyber chatroom replaces the neighbourhood fence as the place for a social conversation.

The dazzling array of choices means that the level of shared experiences tend to be less. Even our shared information may be declining. Our information is not declining. Maybe our shared information is. Once upon a time, the widely read newspaper gave a town or a city a common reference point. Newspapers basically choose content; they prioritise information. Each morning a paper would put a range of information or opinions to its citizens. They might have different views but it gave them a shared reference to discuss or debate. But if I am getting my infotainment from one web page and others I deal with are getting theirs from different web pages, there is no commonality, no common reference to discuss. We don't start with the same menu. So while we are creating more individual choices than ever before, this may be leading to a loss of the shared experience. And a feeling of belongingness goes with shared experience.

At this point somebody is going to ask, 'Well, what is the Government going to do about that?'

And here lies one of our biggest problems. The expectation that the Government should solve all of our problems or can solve all of our problems is a big problem.

Governments can deliver services, they should deliver reliable transport services, and high-quality health services, and strong educational services. But Governments can't deliver friendly relationships, harmony between parents and children, happy marriages.

I think there has been a tendency for Government to encourage the belief that it can solve any kind of problem. This inevitably leads to disappointment. People should not look to Government to deal with issues that it is not designed to deal with. I have always been a believer in limited Government. I don't think it can solve the deep core issues of personal relationships, identity, family and love. If you limit the Government to what it can do it is likely to do that better and likely to do less damage than if it intervenes in areas where it has no competence.

I can remember that under some Whitlam scheme the Government began building community centres in local areas. Now, I have nothing against community centres and believe that fine facilities for games and meetings is a good thing. But there are community halls and mechanics institutes and CWA halls in country towns all across Australia. I'll bet that in the early days the citizens in the community came together and built them, physically built them, laid foundations and put up the frame and nailed on the boards. And in later years the community would come together and fundraise and employ a builder to build them. And I'll warrant that if there wasn't a community before the construction started, there certainly was after the locals had spent hours together at fetes and raffles and pie drives, working together to realise a common goal which they owned.

And then the Government began building community centres. And this was no doubt on the theory that if you built a centre a community would materialise to fill it. If you build it they will come. Individuals can build buildings but I don't know that buildings can build individuals and their relationships. Individuals with a sense of personal responsibility and a shared experience and a commitment beyond themselves build a community.

And that is a phrase that you don't hear too often in the political lexicon these days: personal responsibility. There was Henry Bolte at eighteen, secretary of the local race club and the church and captain of the football team. He wasn't sitting around in Skipton waiting for the Government to build the community.

We need to remind ourselves that there is a whole sphere of life outside Government. And this is where important personal decisions are made and personal emotions are felt. There is a place where Government ends and the local church, or the family, or the Immigrant Elderly Citizen Association takes over. This is the place of the shared experience and the voluntary commitment. This is the place of the community. This is the place of the volunteer.

One of the most memorable features of the Sydney Olympics was that of the volunteers, the people who directed the spectators as they got off the train and went into the stadium. I met one lady I knew from Dubbo who had become a volunteer and was standing outside the stadium putting people's bags through an X-ray machine. She didn't go to watch the events or cheer in the stadium or earn a little part-time income. She went to Sydney from Dubbo and worked long hours for free because she wanted to give something to the Games. She wanted visitors to have a good time and to like Australia. She wanted to be proud of her country. After the Games were over there was a tickertape parade to thank those volunteers.

Last week at the Stonnington Town Hall I presented badges to volunteers in my electorate. There were over 500 people there, people who don't get paid and people who voluntarily choose to be involved in all host and manner of activities. This is beyond Government. This is the volunteer spirit. This is community. This is personal responsibility.

Community is shared experience. These days when schools want to build a shared experience between their students they take them out of their comfortable homes and throw them together on a camp to experience a bit of adversity. Going outside our homes to share an experience with the volunteer organisations of society is a big part of building community. We could revive the volunteer spirit in Australia—we could revive all these non-Government community organisations—if each of us were to spend one hour per week in volunteer activity.

I'm not talking exclusively about charity work here, although that is a special kind of volunteer activity. I'm talking about the non-Government voluntary organisations of Australia, the Rotary and Lions group, the churches and synagogues, the local sporting clubs, the Neighbourhood Watch, opportunity shops, the Scouts and Guides, political parties, the CFA and SES, the Young Farmers' Associations, and local libraries and school canteens and school councils, cultural associations and arts auxiliaries, Landcare groups, and RSLs, the book group, the thousands of non-Government voluntary organisations that bring people together in a shared experience and build relationships and form a network of joining together, and mutual support, and human contact. It might be an hour a week talking to a neighbour or spending an hour with a child or older relative.

But it has to be freely chosen and in that sense voluntary. If someone says to me that the Government should do this or that to make this work then I have not made my point. This is something outside Government. We have to celebrate individuals, individuals doing something they want to, which together creates community: practical, hands-on, on-the-ground community. This is the way to recover a little of what we feel might be lacking—people who are friendly, neighbours who know each other, individuals that share experience together.

In the midst of our substantial economic improvements we should not forget to celebrate and cultivate the role of the volunteer.

Our economic policy is crucial but we should remember that life consists of other things beyond the economic dimension and beyond Government. To realise those many other aspirations of a fulfilling life we need to recover the spirit of the volunteer.

15 August 2001

4 Lone Pine Memorial: Gallipoli Peninsula, Turkey

*My greatest honour as an Australian Minister was to deliver the speech
at Anzac Cove on Anzac Day 2003. To see young Australians halfway
around the world come and stay up all night through bitter cold on that
small beach to honour the sacrifice of their forebears moved me to the core.
After the Dawn Service we walked up the hill to Lone Pine
to honour the Australians who died there.*

We stand in a place of solemn remembrance. We think of the fallen resting in their graves. We see their headstones. We see their names, each one a life full of hope and possibility cut down before its time.

But there are those who lie in the ground and in the sea—where they fell. Those whose graves are indistinguishable from the sand, water and soil that claimed them. 4,228 Australians and 708 New Zealanders with no known graves are commemorated at this memorial.

Lone Pine was a place of particular carnage and bravery. It has been said that the dead were so thick on the ground that the only respect that could be shown was to avoid treading on their faces.

Lone Pine was one of a series of diversionary attacks. It was an exercise in putting oneself in harm's way for the benefit of other soldiers. It was not a task sought by Australians, but it was one they discharged with unrivalled heroism.

This is a cathedral to courage.

Of the nine Victoria Crosses awarded to Australians during the Gallipoli campaign, seven were awarded to Australians during the fighting here. Five VCs were awarded on one day alone—9 August.

The first Lone Pine VC was awarded to Lance Corporal Leonard Keysor. For two days he threw back grenades. Some he caught in mid-air.

It is hard to imagine chaos here, where now there is order. The foe prevailed. The dead were buried or lay where they fell.

The guns did not stop here at Gallipoli until the complete withdrawal of the Imperial Forces on the nights of 18 and 19 December 1915. The withdrawal was an entire success. Not a single life was lost.

Company Quarter Master Sergeant AL Guppy wrote in his diary on the day of withdrawal:

Not only muffled is our tread
To cheat the foe,
We fear to rouse our honoured dead
To hear us go.
Sleep sound, old friends—the keenest smart
Which, more than failure, wounds the heart,
Is thus to leave you—thus to part,
Comrades, farewell!!

The spirit that was forged here has inspired generations of Australians. Other Australian servicemen and -women have fought with similar valour. But this site is, in our imaginings, its home.

The young soldiers that fell here were full of passion, spirit and love. And so they will always remain.

We remember the families, the parents, the wives and the children—those who live, until they die, with the pangs of loss. For those left behind, it was often the small things from which they took comfort—a badge or button from a uniform or the last letter received.

We stand here to honour sacrifice. We do so because sacrifice is an uncommon virtue. And a virtue that we, successive generations of Australians can take from and learn from and in a much smaller way return.

It is difficult to leave those who have paid so high a price. In spirit Australia has never left this site. And we never will. Australia will never forget its fallen.

25 April 2003

5 National Day of Thanksgiving

*The churches proclaimed a National Day of Thanksgiving in Australia
in May 2004. I was asked to give the inaugural address in Melbourne.
I spoke of the importance of faith and the Judeo–Christian tradition in
our society.*

When Jesus told his disciples that they would be witnesses in
Jerusalem, Judea, Samaria and the uttermost parts of the earth, the
known world consisted of the Roman Empire—the Mediterranean
and surrounds.

No one in the Roman world, no one in the Jewish world, knew of
Australia. From the then known world of the Mediterranean, Australia
was beyond even the uttermost parts of the earth.

And yet the teaching of Jesus came to Australia. It took nearly
eighteen centuries. And we can pinpoint quite accurately the first
time a Christian service was held on Australian soil. The sermon was
preached by the Rev. Richard Johnson, chaplain of the First Fleet.
It was preached on Sunday 3 February 1778 under a large tree in
Sydney. His text was from Psalm 116, verse 12: 'What shall I render
unto the Lord for all his benefits toward me?'

The first Australian Christian service was a thanksgiving service.
It was thanksgiving for a safe passage in dangerous sailing ships, on a
dangerous mission half way around the world.

Two hundred and twenty-six years later we meet tonight to mark
a National Day of Thanksgiving for all the benefits rendered to us, in
the modern Australia.

Of course, the members of the First Fleet were not the first
people to come to Australia. The Aboriginal people were here long
before that. And I am so proud that we have descendants of those first
Australians who are here tonight and who we have just honoured.

But it was the First Fleet that brought the first chaplain and first
knowledge of the Christian faith to Australia. This was the critical and
decisive event that shaped our country.

If the Arab traders that brought Islam to Indonesia had brought
Islam to Australia and settled, or spread their faith, among the indig-

enous population, our country today would be vastly different. Our laws, our institutions, our economy would all be vastly different.

But that did not happen. Our society was founded by British colonists. And the single most decisive feature that determined the way it developed was the Judeo-Christian Western tradition.

As a society, we are who we are because of that heritage.

I am not sure this is well understood in Australia today. It may be that a majority of Australians no longer believes the orthodox Christian faith. But whether they believe it or not, the society they share is one founded on that faith and one that draws on the Judeo-Christian tradition.

The foundation of that tradition is, of course, the Ten Commandments. How many Australians today could recite them? Perhaps very few. But they are the foundation of our law and our society, whether we know them or not.

The first commandments—'Thou shalt have no other God before me'; 'Thou shalt not make any graven image'; 'Thou shalt not take the name of the Lord in vain'; 'Remember the Sabbath and keep it holy'—are the foundation of monotheism.

The commandments 'Honour thy father and mother'; 'Thou shalt not commit adultery' are the foundation of marriage and the family.

The commandment 'Thou shalt not kill' is the basis for respect for life.

The commandment 'Thou shalt not steal' is the basis for property rights.

The commandments 'Thou shalt not bear false witness against thy neighbour' and 'Thou shalt not covet thy neighbour's property' are the basis of respect for others and their individual rights.

These are the great principles of our society. On them hang all of the laws and institutions that make our society what it is.

When Moses gave the Ten Commandments he initiated the rule of law. From the moment that he laid down these rules it followed that human conduct was to be governed according to rules—rules which were objectively stated, capable of being understood and, if necessary, enforced by the Hebrew judges. Prior to that the people of the ancient world were governed by rulers rather than rules. The ruler was much more subject to whim and capricious behaviour. Rulers were not subject to independent review or interpretation. The rule of law is the basis for our constitution and justice system.

And so we have the rule of law, respect for life, private property rights, respect of others—values that spring from the Judeo-Christian tradition.

Tolerance under the law is a great part of this tradition.

Tolerance does not mean that all views are the same. It does not mean that differing views are equally right. What it means is that where there are differences, no matter how strongly held, different people will respect the right of others to hold them.

… We have such a rich heritage. But in so many ways it is being run down. The values which it has given us—respect for life, respect for others, for property, respect for family—seem to be undermined in many ways.

What should we do?

At this point it is usual for some leading churchman from some well-known denomination to appear in the media to call on the Government to fix things.

I do not want to suggest that there are no initiatives the Government should take. And what Government can do, it should do. But I do want to suggest something much more radical and far-reaching. I want to suggest that a recovery of faith would go a long way to answering this challenge. A Government should never get into religious endeavours. But if our church leaders could so engage people as to lead them to genuine faith we should be much richer and stronger for it.

The Bible tells the story of the prophet Elijah, who got despondent about the state of decay all around him. He was running for his life. He fled out to the wilderness. He sat under a juniper tree and asked to die. He felt alone and let down. He had no supporters. He thought he was the only person left that was true.

But the still small voice of God came to him and lifted him and told him that there were still thousands that had not lowered the knee to the spiritual and moral decay all around him (1 Kings 19).

And this is the point I would like to make to those who have gathered here tonight. There are many that have not, in their hearts, acquiesced to the kind of decay which is apparent around us. They do not believe it is right. They earnestly pray for the expansion of faith and yearn for higher standards.

They will get up tomorrow and go to their places of worship in suburbs and towns across the country, affirm the historic Christian faith and go to work on Monday as law-abiding citizens who want their marriages to stay together, their children to grow up to be healthy and useful members of society and their homes to be happy. They care deeply about our society and where it is going.

These people will not get their names in the media. They will not be elected to anything. They will not be noisy lobbyists. But they are the steadying influence, the ballast, to our society when it shakes with moral turbulence. They give strength and stability and they embody the character and the traditions of our valuable heritage. It is their inner faith which gives them strength. Our society won't work without them.

All citizens share in the heritage and the blessings that heritage brought to our country, something for which we can all give thanks. We should not take these blessings for granted. We should not become complacent. We should genuinely give thanks because we have been genuinely blessed. And each, to our own ability, should nurture the values which were so important in bringing us to where we are today and which we need so badly to take us on.

29 May 2004

6 Worth Promoting, Worth Defending: Australian Citizenship

After the London Underground bombing of 2005 I was troubled by the fact that young people born and raised in a democratic society could turn to terrorism and kill their fellow citizens in the name of Islam. I gave a speech at the Sydney Institute in which I argued that freedom and tolerance can be protected only within a legal framework that is accepted by all.

... Outside Australia's indigenous people, we are all immigrants or descendants of immigrants—some earlier than others—but all with an experience of immigration during the foundation of modern Australia. Australia is part of the New World, the world of immigrants, not part of the Old World or the places they embark from. This is why we are suspicious of inherited titles and privileges. Nobody can afford to get too precious about their position or entitlements in this country because we all know that position and entitlements are comparatively new.

Australia's immigration experience is also a broad one. Originally it was Anglo-Celtic but after the war our immigrants came increasingly from southern Europe. In more recent times, Vietnamese and Chinese immigrants have grown considerably in numbers. And all these immigrant communities have made successful contributions to Australian life.

Australia is often described as a successful multicultural society. And it is, in the sense that people from all different backgrounds live together in harmony. But there is a predominant culture just as there is predominant language. And the political and cultural institutions that govern Australia are absolutely critical to that attitude of harmony and tolerance. Within an institutional framework that preserves tolerance and protects order we can celebrate and enjoy diversity in food, in music, in religion, in language and culture. But we could not do that without the framework which guarantees the freedom to enjoy diversity.

... The Australian Citizenship Oath or Affirmation tries to capture the essence of what it means to be Australian. It reads as follows: 'From this time forward [under God] I pledge my loyalty to Australia and its people, whose democratic beliefs I share, whose rights and liberties I respect and whose laws I will uphold and obey.' To be an Australian citizen one pledges loyalty first: loyalty to Australia. One pledges to share certain beliefs—democratic beliefs—to respect the rights and liberty of others and to respect the rule of law.

There is a lot of sense in this pledge. Unless we have a consensus of support about how we will form our legislatures and an agreement to abide by its laws, none of us will be able to enjoy our rights and liberties without being threatened by others. We have a compact to live under a democratic legislature and obey the laws it makes. In doing this the rights and liberties of all are protected. Those who are outside this compact threaten the rights and liberties of others. They should be refused citizenship if they apply for it. Where they have it they should be stripped of it if they are dual citizens and have some other country that recognises them as citizens.

Terrorists and those who support them do not acknowledge the rights and liberties of others—the right to live without being maimed, the right to live without being bombed—and as such they forfeit the right to join in Australian citizenship. The refusal to acknowledge the rule of law as laid down by democratic institutions also stabs at the heart of the Australian compact. The radical Muslim cleric Ben Brika was asked in an interview on the *7.30 Report* in August last year: 'But don't you think Australian Muslims—Muslims living in Australia—also have a responsibility to adhere to Australian law?' To which he answered: 'This is a big problem. There are two laws—there is an Australian law and there is an Islamic law.'

No, this is not a big problem. There is one law we are all expected to abide by. It is the law enacted by the Parliament under the Australian Constitution. If you can't accept that then you don't accept the fundamentals of what Australia is and what it stands for. Our State is a secular State. As such it can protect the freedom of all religions for worship. Religion instructs its adherents on faith, morals and conscience. But there is not a separate stream of law derived from religious sources that competes with or supplants Australian law in governing our civil society. The source of our law is the democratically elected legislature.

There are countries that apply religious or sharia law—Saudi Arabia and Iran come to mind. If a person wants to live under sharia law these are countries where they might feel at ease. But not Australia. And the citizenship pledge should be a big flashing warning sign to those who want to live under sharia law. A person who does not acknowledge the supremacy of civil law laid down by democratic processes cannot truthfully take the pledge of allegiance. As such they do not meet the pre-condition for citizenship.

Before entering a mosque visitors are asked to take off their shoes. This is a sign of respect. If you have a strong objection to walking in your socks, don't enter the mosque. Before becoming an Australian you will be asked to subscribe to certain values. If you have strong objections to those values, don't come to Australia.

We need to be very clear on these issues. There are some beliefs, some values, so core to the nature of our society that those who refuse to accept them refuse to accept the nature of our society. If someone cannot honestly make the citizenship pledge, they cannot honestly take out citizenship. If they have taken it out already they should not be able to keep it where they have citizenship in some other country.

Of course, this is not possible for those that are born here and have no dual citizenship. In these cases we have on our hands citizens who are apparently so alienated that they do not support what their own country stands for. Such alienation could become a threat to the rights and liberties of others. And so it is important to explain our values, explain why they are important and engage leadership they respect to assist us in this process. Ultimately, however, it is important that they know that there is only one law and it is going to be enforced whether they acknowledge its legitimacy or not.

It will be a problem if we have a second generation—the children of immigrants who have come to Australia—in a twilight zone where the values of their parents' old country have been lost but the values of the new country not fully embraced. To deal with this we must clearly state the values of Australia and explain how we expect them to be respected. I suspect there would be more respect for these values if we made more of the demanding requirements of citizenship. No one is going to respect a citizenship that is so undemanding that it asks nothing. In fact, our citizenship is quite a demanding obligation. It demands loyalty, tolerance and respect for fellow citizens and support for a rare form of Government—democracy.

… We are more likely to engender respect by emphasising the expectations and the obligations that the great privilege of citizenship brings. We have a robust tolerance of difference in our society. But to maintain this tolerance we have to have an agreed framework which will protect the rights and liberties of all. And we are asking our citizens—all our citizens—to subscribe to that framework.

I do not like putrid representations like *Piss Christ*. I do not think galleries should show them. But I do recognise they should be able to practise their offensive taste without fear of violence or a riot. Muslims do not like representations of the Prophet. They do not think newspapers should print them. But so too they must recognise this does not justify violence against newspapers or countries that allow newspapers to publish them.

We are asking all our citizens to subscribe to a framework that can protect the rights and liberties of all. These are Australian values. We must be very clear on this point. They are not optional. We expect all those who call themselves Australians to subscribe to them. Loyalty, democracy, tolerance, the rule of law: values worth promoting, values worth defending. The values of Australia and its citizens.

23 February 2006

7 Challenges and Benefits of Globalisation

The disruption at the World Trade Organization Ministerial Meeting in Seattle in 1999 led to flow-on demonstrations against globalisation, including a violent one against the World Economic Forum on 11 September 2000 in Melbourne. I wanted to respond and to explain the process when I addressed the Sydney Institute in July 2001.

… Globalisation is a description of the fact that countries and their citizens are affected by other people, or Governments, or businesses, or decision-makers all around the world. And because communication is faster and transport cheaper, the connections are more immediate and more intense than ever before. The telephone, which first connected suburbs, now connects the world, and optic fibre transmits data, money, email, knowledge from business to business, home to business, home to home across the world.

As I have previously argued, globalisation is not a value; it is a process. Globalisation describes what is happening. And ranting against globalisation is like ranting against the telephone. You can use the telephone for good or for ill. So too the wider process (of which the telephone is part) can be a force for good or ill.

Rant against globalisation and you might as well rant against the telephone. And, what is more, you will not reverse this process.

Of all the countries in the world where this should be well understood, it should be in Australia. The founding of the colonies in Australia was an example of globalisation. At the end of the eighteenth century, as its economy strengthened, its technological capacity developed, Britain was able to establish and maintain a settlement 12 000 nautical miles from its global centre in London. It couldn't do this in the sixteenth century, when its capacity to maintain colonies extended only 3000 nautical miles to North America.

Foreign investment arrived here in Port Jackson in 1788 with the First Fleet. It was investment in construction, agriculture, livestock and Government infrastructure. Of course, at that stage it was Government rather than private investment, but overseas private investment followed thereafter. In the early years it came principally from London. We used the savings of others to invest in and build our economy. Australia is here as a result of globalisation and foreign investment.

None of this is to say that all the consequences have been without blemish, nor to say that we should not try to direct this process to maximise our benefits in the future. In fact I think we should. But we should come at it from the right starting point. A country which is open to trade, investment, technological transfer, is going to be more prosperous and a better place to live than one that is not.

There is a self-styled anti-globalisation movement that pretends to the contrary. This movement likes to protest against the meeting of any organisation that has the word *world* in its name—the *World* Trade Organization (Seattle, December 1999), the *World* Bank (Washington, April 2000), the *World* Economic Forum (Melbourne, September 2000).

Yet these demonstrations are organised on the internet, otherwise known as the *world* wide web, its members fly the One *World* airline network to get to anti-globalisation rallies and once there they organise demonstrations for *world*wide television coverage.

Some of these people are committed leftists. They are not against internationalism. They are against international markets for capital. They wouldn't mind a bit of internationalism of the socialist variety. Some of the protestors are Christians who are members of the Roman Catholic church (which has a global hierarchy here on earth) or the worldwide Anglican Communion. Some are environmentalists who protest against globalisation, and demand international agreement on global warming. They think 'global' and act 'global' and protest against globalisation.

Of course, there are countries that have sought to close their borders to foreign investment and erect barriers to trade. But it is unlikely you will hear the demonstrators extolling the virtues of them: countries like North Korea, Albania or Cuba. And one wouldn't want to run an anti-globalisation demonstration, indeed any demonstration, in a country that prefers the closed—as opposed to the open—society.

One of the constant claims made against the process described as 'globalisation' is that it is making the world's rich richer and the world's poor poorer. Let me say at the outset that I am interested in making the world's poor richer. If there are policies that can pull the world's poor out of poverty and increase their standards of health care and education, it does not concern me that in the process the world's rich become richer too. Rising living standards in the developed world would be another reason to pursue these policies. However, it would concern me if rising living standards in the developed world were the cause of deterioration for the world's poor.

Experience shows us that open markets, trade liberalisation and the economic growth which it has facilitated is boosting the living standards of the world's poor.

In the twentieth century, the poorest quarter of the world's population became almost three times richer. Economic development lifted more people out of poverty than ever before and gave them better health and education and better opportunities in life. Gains of this magnitude are unprecedented in previous human history.

A clear majority of those who were poor as recently as 1970 have got richer, in both absolute and relative terms: over the last thirty years, about 70 per cent of the population of developing countries have experienced sufficiently fast growth in real per capita GDP to converge towards rich countries' levels. Poverty has worsened in some nations, particularly in Africa. But there are major developing countries, particularly in Asia, with large populations that have been growing quite strongly and lifting millions out of poverty.

In our part of the world—East Asia—economic policies which encouraged foreign investment, more open trade and economic growth have halved the number of people living in extreme poverty in less than two decades. The dispersion of living standards has been slowly narrowing, not widening. The only halt in this process was the Asian economic crisis of 1997–98. Economic growth is the best poverty-buster yet discovered.

But there have not been many successes in sub-Saharan Africa.

Those countries where poverty is worsening are not those which have participated in free capital flows and foreign investment. On the contrary, they are those that have been unable to participate in globalisation because of war, corruption or maladministration. And their economic institutions are weak. Their share of global trade has actually halved over the last twenty years. They are isolated from global trade opportunities.

This indicator of falling trade shares for the poorest countries is not a sign they are exploited by globalisation, but rather an indicator they are missing out on the opportunities that can be created.

Many of the problems attributed to international trade rules or international institutions, such as apparently intractable poverty in the poorest countries, are in fact failures of national policies and institutions. If only things were easy. If only we could defeat poverty by halting the proceedings of the World Trade Organization. The truth is much more pessimistic than the fantasy that the developed world can fix all the problems of the developing world. Ending war, tribal conflict, corruption and building legal and economic institutions is so much harder.

The greatest victims of the anti-globalisation demonstrators who want to stop more liberal world trade would be the poor. Protectionist policies followed in developed countries would lock the poor out of markets for agriculture and textiles where they could actually develop trade and earnings. It is not open markets and free trade, it is protection that will damage the world's poor.

25 July 2005

8 *The Bulletin*'s Top 100 Most Influential Australians Luncheon

In June 2006 I was asked to address a luncheon organised by Australian's then oldest continuous magazine, The Bulletin, *at which it named its list of the 100 most influential Australians. Rupert Murdoch was there to be honoured as* The Bulletin's *most influential Australian.*

… When you see a list of the 100 most influential Australians that have ever lived, you begin looking down that list starting with the letter that your own surname begins with. I went to 'C'—no joy there—and I thought maybe they were doing it on the basis of first names, so I went to 'P'. I couldn't find anything there. I thought, 'What about occupations?' So I went to 'T' and I didn't find anything there.

But alas, you look in vain to see my name on this list of 100 influential Australians. I turn up here today and I see so many of them in the room … I say to those influential people, thank you for letting me in here today.

The Bulletin of course is one of Australia's most influential organs itself, nurturing a talented stable of writers such as Henry Lawson, Banjo Paterson, and paying the wages of distinguished editors such as Peter Coleman, whose daughter is my wife. *The Bulletin* championed causes such as the republic (unsuccessfully) and White Australia, which for many years was part of the masthead itself. And isn't it fitting that we are sitting here in a restaurant bearing the name of a Florentine who lived 500 years ago, certainly one of Italy's 100 most influential people?

… Of course, since European settlement Australia has been one of the most successful societies on earth in every way—politically, economically, in the quality of life. A colony which started as a penal settlement has led the world. There is so much that we can be proud of.

And we have certain characteristics which people throughout the world will always remark on. The great travel writer Bill Bryson, in his book *Down Under*, said these words:

> The Australian people are immensely likeable—cheerful, extroverted, quick-witted and unfailingly obliging. Their cities

are safe and clean and nearly always built on water. They have a society that is prosperous, well ordered and instinctively egalitarian.

You read that word a lot, that word *egalitarian*, when you read about Australians and Australian values.

… We would expect that the values of our country would reflect the values of influential people; after all, they are the people who have influenced those values. If you were doing the 100 most influential people in British history you would have kings and you would have queens, but you won't find kings or queens on our list today. If you were doing the 100 most influential people of the United States, you would have Revolutionary War heroes and generals from the Civil War era, but you won't find them on our list today. You will find pioneers and settlers and founders of industries. And people who interpret ourselves and our nation back to ourselves.

We would all agree that one of the most decisive events in our national history was the landing at Gallipoli in 1915. This was the first great event since Federation which shaped our sense of identity and the nation like no other. But the people on today's list who come to us enshrining that legend in our consciousness are not the actual soldiers who went ashore on that fateful day. No Albert Jacka VC, no Major-General Bridges. Monash is on our list, but his moment of greatness was still to come, after 1915.

The legend of Gallipoli comes to us through a *Sydney Morning Herald* journalist turned war historian, CEW Bean. The legend of the outback comes to us not through the people who went through great privation and suffering but through the poets Lawson and Paterson. Our fascination with the Snowy River—which even as recently as this month defeated Government policy—comes through a poet and the Cinesound news-reels recording great Australian achievements.

And so the writers and the poets and the artists become important because they fire our imagination and our emotion. You have heard the expression 'movers and shakers'. Perhaps we could call this list 'Australia's 100 Movers and Shakers'. But do you know where the term 'movers and shakers' comes from? Arthur William Edgar O'Shaughnessy, a poet, wrote these words:

> We are the music-makers,
> And we are the dreamers of dreams,
> Wandering by lone sea-breakers,
> And sitting by desolate streams;
> World-losers and world-forsakers,
> On whom the pale moon gleams;
> Yet we are the movers and shakers,
> Of the world for ever, *it seems.*

The poets in O'Shaughnessy's mind were the movers and shakers. And so we find on this list artists (not enough artists in my view); we have artists like Sidney Nolan and Albert Namatjira. I think we should have had more artists. We don't have Roberts or Dobell or Fred Williams or Arthur Boyd: people who helped us see ourselves and our country in a new light.

Now, one of my predecessors as Treasurer complained about the lack of leadership in this country. 'We've never had a Lincoln,' he said, 'we've never had a Roosevelt.' And I think the reason he used to talk like this is he rather thought he might fill the vacancy. Will Australia ever have a Lincoln? Well, if we have a civil war over a great moral question, where our national Leader manages to get on the right side of the moral question, lead the nation to victory, preserve the Federation and lose his life in the process, we may have a Lincoln.

Let us suppose that the South had not seceded in the United States for another twenty years. Would we remember Lincoln any more than we remember Rutherford Hayes or James Garfield? Events make the man or woman just as the men or the women make the events.

For much of his life Churchill was considered a failure, shamelessly chasing wars around the globe, a struggling Home Secretary, a propagator of failed military strategy in the First World War, an undistinguished Chancellor; but his moment came in 1940. If it had not, his career could well have been marked as a failure.

Which brings me to my next point. A person's influence can only be judged at the end of their career, preferably judged hundreds of years thereafter. Influential Australians are those who will stand the test of time. Richard Nixon used the quote of Sophocles, saying: 'One must wait until the evening to see how splendid the day has been.'

And so, as I think of these 100 most influential people in Australia's history, four tips come to mind for those wishing to join the list. The first is become a poet, writer or artist. Second, if you can't become a poet, writer or artist, have a poet, writer or artist at close hand as you do your deeds. My third tip is to time your contribution to coincide with great events. Great events can make the great man or woman. My fourth tip is: overcome great odds; the greater the odds, the greater the achievement.

And now let me conclude by asking this question: Who will be on our list of the most influential Australians in 2100, when we get our cyber edition of *The Bulletin* magazine?

For those of you who have not made this list but would like to, can I suggest some avenues that you might like to explore? I come from the field of politics and public policy, so let me suggest a few here.

The person who can solve the problem bedevilling Australian political life in every area, the problem of federalism, will be there. In 1900 Federation was a great success, the coming together of colonies in a customs and economic union within an empire. But the empire has faded and the nation now has consciousness of itself. We are no longer dealing with self-governing sovereign colonies. I believed that by giving the states a revenue base—a financial free kick—we would restore that sense of sovereignty. It was a failed hope. States are moving towards the role of service delivery more on the model of divisional offices than sovereign, independent Governments. Legally, constitutionally and practically we must fix the problem of federalism.

The second person who might be on this list in 2100 is the person who can solve our water problem. We are the driest continent on earth; water storage has not been the subject of proper investment; we have wasted water and we have not properly priced it. Scientific, economic and engineering reform will be essential to fix this problem.

The third problem-solver who could be on our list in 2100 is the person who arrests Australia's fertility decline. We are an ageing society;

we need to rebalance—hopefully not just rebalance but have a larger population, which is essential for our national aims and our ambitions. Arresting our fertility decline will be of enormous importance to Australia's future. Hence my frequently stated refrain to have one for Mum, one for Dad and one for the country.

Fourth, the person who provides a model capable of winning genuine public support to improve and preserve our democracy and translate our current legal arrangements into those of a republic will be a person recognised as influential. A republic is where we are already, in our sympathies and in our imagination. And the person who can accomplish this in a legal and a constitutional sense will win a place in the list of 2100.

Fifth, there will be a place for a person on the list in 2100 who has a genuine workable way of lifting our indigenous people from the margin to the mainstream. Many have tried—many people of goodwill have tried—and there have been no shortage of resources; this is not a question of spending. There has been no area where we have had more ideological experimentation and more failure. There will be a place on the list in 2100 for that person.

But because we are a young country our greatest glories are still in front of us. That gives the people in this room plenty of capacity to win a place as an influential Australian in the years that lie ahead. We have been served well as a country. Although we have had failures and although we have not on every occasion lived up to the best practice, the Australian achievement—political, economic and in lifestyle—is one of the great successes of the world. And there is still plenty more room on that list of influential people in the years which lie ahead.

Congratulations to those people who are with us today. I acknowledge the debt to those that went before that made this country what it has become. A reminder to those who will take us into our future: there are still many glories to be won in every sphere of life as long as our country continues.

26 June 2006

9 Benchmarking Tax and Spending

(and How Australia Became a Leaner Government than the United States)

People don't realise how we cut the size of Government in Australia (in proportion to the economy), making it smaller than the United States and the second lowest among the world's developed nations in the OECD.

Tax and spending should be viewed as two sides of the same coin. If we want to tax less we will have to spend less. The only way to tax less and spend more is by borrowing and driving the Budget into deficit—a policy which brings worse problems when the consequences begin to catch up.

One of the values that Liberals hold dear is to be disciplined with Government spending. We should be careful about spending taxpayers' money—because it is their money and because the less we spend the less we have to raise.

Lower Spending ...

When we compare how much we spend now to how much Government spent ten years ago it is clear that the size of the Government as a proportion of the economy has fallen.

From 1995–96 through the ten years to 2005–06 the Australian Government's spending has declined from 25.3 per cent of GDP to 21.6 per cent of GDP.

I should add that this spending discipline has been achieved at some political cost. Our opponents have opposed every sensitive area of spending restraint or cuts.

How do we compare internationally?

In their latest statistics, the OECD ranks Australia as the second-lowest spending Government amongst twenty-eight developed countries of the world. That's right: second-lowest.

Over ten years the all-Government spending to GDP ratio has declined from 38.0 per cent to 35.7 per cent.

Over these ten years Australia has become leaner, while Japan, Korea and the United Kingdom have been creating bigger Governments.

In fact, an historic milestone was passed three years ago—which few people noticed—but Government spending in Australia became lower than the United States.

This is a fascinating development. Many people hold the United States up as the acme of lean Government, but in 2003 Australian Government spending as a proportion of GDP actually went below that of the United States and has stayed underneath.

Our paths have been converging but Australia now has a leaner Government than the United States.

Some people may wonder—if spending in Australia has declined as a proportion of GDP, how is it that the Government can still be spending more in certain areas? This is an important point to understand—the Government has been spending more, but not at the same rate as the economy has been growing. Government spending is declining as a proportion.

It is hard to restrain expenditure at any time and especially hard to restrain it in a growing economy. Every interest group has a good idea for new or expanded programs. And they usually argue that in a strong economy the Government can afford it. Keeping control of costs requires daily vigilance. But Australia has managed to do so and locked in Budget surpluses which will help us in the future, when the ageing of the population will really give us trouble on the spending front.

... Means Lower Taxes

If you are disciplined on spending it allows you to cut the tax burden. And the record shows that the Australian Government has reduced its tax as a proportion of the economy.

The Commonwealth's tax take to GDP peaked in Australia in 1986–87 at 23.7 per cent of GDP. In 1996–97 it was 22.8 per cent of GDP, and since then we have brought it down to its current level of 21.0 per cent. The Commonwealth Government has become smaller relative to our economy.

You can have endless arguments about the tax burdens in various countries. The only way to properly compare them is to take all levels of Government and measure that tax as a proportion of the economy.

How do we rank internationally?

When we compare ourselves to developed countries, the total Government tax take of 31.6 per cent of GDP is the eighth-lowest tax to GDP ratio of the thirty countries in the OECD.

Our recent performance has put us in an even better position than the OECD rankings would indicate, because our Government Budget is in surplus. Many of those countries that in the OECD rankings have lower tax than Australia, like the United States and Japan, have massive Government deficits. This means that while they may have a lower tax take now, they are doing it in some part by postponing tax collection into the future.

Let me illustrate how this occurs. Suppose the tax take to GDP ratio is 32 per cent. You can reduce it by 1 percentage point or 2 percentage points to 30 per cent and fund it by running a budget deficit of 1 per cent or 2 per cent of GDP. The budget deficit is financed by borrowing. The borrowing will have to be serviced and repaid by future Governments, who will have to raise it by taxing future citizens. The current generation lowers its tax bill, sure, but only by increasing the tax bill of the next generation. Has tax been cut? Well, only in the sense that one generation has transferred its liability to the next.

So what conclusions can we draw from these comparisons?

First, amongst developed countries, Australia is at the low end of both taxing and spending comparisons. Second, that over the 10-year period of Coalition Government both taxes and spending have declined as a proportion of GDP.

People can quarrel about subset arguments, but they should not allow subset gripes to cloud the big facts.

Let me just cover off a few subset arguments.

First, some people say that we should not compare ourselves to OECD countries because it makes our position look favourable. But this is the world league of developed countries. It has gathered international statistical comparisons. Historically, we have always compared ourselves with our peers in the other rich countries. This doesn't negate other comparisons. There is no point comparing ourselves to developing countries because we aren't one and we don't want to become one. We are not going to have a developing country's tax system unless we decide to scale down to the standards of social services that are delivered in developing countries. The health, education, aged care, pharmaceutical services of a developing economy is not what we have and not what we want.

Second, some people say that the federal Government's tax take should include GST. The trouble is that the same people who count GST as a federal tax then want to count all the state taxes it replaced as a reduction in state taxes. This asks you to believe that in 2000 all the states unilaterally cut taxes (without losing a dollar) while the Commonwealth unilaterally increased them (without gaining a dollar). It is statistical nonsense. If you want to compare like with like then you have to include GST and all those state taxes as federal taxes, or GST and all those state taxes as state taxes. Redoing the classifications on this basis still leads to the same general conclusions.

As I said earlier, the only way to avoid the effect of shifts of taxes between federal, state and local Government is to compare overall tax burdens against similar calculations in other countries.

None of this should be taken to mean that it is time to rest on our laurels. My view is that we should strive to be amongst the first row, and an International Benchmarking Study will assist us to look at those areas where we lead and those areas where we lag.

We are in a relentlessly competitive world and we should aim to have taxes and spending as low as possible, consistent with the standard of health, education, defence and security that our public is justly entitled to receive.

Autumn 2006

10 Comparative Economic Statistics

Key Indicator	Labor	Liberal
Net Government Debt	$95.8 billion (95–96)	ZERO (07–08)
Interest on Government Debt	$8.4 billion (95–96)	ZERO (07–08)
Average Mortgage Rates	12.75%	7.25%
Average Real Wages Growth	−1.8% (Mar 83–Mar 96)	21.5% (Mar 96–Jun 07)
Average Small Business Lending Rates	14.25%	8.90%
Unemployment Rate	8.2% (Mar 96)	4.2% (Sep 07)
Long-Term Unemployed	197 900 (Mar 96)	66 700 (Aug 07)
Australians in Work	8.3 million (Mar 96)	10.5 million (Sep 07)
Average Inflation	5.2%	2.5%
Tax Burden	22.3% of GDP (95–96)	20.7% of GDP (07–08)
Middle Tax Bracket	34%—up to $38 000	30%—up to $80 000 (from 1/7/08)
Top Tax Bracket	47%— 50 001+	45%— $180 001+ (from 1/7/08)
Waterfront Crane Rates (per hour)	$16.9 (Mar 96)	$26.8 (Dec 06)
Industrial Disputes (days lost per 1000 employees, per year)	193 (Avg 83–95)	59 (Avg 96–06)

Key Indicator	Labor	Liberal
Direct Investment in the Environment	AA Downgraded twice	AAA Upgraded twice
Investment in Climate Change Programs	$379 million (95–96)	$1724 million (07–08)
Total Spending on Health and Ageing	$16 million (96–97)	$666 million (07–08)
Australians with Private Health Insurance	$19.5 billion (95–96)	$51.8 billion (07–08)
Immunisation Rates	34% (1996)	44% (2007)
Investment in Vocational Education and Training	52% (0–6 year olds as at 1995)	90% (12–15 month olds)
Apprentices in Training	$1.1 billion (95–96)	$2.9 billion (07–08)
Mandatory Literacy Testing for Children	154 800 (Mar 96)	414 390 (Mar 07)
Federal Investment in Government Schools	NONE	Yrs 3, 5, 7, 9
Work for the Dole Participants	$1.4 billion (95–96)	$3.5 billion (07–08)
Total Number of Aged Care Places	NONE	599 613
Total Number of Aged Care Places	141 292 (June 96)	208 698 (Dec 06)

In comparing levels of funding and numbers of places, it should be noted that between March 1996 and June 2007, Australia's population increased around 15 per cent and CPI (inflation) increased just 32.4 per cent. Facts sourced from official Government documents, with information accurate at September 2007.

INDEX

A New Tax System (Commonwealth–state Financial Arrangements) Bill 1999, 134–5, 141–2

A New Tax System (Goods and Services Tax) Bill 1998, 134–5, 141–2

Abbott, Tony, 27, 54–5, 232, 244, 249–50, 252, 303, 327

Abetz, Eric, 27

Aboriginal people; alcohol, sexual abuse and violence, 206, 207, 213–15; assimilation policy, 207–8; Family Income Management Scheme, 221–2; health and education, 214, 221, 222; housing and income support, 220–2; Howard committed to reconciliation, 148; *Little Children Are Sacred*, 213, 214–15, 293; native title and Wik decision, 218–19; permit system, 215; Reconciliation Convention, 211; Reconciliation Walks, 149, 216–17, 218; 'stolen generations', 148, 207–13

Aboriginal and Torres Strait Islander Commission, 214

Accord, 33–4, 40

ACTU (Australian Council of Trade Unions), 34, 100–1

Afghanistan; Australian troops in, 163, 192, 193, 336; Soviet invasion, 29

Akerman, Piers, 256

Albrechtsen, Janet, 249

Aldred, Ken, 46

Alexander, Dave, 3, 4, 134, 238

Anderson, John, 80, 95, 156, 258, 259–60, 261, 313

Andrews, Kevin, 250, 261

APEC (Asia-Pacific Economic Cooperation); Australia one of strong economies of Asia, 117, 118; Australia tolerated but not respected, 117; Sydney meeting, 248, 249, 251, 252

Arbitration Commission and Dollar Sweets, 33–4, 35, 36

Ashmore Reef, 160, 163

Asian financial crisis; Australian assistance, 173, 174, 175, 177, 181–2; implications for Australia, 93, 117, 175, 176; Indonesia, 174–8, 180; IMF assistance, 171, 174–5, 176, 177–9, 180, 182;

Korea, 175–7, 179, 180; Thailand, 172–3, 180; US view of aid, 176, 179, 185–6

Asian Monetary Fund, 174

Asprey, Justice Kenneth William, 119

Aston by-election, 159–60, 163

AusLink program, 293

Australia Council, 165

Australia Institute, 135

Australian Business Numbers, 142

Australian Democrats, 19, 138–40

Australian Greenhouse Office, 140

Australian Labor Party; anti-communist but some fellow travellers, 29; campaigned against GST, 121; changing the face of Government at state level, 332–3; and conscription, 16, 22–3; dominating the media, 332; election loss and children overboard story, 164–5; opposes Australian troops in Iraq, 201, 202, 204; 134; power of the union bosses, 28; privatisation does not include Telstra, 79; proceeds of asset sales to pay for recurrent expenditure, 79; public thinks Keating has swindled them with 1993 Budget, 70; reaction to Statement on the Conduct of Monetary Policy, 110–12; return to power in 2007 started at state level, 331–2; 'rolling back the GST' in 2001, 163, 167; Rudd new Leader, 248, 290–2; and union membership, 28; and Vietnam War, 23; *see also* Hawke Government; Keating, Paul; Rudd, Kevin; Whitlam Government

Australian League of Rights, 151

Australian Liberal Students Federation, 27–8, 29

Australian Prudential Regulatory Authority, 115

Australian Republican Movement, 322, 325, 327

Australian Stock Exchange, 51

Australian Tax Office, 143–4

Australian Union of Students, 25–7

Australian Water Fund, 313

Australian Wheat Board scandal, 290–1

Australian Workers' Union, 38

Australian Workplace Agreements, 271

awards-based system, 271

INDEX

Baby Bonus, 274, 318, 319
Bailey, Fran, 148
Bailey, Nigel, 128, 131, 299
Bali bombing, 193, 194
Barresi, Phil, 8
Barrie, Admiral Chris, 165
Bartlett, Andrew, 139
Beale, Julian, 30, 46
Beattie Government, 153
Beazley, Kim, 76, 95, 100, 159, 230, 233, 292;
   claims GST will undo Coalition, 143; good
   debater, 164; interest in defence, not the
   economy, 81; Labor Leader at the wrong
   time, 164
Bill of Rights, 322, 328
Billson, Bruce, 293
biological weapons, 198, 199
Bishop, Bronwyn, 62
Bishop, Julie, 251, 261, 262, 333, 334
Bjelke-Petersen, Sir Joh, 43, 95, 150
Blix, Dr Hans, 199
Bolt, Andrew, 256
Bolte, Henry, 333
Bongiorno, Paul, 235
Bono (rock star), 184
Boswell, Ron, 261
Boxall, Peter, 107
bracket creep, 273
Brennan, Gabrielle, 4
Bretton Woods institutions, 168
Bringing Them Home report, 209–11
Broadbent, Russell, 147
Brough, Mal, 8, 215, 251, 252, 254, 261, 293, 299,
   301
Brown, Bob, 140
Brown, Dean, 212
Brown, Gordon, 170
'Brutopia', 334
Budget process; aim for at least 1 per cent Budget
   surpluses, 278, 288; in balance by 1998 election,
   148; Charter of Public Honesty, 80–1, 95–6,
   97, 297, 300, 317; Costello's achievements, 262;
   debated day after presentation, 280; mid-year
   reviews, 96; Ministers' proposals to ERC, 277–8;
   national tour to explain, 126; rating, 293; started
   six months before delivery, 277; tax cut details
   kept confidential, 278; turned from deficit to
   surplus, 267
Budget 1996; election promises based on inheriting
   slight deficit, 91, 96; no proposals for spending,
   only saving, 97; nursing home bonds, 147;
   one of best-received in Australian history,
   101, 126; two-year program to balance, 101,
   191, 125; union riot in Canberra on eve of,
   100–1

Budget 1997; Howard will not apply for rebate,
   125–6; net approval rate, 126; savings rebate with
   no means test, 125
Budget 2001; compensation to older Australians,
   159
Budget 2002; Baby Bonus, 318; narrow deficit due
   to defence spending for Afghanistan, 193; only
   deficit since Budget balanced in 1997, 193
Budget 2003; income tax cuts, 272–3
Budget 2004; Baby Bonus, 274, 318, 319; Family
   Tax Benefit, 274; raised marginal tax thresholds,
   274
Budget 2005; employers passing on tax cuts, 280–1;
   feeble response from Opposition, 280; Future
   Fund, 276, 278; Labor squibs on disallowing
   schedules, 281; press calls 'Bringing Home the
   Bacon', 277; tax cuts criticised for not going far
   enough, 281–2, 285; tax cuts for high income
   earners, 276–80
Budget 2006; Beazley does not oppose tax cuts,
   286; cutting top tax rates, 284; Howard opposes
   thresholds, 284–5; superannuation streamlined,
   285–6
Budget 2007; best received of Costello Budgets,
   293; no opposition from Labor to tax cuts, 287;
   tax thresholds lifted, 286–7
Burke, Brian, 294–5
Business Activity Statements, 153, 157
Business Council, 131
business tax system changes, 272

Cain, John, 34–5, 60
Cameron, Ross, 232
Campbell, Ian, 261–2, 295
Campbell, Philippa, 6
Camdessus, Michel, 172, 177, 179, 188
capital gains tax, 272
Carney, Shaun, 233
Carpenter, Alan, 294
cash rate target, 102–3, 114
centralised wage fixation, 33–4, 41
Centre for Independent Studies, 42
Charter of Budget Honesty, 81, 95–6, 97, 297,
   300, 317
children overboard (SIEV 4 case), 164–5, 166
Chipp, Don, 139
Christmas Island, 161, 162, 163
Clarke, Philip, 228
Clinton, President Bill, 182
Coalition Government; balancing the Budget,
   117; built an Age of Prosperity, 2–3, 335;
   Commonwealth net debt eliminated, 3;
   economic performance under Howard, 2,
   335; Howard–Peacock rivalry destabilising,
   84; independence of RBA established, 117;

interest rates lowered, 3; legacy regionally and internationally, 3, 336; majority reduced to six in 1996, 148; new ideas still in 2007, 292–3 57; targeting inflation, 111, 117; unemployment at historic low, 3, 111; *see also* Budgets; elections; leadership change; particular politicians

Cole, Tony, 90

Coleman, Peter, 31

Coleman, Verna, 31

collective bargaining, 271

Collins, Peter, 152

Colston, Mal, 73, 135

Commonwealth Bank privatisation, 79

Commonwealth Government Securities market, 263

Community Cultural Recreational and Sporting Facilities Program, 59

company tax and GST, 142–3

Conran, Peter, 299

conscription, 16, 22–3, 24

Constitution Preamble referendum, 320, 328–9

Constitutional Convention, 322, 324–7, 329

Conybeare, Chris, 90

Coombs, 'Nugget', 102

Coote, Andrea, 5

Core, Peter, 90

Cosgrove, General Peter, 189

Costello, Anne (née Northrop), 10, 11–12, 15, 16, 20–1, 205

Costello, Christopher, 18

Costello, Janet, 20

Costello, Madeleine, 5, 6, 31–2, 166

Costello, Michael, 90

Costello, Peter; Blackburn South Primary, 13–14; Carey Baptist Grammar, 205; childhood, 10–15; corporal punishment, 14–15; declines to stand for election (1987), 42–3, 45; Essendon Football Club, 53; on failure of federalism, 310–12; family background, 17–19; family life separate from politics, 225–6; fascinated by tax, 119; first campaign at Monash University, 26–7; first vote (for Liberal Party), 24; on Fraser blocking Supply, 24; the future, 336; impressions of Eastern Europe, 28–9; Irish ancestry, 16–17; joins Liberal Party, 29; law practice, 30, 33–7, 39, 40; marriage, 30–1; Monash arts/law degree, 21–2; music tastes, 89; owns no company shares, 72; part-time tutor in industrial law, 35; religious education, 15–16, 19, 20; speech in event of 2007 win, 1–2; student politics, 25–8; Young Liberals state executive, 30

Costello, Peter (in Opposition); advantages of starting in Opposition, 52; attacked by Kennett, 60–2; debate with Willis before 1996 election, 82; Deputy Leader, 62, 65; discovers 'Sports

Rorts', 59; and Fightback!, 53–4, 57; first wins Higgins, 47; good relations with Howard, 54; Hewson wary of, 50, 52, 54, 55–6; Howard asks to stand aside, 66, 67–8; interest in corporate law, 51; interest in economic issues and foreign affairs, 52; on Labor's 1993 Budget, 70; shadow Attorney-General, 52, 53, 55; shadow Minister for Corporate Law and Consumer Affairs, 51–2; shadow Minister for Finance, 59; staff, 52; support for Howard, 43, 54, 58, 61, 223; 'The Things That Matter', 65; unsuccessful nomination for deputy, 58

Costello, Peter (Treasurer); achievements, 8; addresses Constitutional Convention, 325–6; and Statement on the Conduct of Monetary Policy, 106–8; appoints Macfarlane to replace Fraser at RBA, 107; appoints new RBA governor, 105–7; attempts at humour in parliament, 75, 76; balancing the Budget, 93, 95, 117; blamed for collapse of the currency, 155; commissions inquiry into the financial system, 115; corporate law reforms, 51; criticised for not encouraging dot-com companies, 155; on disclosure of parliamentarians' financial interests, 72–4; first press conference, 95–6; gold card for returned WWII servicemen, 12; IMF representative, 169–70; keeping election promises despite large deficit, 91; learns true state of Budget on taking office, 90, 91, 92–3, 95; and Nick Sherry's 'travel rort', 74–6; parliamentary performances toned down, 76; preferred treasurer, 2007 election, 304; RBA independence recognised, 108–9, 114, 116, 117; speech on Australian citizenship, 196–7; speech at campaign launch, 2007 election, 305; Statement on the Conduct of Monetary Policy, 106, 108–10, 111, 112; sworn in, 93, 94–5; thanked by Howard in 1998, 149; *see also* GST; leadership change; particular budgets

Costello, Phoebe, 4, 9, 32

Costello, Russell, 10, 11, 12, 16, 19, 20, 21, 94

Costello, Sebastian, 1, 4, 31, 101–2

Costello, Tanya (née Coleman), 1, 4, 6, 8–9, 27, 30–3, 72, 101

Costello, Tim, 19–20

Council for Reconciliation, 216

Cousins, Geoffrey, 302

Crean, Simon, 100, 143, 204

Crosby, Lynton, 147, 156

Cubillo, Lorna, 208

Davey, Alistair, 77, 78, 101

Dawkins, John, 70

Day, Bob, 239–40

Deane, Sir William, 93, 94, 95

Debt-Free Day (21 April 2006), 265–7

de Crespigny, Robert Champion, 241

defence expenditure, 99, 100, 190, 193

demonstrations; left-wing student politics, 23–7; in One Nation campaign, 150; opposing globalisation, 185; violence, G–20 meeting, 184–5

departmental heads, 98

detention centres, 160–1

disability assistance package, 293

disability pension indexation, 293–4

disclosure of financial interests by parliamentarians, 72–6

Dodson, Pat, 148

Dollar Sweets case, 33–7

Downer, Alexander, 58, 224, 258, 299, 322; Costello supports in leadership spill, 62–3, 64; days of leadership numbered, 65; influence of Fraser, 63, 64; Kennett's opinion on as Leader, 62; replaces Hewson as Leader, 64; second chance as Leader, 66–7; shadow Minister for Foreign Affairs, 67; shadow Treasurer, 59; stands down as Leader, 67, 226–7; tells Howard Cabinet want him to go, 249, 251; understands Liberal Party culture, 64

Duckett, Dr Stephen, 90

Duffy, Michael, 53

Durack, Peter, 52

East Timor, 336; ADF deployment, 189–90, 191; Australian journalists murdered, 188; independent sovereign state, 189, 190; INTERFET a success, 189–90; Whitlam approves Indonesian annexation, 188

Easton Royal Commission, 71

economic growth drivers (Three Ps), 320

Election 1990; Coalition's fourth successive defeat, 48; Costello wins Higgins, 47; interest rates the issue, 46–7; Peacock's second defeat as Leader, 48; reasons for defeat, 58

Election 1993; funding the promises, 77, 79, 80; Jobsback, 57; Labor makes promises it cannot keep, 69; Liberals lose 'unlosable election', 57–8; private health insurance rebate, 79; privatisation, 79, 80; settling the policies, 78–80; youth wage controversial, 57, 58; see also Fightback!

Election 1996; campaign on Labor's broken promises, 69–70, 82; Costello debates Willis, 82; costings released, 80–1; Family Tax Initiative, 77–8, 79, 83–4; forged letter affair damages Labor, 2, 85–7; funding election promises, 77–8, 79, 80; Howard's address to Press Club, 85; Howard stumbles over Family Tax Initiative, 83–4; incentives for private health insurance, 79; Keating off-message at start of campaign, 83; Keating wants Ministers debating their shadows, 82; Labor campaign, 82, 85–8; 'Meeting

Our Commitments' document, 80; Natural Heritage Trust funding and projects, 79; policy decisions, 78–9; privatisation of Telstra, 79; racist issues avoided, 84; tight rein on ill-disciplined candidates, 84; use of funds from privatisation, 79; win with a majority of 30, 89

Election 1998; Coalition scrapes home, 133, 147–8; good economic performance a factor in win, 148; GST the central issue, 133; Hanson and One Nation, 149, 150–1, 152; Howard's victory speech, 148; Labour polls majority of votes but not seats, 148; Liberal preferences and One Nation, 152–3; seats lost, 147–8

Election 2001; decision to send troops to Afghanistan, 163; domestic issues become important, 163; Coalition gains four seats, 163; Labor 'rolling back the GST', 163, 167; importance of Aston by-election, 159–60; Tampa and SIEV 4 in lead-up, 162, 163, 164–5, 166; 'Two Brothers' play, 265–6; US terrorist attacks in lead-up, 163

Election 2004; foreign affairs and defence issues, 204; Future Fund, 264; Howard the face of the Government, 262; Howard to lead party, 232; win helped by ALP choice of Latham, 233, 276

Election 2007, 290; campaign launch, 305–7; Charter of Public Honesty effective, 96; Coalition ahead in economic management, 3; Coalition policy, 299–300; Coalition wins only first week of campaign, 300–1; Costello the preferred treasurer, 304; Costello speech at campaign launch, 305; Costello's last speech of campaign, 2–3; Election Day, 4–6; education rebate, 299, 305; election team the best ever, 3; electorate tired of Government and Howard, 294; expecting defeat before the event, 1; Government represented as out of touch and stale, 296–7; Howard handicapped by small circle of advisers, 307; Howard's speech at campaign launch, 306; Kyoto Protocol issue, 302; Labor adopts Coalition tax policy, 287, 300–1; Labor always ahead in two-party preferred vote, 292; Labor inherits built-in Budget surpluses, 287; Leaders' Debate won by Rudd, 301–2; Lindsay leaflet bogus, 2, 309; many Coalition class of 1996 lose seats, 237; mid-year review issued on first day of campaign, 300; new tax plan, 297–300; pre-election statement on the Budget, 297; RBA announces interest rate rise, 304–5; Rudd always preferred Leader, 249; Rudd's speech at ALP campaign launch, 306–7; succession issue, 308

Election 2007 aftermath; Costello's speech in event of win, 1–2; Costello will not seek leadership, 6, 7–8; tribute to Howard as Prime Minister, 7

INDEX

Elliott, John, 44, 45–6
Ellison, Chris, 250
emissions trading system, 315, 316
Equal Opportunity Board, 39
Evans, Gareth, 72, 88, 100
Evans, Ray, 40, 41
Evans, Ted, 90, 91, 92, 114, 180
excise and GST, 143
Expenditure Review Committee (ERC), 96–9, 100

Fahey, John, 95, 98, 131–2
family benefits simplification, 132
Family Income Management Scheme, 221–2
Family Tax Benefit, 274
Family Tax Initiative, 77–8, 79, 83–4
Farr, Malcolm, 233, 237
federalism, failure of, 310–12
Federated Confectioners' Association, 33–6
Fels, Alan, 146
fertility decline problem, 318–19
Fightback!; Costello's views on, 57; election lost
    on, 78; GST component, 53–4, 57, 58; Hewson
    dumps after losing election, 59–60; Keating on,
    54; privatisation issue, 79; should have been a
    winner, 57–8; 20-point plan, 53–4
Financial Assistance Grants, 141
Fischer, Tim, 94–5, 126, 149, 239, 259
Fitzgibbon, Joel, 280
flexible exchange rate, 169, 186
Fraser, Bernie, 102, 104–5, 106, 110, 116–17
Fraser, Malcolm, 24–5, 29, 30, 49, 63, 64, 120, 232
Free Trade Agreement with US, 260
Friedman, Milton, 187
Frizziero, Carlo, 33, 34
fully funded superannuation, 265, 288
Future Fund, 8, 264, 265, 267, 276, 278, 288

G–7, 179, 182
G–20, 182–5
Gaetjens, Phil, 3, 132, 134, 155
Garnaut, Ross, 316
Garrett, Peter, 76, 303
Gazard, David, 3, 318
General Agreement on Tariffs and Trade, 168
Georgiou, Petro, 61
Gersh, Joe, 26
Gibson, Brian, 72–3, 75
Gillard, Julia, 292, 308
globalisation, 185, 186
Goldberg QC, Alan, 35, 37
Gordon, Michael, 233
Gorton, John Grey, 44–5, 232
Goss, Wayne, 70
governor-general, 321; Deane, 93, 94, 95; Howard's
    view on role, 94

Grattan, Michelle, 231, 235, 236
Greens Party, 140–1
Greenspan, Alan, 109, 263
Grenville, Stephen, 179
GST, 126–7; answering questions on, 149;
    briefing Cabinet, 130; briefing Treasury, 125;
    central issue in 1998 elections, 133; central to
    Coalition defeat in 1993, 124; Day One, 145–6,
    153; in Fightback!, 53–4, 57, 58, 121–3, 124;
    forerunners, 121; hostility at paperwork, 153;
    Howard rejects idea in 1995, 124, 126; Howard
    wants 8 not 10 per cent, 132–3; immediate
    effects, 153–4; implementing, 142–5, 227;
    introducing to the public, 130–1; launch, 133;
    legislating the program, 134–42; MPs critical of
    small business problems, 156–7; press statement
    on, 139; rate to be 10 per cent, 128, 132–3;
    revenue allocated to states, 128, 129–30, 141,
    311; taxation task force, 128–30
gun lobby and One Nation, 150, 151
Gunner, Peter, 208–9, 210

Habibie, President BJ, 180, 188, 189
Hamilton, Stuart, 90
Hanson, Pauline, 84, 149, 150–1, 152, 261
Harradine, Brian, 135–8
Hasluck, Paul, 207
Hawke, Bob; and Accord, 33; and Dollar
    Sweets, 34; response to Fightback!, 54
Hawke Government; floating the dollar, 169;
    Keating's Option C, 120; Keating takes the flak
    for Hawke, 70–1; interest rate, 103–4
Hay, Andrew, 35, 37, 43
Hayes, Barbara, 85, 86
Health and Medical Investment Fund, 293
Heath, Sister Eileen, 206–7, 208, 209
Hein, Franz, 39
Henderson, Gerard, 37, 41
Hendy, Peter, 284
Henry, Dr Ken, 91, 123, 128, 130, 315, 316
Herman, Pat, 52
Hewson, John, 224; apprenticeship under Lynch,
    49; background not in Liberal Party, 49–50;
    confrontation with Costello, 55–6; contemplates
    re-introducing death penalty, 56; drops GST
    after 1993 defeat, 58; elected 1987 (Wentworth),
    50; front bench, 50–1; replaces Peacock as
    Leader, 48; reshuffles front bench, 52; sacked
    by Downer, 67; shadow Treasurer, 50; wary of
    Costello, 50, 52, 54, 55–6, 58; wins leadership
    over Reith, 50; see also Fightback!
Hicks, David, 192–3, 197–8
Higgins, Henry Bournes, 36, 40–1
Higgins electorate, 44–6
Higher Education Endowment Fund, 293

INDEX

Hill, Robert, 258, 261, 302
Hockey, Joe, 232, 250, 261, 262
Holt, Harold, 44
housing affordability package, 298–9
Howard, John; background, 49, 225; champion of
    stay-at-home mothers, 78; 'cricket tragic', 225;
    described as 'mean' and 'tricky', 158, 159; family
    involvement in his politics, 225; role at times
    of national suffering, 94; works for Treasurer
    Lynch, 49
Howard, John (in Opposition); dumped as Leader,
    46, 49; elected Leader unopposed 1995, 77; good
    relations with Costello, 54; leadership chances
    better when Peacock retires, 65, 225; leadership
    unopposed when Downer steps down, 67–8;
    never stopped dreaming about leadership, 224–6;
    Reith spoils 1990 leadership bid, 50; rivalry with
    Peacock destabilises party, 84; supports Downer
    and Costello against Hewson, 64; rejects GST
    after 1993 election loss, 124–5
Howard, John (Prime Minister); address to
    the Press Club, 1996, 85; commitment to
    Aboriginal reconciliation, 148; each election
    a little harder, 167; loses Bennelong, 5, 8, 257,
    307; negotiates with Democrats over GST,
    139; relationship with Bush, 193; relationship
    with Kennett, 62, 149; saying 'sorry' to 'stolen
    generations', 211–12; small circle of advisers
    a handicap, 307; social conservative, 49;
    speech at campaign launch (2007), 306; *Tampa*
    incident, 160–2, 163; tension with governor-
    general, 94; thanks Costello in 1998, 139,
    149; in US on September 11th, 191, 192,
    193; victory speech (1998), 148; vilified in
    'Two Brothers' play, 265–6; *see also* leadership
    change
HR Nicholls Society, 40, 41–2
Hussein, Saddam, 198, 199–200, 201, 202, 203, 291
Hyde, John, 41

'In Need of Reform' document, 130–1
income tax rates, 284
indirect tax complexity, 128
Indonesia; Australian Embassy attacked, 204; and
    East Timor, 188–9; end of Suharto regime,
    177–8, 180; financial crisis, 174–8, 180
'Industrial Relations Club', 37–8, 41
industrial relations system, 271
inflation target, 104, 105, 109, 110, 111
Institute of Public Affairs, 42
interest rates; advantage of a target rate, 104;
    Costello view that rates cut too late rather than
    too early under Hawke, 104; in lead-up to 1990
    election, 103–4; in lead-up to 1996 election,
    103; Labor mismanagement, 103; power to cut

no longer with Government, 112; transmitting
    in the real economy, 114
Intergenerational Report, 265, 317–18
International Monetary Fund; in Asian financial
    crisis, 171, 174–5, 177–9, 180–1, 182; Costello
    represents Australia, 156, 169–70; diminished
    influence on global economy, 170–1; member-
    ship, 169; role, 168–9, 171; US influence, 171
Investing in Our Schools Program, 290
Iraq, 336; Australian troops in, 200–4; chemical and
    biological weapons, 198–9; weapons of mass
    destruction, 198–200, 201, 202, 203–4

Jarman, Alan, 30
Jeremenko, Rob, 134
'Jobsback' policy, 57
Joh-for-PM campaign, 43, 150, 261
Jones, Barry, 89
Joske, Stephen, 78
Joyce, Barnaby, 260–1
Jull, David, 73

Katter, Bob, 261
Keating Dr Michael, 90
Keating, Paul; on Fightback!, 54; Prime Minister,
    71, 77, 87, 91, 322–3; Treasurer, 70, 71, 120
Kelly, Fran, 81
Kelly, Jackie, 2, 236–7, 309
Kelly, Ros, 59, 77
Kelty, Bill, 100, 120
Kemp, David, 46, 51, 99, 258, 261
Kemp, Rod, 80, 154–5
Kennett, Jeff, 152; apology to 'stolen generations',
    210, 212; attacks Costello for undermining
    Hewson, 60, 61–2; enthusiastic about GST
    revenue, 149; and forged letters before 1996
    election, 85, 87; relationship with Howard, 61,
    149; shock defeat, 149
Kernot, Cheryl, 19, 100
Kerr, Sir John, 41
King, Richard, 134
Kirner, Joan, 60, 61
Korean financial crisis, 175–7, 179, 180
Koutsoukis, Jason, 233, 234
Kroger, Michael, 25, 39, 30, 35, 37, 61
Kyoto Protocol, 302

Latham, Mark, 20, 204, 262, 344; background, 275;
    campaign in 2004, 275; Labor Leader, 233, 275;
    public worries about, 276; shadow Treasurer, 100
Lawrence, Carmen, 71, 77
leadership change (Costello); will not seek after
    2007 election defeat, 6, 7; assesses chances
    in ballot, 244–5; questioned by press about
    McLachlan, 241–3; speech prepared in case

Howard steps down, 1–2; wants an orderly transition, 240, 245; will stay as deputy for 2007 election, 247

leadership change (Howard); asks Cabinet if they want him to go, 254; Athens Declaration, 233–4, 237; change too late for Party, 250, 257; to consider options at 64, 228, 229; does not want to announce too far ahead, 229; Downer initiates Cabinet discussions, 250; Downer tells him Cabinet want him to go, 249, 250–1, 253; family don't want him to go, 253; finds reasons to stay on, 248; GST implementation not the right time, 227, 228; Ministers angered when put on the spot, 253–4; not likely to leave before APEC summit, 248; not to serve full term from 2007, 255; press speculation, 223–4, 235–6, 237–8, 239, 240; stays beyond 64 in party's best interest, 230, 231; stays despite bad polls, 254–5; wants orderly transition to Costello, 255; wants party to tell him to go, 251; will contest 2007 election, 245–6

leadership change (McLachlan meeting); Costello confirms the arrangement, 241–3, 244; Costello unwilling to disclose conversation, 234; Howard asks Costello to stand aside when Downer goes, 226; Howard indicates he wants one term only, 227; Howard says it was not a 'deal', 240–1; Howard wants only one term, 227; McLachlan makes note of undertaking, 239; McLachlan's note of undertaking becomes public, 239; McLachlan witnesses Howard's offer to stand aside, 226; Milne's story on McLachlan meeting, 238–9, 240; original date of departure to be during 2000, 227; witnesses Howard and Costello leadership arrangement, 66, 239

Lee, Kuan Yew, 335

Lee, Michael, 125

Lees, Meg, 138, 139, 140

Lewis, Steve, 233, 237–8

Liberal Party; beliefs, 28; concentration on social activities, 29, 30; Costello joins, 29; culture of the Leader rather than culture of the party, 331, 333; Downer given second chance, 66–7; Downer replaces Hewson as Leader, 64; early 1980s a bad period, 30; factionalism in Queensland, 155–6; federal executive, 158; formation, 330; Fraser represents Right, 49; generational renewal needed, 335; Hewson flounders as Leader, 59; Hewson replaces Peacock, 48, 50; Howard dumped as Leader, 46; Howard's chance when Downer goes, 66; Howard elected unopposed, 67, 68; influence of MPs in, 330–1; Kennett attacks Costello for undermining Hewson, 60–2; loses Government in Victoria, 30; media dominated by Labor, 332; membership not run by big business, 28; new leadership sought after 1987 defeat, 44; New Right (Costello, Beale and Kemp), 46; no big differences from National Party, 261; no extra-parliamentary apparatus, 330, 331; no misapprehensions about communism, 29; opportunity for new leaders, 333; Peacock's second defeat as Leader, 48; preferences in 1998, 152–3; and republic question, 322, 323, 325, 326, 327–8; retains few departmental heads on winning, 90–1; Stone's memo to Howard leaked, 156–9; structural problems, 330–1; 'The Things That Matter', 65; voluntary organisation, 330; Young Liberal Movement, 27, 29

Lindsay, Phil, 144

Little Children Are Sacred, 213, 214–15, 293

Loosley, Stephen, 42

Loughnane, Brian, 296

Low Income Tax Offset, 297

Lynch, Philip, 49

Mabo case, 218

McCrann, Terry, 256

Macfarlane, Ian, 106, 108, 115–16, 250

McGarvie, Richard, 324

McGauran, Peter, 73

McGuinness, Paddy, 27–8

McKew, Maxine, 307

McLachlan, Ian, 41, 51, 52, 56, 57, 63; note of Howard's undertaking, 239; retires from parliament, 229; tells Howard to give Costello a go, 240; witness to Howard and Costello leadership arrangement, 66, 239

McMullan, Bob, 100

Macphee, Ian, 45, 46

Mahlab, Eve, 45

Mannix, Archbishop Dr Daniel, 16

Marrett, Frank, 39–40

Meat Workers' Union, 38

media; broadcasting political indiscretions, 76; claiming scalps of Ministers, 73–4; dominated by Labor, 332; speculation about leadership issue, 223–4, 235–6, 237–8, 239, 240

'Meeting Our Commitments', 80

Melbourne Chamber of Commerce, 35

Menzies, Dame Pattie, 337

Menzies, Sir Robert, 7, 23, 48, 257, 321, 330–1, 333, 336

Miles, Chris, 74

Milne, Glenn, 235, 236, 238–9, 240

Minchin, Nick, 64, 239, 250, 299

'mission creep', 184

Mitchell, Alan, 113

Monash University student activism, 22, 23, 25–7, 28

Moore, John, 155–6, 228

Moore-Wilton, Max, 131, 158, 307
Morgan, Hugh, 35, 37, 40, 41
Morris, Grahame, 73, 125, 307
mortgage rates, 148
Moylan, Judi, 147
Mudginberri Abattoir case, 38
Murphy, Mr Justice Peter, 36
Murray, Andrew, 138
Murray, Les, 329

National Commission of Audit, 96
National Companies and Securities Commission, 51
National Party; differences within party, 261; no
    big differences from Liberal Party, 261; relief
    at defeat of Hanson in 1998, 149–50; and Wik
    decision, 218
National Plan for Water Security, 292–3, 314
National Security Committee, 162, 164, 195, 200,
    201, 203
national service, 23
National Tax and Accountants Association, 135
National Taxation Summit 1985, 120
National Water Initiative, 293, 313–14, 316
Nationalist Party, 18
Native Title Act 1993, 218
Natural Heritage Trust, 79
Nelson, Brendan, 250, 252, 261, 293, 333–4
New Business Tax System, 272
'new economy', 155
New Right, 41, 42
Newman, Jocelyn, 258
Nicholls, Henry Richard, 40–1
Northrop, Frances, 205–6, 207
Northrop, Raymond, 17–18
Nugent, Peter, 159
Nutt, Tony, 158

O'Brien, Kerry, 255, 283
Oakes, Laurie, 56, 64, 84, 101, 152, 156, 157
Officer, Professor Bob, 96
oil prices, 154, 271
One Nation, 69, 77, 149–50, 151, 152–3, 218, 261

Pacific Solution, 163
Packer, Kerry, 57–8
Parkinson, Martin, 316
parliamentary register of Members' interests, 72–4
participation in the workforce, 318, 319
Patterson, Kay, 261
Peacock, Andrew, 46, 52, 104; background, 49;
    charmed entry into politics, 48; Kennett's
    opinion on as Leader, 62; resigns from
    Parliament, 65, 225; rivalry with Howard
    destabilises party, 84; second defeat as Leader, 48;
    in Young Liberals movement, 29

Pearce, Chris, 159–60
Pearson, Noel, 220
people-smuggling, 160–1, 163
petrol price rise, 154, 271
pharmaceutical costs, 317, 319
ports infrastructure, 269–70
Pre-Election Economic and Fiscal Outlook, 297
preferred prime minister poll, 292
Price, Matt, 231
prudential regulation, 115
Puplick, Christopher, 223
Purvis, Barry, 41
Pyne, Christopher, 232, 262

Qantas privatisation, 79
Quadrant, 28, 37, 42
Queensland, 210, 211; Beattie Government re-
    election a warning, 153; factionalism in Liberal
    Party, 155–6; Liberal anger after losing state
    election, 156; Ryan by-election loss, 155–6, 159,
    228, 229

rail links, 270
Rayson, Hannie, 165, 167
recession, 103, 154–5, 159, 268
Reconciliation Convention, 211
Reconciliation Council, 148
Reconciliation Walks, 149, 216–17, 218
refugees see detention centres; Tampa
Regional Assistance Mission to the Solomon
    Islands, 204
registering for GST, 142
Reid, Bruce, 148, 223, 224
Reith, Peter, 48, 58, 99, 327; an ally for Costello,
    224–5; and children overboard pictures, 164–5;
    loyalty to Hewson through Fightback! not
    repaid, 224; runs for leadership, 50; unsuccessful
    deputy nomination, 224
republic debate, 320–5
Reserve Bank Act, 110, 111
Reserve Bank of Australia; Australia considered
    a high inflation risk, 105; concern overseas
    about independence of bank, 105; focus
    on monetary policy and payments system,
    115; Government guarantees independence
    of decision, 108–9, 112, 114, 116, 117;
    Government retains right of veto, 107;
    Government has right to comment on
    monetary policy, 108; independent but subject
    to scrutiny, 112; interest rate rise during 2007
    campaign, 304–5; loses responsibility for
    prudential supervision, 115; press scrutiny
    important, 113–14; Statement on the Conduct
    of Monetary Policy, 106, 108–10, 111, 112;
    talking to journalists off the record, 113

Index

Reserve Bank of Australia governor; agreement with Government on inflation target, 106; announcements about change in monetary policy, 105, 107–8; appointment process, 106; briefing the Treasurer, 106; Fraser appointed from Treasury, 102; Macfarlane a successful governor, 115–16; Macfarlane replaces Fraser, 106, 107; quarterly Statement on the Conduct of Monetary Policy, 108; Stevens succeeds Macfarlane, 116; usually a career officer, 102

Reserve Bank of New Zealand, 105

restrictive work practices, 38–9

Revenue Committee of Cabinet, 97

Ridgeway, Aden, 329

Ritchie, Eda, 42

Robb, Andrew, 56, 78, 84, 255, 256

Robe River dispute, 38–9

Rocher, Allan, 65, 66, 334

Rogers, Nanette, 213

Roxon, Nicola, 303

Rudd, Kevin (in Opposition), 201, 250, 334; campaigns on new leadership, fresh ideas, 262; *Sunrise* program with Hockey, 232; Coalition focus on his capacity in election, 294; misleading about dealings with Burke, 294–5; becomes Leader, 248, 290–1; not a good speaker in the House, 291; on injustice of GST reform, 141–2; polls well as preferred Prime Minister, 292; press unwilling to damage as wanting change of Government, 295–6; shadow Minister for Foreign Affairs and AWB scandal, 290–1; speech at 2007 campaign launch, 306–7

Rudd, Kevin (Prime Minister); saying 'sorry' to 'stolen generations', 213; no collective memory of problems of expenditure, 100

Ruddock, Philip, 166–7, 250

Rundle, Tony, 212

Ryan, Scott, 87–8

Ryan by-election 2001, 155–6, 159, 228, 229

Sakakibara, Eisike, 118, 174

Samuel, Graham, 45

Santoro, Santo, 293

Savva, Niki, 156

Schubert, Misha, 233

Securing the Future of Aged Care for Australians, 293

September 11 terrorist attack, 163, 190–1, 192, 193, 198

Shack, Peter, 223

Shanahan, Dennis, 233, 256, 304

Sharp, John, 73

Shepherd, Bruce, 43

Sheridan, Rourke, 290

Sherry, Nick, 72, 74–5, 76

Shipton, Roger, 44, 45, 46

Short, Jim, 72, 75, 95

SIEV 4 (Suspected Illegal Entry Vessel 4) controversy, 164–5, 166

SIEV X, 166

Simpson, Kim, 89

Simpson, Peter, 128

Singleton, John, 27–8

Sinodinos, Arthur, 85, 307

small business and GST, 143

Smith, Alan, 24, 40

Smith, Tony, 40, 52, 53, 59, 63, 72, 78, 82, 143, 149, 232, 262

Smith, Warwick, 147

Snow, Jim, 69

Solomon Islands, 204, 336

Somlyay, Alex, 43, 239

'Sports Rorts', 59, 77

Staley, Tony, 65

Starkins, Anthony, 46

state indirect taxes, 127

Statement on the Conduct of Monetary Policy, 106, 108–110, 111, 112

states; briefing on GST, 129; effect of change in state Governments, 141; failure of federalism, 310–12; indirect taxes replaced by GST revenue, 128, 130, 149; negotiations with over GST, 141; responses to *Bringing Them Home*, 209–11

Stauder, Fred, 33–7

Stevens, David, 128

Stevens, Glenn, 116

'stolen generations', 148, 207–9; *Bringing Them Home*, 209–11; Cubillo and Gunner test cases, 208–9, 210; Rudd Government apologises, 213; state responses to report, 210–11; symbolism of saying 'sorry', 210–12

Stone, John, 41, 43, 47, 104, 105

Stone, Shane, 156–7

Stott-Despoja, Natasha, 139

Stutchbury, Michael, 281–2

Suharto, President, 177–8, 180, 188

suicide attempts by parliamentarians, 76

Summers, Larry, 117–18, 180

superannuation reform, 285–6, 319–20

superannuation surcharge, 279

Swan, Wayne, 10, 275, 280, 292

Takeovers Panel, 51

Tampa, 160–2, 163

tax reform *see* GST

Tax Reform: Not a New Tax, A New Tax System, 133

Taxation Review, 119–20

taxation, a necessary evil, 121

INDEX

Telstra float, 267
Telstra privatisation, 79, 80
terms of trade improvement, 268–9, 270–1
terrorism; anthrax scares, 194–5; Australian Embassy
  Jakarta attacked, 204; Bali bombing, 193, 194;
  Costello speech on Australian citizenship, 196–7;
  London Underground bomb, 195–6; security
  and defence upgraded, 194; September 11th,
  163, 190–1, 192, 193, 198
Thailand; financial crisis, 172–3; political troubles,
  180
'The Industrial Relations Club', 37–8
'The Things that Matter', 65
Thompson, Cameron, 255
Thompson, Kathy, 52
'three Ps' of economic growth, 320
'travel rorts', 74–6
treasury bonds, 262–4
tsunami, 19–20
Tuckey, Wilson, 223
Turnbull, Malcolm, 250, 251–2, 261, 262, 282, 283,
  302, 315, 323, 333–4
'Two Brothers' play, 165–6
two-party preferred vote, 292

unemployment, 111, 112, 148, 288–9
unfunded Commonwealth superannuation, 264–5,
  267, 288
unions; Costello represents victims of
  discrimination, 39–40; milestone cases against,
  38–9; power in ALP, 28; riot before first
  Coalition Budget, 100–1
United States; and Asian economic crisis, 176, 179,
  185–6; Free Trade Agreement, 260; moves dollar
  off gold standard, 169; September 11, 2001, 163,
  190–1, 192, 193, 198

Vaile, Mark, 250, 259, 260, 299, 305
Vanstone, Amanda, 258–9, 261, 272–3
Victorian Liberal Party, 61; see also Kennett, Jeff

Victorian Liberal Students' Association, 40
Vietnam War, 22, 23
Viner, Ian, 148
Volker, Derek, 90

Walker, Ron, 71–2, 157–8
Wallis, Stan, 115
Warburton, Dick, 284
Water Agreement, 293, 313
water management, 292–3, 312–15, 316
Watt, Dr Ian, 128
weapons of mass destruction, 198–200, 201, 202,
  203–4
Webster, Alistair, 50
Welfare to Work, 288
Whitlam Government; dismissal, 23–4;
  Government borrowing, 266; and Indonesian
  annexation of East Timor, 188
wholesale sales tax, 121, 123–4, 125, 129
Whybin, Scott, 143
Wide Comb issue, 38
Wik decision, 218–19
Willard Group, 182
Willesee, Michael, 122–3
Williams, Daryl, 70, 261
Willis, Ralph, 34, 82, 85, 86–7, 89, 91–2
Wilton, Greg, 76
Wood, Alan, 113
Woolcock, Vincent, 25
Wooldridge, Michael, 42–3, 58, 64, 95, 136,
  147–8, 224
World Bank, 168–9, 170
World Trade Organization, 168
'Worth Promoting, Worth Defending—Australian
  Citizenship', 196–7
Wran, Neville, 324

Yabsley, Michael, 51
Young Liberal movement, 27, 29
YouTube, 76